OUT OF MY LIFE

Marshal von Hindenburg

OUT OF MY LIFE

Translated by F. A. Holt

The Naval & Military Press Ltd

Published by
The Naval & Military Press Ltd
Unit 10, Ridgewood Industrial Park,
Uckfield, East Sussex,
TN22 5QE England
Tel: +44 (0) 1825 749494
Fax: +44 (0) 1825 765701
www.naval-military-press.com
© The Naval & Military Press Ltd 2005

*In reprinting in facsimile from the original, any imperfections are inevitably reproduced
and the quality may fall short of modern type and cartographic standards.*

Printed and bound by Antony Rowe Ltd, Eastbourne

CONTENTS

PAGE

A FOREWORD xiii

PART I
Days of Peace and War Before 1914

CHAPTER I
MY YOUTH

Hindenburg-Beneckendorff—My Parents and Early Years
—In the Cadet Corps 3

CHAPTER II
IN BATTLE FOR THE GREATNESS OF PRUSSIA AND GERMANY

In the Third Regiment of Foot-Guards — 1866 — In the
Field—At Soor—Königgrätz—After Königgrätz—Back
Home Again—At Hanover—In the Field Once More—
St. Privat—After the Action at St. Privat—The Battle
of Sedan—Sedan—Outside Paris—The Proclamation of
the Empire—Paris—The Commune—My Second Entry
Into Berlin 17

CHAPTER III
WORK IN PEACE-TIME

At the *Kriegsakademie* —In the General Staff—At Corps and
Divisional Headquarters—In Command of a Company—
The Great General Staff—Teaching at the *Kriegsakademie*
—At the War Ministry—In Command of a Regiment—
Chief of Staff to a Corps—Commanding a Division—I
Become a Corps Commander—Retirement . . . 53

v

Contents

CHAPTER IV

RETIREMENT

The German Army and the German Nation—A Glance into
the Future 71

PART II

The Campaign in the East

CHAPTER V

THE STRUGGLE FOR EAST PRUSSIA

1. THE OUTBREAK OF WAR AND MY RECALL . . . 77
   German Policy and the Triple Alliance—Mobilisation

2. TO THE FRONT 81
   In Command of an Army—General Ludendorff—The
   Situation in the East—My Relations with General
   Ludendorff

3. TANNENBERG 86
   At Army Headquarters—Russian Plans—The Evolution
   of Our Battle-plan—Danger from the Side of Rennen-
   kampf—A Numerical Comparison—The Marienburg
   —Tannenberg—The Battle Develops—A Decision—
   The Results

4. THE BATTLE OF THE MASURIAN LAKES 99
   Fresh Problems—Rennenkampf—The Attack Begins—
   The Course of the Battle

CHAPTER VI

THE CAMPAIGN IN POLAND

1. I LEAVE THE EIGHTH ARMY 110
   Co-operation with the Austro-Hungarian General Staff—
   I Go to Silesia

2. THE ADVANCE 114
   The Strategic Situation—Affairs in Poland—The Battles
   at Ivangorod and Warsaw—Russian Counter-
   Measures

Contents

PAGE

3. THE RETREAT 120

    Fresh Plans—Further Resistance in Poland—The Retreat to the Silesian Frontier—I Become Commander-in-Chief in the East

4. OUR COUNTER-ATTACK 124

    Confusing Operations—The Conclusion of the Fighting in Poland

CHAPTER VII
1915

1. THE QUESTION OF A DECISION 129

2. BATTLES AND OPERATIONS IN THE EAST 135

    The Intentions of the Austro-Hungarian General Staff—The Winter Battle in Masuria—Russian Counter-Attacks—Our General Offensive in the East—The Rôle of the Commander-in-Chief in the East—Our Own Plans—Novo-Georgievsk—Vilna

3. LÖTZEN 144

4. KOVNO 147

CHAPTER VIII
THE CAMPAIGN OF 1916 UP TO THE END OF AUGUST

1. THE RUSSIAN ATTACK ON THE GERMAN EASTERN FRONT . 149

    The Winter of 1915—The Battle of Lake Narocz

2. THE RUSSIAN OFFENSIVE AGAINST THE AUSTRO-HUNGARIAN EASTERN FRONT 154

    Verdun and Italy—Wolhynia and the Bukovina—My Sphere of Command is Extended

PART III
From Our Transfer to Main Headquarters to the Collapse of Russia

CHAPTER IX
MY SUMMONS TO MAIN HEADQUARTERS

1. CHIEF OF THE GENERAL STAFF OF THE FIELD ARMY . 163

2. THE MILITARY SITUATION AT THE END OF AUGUST, 1916 . 164

Contents

PAGE

3. THE POLITICAL SITUATION 167

4. THE GERMAN HIGH COMMAND 171
The Austro-Hungarian Army—The Bulgarian and
Turkish Armies—Our Achievements in the War

5. PLESS 178
King Ferdinand of Bulgaria—The Emperor Francis
Joseph—General Conrad von Hötzendorf—Enver
Pasha—General Jekoff—Talaat Pasha—Radoslavoff

CHAPTER X

LIFE AT HEADQUARTERS

THE DAILY ROUTINE—VISITORS 186

CHAPTER XI

MILITARY EVENTS TO THE END OF 1916

1. THE RUMANIAN CAMPAIGN 194
Our Political and Military Situation with regard to
Rumania—The Bulgarian Offensive in Macedonia
—Rumania Declares War—Previous Plans of
Campaign—The Overthrow of Rumania

2. THE FIGHTING ON THE MACEDONIAN FRONT . . . 206

3. THE ASIATIC THEATRES 209

4. THE EASTERN AND WESTERN FRONTS TO THE END OF 1916 211
Russian Help to Rumania—The Battles at Verdun Continue—I Pay my First Visit to the Western Front

CHAPTER XII

MY ATTITUDE ON POLITICAL QUESTIONS

1. FOREIGN POLICY 219
Statesmanship and the Conduct of Operations—The
Polish Question—The Polish Volunteers—False
Hopes—The Question of the Dobrudja—Political
Agitation in Bulgaria—The Policy of Turkey

2. THE PEACE QUESTION 231

Contents

PAGE

3. HOME POLITICS 236

   The Hindenburg Programme—The Auxiliary Service
   Law

CHAPTER XIII

PREPARATIONS FOR THE COMING CAMPAIGN

1. OUR TASKS 241

   The General Situation in the Winter of 1916-17—We are
   forced to the Defensive—The Siegfried Line—I
   Reject the Idea of an Offensive in Italy and Macedonia—Turkey's Task for 1917

2. THE U-BOAT WARFARE 250

   The Blockade from the Humanitarian Point of View—
   American Munitions—Our Confidence in the U-Boat
   Campaign—The Arguments and Our Decision—The
   Supreme Effort

3. KREUZNACH 258

CHAPTER XIV

THE HOSTILE OFFENSIVE IN THE FIRST HALF OF 1917

1. IN THE WEST 261

   Preparations for Defence—The Spring Battle at Arras—
   The Double Aisne-Champagne Battle

2. IN THE NEAR AND FAR EAST 268

3. ON THE EASTERN FRONT 269

   The Russian Revolution—We Maintain an Attitude of
   Reserve—Further Developments of the Russian
   Upheaval—The Last Russian Offensive

CHAPTER XV

OUR COUNTER-ATTACK IN THE EAST 276

The Risks Involved in a Counter-Attack—Tarnopol—
Riga and Oesel

CHAPTER XVI

THE ATTACK ON ITALY 283

Contents

CHAPTER XVII

FURTHER HOSTILE ATTACKS IN THE SECOND HALF OF 1917

1. IN THE WEST 288
The End of the Battles in Flanders—Cambrai—Its Lessons
—French Attacks

2. THE BALKANS 292

3. ASIA 293
English Operations in Asia—Plans for the Recovery of
Bagdad—The Condition of the Turkish Army—Our
Reinforcements

CHAPTER XVIII

A GLANCE AT THE INTERNAL SITUATION OF THE STATES AND
NATIONS AT THE END OF 1917 302
The Turkish Empire—Bulgaria—Austria-Hungary—Ger-
many—France—England—Italy—The United States
—The Prolongation of the War

PART IV
The Fight for a Decision in the West

CHAPTER XIX

THE QUESTION OF AN OFFENSIVE IN THE WEST

1. OUR INTENTIONS AND PROSPECTS FOR 1918 . . . 325
Our Views and Hopes—The Intention to Attack—The
Situation and the Decision—Training the Troops—
Concentrating in the West—Difficulties in the East—
The Finnish Expedition—Help from Austria-Hungary
—Troops from Bulgaria and Turkey—Should We
Remain on the Defensive in 1918?

2. SPA AND AVESNES 341

CHAPTER XX

OUR THREE GREAT OFFENSIVE BATTLES

1. THE " GREAT BATTLE " IN FRANCE . . . 344

2. THE BATTLE ON THE LYS 351

Contents

PAGE

3. THE BATTLE OF SOISSONS—RHEIMS 356

    The Battle—Fellow-feeling on the Battlefield

4. RETROSPECT AND PROSPECTS AT THE END OF JUNE, 1918 . 364

CHAPTER XXI

OUR ATTACK FAILS

1. THE PLAN OF THE RHEIMS BATTLE 370

2. THE RHEIMS BATTLE 374

    Our Attack—Its Results—The Enemy's Counter-Attack
    —We Decide to Evacuate the Marne Salient—The
    Behaviour of the Troops—The Meaning of the Battle

PART V

Beyond Our Powers

CHAPTER XXII

ON THE DEFENSIVE

1. AUGUST 8 389

2. THE CONSEQUENCES OF AUGUST 8 AND FURTHER BATTLES IN
    THE WEST UP TO THE END OF SEPTEMBER . . 394

CHAPTER XXIII

THE LAST BATTLES OF OUR ALLIES

1. THE COLLAPSE OF BULGARIA 400

2. THE OVERTHROW OF TURKISH POWER IN ASIA . . . 411

3. MILITARY AND POLITICAL ISSUES IN AUSTRIA-HUNGARY . 418

    Austrian Reinforcements on our Western Front—The
    Fighting in Albania—Efforts to End the War—
    Count Czernin — Count Burian — The Last Austro-
    Hungarian Peace Efforts

Contents

CHAPTER XXIV

TOWARDS THE END

1. FROM SEPTEMBER 29 TO OCTOBER 26 426
   The Situation on the Battle Front—Our Hardest Decision
   —The Armistice and Our Peace Offer—The Progressive
   Disintegration at Home

2. OCTOBER 26 TO NOVEMBER 9 433
   The Collapse of Our Allies' Resistance—The Great Crisis
   and the Final Crash

MY FAREWELL 440

INDEX 445

MAPS

(In pocket at end)

1. THE EASTERN FRONT   2. THE POLISH FRONT

3. THE WESTERN FRONT

A FOREWORD

THE memoirs that follow owe their inception not to any personal inclination to authorship, but to the many requests and suggestions that have been made to me.

It is not my intention to write an historical work, but rather to interpret the impressions under which my life has been spent, and to define the principles on which I have considered it my duty to think and act. Nothing was farther from my mind than to write an apology or a controversial treatise, much less an essay in self-glorification. My thoughts, my actions, my mistakes have been but human. Throughout my life and conduct my criterion has been, not the approval of the world, but my inward convictions, duty and conscience.

The following pages of reminiscences, written in the most tragic days of our Fatherland, have not come into being under the bitter burden of despair. My gaze is steadfastly directed forward and outward.

I gratefully dedicate my book to all those who fought with me at home and in the field for the existence and greatness of the Empire.

September, 1919.

PART I

Days of Peace and War before 1914

OUT OF MY LIFE

CHAPTER I

MY YOUTH

ONE spring evening in the year 1859, when I was a boy of eleven, I said good-bye to my father at the gate of the Cadets' Academy at Wahlstatt, in Silesia. I was bidding farewell not to my dear father only, but to my whole past life. Overwhelmed by that feeling, I could not prevent the tears from stealing from my eyes. I watched them fall on my uniform. " A man can't be weak and cry in this garb," was the thought that shot through my head. I wrenched myself free from my boyish anguish and mingled, not without a certain apprehension, among my new comrades.

That I should be a soldier was not the result of a special decision. It was a matter of course. Whenever I had had to choose a profession, in boys' games or even in thought, it had always been the military profession. The profession of arms in the service of King and Fatherland was an old tradition in our family.

Our stock—the Beneckendorffs—came from the Altmark, where it had originally settled in the year 1289. From there, following the trend of the times, it found its way through the Neumark to Prussia. There were many who bore my name among the Teutonic Knights who went out, as Brothers of the Order, or " War

3

Guests," to fight against heathendom and Poland. Subsequently our relations with the East became ever closer as we acquired landed property there, while those with the Marches became looser and ceased altogether at the beginning of the nineteenth century.

We first acquired the name " Hindenburg " in the year 1789. We had been connected with that family by marriage in the Neumark period. Further, the grandmother of my great-grandfather, who served in the von Tettenborn Regiment and settled at Heiligenbeil in East Prussia, was a Hindenburg. Her unmarried brother, who once fought as a colonel under Frederick the Great, bequeathed to his great-nephew, on condition that he assumed both names, his two estates of Neudeck and Limbsee in the district of Rosenberg, which had originally fallen to Brandenburg with the East Prussian inheritance but had subsequently been assigned to West Prussia. This received King Frederick William II's consent, and the name " Hindenburg " came into use through the abbreviation of the double name.

As a result of this bequest the estate at Heiligenbeil was sold. Further, Limbsee had to be disposed of as a matter of necessity after the War of Liberation. Neudeck is still in the possession of our family to-day. It belongs to the widow of one of my brothers who was not quite two years younger than I, so that the course of our lives kept us in close and affectionate touch. He too was a cadet and was permitted to serve his King as an officer for many years in war and peace.

During my boyhood my grandparents were living at Neudeck. They now rest in the cemetery there with my own parents and many others who bear my name. Almost every year we paid my grandparents a visit in the summer, though in the early days it meant difficult journeys by coach. I was immensely impressed when my grandfather, who had served in the von Langen Regiment after 1801, told me how in the winter of 1806-7 as *Landschaftsrat* he had visited Napoleon I. in the castle of Finckenstein nearby to beg him to remit the levies, but had been coldly turned away. I also heard how the French were quartered in and marched through Neudeck. My uncle, von der Groeben, who had settled on the Passarge, used to tell me of the battles that were fought in this region in 1807. The Russians pressed forward over the bridge, but were driven back again. A French officer who was defending the manor with his men was shot through the window of an attic. A little more, and the Russians would have been crossing that bridge again in 1914!

After the death of my grandparents my father and mother went to Neudeck in 1863. There, after a removal which was over familiar ground, we found the home of our ancestors. In that home where I spent so many happy days in my youth I have often, in later years, taken a rest from my labours with my wife and children.

Thus for me Neudeck is " home," and for my own people the firm rock to which we cling with all our hearts. It does not matter to what part of our German Fatherland my profession has called me, I have always felt myself an " Old Prussian."

The son of a soldier, I was born in Posen in 1847. My father was then a lieutenant in the 18th Infantry Regiment. My mother was the daughter of Surgeon-General Schwichart, who was also then living in Posen.

The simple, not to say hard, life of a Prussian country

gentleman in modest circumstances, a life which is virtually made up of work and the fulfilment of duty, naturally set its stamp on our whole stock. My father too was heart and soul in his profession. Yet he always found time to devote himself, hand in hand with my mother, to the training of his children—for I had two younger brothers as well as a sister. The way of life of my dear parents, based on deep moral feeling and yet directed to practical ends, revealed a perfect harmony within as without. Their characters were mutually complementary, my mother's serious, often anxious view of life pairing with my father's more peaceful, contemplative disposition. They both united in a warm affection for us and thus worked together in perfect accord on the spiritual and moral training of their children. I find it very hard to say to which of them I should be the more grateful, or to decide which side of our characters was developed by my father and which by my mother. Both my parents strove to give us a healthy body and a strong will ready to cope with the duties that would lie in our path through life. But they also endeavoured, by suggestion and the development of the tenderer sides of human feeling, to give us the best thing that parents can ever give—a confident belief in our Lord God and a boundless love for our Fatherland and—what they regarded as the prop and pillar of that Fatherland—our Prussian Royal House.

From our earliest years our father also brought us into touch with the realities of life. In our garden or on our walks he wakened the love of Nature within us, showed us the countryside, and taught us to judge and value men by their lives and work. By "us" in this connection I

mean my next brother and myself. Of course the training
of my sister, who came after this brother, was more in
the hands of my mother, while my youngest brother
appeared on the scene just before I became a cadet.

The soldier's nomadic lot took my parents from Posen
to Cologne, Graudenz, Pinne in the Province of Posen,
Glogau and Kottbus. Then my father left the service
and went to Neudeck.

I do not remember much about those Posen days. My
grandfather on my mother's side died soon after I was
born. In 1813 he had, as a medical officer, won the Iron
Cross of the combatant services at the Battle of Kulm.
He had rallied and led forward a leaderless Landwehr
battalion which was in confusion. In later years my
grandmother had much to tell us of the " French Days "
which she had known when she was a girl in Posen. I
have vivid memories of a gardener of my grandparents
who had once served fourteen days under Frederick the
Great. In this way it may be said that a last ray of the
glorious Frederickian past fell on my young self. In the
year 1848 the rising in Poland had its repercussion on the
province of Posen. My father went out with his regiment
to suppress this movement. For a time the Poles actually
got control of the city. They ordained that every house
should be illuminated to celebrate the entrance of their
leader, Miroslavsky. My mother was in no position to
resist this decree. She retired to a back room and, sitting
on my cot, consoled herself with the thought that the
birthday of the " Prince of Prussia " fell on that very
day, March 22, so that to her eyes the lights in the
windows of the front rooms were in honour of him.

Twenty-three years later that same child in the cradle

B

witnessed the proclamation of William I, that same
"Prince of Prussia," as Emperor in the Hall of Mirrors
at Versailles.

We did not reside very long in Cologne and Graudenz.
From the Cologne period the picture of the mighty,
though then still unfinished, cathedral is ever before my
eyes.

At Pinne my father, in accordance with the custom
then obtaining, commanded a company of Landwehr as
supernumerary captain. His service duties did not make
very heavy demands on his time, so that just at the very
period when my young mind began to stir he was able to
devote special attention to us children. He soon taught
me geography and French, while the schoolmaster Kobelt,
of whom even now I preserve grateful memories, in-
structed me in reading, writing and arithmetic. To this
epoch I trace my passion for geography, which my father
knew how to arouse by his very intuitive and suggestive
methods of teaching. My mother gave me my first religious instruction in a way that spoke straight to the heart.

In these years, and as result of this method of training,
there gradually developed for me a relation to my parents
which was undoubtedly based on unconditional obedience,
and yet gave us children a feeling of what was unlimited
confidence rather than blind submission to too firm a
control.

Pinne is a village bounded by a manor. The latter
belonged to a certain Frau von Rappard, at whose house
we were frequent visitors. She had no children, but was
very fond of them. Her brother, Herr von Massenbach, owned the manor of Bialakesz quite near. I found
many dear playmates among his numerous family. My

memories of Pinne have always remained very vivid. I
visited the place when I was at Posen in the late autumn
of 1914, and was greatly moved on entering the little
modest house in the village in which we had once passed
so many happy days. The present owner of the property
is the son of one of my erstwhile playmates. His father
has already gone to his long rest.

It was while I was at Glogau that I entered the
Cadet Corps. For the previous two years I had
attended the higher elementary school and the Protestant
Gymnasium. I hear that Glogau has preserved so kindly
a memory of me that a plate has been affixed to the house
we then lived in to commemorate my residence there.
To my great joy I saw the town again when I was a company officer in the neighbouring town of Fraustadt.

Looking back over the period I have referred to I can
certainly say that my early training was based on the
soundest principles. It was for that reason that at my
departure from the house of my parents I felt that I was
leaving a very great deal behind me, and yet that I was
taking a very great deal with me on the path that was
opening out before me. And it was to remain thus my
whole life. Long was I to enjoy the anxious, untiring
love of my parents, which was later to be extended to my
own family. I lost my mother after I had become a regimental commander; my father left us just before I was
appointed to the command of the 4th Army Corps.

It can certainly be said that in those days life in the
Prussian Cadet Corps was consciously and intentionally
rough. The training was based, after true concern for
education, on a sound development of the body and the
will. Energy and resolution were valued just as highly

as knowledge. There was nothing narrow, but rather a certain force in this method of training. The individual should and could develop his healthy personality in all freedom. There was something of the Yorck spirit in the method, a spirit which has often been misjudged by superficial observers. Yorck was undoubtedly a hard soldier and master, to himself no less than to others, but it was he, too, who demanded unlimited self-reliance from each of his subordinates, the same self-reliance he himself displayed in dealing with everyone else. For that reason the Yorck spirit, not merely in its military austerity, but also in its freedom, has been one of the most precious traits of our army.

I have but little sympathy for the humanistics of other schools so far as they are principally concerned with dead languages. Their practical value in life has always been obscure to me. Considered as a means to an end, I am of opinion that the dead languages take up too much time and energy, and as a special study they are for the later years of life. At the risk of being pronounced an ignoramus I could wish that these schools would give greater prominence to modern languages, modern history, geography and sports, even at the expense of Latin and Greek. Must that which was the only thing to which civilisation could cling in the Dark Ages really be regarded as all-important even in modern times? Have we not, since those days, made our own history, literature and art in hard fighting and ceaseless toil? Do we not need living tongues far more than dead ones if we are to hold our just position in world trade?

What I have said is not intended to convey any contempt of classical antiquity in itself. Quite the contrary.

From my earliest years classical history has had a very great attraction for me. Roman history, in particular, had me in its grip. It seemed to me to be something mighty, almost demoniacal, and this impression possessed me particularly strongly when I visited Rome in later years, and expressed itself, *inter alia*, in the fact that the monuments of the ancient Eternal City appealed to me more than the creations of the Italian Renaissance.

Rome's clever recognition of the advantages and disadvantages of national peculiarities, her ruthless selfishness which scorned no method of dealing with friend or foe where her own interests were concerned, her virtuous indignation, skilfully staged, whenever her enemies paid her back in her own coin, her exploitation of all emotions and weaknesses among enemy peoples (the method which was used adroitly and with special effect in dealing with the Germanic peoples, and proved more effective than arms)—all this, as I was to learn later, found its mirror and perfection in British statesmanship, which succeeded in developing all these aspects of the diplomatic art to the highest pitch of refinement and duplicity.

But though I held the classic world in high honour I sought my youthful heroes among my own countrymen. I publicly state my honest opinion that in our admiration of an Alcibiades or a Themistocles, of the various Catos or Fabii, we ought not to be so narrow-minded and ungrateful as quite to lose sight of those men who played every bit as great a part in the history of our Fatherland as these did in the history of Greece and Rome. In this connection I am sorry to say I have often noticed, in conversation with German youths, that with all their learning there is something parochial about their outlook.

Our tutors and lecturers in the Cadet Corps guarded us against such limitation of vision, and I thank them for it now. My thanks are due more especially to the then Lieutenant von Wittich. I had been recommended to him by a relation of mine when I first went to Wahlstatt, and he always took a particularly friendly interest in me. He had left the Cadet Corps himself only a few years before, and he regarded himself as quite one of us, gladly took part in our games, especially snowballing in winter, and was a man of character and ideas. Above all he possessed a wonderful talent for teaching. In 1859 he taught me geography in the lowest form, and six years later he taught me land survey in the special class in Berlin. When I attended the *Kriegsakademie* some years after I found that Major von Wittich of the General Staff was once more one of my tutors.

Wittich was interested in military history even in his lieutenant days, and on our walks on fine days often set us little exercises in suitable spots to illustrate the battles which had just been fought in Upper Italy—Magenta and Solferino, for example. Later, in Berlin, he encouraged me, now a cadet, to take up the study of military history, and aroused my youthful interest in railways, which was important for my future progress. Who can doubt that military history is the best training for generalship? When I was subsequently transferred to the General Staff, Lieutenant-Colonel von Wittich was still attached to it in an important position, and finally we were simultaneously appointed G.O.C.'s—that is, to the command of an Army Corps. The little lowest-form boy at Wahlstatt hardly suspected *that* when Lieutenant von Wittich gave him a friendly whack with a ruler because he mixed up Mont Blanc and Monte Rosa.

Our high spirits did not suffer from the hard schooling of our cadet life. I venture to doubt whether the boyish love of larking, which no doubt at times reached the stage of frantic uproar, showed to more advantage in any other school than among us cadets. We found our teachers understanding, lenient judges.

At first I myself was anything but what is known in ordinary life as a model pupil. In the early days I had to get over a certain physical weakness which had been the legacy of previous illnesses. When, thanks to the sound method of training, I had gradually got stronger, I had at first little inclination to devote myself particularly to study. It was only slowly that my ambitions in that direction were aroused, ambitions which grew with success, and finally brought me, through no merit of mine, the calling of the specially gifted pupil.

Notwithstanding the pride with which I styled myself " Royal Cadet," I hailed my holidays at home with uncontrollable delight. In those days the journeys, especially in winter, were anything but a simple matter. According to one's destination, slow journeys in a train (the carriages were not heated) alternated with even slower journeys in the mail-coach. But all these difficulties took a back seat compared with the prospect of seeing my home, parents, and brothers and sister again. Her son's longing for home filled my mother's heart with the deepest joy. I can still remember my first return to Glogau for the Christmas holidays. I had been travelling with other comrades in the coach from Liegnitz the whole night. We were delayed by a snowstorm, and it was still

dark when we reached Glogau. There, in the so-called
" waiting-room," badly lit and barely warmed, my dear
mother was sitting knitting stockings just as if, in her
anxiety to please one of her children, she were afraid of
neglecting the others.

In my first year as cadet, the summer of 1859, we
had a visit at Wahlstatt from the then Prince Frederick
William, later the Emperor Frederick, and his wife. It
was on this occasion that we saw for the first time almost
all the members of our Royal House. Never before had
we raised our legs so high in the goose-step, never had
we done such break-neck feats in the gymnastic display
which followed as on that day. It was a long time before
we stopped talking about the goodness and affability of
the princely pair.

In October of the same year the birthday of King
Frederick William IV. was celebrated for the last time. It
was thus under that sorely tried monarch that I put on the
Prussian uniform which will be the garb of honour to me as
long as my life lasts. I had the honour in the year 1865 to
be attached as page to Queen Elizabeth, the widow of the
late King. The watch which Her Majesty gave me at that
time has accompanied me faithfully through three wars.

At Easter, 1863, I was transferred to the special class,
and therefore sent to Berlin. The Cadet School in that
city was in the new Friedrichstrasse, not far from the
Alexanderplatz. For the first time I got to know the
Prussian capital, and was at last able to have a glimpse
of my all-gracious sovereign, King William I., at the
spring reviews when we paraded on Unter den Linden
and had a march past in the Opernplatz, as well as the
autumn reviews on the Tempelhofer Feld.

The opening of the year 1864 brought a rousing, if serious atmosphere into our lives at the Cadet School. The war with Denmark broke out, and in the spring many of our comrades left us to join the ranks of the fighting troops. Unfortunately for me I was too young to be in the number of that highly envied band. I need not try to describe the glowing words with which our departing comrades were accompanied.

We never troubled our heads about the political causes of the war. But all the same we had a proud feeling that a refreshing breeze had at last stirred the feeble and unstable structure of the German union, and that the mere fact was worth more than all the speeches and diplomatic documents put together. For the rest we followed the course of military events with the greatest eagerness, and, quivering with excitement, were joyful spectators when the captured guns were paraded round and the troops made their triumphal entry. We thought we were justified in feeling that within us resided something of that spirit which had led our men to victory on the Danish battlefields. Was it to be wondered at that henceforth we were all impatience for the day on which we ourselves would enter the army?

Before that day came we had the honour and good fortune to be presented personally to our King. We were conducted to the castle, and there had to tell His Majesty the name and rank of our fathers. It is hardly surprising that many of us, in our agitation, could not get a word out at first, and then poured them out pellmell. Never before had we been so close to our old sovereign, never before had we looked straight into his kind eyes and heard his voice. The King spoke very

earnestly to us. He told us that we must do our duty
even in the hardest hours. We were soon to have an
opportunity of translating that precept into action. Many
of us have sealed our loyalty with death.

I left the Cadet Corps in the spring of 1865. My own
personal experiences and inclinations throughout my life
have made me grateful and devoted to that military
educational establishment. It is a joy to think of my
hopeful young comrades in the King's uniform. Even
during the World War I was only too happy to have an
opportunity of having sons of my colleagues, acquaint-
ances and fallen comrades as guests at my table. A more
favourable occasion, the celebration of my seventieth birthday, which fell during the war, gave me an opportunity
of beginning the ceremonies by having three little cadets
brought out of the streets of Kreuznach to my luncheon
table, piled high with edible gifts. They came in before
me cheery and unembarrassed, exactly as I would have
boys come, the very embodiment of long-past days,
living memories of what I myself had been.

CHAPTER II

ON April 7, 1865, I became a second-lieutenant in the 3rd Regiment of Foot Guards. The regiment belonged to those troops which had been re-organised when the number of active units was greatly increased in 1859-60. When I joined it the young regiment had already won its laurels in the campaign of 1864. The historic fame of any military body is a bond of unity between all its members, a kind of cement which holds it together even in the worst of times. It gives place to an indestructible something which retains its power even when, as in the last great war, the regiment has practically to be reconstituted time after time. The old spirit very soon permeates the newcomers.

In my regiment, which had been formed out of the 1st Regiment of Foot Guards, I found the good old Pots-dam spirit, that spirit which corresponded to the best traditions of the Prussian Army at that time. The Prussian Corps of Officers in those days was not blessed with worldly goods—a very good thing. Its wealth consisted of its frugality. The consciousness of a special personal relation to the King—"feudal loyalty," as a German historian has put it—permeated the life of the officer and compensated for many a material privation. This ideal point of view was of priceless advantage to the army. The words "I serve" took on a quite special meaning.

It is frequently said that this point of view has led to the isolation of the officer from the other professional classes. Personally I have not found the sentiment of exclusiveness more noticeable among the officer class than in any other profession, the members of which keep to themselves and prefer the society of their equals. A picture, very accurate in its broad outlines, of the spirit of the Prussian Corps of Officers in those days may be found in a book on the War Minister, von Roon. In that work the Officer Corps is shown as an aristocratic professional class, very exclusive and jealous, but not in any sense hidebound or remote from ordinary life. Nor was it without a sprinkling of liberal elements. The new ideal of a severe professional training had revolted against the old ideal of broad humanitarianism. It found its most zealous representatives in the sons of the old monarchical-conservative stock of Prussia. It had been borne along by a strong conviction of the power of the State and by the Frederickian tradition, which longs to give Prussia an ever greater rôle in the world through her army.

At the time I joined the regiment, which was then stationed at Danzig, the political events of the following months were already casting their shadows before. It was true that mobilisation had not yet been ordered, but the decree for the increase of establishments had already been issued and was in course of execution.

In face of the approaching decisive conflict between Prussia and Austria our political and military ideas travelled over the tracks of Frederick the Great. It was in that train of thought that when we were in Potsdam, to which the regiment was transferred immediately our mobilisation was complete, we took our Grenadiers to the tomb of that immortal sovereign. Even the Order of the Day which was issued to our army before the invasion of Bohemia was inspired by thoughts of him, for its closing words ran : " Soldiers, trust to your own strength, and remember that your task is to defeat the same foe which our greatest King once overthrew with his small army."

From the political point of view we realised the necessity of settling the question of Prussian or Austrian supremacy, because within the framework of the Union, as then constituted, there was no room for two great Powers to develop side by side. One of the two had to give way, and as agreement could not be reached by political methods the guns had to speak. But beyond that train of ideas there was no question of any national hostility against Austria. The feeling of community of race with the German elements in the Danube Monarchy, which at that time still predominated, was far too strong to allow sentiments of hostility to prevail. The course of the campaign proved the truth of this time after time. On our side we generally treated our prisoners as fellow-countrymen with whom we were only too glad to resume friendly relations after our little dispute had been fought out. The inhabitants of the enemy's country, especially the Czech population, showed themselves well disposed towards us, so much so that in our billets we lived and acted much as we did while on manœuvres at home.

In this war we trod in the footsteps of Frederick the Great—in actual fact as well as in a metaphorical sense. The Guard Corps, for example, in invading Bohemia from Silesia by way of Branau was taking a route that had often been taken before. And the course of our first action, that at Soor, led us on June 28 into the same region and in the same direction—from Eipel on Burkersdorf—against the enemy as that in which, on September 30, 1747, Prussia's Guard had moved forward in the centre of the great Kíng's army which was advancing in the rigid line of that time during the Battle of Soor.

Our 2nd Battalion, of which I was commanding the first skirmishing section (formed out of the third rank in accordance with the regulations of those days), had no opportunity that day of appearing in the front line, as we formed part of the reserve, which had already been separated from the rest before the battle, as the tactical methods of those days decreed. But all the same, we had found an opportunity of exchanging shots with Austrian infantry in a wood north-west of Burkersdorf. We had made some prisoners, and later on we drove off and captured the transport of about two squadrons of enemy Uhlans who were resting, all unsuspecting, in a glen. Among the transport we found, *inter alia*, the regimental safe, which was handed over, large supplies of bread, which our Grenadiers brought into our camp at Burkersdorf stuck on their bayonets, and the regimental diary which was kept in the same book as that of the Italian campaign of 1859. About twelve years ago I came across an old gentleman from Mecklenburg who was a lieutenant in the service of Austria in one of those very squadrons of Uhlans. He confided to me that in this affair he had lost his brand-new Uhlan uniform which he was to wear at the entry into Berlin.

As I had had so little to do at Soor I had to be content with having smelt powder and gone through some of the emotional experiences which are the lot of the soldier when he first comes face to face with the enemy.

Straight from the excitement of battle, I was familiarised on the very next day with what I may call the reverse side of the medal. I was assigned the sad duty of taking sixty grenadiers to search the battlefield and bury the dead—an unpleasant task, which was all the more difficult because the corn was still standing. By dint of enormous exertions and at times passing other units by running in the ditches by the roadside, I and my men caught up my battalion about midday. The battalion had already joined the main body of the division and was on the march to the south. I came up just in time to witness the storming of the Elbe crossing at Königinhof by our advance guard.

On June 30 I was brought face to face with the sober realities of war's more petty side. I was sent with a small escort to take about thirty wagons, full of prisoners, by night to Tartenau, get a load of food supplies for the empty wagons, and bring them all back to Königinhof. It was not before July 2 that I was able to join my company again. It was high time, for the very next day summoned us to the battlefield of Königgrätz.

The following night I went out on a patrol with my platoon in the direction of the fortress of Josephstadt, and on the morning of July 3 we were in our outpost camp, wet and cold and apparently unsuspecting, by the southern outskirts of Königinhof. Soon the alarm was given, and shortly after we received the command to get our coffee quickly and be ready to march. Careful listeners could hear the sound of guns in the south-west. Opinions as to the reasons for the alarm being given were divided. The generally accepted view was that the 1st Army, under Prince Frederick Charles, which had invaded Bohemia from Lausitz—we formed part of the 2nd Army commanded by the Crown Prince—must have come into contact with a concentrated Austrian corps somewhere.

The order to advance which now arrived was greeted with joy. The Guardsmen, green with envy, remembered the brilliant victories which had previously been won by the 5th Corps, under General von Steinmetz, on our left. In torrents of rain and bathed in perspiration, though the weather was cold, our long columns dragged themselves forward along the bottomless roads. A holy ardour possessed me, and reached the pitch of fear lest we should arrive too late.

My anxiety soon proved to be unnecessary. After we had ascended from the valley of the Elbe we could hear the sound of guns ever more clearly. Further, about eleven o'clock we saw a group of the higher Staff on horseback standing on an eminence by the roadside and gazing south through their glasses. They were the Headquarters Staff of the 2nd Army, under the supreme command of our Crown Prince, subsequently the Emperor Frederick. Some years later General von Blumenthal, his Chief of Staff at that time, gave me the following account of what transpired at that moment:

" Just when the 1st Guards Division was passing us on the impossible roads I was asking the Crown Prince to give me his hand. As he looked at me questioningly I added that I wished to congratulate him on the victory that had been won. The Austrian artillery fire was now directed everywhere to the west, a proof that the enemy was held by the 1st Army along the whole line, so that we should now take him in the flank and partly in the rear. In view of this position it only remained for us to order the Guard Corps to advance to the right, and the 6th

Corps to the left of a hill by Horonowes, crowned by two huge lime trees which were visible in the far distance in spite of the mist. The 1st and 5th Corps, which were still on their way to the battlefield, would have to follow these corps. Scarcely any other orders were required from the Crown Prince that day.''

Our advance took us at first straight across country; then we deployed, and before long the first shells began to arrive from the heights by Horonowes. The Austrian artillery justified its old excellent reputation. One of the first shells wounded my company commander, another killed my wing N.C.O. just behind me, while shortly after another fell into the middle of the column and put twenty-five men out of action. When, however, the firing ceased and the heights fell into our hands without fighting, because they were only an advanced position lightly held by the enemy for the purpose of surprise and gaining time, there was quite a feeling of disappointment among us. It did not last for long, for we soon had a view over a large part of a mighty battlefield. Somewhat to our right heavy clouds of smoke were rising into the dull sky from the positions of our 1st and the enemy's army on the Bistritz. The flashes of the guns and the glow of burning villages gave the picture a peculiarly dramatic colouring. The mist, which had become much thicker, the high corn, and the formation of the ground apparently hid our movements from the enemy. The fire of the enemy batteries which soon opened on us from the south, without being able to stop us, was therefore remarkably innocuous. Later on most of them were captured after putting up a brave defence. And so we pressed on as fast as the formation of the country, the heavy, slippery ground, and the corn,

c

rape and beet would allow. Our attack, organised according to all the rules of war then in vogue, soon lost cohesion. Individual companies, indeed individual sections, began to look for opponents for themselves. But everyone pressed on. The only co-ordinating impulse was the resolution to get to close quarters with the enemy.

Between Chlum and Nedelist our half battalion—a very favourite battle formation in those days—advancing through the mist and high-standing corn, surprised some enemy infantry coming from the south. The latter were soon forced to retire by the superior fire of our needle-guns. Following them with my skirmishing section in extended order, I suddenly came across an Austrian battery, which raced past us with extraordinary daring, unlimbered and loosed off case-shot at us. A bullet which pierced my helmet grazed my head, and for a short time I lost consciousness. When I recovered we went for that battery. We captured five guns, while three got away. I felt a proud man and gave a sigh of relief when, bleeding from a slight wound in the head, I stood by my captured gun.

But I had little time to rest on my laurels. Enemy jäger, easily recognisable by the feathers in their caps, sprang up from among the wheat. I beat them off and followed them up to a sunken road.

As luck would have it, this, my first battle experience, became known in Austria during the last great war. A retired Austrian officer, a veteran of 1866, wrote to me from Reichenberg in Bohemia that at the battle of Königgrätz he had been a regimental cadet in the battery I had attacked, and illustrated his statement with a sketch map. As he added a few kind words I thanked him warmly, and so between the two former enemies a most friendly exchange of letters took place.

When I reached the sunken road to which I have referred I took a good look round. The enemy jäger had vanished in the rain and mist. The villages in the neighbourhood—Westar was immediately in front, Rosberitz on my right, and Sweti on my left—were obviously still in possession of the enemy. Fighting was already going on for Rosberitz. I was quite alone with my section. Nothing was to be seen of our people behind me. The detachments in close order had not followed me southwards, and appeared to have veered to the right. I decided to bring my isolation on that far-flung battlefield to an end by following the sunken road to Rosberitz. Before I reached my goal several more Austrian squadrons shot past us, not noticing me and my handful of men. They crossed the sunken road at a level place just ahead of me, and shortly after, as the sound of lively rifle fire showed me, came into contact with some infantry north of Rosberitz, whom I could not see from where I was. Soon a number of riderless horses swept back past us, and before long the whole lot came pelting by again in wild confusion. I sent a few shots after them, as the white cloaks of the riders made an excellent target in the poor light.

When I reached Rosberitz I found the situation there very critical. Sections and companies of different regiments of our division were dashing themselves furiously against very superior forces of the enemy. At first there were no reinforcements behind our weak detachments. The bulk of the division had been drawn away to the village of Chlum, situated on a height, and was violently engaged there. My half battalion, which I had been lucky enough to rejoin at the eastern outskirts of Rosberitz, was therefore the first reinforcement.

I really cannot say which was the more surprised, the Austrians or ourselves. However, the enemy masses concentrated and closed in on us from three sides in order to recover complete possession of the village. Fearful as was the effect of the fire from our needle-guns, as each wave collapsed a fresh one came to take its place. Murderous hand-to-hand fighting took place in the streets between the thatched cottages on fire. All idea of fighting in regular units was lost. Everyone shot and stabbed at random to the best of his ability. Prince Anthony of Hohenzollern was seriously wounded and collapsed. Ensign von Woyrsch—now a field-marshal—remained with a handful of men by the prince while the battle swayed this way and that. The prince's gold watch was handed over to me to prevent its falling into the hand of enemy looters. Before long we were in serious danger of being cut off. Austrian bugles were being blown in a side street which came out behind us, and we could hear the roll of the enemy's drums, which made a more hollow sound than ours. We were hard pressed in front as well, and there was nothing for it but to retire. We were saved by a burning roof which had fallen into the street and formed a barrier of flame and thick smoke. We escaped under its protection to the shelter of a height just northeast of the village.

We were furiously disappointed, and refused to withdraw any further. As the most senior officer present, Major Count Waldersee of the 1st Regiment of Foot Guards—who fell before Paris in 1870 at the head of the

" Queen Augusta " Guard Grenadier Regiment—ordered the two standards we had to be planted in the ground. The men flocked to them, and the units were reorganised. Reinforcements were already coming up from the rear, and so, with drums beating, we all stormed forward once more against the enemy, who had contented himself with recovering possession of the village. However, he soon evacuated it in order to conform to the general retreat of his army.

In Rosberitz we found the Prince of Hohenzollern again, but unfortunately he shortly afterwards succumbed to his wounds in hospital at Königinhof. The enemy had carried off his faithful guard as prisoners with them. I lost several grenadiers from my section in that way. They had defended themselves very bravely in a brickworks. Two days later, as we were pitching our camp south-west of the fortress of Königgrätz in the course of our march to the south, these men came up and rejoined us. The Commandant of the fortress had sent them out in the direction of the Prussian camp-fires in order to be relieved of the responsibility of feeding them. They were lucky enough to strike their own unit at once.

In the evening of the battle we proceeded to Westar, and remained there until we left the battlefield for good. The doctor wanted to send me to hospital on account of my head wound, but as I expected there would be another battle behind the Elbe I contented myself with poultices and a light bandage, and for the rest of the march had to wear a cap instead of my helmet.

The feelings which assailed me on the evening of July 3 were of a very special kind. Next to thankfulness to our Lord God, the dominant emotion was a certain proud consciousness that I had co-operated in a feat which added a new page of glory to the history of the Prussian Army and our Prussian Fatherland. We had not yet appreciated the full extent of our victory; but it was already clear to us that it was a very different matter from the previous battles. I had kind thoughts for my fallen and wounded comrades. My section had lost half its strength—sufficient proof that it had done its duty.

When we crossed the Elbe by a temporary bridge at Pardubitz on the evening of July 6 the Crown Prince was waiting there for the regiment, and gave us his thanks for our behaviour in the battle. We thanked him with loud cheers and continued our march, proud of the praise lavished upon us by the Commander-in-Chief of our army, who was also the heir to the Prussian throne, and prepared to follow him to further battlefields.

However, the rest of the campaign brought us nothing but marches, certainly no events worth mentioning. The armistice which followed on July 22 found us in lower Austria about 30 miles from Vienna. When we began our homeward march soon after, we were accompanied by an unwelcome guest, cholera. We only got rid of it by degrees, and then not before it had exacted a large toll of victims from our ranks.

We remained a few weeks on the Eger. During that period I met my father in Prague. As a member of the Order of St. John he was employed in a hospital on the battlefield of Königgrätz. We did not let slip such an opportunity of visiting the neighbouring battlefield of our great King. To our intense surprise we found that adjacent to the monument to Field-Marshal Count Schwerin (who fell at Prague) erected by the State of Prussia after the War of Liberation, there was another which the Emperor Joseph II., a great admirer of Frederick the Great, had had erected to the memory of his enemy hero.

In the course of the last war I was again specially reminded of the visit to this battlefield. There was a close parallel between the situation of Prussia in 1757 and that of Germany in 1914. Just as Kolin followed Prague, so the failure of our great offensive in the battle of the Marne, which followed a succession of victories, involved a fateful prolongation of our Fatherland's fight for existence. But while the conclusion of the Seven Years' War showed us a mighty Prussia, we behold a shattered Germany at the end of the four years' desperate struggle. Have we been unworthy of our fathers?

Continuing our march home, we crossed the frontiers of Bohemia and Saxony on September 2, and on the 8th the frontier of the Mark of Brandenburg at the Grosenhain—Elster road. A triumphal arch greeted us. We marched through it on our homeward way to the strains of " Heil dir im Siegerkranz." I need not try to describe our feelings!

On September 20 we made our triumphal entry into Berlin. The grand review followed on what is now the Königsplatz, but was then a sandy parade-ground. The site of the present General Staff building was occupied by a timber yard, which was connected with the town by a lane bordered with willows. Starting from the parade-ground, the troops marched under the Brandenburger Tor, up the Linden to the Opernplatz. Here took place the march past His Majesty the King. Blücher, Scharnhorst and Gneisenau looked down from their pedestals. They might well be pleased with us!

My battalion had assembled in the Floraplatz in order to take its place in the column. It was here that my Commanding Officer handed me the Order of the Red Eagle, 4th Class, with swords, and told me to put it on at once, as the new decorations were to be worn for the triumphal march. As I looked about me, apparently in some embarrassment, an old lady stepped out of the crowd of spectators and fastened the decoration to my breast with a pin. So whenever I have crossed the Floraplatz in later years, whether walking or riding, I have always gratefully remembered the kind Berlin lady who once gave the eighteen-year-old lieutenant his first order there.

After the war Hanover was assigned to the 3rd Guards Regiment as peace station. The intention was to pay the former capital a special compliment. We were not pleased to be sent there, but when the hour of parting struck, twelve years later, as the regiment was transferred to Berlin, there was not a man in its ranks who did not regret leaving it. I myself had to leave the beautiful town as early as 1873, but I had then grown so fond of it that I took up residence there after my retirement from the service later on.

We had soon made friendships in our new station. Of course, many Hanoverians held completely aloof from us for political reasons. We never condemned anyone for loyalty to the hereditary reigning House, however deep was our conviction that the union of Hanover with Prussia was essential. We regarded Guelph feeling as hostile only where, as illustrated by the conduct of individuals, it showed that it did not bear its sorrow with dignity, but expressed it in ill-mannered behaviour, insults or insubordination.

As the years rolled by we made ourselves ever more at home in Hanover, which, in the happiest way, seems to have all the advantages of a big town with none of its disadvantages. A lively, aristocratic social life, which attained its climax after the war with France when their Highnesses Prince Albert of Prussia and his wife resided there for several years, alternated with visits to the excellent Court Theatre which was made very cheap to the young officer. Splendid parks and one of the finest of German forests, the Eilenriede, surround the town, and in them we could enjoy ourselves, walking or riding in our spare time. And if, instead of going to the autumn exercises of the Guard Corps at Potsdam, we attended manœuvres in the province, we gradually got to know and appreciate the peculiar charm of all Lower Saxony from the mountains to the sea. The Waterloo Platz was the scene of such duties as there were. It was there that for three years I trained my successive batches of recruits, and had my first quarters—living and sleeping room—in one of its barracks. Even to-day, whenever I visit that part of the town, I go back in thought to the golden hours of youth. Almost all my comrades of that time have joined the great army. Quite recently I have had an opportunity of seeing Major von Seel (retired), who was my Company Commander for many years. I owe this man of more than eighty years more than I can say.

In the summer of 1867 His Majesty the King visited Hanover for the first time. When he arrived I was in the guard of honour which was drawn up before the palace in George's Park, and my War Lord made me happy by asking me on what occasion I had won the Order of

Swords.   In later years, after I had also won the Iron
Cross in 1870-1, my Kaiser and King has often asked me
the same question when I have been reporting for transfer
or promotion.   I always thought of this first occasion with
the same joy and pride as possessed me then.

The political, military and social circumstances of
Hanover became ever more stable.   Before long this new
province, too, was to prove on many a bloody battlefield
that it was equally part and parcel of Prussia!

When the war of 1870 broke out I took the field as
adjutant of the 1st Battalion.   My Commanding Officer,
Major von Seegenberg, had gone through the campaigns
of 1864 and 1866 as a company commander in the regiment.   He was a war-hardened old Prussian soldier of
irresistible energy and tireless concern for the welfare of
his troops.   The relations between us were good on both
sides.

The opening of the campaign brought my regiment,
as indeed the whole Guard Corps, bitter disappointment,
inasmuch as we marched for weeks and yet did not come
into contact with the enemy.   It was not until after we
had crossed the Moselle above Pont à Mousson and nearly
reached the Meuse that the events west of Metz on August
17 summoned us to that neighbourhood.   We turned
north, and after an extraordinarily tiring march reached
the battlefield of Vionville in the evening of that day.
Relics of the fearful struggle of our 3rd and 10th Corps
on the day before met our eyes at every turn.   Of the
military situation as a whole we knew next to nothing.
Thus it was in an almost complete mental fog that on
August 18 we marched from our camp at Hannonville,
west of Mars la Tour, and reached Doncourt about mid-

day. Although this was a relatively short march, it required an enormous effort owing to the fact that it was carried out in close mass formation, and that we unfortunately crossed the Saxon (12th) Corps. Besides, the heat was terrific, the dust awful, and we had been unable to get enough water since the previous day. On the march I had visited the cemetery of Mars la Tour to see the grave of a cousin of mine in the 2nd Guard Dragoons who had fallen; and I availed myself of the opportunity of riding over the ground across which the 38th Infantry Brigade and the 1st Guard Dragoon Regiment had made their attack. Groups, in places whole mounds, of corpses, both Prussian and French, showed what a murderous encounter had taken place only quite a short distance away from us.

We halted at Doncourt, and began to think of cooking a meal. Rumours ran round that Bazaine had marched west and so got away. The enthusiasm of the previous day had somewhat waned. Suddenly a tremendous cannonade started in the east. The 9th Corps had got into touch with the enemy. The " stand to " cheered us all up. Our nerves began to brace themselves up again and our hearts to beat faster and stronger. We resumed our march to the north. The impression that we were on the eve of a great battle grew stronger from minute to minute. We went on, and quite close to Batilly received orders to unfurl our colours. This was done to the accompaniment of a threefold " hurrah." What a moving moment that was! Almost simultaneously some Guard batteries galloped past us, going east towards the enemy's positions. The main features of the battle became more distinct. From the heights of Amanweiler right to St.

Privat thick, heavy clouds of smoke were rising. Enemy infantry and artillery were posted there in several successive lines. For the time being their fire was directed with extreme fury against our 9th Army Corps. Its left wing was apparently commanded by the enemy. We could not make out more.

To avoid a frontal attack against the enemy's lines we took a gulley which ran parallel to the enemy's front for about three miles, and turned north to Ste. Marie aux Chênes. This village had been attacked and captured by the advance guard of our division and part of the 12th Corps, which was marching on Auboué on our left. After the capture of Ste. Marie our brigade deployed immediately south of the village and on a front facing it. We rested. Truly a peculiar kind of rest! Stray bullets, from enemy riflemen pushed forward from St. Privat, fell here and there among our formations in close order. Lieutenant von Helldorf, of the 1st Guards Regiment, was shot quite close to me. His father, commanding a battalion of the same regiment, had fallen, also not far from where I stood, at Rosberitz in the Battle of König-grätz in 1866. Several men were wounded.

I turned the situation over in my mind. Away to the east, almost on the right flank of our present front, lay St. Privat, crowning a gentle sloping hill and connected with Ste. Marie aux Chênes, about a mile and a quarter away, by a dead-straight road bordered with poplars. The country north of this road was for the most part concealed by the trees, but gave the same impression of lack of cover as that south of the road. On the height itself an almost unearthly silence reigned. Our eyes strove involuntarily to pierce the secrets we suspected there. Apparently it was not thought necessary on our side to try and pierce the veil by reconnaissance. So we remained quietly where we were.

About half-past five in the afternoon our brigade received orders to attack. We were to press forward in a northerly direction on the east side of Ste. Marie, and when we had crossed the road, wheel to attack St. Privat. The thought that these skilful movements could be taken in the right flank from St. Privat sprang to one's mind at once.

Just before our brigade rose up, the whole neighbourhood of St. Privat sprang to life and shrouded itself in the smoke of lines of French infantry. What had happened was that the 4th Guards Brigade, which was not in our division, was already pressing on south of the road. For the time being the whole force of the enemy's fire was turned against it. These troops would have been reduced to pulp in a very short time if we, the 1st Guards Brigade, had not immediately attacked north of the road, and thereby taken the burden off them. Indeed, it seemed almost impossible to get forward at all. My Commanding Officer rode forward with me to reconnoitre the country ahead and give the battalion its route direction within the orbit of the brigade. A hurricane of continuous fire now swept over us from every quarter. Yet we had to try and execute the movement which had been begun. We managed at length to cross the road. Once across, the compact columns formed a front against the enemy lines, and in open order stormed forward towards St. Privat. Every man tried his hardest to get to close quarters with the enemy in order to use his rifle, which was inferior to the *chassepot*. The sight was as terrible as impressive.

The ground behind the mass surging forward, as if against
a hailstorm, was strewn with dead and wounded, and yet
the brave troops pressed on without stopping. They were
gradually deprived of their officers and N.C.O.s, who had
to be replaced by the best of the fusiliers and grenadiers.
As I was riding forward I saw the general of the Guard
Corps, Prince Augustus of Würtemberg, on horseback at
the outskirts of Ste. Marie. He was following the terrible
crisis in which his splendid regiment was involved and
looked like being destroyed. It is said that just opposite
him Marshal Canrobert was standing at the entrance to
St. Privat.

To get his battalion out of the vortex of the masses
north-east of Ste. Marie and give it the necessary room to
fight, my Commanding Officer did not make it form a
front against St. Privat, but at first made it follow a fold
of the ground, and continue the original movement to the
north. We had thus a certain amount of cover, but we
made so great a detour that after wheeling we formed the
left wing of the brigade. In these circumstances we
managed, with increasing losses, to get half-way to Ste.
Marie Roncourt.

Before we could prepare to envelop St. Privat we had
to see what the situation was at Roncourt, which the
Saxons from Aboué did not yet seem to have reached. I
rode forward, found the village unoccupied either by friend
or foe, but noticed that there was French infantry in the
quarries east of the village. I was successful in getting
two companies of my battalion into Roncourt in time.
Soon after the enemy made a counter-attack from the
quarry, but was beaten off. It was now possible for the
two other companies, no longer anxious about their flanks

and rear, to turn against the northern exit from St. Privat to relieve—at least to some extent—the fearful frontal attack of the rest of the brigade. Later, after Roncourt had been occupied by parts of the 12th Corps, the two companies we had used there were brought up.

Meanwhile the bloody struggle continued uninterruptedly in the front.

On the enemy's side it was an unceasing storm of rifle-fire from several lines of infantry, fire which strove to make all life impossible on the broad, exposed field of attack. On our side it was a line—a line with innumerable gaps—formed by remnants of units which did not merely cling to the ground, however, but strove time after time to close with the enemy in spasmodic rushes. I held my breath as I watched the scene in utter anguish lest an enemy counter-attack should hurl our men back. But except for an attempt to break out with cavalry north of St. Privat, an attempt which did not survive the first charge, the French did not leave their positions.

There was now a pause in the infantry action. Both sides were exhausted and lay facing one another, firing but seldom. The halt in the hostilities on the battlefield was so marked that I rode along the firing line from the left wing almost to the centre of the brigade without feeling I was running any risk. Now, however, our artillery which had been brought up began its work of preparation, and before long fresh forces, the 2nd Guards Brigade from Ste. Marie, made their appearance among the fast vanishing remnants of the 4th and 1st, while Saxon reinforcements approached from the north-west. The pressure on the tortured infantry was sensibly relieved. There, where death and ruin seemed the only prospect, a fresh battle spirit seemed to stir, a new will to victory was born, which reached its heroic climax in a fierce charge at the enemy. It was an indescribably moving moment when our foremost lines rose for the final assault just as the sun was going down. No orders urged them on. Spiritual enthusiasm, a stern resolve to conquer and the holy lust of battle drove them forward. This irresistible impetus carried everything away with it. The bulwark of the foe was stormed as darkness descended. A fierce exultation seized all our men.

The softer sides of human emotion came to the surface when, late in the evening, I counted the remnants of our battalion and on the next morning visited the yet smaller fragments of the other units of my regiment. At such times we think not only of the victory that has been won, but of the price which has been paid for it. The 3rd Guards Regiment had suffered losses of 36 officers and 1,060 non-commissioned officers and men, of which 17 officers and 306 men were killed. All the Guards infantry regiments had similar losses to show. During the last great war the losses in battle of our infantry regiments repeatedly reached the level of those suffered by the Guards at St. Privat. I was able to appreciate from my own experience what that meant to the troops. What a mass of the best, frequently irreplaceable, human energy has sunk into the grave. And, on the other hand, what a superb spirit must have lived in our people to enable them to keep our army resolute in a struggle lasting years!

On August 19 we buried our dead, and in the afternoon of the 20th we marched away to the west. On the way our divisional commander, Lieutenant-General von Pape, gave us his thanks for our victory, but laid special emphasis on the fact that we had only done our bounden duty. He concluded with these words, "In short, what applies to us is the old soldier's hymn : ' Whether thousands to left, Or thousands to right, Of all friends bereft, A soldier must fight.' " Our reply was a thunderous cheer for His Majesty the King.

Whatever military criticisms may be levelled at the Battle of St. Privat, they detract in no way from its inward grandeur. That grandeur lies in the spirit with which the men bore the terrible crisis for hours on end and finally overcame it victoriously. That feeling was thenceforth paramount in our minds whenever we remembered August 18. The stern mood which had possessed our men throughout the battle soon faded away. In its place came a sense of pride in individual prowess and collective achievement which lives to-day. Once more, in the year 1918, and again on hostile soil, I celebrated the anniversary of St. Privat with the 3rd Guards Regiment of which I was once more a member by the favour of my King. Many "old gentlemen" who fought with me in 1870, among them Major von Seel, whom I have mentioned, had come from home to the Front for the anniversary. It was the last time that I was to see the proud regiment !

I hear that the monuments to the Prussian Guard on the heights of St. Privat have now been thrown down by our enemies. If it really is so, I do not believe that German heroism can be degraded by acts of that kind. Many a time have I seen German officers and men standing before French monuments, even those on German

D

soil, and giving expression to their respect for an enemy's achievements and sacrifices.

After the battle the commander of my battalion, as the only unwounded Staff officer, took over the command of the regiment. I remained his adjutant in his new post.

The course of the operations which came to such a memorable conclusion at Sedan brought little of note in my way. We were present at the prelude, the Battle of Beaumont, on August 30, but being in the reserve were only spectators. On September 1 also, I followed the course of the battle mainly in the rôle of a looker-on. The Guard Corps formed the north-eastern section of the iron ring which closed in on MacMahon's army during that day. In particular the 1st Guards Brigade was held in readiness behind the heights east of the Givonne valley from the morning to the afternoon. I used this period of inactivity to visit the long line of Guard batteries posted at the edge of the heights. They were firing across the valley at the French lying on the wooded heights on the far side. From this point we had a comprehensive view of the whole region from the Forest of Ardennes to the valley of the Meuse. I felt as if I could almost touch the heights of Illy and the French positions west of the Givonne stream, including the Bois de la Garonne. The catastrophe to the French Army thus developed practically before my eyes. I was able to observe how the German ring of fire gradually closed in on the unhappy enemy and watch the French making heroic efforts, though these were doomed to failure from the start, to break through our encircling lines by thrusts at different points.

The battle had a quite special interest for me. The fact is that on the previous day, as we were going through Carignan, a talkative French harness-maker from whom I had bought a riding-whip as we passed had told me that the French Emperor was with his army. I had handed this piece of news on, but no one would believe it. On the day of the battle, when speaking of the destruction of the enemy which was becoming more complete from minute to minute, I remarked : " Napoleon too is stewing in that cauldron." My remark was greeted with laughter. My triumph was great when my statement was subsequently confirmed.

That day my regiment took no more active share in the battle. About three o'clock in the afternoon we followed the 1st Guards Regiment over the Givonne sector. By that time the bottom had been knocked out of the French resistance by the fire of our artillery, coming as it did from all sides. All that remained to be done was to press the enemy back into Sedan to convince him once and for all that further resistance was perfectly hopeless. The picture of destruction which I beheld during this process from the north-eastern edge of the Bois de la Garonne surpassed all the horrors that had ever met my gaze, even on the battlefield.

Between four and five we went back to our bivouac. The battle was over. Only towards evening a shell flew by and a bullet whistled over our heads. When we looked towards the edge of the forest a scowling Turco waved his rifle threateningly at us and disappeared with great bounds into the darkness of the trees.

Never, either before or since, have I spent the night on a battlefield with the same feeling of quiet satisfaction as possessed me now. For after "Now thank we all our God" had resounded through the darkness, every man lay down to dream of a speedy end to the war. Of course, we were bitterly deceived so far as that was concerned, The war continued. There are those among us who have represented the continuation of the French resistance after the battle of Sedan as merely a piece of useless French self-mutilation. I was not able to share that view, for I cannot but approve the far-reaching views which animated the dictators of France at that time. In my opinion the fact that the French Republic took up arms at the point where the Empire had been compelled to lay them down was not only a proof of ideal patriotic spirit, but of far-seeing statesmanship as well. I firmly believe, even to-day, that if France had abandoned her resistance at that moment she would have surrendered the greatest part of her national heritage, and with it her prospects of a brighter future.

In the morning of September 2 we had a visit from the Crown Prince, who brought us the first news of the capture of Napoleon and his army, and in the afternoon it was followed by that of our King and military leaders. It is impossible to form any conception of the unexampled enthusiasm with which the monarch was received. The men simply could not be kept in the ranks. They swarmed round their dearly-loved master, and kissed his hands and feet. His Majesty saw his Guards for the first time in the campaign. With tears streaming down his face he thanked us for all we had done at St. Privat. This was indeed a rich reward for those fateful hours! Bismarck was also in the King's suite. In Olympian calm he was riding at the end of the cavalcade, but he was recognised and received a special cheer, which he accepted with a smile. Moltke was not present.

In the morning of September 3 my regiment received an order to advance on Sedan and drive any French who happened to be outside the fortress within its walls. The idea of this was to prevent the large bodies of our enemy who were roving round the outskirts from being tempted to pick up the enormous numbers of rifles that were lying about, and make the attempt, however hopeless, to cut their way through. I rode on ahead through the Bois de la Garonne to the heights immediately above the town. There I discovered that the " Red-Trousers," which added such a picturesque touch to the landscape, were merely harmless searchers for cloaks and coats which they wanted to take with them into captivity.

The intervention of my regiment was therefore unnecessary ; a few patrols from other troops which were encamped nearby were all that was required. When I rode back with this news to my regiment, which was coming up behind, I saw a cloud of dust in the woods on the road going north. A French military doctor who was standing in front of Quérimont Farm (which had been converted into a hospital), and accompanied me part of the way, told me that in that cloud of dust was the Emperor Napoleon, who was on his way to Belgium with a guard of Black Hussars. If I had reached that road a few minutes earlier I should have been an eye-witness of the historic spectacle.

In the evening of that day we left the battlefield and returned to our quarters. Then, after a day's rest, we resumed our march on Paris. Our advance brought us first over the battlefield of Beaumont, and then through districts which have been the scene of fateful encounters in the last great war. On September 11 and 12 the regiment was at Craonne and Corbény, two pretty little villages lying at the foot of the Mont d'Hiver. Once more, on May 28, 1918, I stood on that same Mont d'Hiver with my All-Highest War Lord, while the battle of Soissons—Rheims was in progress. I told His Majesty that I had encamped there forty-eight years before. The two villages were now little more than heaps of rubbish. The house at the corner of the market-place of Corbény in which I had had my quarters had vanished under rubble and ashes. The Mont d'Hiver, which was a green, partly wooded ridge in 1870, was now nothing but a bare, steep chalk cliff from which guns, the spade and the entrenching tool had removed every vestige of soil. What a melancholy return, even in that hour of triumph.

On September 19, from the plateau of Gonesse, five miles north-east of St. Denis, we had our first glimpse of the French capital. The gilded domes of the Invalides and other churches sparkled in the morning sunlight. I am sure that when the Crusaders gazed for the first time on Jerusalem their feelings were the same as ours when we saw Paris lying at our feet. We started off at three o'clock in the morning, while it was still dark, and spent the entire day—a beautiful autumn day—lying in the stubble fields ready to intervene if we or the neighbouring divisions met with difficulty in placing and occupying our outpost line. It was not until late in the afternoon that we got back to billets. We remained for some time in quarters at Gonesse, a place which enjoys some historical note from the fact that in 1815 Blücher and Wellington, who had reached Paris, met here to discuss the future course of the operations.

Instead of a complete and speedy victory, we were to be faced with many months of thoroughly exhausting and thankless investment operations, which were but seldom interrupted on our front by any noteworthy sortie. Their monotony was first broken about Christmas, when the bombardment of the forts made things a little more lively in a military sense.

The middle of January brought me a special event. I was sent, with a sergeant, as representative of my regiment to the proclamation of the Emperor at Versailles. I received the order in question in the evening of January 16. Before the night was out I was to get to Margency, twelve miles away, where the Headquarters Staff of the Meuse Army had made arrangements for the billeting of all deputations coming from the east. From there we were to proceed to Versailles on the 17th, passing through St. Germain. I could not negotiate the distance—about twenty-five miles—on horseback, as I had my kit to take with me. I therefore promptly planted myself, with my sergeant and soldier servant, on the transport wagon of the Body Company of the 1st Guards Regiment, which happened to be where I was and had also been summoned to Versailles. Off we went at a snail's pace in the dark, freezing night to Margency, where a warm fireside, a good bed of straw and tea were awaiting us.

Early on the 18th the commander of the Body Company told me that he had just received orders not to proceed to Versailles but to return to the regiment. Fortunately another comrade took me and my servant in his dogcart, and my sergeant met with a welcome reception somewhere else. So we trotted off on a bright winter morning to our next stage, St. Germain. But there is no such thing as a lasting compact with Fate. Our dogcart, piled high with our belongings, suddenly lost a wheel and pitched the whole lot of us on to the road. Fortunately we soon came across a field-smithy which repaired the damage, so that we were able to join the rest of our fellow-travellers at breakfast in the Pavillon d'Henri Quatre, splendidly situated on the terrace above the Seine.

It was a peculiar collection of carriages which made its entrance into Versailles as the sun was setting. There were representatives of every type of vehicle which could be scraped up from the châteaux, villas and farms round Paris. The greatest sensation was made by a potato-wagon the driver of which was celebrating the day by displaying a huge Prussian flag—there was no German flag as yet—to right and left of his seat. I soon found myself in a good billet in the Avenue de Paris kept by a cheerful old lady, and in the evening we all assembled for an excellent supper—a luxury we had not known for ages—in the Hôtel des Reservoirs.

The ceremony of the 18th is familiar enough. I have countless impressions of it. It goes without saying that the personality of my all-gracious King and master had the most inspiring and yet the most touching effect upon me. His calm and simple, yet commanding presence gave the ceremony a greater sanctity than all external pomp. The affectionate enthusiasm for the illustrious sovereign was fully shared by all present, no matter to what German tribe they belonged. Indeed our South German brothers gave the most vociferous expression to their joy at the foundation of the " German Empire." For historic reasons we Prussians were somewhat more reserved, for we had learned to know our own value at a time when Germany was but a geographical expression. That cannot be said in future!

For the evening of the 18th the generals present in Versailles were invited to His Majesty's table in the *Préfecture*. The rest of us were the Emperor's guests at the Hôtel de France.

January 19 began with an inspection of the old French royal palace with its proud collection of pictures immortalizing the glories of France. We also visited the great park. Then the sudden thunder of cannon from the town burst upon us. The garrison of Versailles had already received the alarm and was on the march. What had happened was that the French had made their great sortie from Mont Valérien. We watched the battle for a considerable time in the capacity of idle spectators. In the afternoon we started out on our homeward journey, and late that night I reached the headquarters of my regiment at Villers le Roi, five miles north of St. Denis, thankful that I had been privileged to witness the great historic event and do honour to him who was now my Emperor.

The fruitless sortie from Mont Valérien was France's last great effort. It was followed on the 26th by the capitulation of Paris and on the 28th by the general armistice. Immediately after the surrender of the forts our brigade was pushed forward into the western bend of the Seine between Mont Valérien and St. Denis. We found good, well-furnished billets just on the bank of the river, opposite Paris and close to the Pont de Neuilly.

There I had an opportunity to make at least a nodding acquaintance with Paris. In the morning of March 2 I went for a ride in the company of an orderly officer of the Guard Hussars, across the Pont de Neuilly, to the Arc de Triomphe. I could not keep away from it any more than my friend Bernhardi, then lieutenant of Hussars and the first man to enter Paris, had been able to the day before. Then I rode down the Champs Elysées, through the Place de la Concorde and the Tuileries to the Louvre, and finally returned home along the Seine and through the Bois de Boulogne. Throughout my ride I let the historical monuments of the past of a great enemy produce their full effect upon me. The few inhabitants who showed themselves adopted an attitude of aloofness.

Although I am little inclined to cosmopolitanism I have always been free from prejudice towards other nations. Though their peculiarities are somewhat foreign to me, I do not fail to see their good side. I admit that the temperament of the French nation is too vivacious, and therefore too capricious for my taste. On the other hand the *élan* which these people display in a fashion all their own even in times of crisis has a particular attraction for me.

But what I appreciate most of all is the fact that strong personalities can produce such an effect on the masses and subject them so completely to their influence that the French nation is able to lay aside every kind of private interest, even to the point of complete self-sacrifice, out of devotion to a patriotic ideal. In contrast to this I must mention the behaviour of the French to defenceless prisoners in the last war, behaviour which frequently approached sheer sadism and could not be condoned on the ground of their vivacious temperament.

The day after my visit to Paris the Guard Corps had the high honour and immense joy of being paraded at Longchamps before His Majesty the Kaiser and King. The war-tried regiments defiled in the old Prussian manner before their War Lord, at whose command they were ever ready to give their lives for the protection and glory of the Fatherland.

There was no longer any question for us of a proper march through Paris, that having been assigned previously to other army corps, because the preliminary peace had meanwhile been signed and Germany had no mind to force a foe, whom she had beaten in honourable fight, to drink the cup of humiliation to the dregs.

It was before Paris too that we celebrated His Majesty's birthday on March 22. It was a lovely, warm spring day, and we had a field service in the open air, a salute of guns from the forts, and banquets for both officers and men. The cheerful prospect of a speedy return home, our duty loyally done, doubled our enthusiasm.

But we were not to leave France quite so soon as we hoped, for at first we had to remain on the northern front of Paris in and around St. Denis, and were thus witnesses of the struggle between the French Government and the Commune.

Even during the siege we had been able to follow the first developments of the new revolutionary movement. We knew of the insubordination displayed by certain circles of political extremists towards the Governor of Paris. When the armistice was concluded the revolutionary movement began to show its head even more openly. Bismarck had said to the French plenipotentiaries : " You came by revolution and a second revolution will sweep you away." It looked as if he were going to be right.

Speaking generally, our interest in this Revolution was small at first. It was only from the beginning of March, when the Commune began to get the upper hand and the development of events seemed to point to an open conflict between Paris and Versailles, that we paid more attention. And now while German corps isolated the capital of France on the north and east, in a certain sense as the allies of the Government troops, the latter began their long and weary attack on Paris from the south and west. Events outside the walls of the fortress could best be followed from the heights above the Seine at Sannois, four miles north-west of Paris. Certain commercially-minded Frenchmen had established telescopes there which they allowed, on payment, any German soldier to use who wished to see the drama of a civil war. I myself made no use of these facilities, but contented myself with getting a peep at what was going on in Paris from a top window in the Cerf d'Or Hotel at St. Denis (when I reported for the daily orders there), or when I went out riding on the island in the Seine by St. Denis. Tremendous fires from the end of April revealed the track of the fighting in the centre of the town. I remember that on May 23, in particular, I had the impression that the whole of the inner quarters of Paris were threatened with destruction.

Refugees painted the situation in the city in the most lurid colours, and the facts did not seem in any way to fall short of the descriptions. Arson, looting, the murder of hostages, in short all those diseases (now called Bolshevism) which are symptomatic of a body politic broken in war were already of common occurrence. The threat of a released Communist leader : "The Government hasn't the courage to havè me shot, but I shall have the courage to shoot the Government," seemed about to be put into practice. How completely the once so strong and sensitive national feeling of the French had been extinguished by the Communists is shown by the following declaration : "We glory in bayoneting our Government in the back under the enemy's nose." It will be seen that the Bolshevist system for the regeneration of the world, the system of which we too have had recent experience, cannot even lay claim to originality.

At long last I saw the end of the Commune one day from my top window in St. Denis. Outside the main walls of Paris Government troops surrounded Montmartre, and from its northern declivity, then unbuilt on, stormed the commanding height which was the last bulwark of the insurgents.

It seems to me a bitter irony of fate that the only political party in Europe which then glorified the movement, in complete ignorance of the true facts as I must presume, is to-day compelled to take the sharpest measures against Bolshevist attempts in our own Fatherland. It is a further proof of what doctrinaire prejudice can lead to until corrected by practical experience.

With the warning example of the events I have just described before our eyes we turned our backs on the French capital at the beginning of June, and after three days in the train reached our happy, victorious Fatherland.

This time the entry into Berlin was made from the

Tempelhofer Feld. For the occasion representatives of all the German troops were present in addition to the Guard Corps. My hope of a third triumphal entry through the Brandenburg Gate, a hope I long cherished not for my own sake but for that of my Kaiser and King and my country, was not to be fulfilled!

CHAPTER III

WITH a rich fund of experiences in every military sphere we had returned home from French soil. With the single Fatherland we had created a single Army, the fundamental form of which was only affected superficially by the demands of State particularism. Uniformity of military plans was now assured as effectively as uniformity of organisation, armament and training. It was in the natural course of German development that Prussian experience and the Prussian system should have decisive weight in the reconstruction of the Army.

Peace training was again resumed in all quarters. For the next few years I was still employed on regimental duty. I then followed my own inclination for a higher military training, sat for the *Kriegsakademie*, and was duly accepted in 1873.

The first year did not quite come up to my expectations. Instead of studying military history and the lessons of recent battles we were mostly regaled on the history of the art of war and the tactics of earlier days. These were secondary matters. In addition we were compelled to take mathematics, which only a few of us would require later in the form of trigonometry in the Survey Department. It was only with the last two years and his posting to other arms that the ambitious young officer could be completely satisfied. Then it was that my horizon was

53

materially extended, thanks to the guidance of splendid
teachers—of whom I must mention, in addition to Major
von Wittich, Colonel Ketzler and Captain Villaume of
the General Staff, as well as the historians, Geheimrat
Duncker and Professor Richter—and in company with
gifted contemporaries such as the later Field-Marshals von
Bülow and von Eichorn as well as the later General von
Bernhardi.

The many-sided social life of Berlin also comes into
the picture. I had the honour to be invited into the exclusive circle of His Royal Highness Prince Alexander of
Prussia, and thereby came into touch not only with leading
soldiers, but also with men of science as well as those in the
State and Court service.

When my time at the *Kriegsakademie* came to an end
I first returned to my regiment at Hanover for six months,
and then in the spring of 1877 was attached to the General
Staff.

In April, 1878, my transfer to the General Staff followed, and I was promoted to the rank of captain. A few
weeks later I was posted to the Headquarters Staff of the
2nd Army Corps at Stettin. My military career outside
regimental duty begins at this point, for subsequently I
was only twice employed with troops until I was appointed
to the command of a division.

The General Staff was certainly one of the most remarkable structures within the framework of our German
Army. Side by side with the distinctly hierarchical form
of the commands it constituted a special element which had
its foundation in the great intellectual prestige of the Chief
of Staff of the Army, Field-Marshal Count von Moltke.
The peace training of the General Staff officer offered a

guarantee that in case of war all the commanders in the field should be controlled from a single source, and all their plans governed by a common aim. The influence of the General Staff on those commanders was not regulated by any binding order. It depended far more on the military and personal qualities of the individual officer. The first requirement of the General Staff officer was that he should keep his own personality and actions entirely in the background. He had to work out of sight, and therefore be more than he seemed to be.

I believe that, taking it all round, the German General Staff has known how to perform its extraordinarily difficult tasks. Its achievements were masterly to the last, though there may have been mistakes and failures in individual cases. I could imagine no more honourable testimony in its favour than the fact that the enemy has demanded its dissolution in the Peace conditions.

It has been suggested in many quarters that there was something mysterious about the work of the General Staff. Nothing more preposterous could be imagined. As has been the case with all our military achievements, those of the General Staff are the result of the application of sound reasoning to the immediate problem in hand. Accordingly it is often necessary for the General Staff officer to turn his attention to all sorts of trivial affairs as well as to high military questions. I have known many most gifted officers who failed in this respect, and were therefore useless as General Staff officers, or proved themselves a positive disadvantage to the troops in that capacity.

As I was the youngest Staff Officer at Corps Headquarters I was naturally mainly occupied with these smaller matters. That was very disappointing for me at first, but

E

then I subsequently acquired a love for the work, because I recognised its importance for the execution of the larger plans and the welfare of the troops. It was only in the annual General Staff rides that I had a chance of interesting myself in higher matters, in my capacity as the handy-man of the Corps Commander. At this time I also took part in the first Fortress General Staff ride at Königsberg conducted by General Count Waldersee, Chief of Staff of the 10th Army Corps. My Corps Commander was General Hans von Weyherrn, an experienced soldier who had fought in the service of Schleswig-Holstein in his youth, commanded a Cavalry Division in 1866, and an Infantry Division in 1870-1. It was a real pleasure to see the old officer, a magnificent rider, on horseback in the uniform of his Blücher Hussars. To both my Chiefs of Staff, Colonel von Petersdorff at first and then Lieutenant-Colonel von Zingler, I owe my thanks for a thorough training in practical General-Staff work.

In the year 1879 the 2nd Corps had Kaiser Manœuvres and received the thanks of His Majesty. It was on this occasion that I met the Russian General Skobeleff, who was then at the pinnacle of his fame after the war with Turkey. He gave me the impression of a man of ruthless energy; alert of mind and undoubtedly a very efficient higher commander. His habit of boasting was a less pleasant characteristic.

I must not omit from my story the fact that I had been married at Stettin. My wife, too, is a soldier's child, being the daughter of General von Sperling, who was Chief of Staff of the 6th Corps in 1866 and Chief of Staff of the 1st Army in 1870-1. He had died after the war with France.

I found in my wife a loving mate who shared with me loyally and untiringly my joys and sorrows, my cares and labours. She presented me with a son and two daughters. The son did his duty in the Great War as an officer on the General Staff. Both daughters are married, and their husbands likewise fought in the Great War.

In 1881 I was transferred to the 1st Division at Königsberg. This change gave me greater independence, brought me into closer contact with the troops, and took me back to my native province.

Of the events of my military life there I must specially mention the fact that the well-known military writer, General von Verdy du Vernois, was for a time my general.

The general was a highly gifted and interesting personality. As a result of his wealth of experience in high Staff posts during the wars of 1866 and 1870-1 he possessed an extraordinary knowledge of the decisive events of that period. Further, he had previously been attached to the Headquarters of the Russian Army in Warsaw during the Polish rising of 1863, and had thus gained a deep insight into the political conditions on our eastern frontier. What he had to tell about his life—and he had brilliant powers of description—was therefore extremely instructive, not only from the military, but also from the political point of view. General von Verdy was a pioneer in the domain of applied war technics. Under his guidance and in the mutual exchange of ideas I learnt very much that was to be useful to me later on when I was myself teaching at the *Kriegsakademie*. This brilliant man thus had a most inspiring influence upon me in many directions. He was always a kind superior who gave me his fullest confidence.

I have also grateful memories of Colonel von Barten-werffer, the Chief of Staff of my Corps at that time. His General Staff rides and exercises for the winter syllabus of the General Staff were masterly conceptions, and his criticisms were particularly instructive.

After three years on the Staff of the 1st Division I was transferred to the command of a company in the 58th Infantry Regiment, stationed at Fraustadt in Posen.

In this return to regimental duty I was taking charge of a company which was recruited almost exclusively from Poles. I thus learned to know the very great difficulties which the ignorance of officers and men of each other's tongue placed in the way of a good understanding between them. I myself did not know Polish except for a few expressions which I had picked up in childhood. It was thus very difficult for me to have any influence on the company, and it was made even more difficult by the fact that the men were distributed in thirty-three civilian billets, even including the windmills on the outskirts of the town. Taking it all round, however, my experiences with Polish recruits were not unfortunate. The men were industrious, willing and—what I must particularly emphasize—devoted so long as I bore in mind their difficulties in learning their work, and also did all I could for their welfare. At that time I considered that the somewhat marked frequency of cases of theft and drunkenness among the Poles was due far less to any moral inferiority than to unsatisfactory training in early years. It is a matter of sincere regret that I have been compelled to revise my favourable opinion of the Poles of Posen since I have heard of all the horrors which the insurgents have perpetrated upon non-combatants. I could never

have expected that from the countrymen of my old
Fusiliers !

My thoughts travel back pleasantly even to-day to the
time, unfortunately only five years and a quarter, when I
was commanding a company. For the first time I was
familiarized with life in a small, semi-rural garrison.
Besides the comrades of my circle I found a kind welcome
in the neighbouring estates, and I was once again in
direct contact with the men. I admit I took great pains
to know the peculiarities of each individual, and thus knit
a firm bond between myself and those under me. For
that reason I found it very hard to part from my company,
in spite of the apparent advantages my recall to the
General Staff brought me.

This event occurred in the summer of 1885 when I
was transferred to the Great General Staff. A few weeks
later I was a major. I was in the department of Colonel
Count von Schlieffen, subsequently General and Chief of
the General Staff of the Army, but I was also placed at
the disposal of the department of Colonel Vogel von
Falkenstein, who was subsequently Corps Commander of
the 8th Army Corps, and then Director of the Corps of
Engineers and Pioneers. In this latter department I
co-operated for more than a year in the first working-out
of the Field Service Regulations, a fundamental code of
instruction issued by His Majesty's command. I thus
came into touch with the most distinguished departmental
heads of that time.

In the spring of 1886 His Royal Highness, Prince
William of Prussia, took part in the manœuvres at
Zossen, which lasted several days. These were intended
to provide a practical test of the soundness of the new

regulations before they were actually introduced. It was the first time I had the honour of meeting him who later was to be my Kaiser, King and Master, William II. In the following winter the Prince attended a war game of the Great General Staff. On this occasion I was the commander of the " Russian Army."

It was in these years that Field-Marshal Count von Moltke handed over all direct business with the departments of the Great General Staff to his assistant, General Count Waldersee. But in spite of the change his spirit and prestige still governed everything. No special guarantee was required that Count Moltke should at all times be held in infinite honour, or that any of us could forget his wonderful influence.

In the circumstances I have described, I myself seldom came into immediate official contact with the Field-Marshal, but I was fortunate enough to meet him unofficially from time to time. At a dinner party in the house of Prince Alexander I once witnessed a scene which throws an interesting light both on his views and his personality. After dinner we were looking at a picture by Camphausen, representing the meeting of Prince Frederick Charles with the Crown Prince on the battle-field of Königgrätz. General von Winterfeldt, who was present, told us from his personal knowledge that at the moment of the meeting Prince Frederick Charles had said to the Crown Prince : " Thank God you've come, Fritz, or it would probably have gone hard with me." As Winterfeldt said this, Count Moltke, who was just then choosing a cigar, came up to us in three great strides, and said very emphatically : " The Prince needn't have said that. He knew quite well that the Crown Prince had been summoned, and was to be expected on the battlefield about mid-day, so that victory was certain." With these words the Field-Marshal returned to the cigars.

On the occasion of the Emperor's birthday the generals and officers of the General Staff were the guests of the Field-Marshal. At one of these gatherings one of the gentlemen asserted that Moltke's toast of the Kaiser would not contain more than ten words, including the speech and the first " Hoch." Bets were laid. I myself did not take any part. The gentleman who took the bet lost, for the Field-Marshal merely said : " Meine Herrn der Kaiser hoch." (" Gentlemen, Hoch der Kaiser.") Words which were certainly enough in our circle, and coming from such a mouth. The same bet was to have been made the next year, but the other side would not close. He would have won this time, for Count Moltke said : " Meine Herrn, Seine Majestat der Kaiser und Königer lebe hoch." (" Gentlemen, I give you the toast of His Majesty the Kaiser and King.") That makes eleven words with the first " Hoch."

On the other hand, in the ordinary relations of life, Count Moltke was not at all uncommunicative, but a charming and challenging conversationalist with a great sense of humour.

In the year 1891 I saw the Field-Marshal for the last time—it was on his death-bed. I was permitted to see him the morning after he had passed peacefully away. He lay in his coffin as if asleep and without his usual wig, so that his splendid head could be seen to perfection ; only a laurel wreath round his temples was wanted to complete the picture of an ideal Cæsar-head. How many great thoughts had emanated from that brain ; what a lofty idealism had had its seat there! What nobility of mind had dwelt there to work unselfishly for the welfare of our Fatherland and its Sovereign! In my opinion, our people have not since produced his equal in intellect and character. Yes, Moltke's greatness was unique in its combination of these qualities.

Our first Emperor—a great Emperor—had left us three years before. I took part in the vigil in the Cathedral, and was permitted to render the last services there to my Imperial and Royal master, whom I so dearly loved. My thoughts took me through Memel, Königgrätz and Sedan to Versailles. They culminated in the memory of a Sunday in the previous year on which I had stood under the historic corner window of the Imperial Palace in the midst of a jubilant throng. Carried away by the general enthusiasm I held up my five-year-old son, and showed him our aged Master, with the words: " If you never forget this moment as long as you live you will always do right." The great soul of a great man and Sovereign had departed to the comrades to whom he had sent his greeting a few years before by the dying Field-Marshal von Roon.

There is a block of grey marble on my desk. It comes from the very spot in the old Cathedral on which the coffin of my Emperor had been laid. No more valued present could have been made to me. I need not attempt to clothe in words the thoughts which rise within me, even to-day, when I look at that piece of stone.

His son, the Emperor Frederick, Germany's pride and hope, was permitted to reign for but a short time. He died of an incurable disease a few months after his father. The Great General Staff was then away on a General

Staff ride in East Prussia. We therefore took the oath to His Majesty the Emperor and King, William II., in Gumbinnen. I thus pledged my fealty to my present War Lord in the same spot at which twenty-six years later I was to translate it into action.

Fate was kind to me in that I found a very great variety of employment within the General Staff. Even while I was attached to the Great General Staff I was assigned the duty of teaching tactics at the *Kriegs-akademie*. I derived great pleasure from this work, and continued it for five years. It is true that the demands on me were very great, as in addition to this I had to do other work simultaneously, both in the Great General Staff and subsequently as the first General Staff Officer with the Headquarters Staff of the 3rd Army Corps. In these circumstances the day of twenty-four hours often seemed too short. It was quite usual for me to work the whole night through.

I got to know many gifted young officers, who justified the brightest hopes, during this period when I was teaching at the *Akademie*. Many of their names now belong to history; I can only mention here Lauenstein, Luttwitz, Freytag-Loringhoven, Stein and Hutier. Two Turkish General Staff Officers were also under me for about two years at this time—Schakir Bey and Tewfik Effendi. The first became a marshal in his own country, the second a general.

At the Headquarters Staff of the 3rd Corps my general was General von Bronsart the younger, a very gifted officer who had been employed on the General Staff in 1866 and 1870-1, and subsequently, like his elder brother, became War Minister.

My transfer to the War Ministry in 1889 brought me a totally different sphere of work. I there took over a section of the Common War Department. This change is attributable to the circumstance that my former divisional general, General von Verdy, had become War Minister, and summoned me to the Ministry when he remodelled it. I was therefore director of a section when I was still a major.

Although at the start this change did not correspond to my wishes and inclinations, I subsequently attached a very high value to the experience I gained by my occupation with affairs and a sphere of work which had hitherto been unknown to me. I had plenty of opportunity of becoming acquainted with formality and red tape (which are scarcely altogether avoidable) and the bureaucratic attitude of the minor officials. But I also came to realize the strong sense of duty with which everyone was imbued, though working at the highest pressure.

The most stimulating part of my work was the issue of Field Engineering regulations, and the initiation of the use of heavy artillery in an ordinary action. Both stood the test of the Great War.

Everything that was done, in peace as well as—and more particularly—in the recent war, deserves the highest recognition. But only a calm, judicial and expert investigation will confirm the justness of that view.

But although I came to realize that my employment at the War Ministry had been extremely valuable to me, I was none the less very glad to be freed from the bureaucratic yoke when I was appointed to the command of the 91st Infantry Regiment at Oldenburg in 1893.

The position of commander of a regiment is the finest

in the army. The commander sets the stamp of his personality on the regiment, and it is the regiment which carries on tradition in the army. The training of his officers, not only in service, but also in social matters, and the control and supervision of the training of the troops are his most important tasks. I endeavoured to cultivate a sense of chivalry among my officers, and efficiency and firm discipline in my battalions. I also fostered the love of work and independence side by side with a high ideal of service. The fact that infantry, artillery and cavalry were all comprised in the garrison gave me an opportunity for frequent exercises with combined arms.

Their Royal Highnesses, the Grand Duke and Grand Duchess, were very gracious to me, and the same applies to the heir and his wife. Indeed, I found a kindly reception everywhere, and thoroughly enjoyed myself in the garden-like town. The quiet, homely character of the Oldenburg people appealed to me. I have pleasant and grateful memories of my time amongst them. By the favour of my Emperor, on my seventieth birthday I was once more, to my great joy, brought into touch with my old regiment by being placed *à la suite*. So I can still call myself an Oldenburger to-day.

On my appointment, in 1896, as Chief of Staff to the 8th Army Corps at Coblenz I came for the first time into close contact with our Rhine Provinces. The high spirits and friendly attitude of the Rhinelanders were particularly pleasant to me. To tell the truth, I had to get used to their habit of sliding over the serious questions of life, as also to their temperament, which is more sentimental than that of the North Germans. The course of our historical development and the difference in geographical and economic conditions entirely explain certain contrasts of thought and feeling. But the view that this involves the necessity of separating the Rhineland from Prussia seems to me an outrage and base ingratitude.

The merry life on the Rhine had me, too, under its spell, and I spent many a happy time there.

At the start my general was General von Falkenstein, who was known to me when I was at the Great General Staff as the head of a section, and also at the War Ministry as the Director of my department. However, he was soon succeeded by His Royal Highness the Grand Duke of Baden.

I was to stand at the side of this royal officer for three and a half years. I remember these years as among the best of my life. His noble mind, in which dignity united with charming cordiality, his typically unflagging sense of duty combined with his soldierly manner and talents, quickly won him the affection and confidence of all his subordinates as well as of the Rhenish population.

It was while I was Chief of Staff that the 8th Corps had Kaiser Manœuvres in 1897. His Majesty the Kaiser and King was satisfied with what he saw both at the review and in the field. The festivities at Coblenz were also marked by the unveiling of the monument to the Emperor William I at the " German Quadrangle," that beautiful spot at which the Moselle joins the Rhine opposite the fortress of Ehrenbreitstein.

As the result of my employment for nearly four years as Chief of Staff of an Army Corps I was so advanced in seniority that there was now no question of my appointment to the command of an infantry brigade. At the conclusion of that period I was therefore appointed to the command of the 28th Division at Karlsruhe in 1900.

I obeyed this command, emanating from His Majesty, with quite special satisfaction. My previous official relations with the Grand Duke's heir secured me the lasting good will of their Royal Highnesses the Grand Duke and Grand Duchess, a good will which was extended to my wife and made us very happy. In addition, we had the splendid country of Baden, with all its natural beauties and its warm-hearted inhabitants, and Karlsruhe with all its wealth of art and science, not to mention its society, less concerned with details, which embraced all professional circles.

In the division all three arms were united for the first time under one command. The duties of a divisional commander are therefore more varied, and demand a sphere of activity which is principally concerned with the great business of war.

With a feeling of deep gratitude I left Karlsruhe in January, 1905, when the confidence of my All-Highest War Lord summoned me to the command of the 4th Army Corps.

In assuming my new duties I took over a position of unlimited responsibility, a position which is usually held longer than other military posts and on which the holder, like the commander of a regiment, sets the stamp of his personality. I myself pursued the principles that had previously guided me, and I think I may claim some success. The affection of my subordinates, to which I had always attached high importance as one of the mainsprings of efficiency, was, at any rate, expressed in the most moving way when I left this splendid post after eight and a quarter

years. As early as the first year I had the honour to
present my army corps to His Majesty in the Kaiser
Manœuvres, which began with a review on the battlefield
of Rossbach. His Majesty expressed his gratitude, which
I gladly attributed to my predecessors and my troops.

I had the distinction of being presented to Her Majesty
the Empress during these manœuvres. This first meeting
was to be followed by others in more serious times, when
I could appreciate more and more how much this noble
lady meant to her exalted husband, her Fatherland, and
myself.

In my time the 4th Army Corps was in the Army
Inspection of His Royal Highness Prince Leopold of
Bavaria. In him I knew a superb leader and splendid
soldier. We were to meet again later in the Eastern
theatre of war. The Prince then placed himself under my
orders, in the most generous manner, in the interests of
the whole situation, although he was substantially senior to
me in the service.

In December, 1908, at His Majesty's command I and
the then General von Bülow, whose corps also belonged to
the Army Inspection of the Prince, took part at Munich
in the celebration of the fiftieth anniversary of the entry of
His Royal Highness into the service. On this occasion we
had the honour to be most graciously received by His
Royal Highness the venerable Prince Regent Leopold.

Magdeburg, our station, is often not appreciated as it
should be by those who do not know it. It is a fine old
town, and its " Broad Way " and venerable cathedral
ought to be of great interest to sightseers. Since its fortifications were dismantled their place has been taken by
imposing suburbs fulfilling all modern requirements.

Extensive parks have been laid out to make up for what the country round Magdeburg lacks in natural beauties. Theatres, concerts, museums and lectures see to the representation of art and science. It will thus be seen that it is possible to have a pleasant time there when off duty, especially if as agreeable society is available as fell to our lot.

Social life in the town was supplemented by social life at the Courts of Brunswick, Dessau and Altenburg, as well as at numerous country houses. It would take too long to mention them all by name. But I have particularly grateful memories of our annual several days' visit to my venerable and fatherly friend, General Count von Wartensleben, now ninety years of age, at Carow.

Nor was there any lack of sport. Quite apart from the well-known excellent hare and pheasant shooting to be obtained in the Province of Saxony, the Court hunting at Letzlingen, Mosugkau near Dessau, Blankenberg in the Hartz and Altenburg, as well as drives and deer-stalking on several private estates, guaranteed us plenty of wild boar, fallow deer, red deer, roe-deer and game shooting.

All this time the resolution to retire from the army was taking shape in my mind. My military career had carried me much farther than I had ever dared to hope. There was no prospect of war, and as I recognised that it was my duty to make way for younger men, I applied in the year 1911 to be allowed to retire. As the hand of legend has descended upon this unimportant event also, I declare emphatically that this step was not the result of any disagreement, whether of an official or private nature.

It was anything but easy for me to put an end to a relationship that had lasted for years, a relationship that

was very dear to me, and more especially to part from my
4th Corps, for which I had a great affection.   But it had
to be !   I never suspected that within a few years I should
gird on the sword again and, like my men, be permitted
to serve my Army Corps, my Emperor and Empire, my
King and Fatherland once again.

In the course of my career I have learned to know
almost all the German tribes.   I believe I am therefore in
a position to judge what a wealth of the most valuable
qualities our nation has at its disposal, and to say that
hardly any other country in the world possesses, in the
versatility of its people, so many conditions precedent to
an abounding intellectual and moral life as Germany.

CHAPTER IV

I HAD said farewell to service on the active list with a feeling of loyal gratitude to my Emperor and King, with the warmest wishes for his army, and in full confidence in the future of our Fatherland. But at heart I always remained the soldier.

Thanks to the wealth of experience I had gained in every department of my profession, I could look back gratefully and feel satisfied with what I had done in the past. There was nothing that could cloud the vision over which lay the magic of youthful dreams come true. My voluntary retirement was therefore not without a certain feeling of home-sickness for the life I had left behind me, nor without many a longing to be back in the army. In the peace of my new life my hope that my Emperor would again summon me if danger threatened the Fatherland, my wish to devote the last ounce of my strength to his service, lost nothing of their force.

At the time I left the army an extraordinarily strong intellectual wave was sweeping over it. The invigorating contest between the old and the new, between ruthless progress and careful conservatism, was reconciled to a happy medium in the practical experiences of the recent war. In spite of the new path which those experiences opened to us, they leave no doubt that with all the increased importance to be attached to material in war, the value of the training and moral education of the soldier is as high as

F

ever.   Stout-hearted action has maintained its precedence
over all the refinements of intellect.   Presence of mind
and strength of character take a higher place in war than
fertility of ideas.   Weapons of destruction have been
brought to perfection, but war has none the less preserved
its simple, I might almost say coarse, forms.   It tolerated
no weaknesses of human nature, and permitted no fas-
tidiousness in military training.   What it demanded as the
primary necessity was that a man should be turned into a
resolute personality.

In peace-time a good many people believed that the
army could be reproached with unproductivity.   That reproach was perfectly justified if by unproductivity the
creation of material values was meant.   But it was certainly false if productivity was regarded from the higher,
moral point of view.

Everyone who does not, either from prejudice or mere
spite, condemn our military work in peace-time offhand,
must admit that the army is the finest school for will and
action.   How many thousands of men have first learnt
under its influence of what physical and moral feats they
were capable, and acquired that self-confidence and inward
strength that have never left them through life?   Where
have the idea of equality and the sense of unity among our
people found more striking expression than in the all-
levelling school of our great national army?   In the army
the human inclination to unlimited egotism, with its
tendency to disintegrate society and the State, is blessedly
purified and transformed by the rigid self-discipline of the
individual for the good of the whole.   The army trained
and strengthened that mighty organising impulse which we
found everywhere in our Fatherland, in the domain of

politics as in that of science, in trade as in technical studies, in industry as in the labour world, in agriculture as in the professions. The conviction that the subordination of the individual to the good of the community was not only a necessity but a positive blessing had gripped the mind of the German Army, and through it that of the German nation. It was only thus that the colossal feats were possible which were needed, and which we performed under the stress of dire necessity and against a world of enemies.

On the battlefields of Europe, Asia and Africa the German officer and the German soldier have given proof that our training was on right lines. Even if the long duration of the last war with its multiplicity of impressions had a demoralising effect on some natures, even if the moral principles of others were confused by the unnerving action of mental and physical overstrain, and characters, hitherto blameless, succumbed to the many temptations, the true core of the army remained sound and worthy of its task in spite of the unprecedented strain.

The reproach has often been cast at the old army that it endeavoured to degrade a free man into an automaton. But the battlefields of the Great War have shown what a strengthening influence our training has had even in the midst of the disintegrating influences of incessant fighting. Innumerable glorious and yet terrible events have shown to what heights of voluntary heroism the German soldier can rise, not because he says, " I must," but because he says, " I can."

It is inherent in the course of events that with the dissolution of the old army new paths for the training of the nation and its defensive forces should be demanded.

As regards that demand I stand by the old tried principles. Even if there are some who do not consider there is anything final about the means by which we are to recover the power to repeat our former achievements, they will certainly agree with me at least in this, that it is vital for the future of our Fatherland that we should recover that power. If not, it means that we should renounce our position in the world, and let ourselves be degraded to the rôle of the anvil because we have neither the courage nor the resolution to be the hammer when the hour comes.

The question how we are to recover the great school of organisation and energy which we possessed in our old army is possibly a fateful one, not only for the future political prosperity of our German Homeland, but even for its economic welfare. Germany can recover and succeed as easily as any other country on earth, and maintain a tolerable place in the world, but only by putting forth and concentrating all her creative energies. Unfortunately there is a marked reaction against the existing strong order, thanks to the disintegrating influences of an unsuccessful war and the fallacious idea that the subordination of all the national forces to one controlling will could not have prevented the disaster to the Fatherland. Resentment against the ancient voluntary or compulsory subjection burst the old barriers, and wandered aimlessly in new paths. Can we hope for success along these lines? Hitherto we have lost far more in moral and ethical values from the effects of political dissolution than from the war itself. If we do not soon create new educative forces, if we continue to exhaust the spiritual and moral soil of our nation as we have done hitherto, we shall soon convert the foundations of our political existence to a barren waste!

PART II

The Campaign in the East

CHAPTER V

THE STRUGGLE FOR EAST PRUSSIA

1

The Outbreak of War and My Recall

THE unruffled course of my life after the year 1911 gave me a chance to devote my spare time to following political events in the world. What I thus saw was not indeed of a nature likely to fill me with satisfaction. I was not in the least anxious, but I could not get rid of a certain oppressive feeling. I was in a sense forced to the conclusion that we were venturing into the distant ocean of world politics before our foundations in Europe itself had been sufficiently secured. Whether the political storm-clouds hung over Morocco or gathered over the Balkans, I shared with the majority of my countrymen a vague feeling that our German foundations were being undermined. In recent years we had unquestionably been in the presence of one of those chauvinistic waves which seemed to recur at regular intervals in France. Their origin was known. They found their support in Russia or England—or both—quite indifferent to who or what was the open or secret, known or unknown driving force there.

I have never ignored the special difficulties with which German foreign policy has been faced. The dangers involved in our geographical situation, our economic necessities, and last, but not least, our frontier provinces with their mixed nationalities, stared us in the face. The policy of our enemies which succeeded in reconciling all their jealousies against us did not, in my opinion, require a high degree of skill. In the long run it was mainly responsible for the war. We neglected to make preparations to meet that danger. From the point of view of procuring allies our policy seemed to be inspired more by a code of honour than a proper regard for the needs of our people and our world situation.

When, even in the 'nineties, a subsequent German Chancellor considered he had to regard the progressive decay of the Danube Monarchy, our Ally, as obvious it is inconceivable that our statesmen should not have drawn the appropriate inferences.

I have always had the liveliest sympathy with the German-Austrian members of our race. All of us have thoroughly understood the difficulties of their position in their Fatherland. But in my opinion this feeling of ours was exploited far too freely by Austro-Hungarian politicians.

The "Nibelung Compact" was certainly solemn enough at the time it was made. It could not, however, blind us to the fact that in the Bosnian crisis, the occasion on which the phrase was coined, Austria-Hungary had precipitately dragged us after her, without that previous understanding due to an Ally, and then summoned us to cover her rear. It was clear that we could not abandon our Allies at that juncture. It would simply have meant that we strengthened the Russian Colossus, with the prospect of being crushed by it all the more certainly and irresistibly in the long run.

To me as a soldier, the contrast between Austria-

Hungary's political claims and her domestic and military resources was particularly striking.

To meet the huge armaments with which Russia had restored her position after the war in Eastern Asia we Germans had certainly increased our defences, but we had not required the same measures of our Austro-Hungarian Allies. It may have been a simple matter for the statesmen of the Danube Monarchy to meet all our suggestions for the increase of Austro-Hungarian armaments with a recital of their domestic difficulties, but how was it that we found no means of presenting Austria-Hungary with a definite alternative in this matter? We already knew of the enormous numerical superiority of our prospective enemies. Ought we to have permitted our Allies to make no use of a large part of their national resources available for the common defence? What advantage was it for us to have Austria-Hungary as a bulwark far to the south-east, when this bulwark was cracked at points innumerable and did not dispose of enough defenders to man its walls?

From the earliest times it seemed to me doubtful to rely on any effective help from Italy. It was an uncertain quantity; questionable even if the Italian statesmen favoured the idea. We had had an excellent opportunity of realising the weaknesses of the Italian Army in the war in Tripoli. Since that war the situation of Italy had improved but little, thanks to the shaky condition of its finances. In any case, it was not ready to strike.

It was along such lines that my thoughts and anxieties moved in those years. I had already had two personal experiences of war, on both occasions under strong and resolute political leadership combined with clear and straightforward military objectives. I was not afraid of war. I am not afraid of it now! But besides its uplifting influence, I knew its wholesale encroachment upon every side of human activity too well not to wish that it should be avoided as long as possible.

And now the war was upon us! The hopelessness of our prospects of compromising with France on the basis of the *status quo*, soothing England's commercial jealousy and fear of rivalry and satisfying Russia's greed without breaking faith with our Austrian Ally, had long created a feeling of tension in Germany, compared with which the outbreak of war was felt almost as a release from a perpetual burden we had carried all our lives.

Then came the Imperial summons to arms, and with it a proud army of whose efficiency the world had seldom seen the like. The hearts of the whole nation must have beat faster at the very sight of it. Yet there was no vainglorious boasting, in view of the task which faced it. As neither Bismarck nor Moltke had left us in any doubt as to what such a war would mean, every intelligent man asked himself whether we should be in a position to hold out, politically, economically and morally, as well as in a military sense.

But confidence was unquestionably stronger than doubt.

The news of the bursting of the storm broke in upon this train of thought and reflection. The soldier within me sprang to life again and dominated everything else. Would my Emperor and King need me? Exactly a year had passed without my receiving any official intimation of this kind. Enough younger men seemed available. I put myself in the hands of Fate and waited in longing expectation.

2

To the Front

THE Homeland listened in suspense.

The news from the various theatres of war realised our hopes and wishes. Liége had fallen, the action at Mülhausen had come to a victorious conclusion, and our right wing and centre were passing through Belgium. The first news of the victory in Lorraine was just reaching the country, rejoicing all hearts. In the East, too, the trumpets of victory were sounding. Nowhere had anything happened which seemed to justify any anxiety.

At three o'clock in the afternoon of August 22 I received an inquiry from the Headquarters of His Majesty the Emperor as to whether I was prepared for immediate employment.

My answer ran : " I am ready."

Even before this telegram could have reached Main Headquarters I received another. It was to the effect that my willingness to accept a post in the field was assumed as a matter of course, and informed me that General Ludendorff was to be assigned to me. Further telegrams from Main Headquarters explained that I was to leave for the East immediately to take command of an army.

About three o'clock in the morning I went to the station, imperfectly equipped, as time had been short, and waited expectantly in the well-lit hall. It was only when the short special train steamed in that I wrenched my thoughts away from the hearth and home which I had had to leave so suddenly. General Ludendorff stepped briskly from the train and reported as my Chief of Staff of the 8th Army.

Before that moment the general had been a stranger to me, and I had not yet heard of his feats at Liége. He first explained the situation on the Eastern Front to me as communicated to him on August 22 at Main Headquarters (Coblenz) by Colonel-General von Moltke, Chief of the General Staff. It appeared that the operations of the 8th Army in East Prussia had taken the following course : At the opening of hostilities the army had left the 20th Army Corps, strengthened by fortress garrisons and other Landwehr formations in a position covering the southern frontier of East and West Prussia from the Vistula to the Lötzen Lakes. The main body of the army (1st and 17th Army Corps, 1st Reserve Corps, 3rd Reserve Division, the garrison of Königsberg, and the 1st Cavalry Division) had been concentrated on the Eastern frontier of East Prussia, and had there attacked the Russian Niemen Army, which was advancing under General Rennenkampf. There had been an action at Stallupönen on August 17, and another at Gumbinnen on the 19th and 20th. During the battle at Gumbinnen news had been received of the approach of the Russian Narew Army, under General Samsonoff, towards the German frontier between Soldau and Willenberg. The Commander of our 8th Army had therefore reason to expect that the Russians would have crossed that stretch of the frontier by the 20th. In view of this threat to their communications from the south, the Headquarters Staff broke off the action at Gumbinnen and reported to Main Headquarters that they were not in a position to hold the country east of the Vistula any longer.

General von Moltke had not approved of that decision. It was his opinion that an attempt must be made to destroy the Narew Army before we could think of abandoning East Prussia, so important from the military, economic and political point of view. The conflict between the views of Main Headquarters and those of the Army Headquarters Staff had necessitated a change in the command of the 8th Army.

At the moment the situation of this army appeared to be as follows : It had successfully shaken off the enemy. The 1st Army Corps and the 3rd Reserve Division were moving west by rail, while the 1st Reserve Corps and the 17th Army Corps were marching for the line of the Vistula. The 20th Army Corps was still in its positions on the frontier.

Before long I and my new Chief of Staff were at one in our view of the situation. Even while at Coblenz General Ludendorff had been able to issue such preliminary orders as brooked no delay, orders intended to secure the continuance of operations east of the Vistula. The most important of these was that the 1st Army Corps should not be brought too far west, but directed on Deutsch-Eylau, that is towards the enemy and behind the right wing of the 20th Corps.

Everything else must and could be left for decision when we reached Army Headquarters at Marienburg.

Our conference had taken scarcely more than half an hour. We then went to bed. I made thoroughly good use of the time at my disposal.

We thus travelled together towards a joint future, fully conscious how serious the situation was and yet with perfect confidence in our Lord God, our brave troops and, last but not least, in one another. From now on we were to be united for years in common thought and action.

At this point I may well say something about my relations with General Ludendorff, then Chief of Staff and subsequently First Quartermaster-General. It has been suggested that these relations find a parallel in those between Blücher and Gneisenau. I will venture no opinion as to how far such a comparison reveals a departure from true historical perspective. As I have already said, I had myself held the post of Chief of Staff for several years. As I knew from my own experience, the relations between the Chief of Staff and his General, who has the responsibility, are not theoretically laid down in the German Army. The way in which they work together and the degree to which their powers are complementary are much more a matter of personality. The boundaries of their respective powers are therefore not clearly demarcated. If the relations between the General and his Chief of Staff are what they ought to be, these boundaries are easily adjusted by soldierly and personal tact and the qualities of mind on both sides.

I myself have often characterised my relations with General Ludendorff as those of a happy marriage. In such a relationship how can a third partly clearly distinguish the merits of the individuals? They are one in thought and action, and often what the one says is only the expression of the wishes and feelings of the other.

After I had learnt the worth of General Ludendorff, and that was soon, I realised that one of my principal tasks was, as far as possible, to give free scope to the intellectual powers, the almost superhuman capacity for work and untiring resolution of my Chief of Staff, and if necessary clear the way for him, the way in which our common desires and our common goal pointed—victory for our colours, the welfare of our Fatherland and a peace worthy of the sacrifices our nation had made.

I had to show General Ludendorff that loyalty of a brother warrior which we had learnt to find in German history from youth up, that loyalty in which our ethical philosophy is so rich. And indeed his work and his determination, his whole great personality were truly worthy of such loyalty. Others may think what they like. For him, as for so many of our great and greatest men, the time will come one day when the whole nation will look to him in admiration. I can only hope that in an equally critical hour of trial our Fatherland may find such a man again, a man who is every bit a man, a host in himself, unapproachable and uncompromising indeed, but created for a gigantic task if anyone ever was.

See how he was hated by his enemies, who rightly knew his worth!

The harmony of our military and political convictions formed the basis for our joint views as to the proper use of our resources. Differences of opinion were easily reconciled, without our relations being disturbed by a feeling of forced submission on either side. The hard work of my Chief of Staff translated our thoughts and plans into action at our Army Headquarters and, later, at Main Headquarters when the responsibilities of that post were entrusted to us. His influence inspired everyone, and no one could escape it without running the risk of finding himself off the common path. How otherwise could the enormous task have been done and full effect given to the driving force? Around us two gathered the wider circle of our colleagues, filled with a resolute soldierly sense of duty and well endowed with ideas. A feeling of deep thankfulness possesses me whenever I think of them!

3

Tannenberg

EARLY in the afternoon of August 23 we reached our Headquarters at Marienburg. We thus entered the region east of the Vistula which was to form the immediate theatre of our operations. At this moment the situation at the front had undergone the following development:

The 20th Corps had been withdrawn from its positions on the frontier by Neidenburg to Gilgenburg and east of it. In touch with this corps on the west the garrisons of the fortresses of Thorn and Graudenz were along the frontier as far as the Vistula. The 3rd Division had arrived at Allenstein as a reinforcement for the 20th Army Corps. After considerable delay the entrainment of the 1st Army Corps for Deutsch-Eylau had begun. The 17th Corps and the 1st Reserve Corps had reached the neighbourhood of Gerdauen on foot. The 1st Cavalry Division was south of Insterburg facing Rennenkampf's army. The garrison of Königsberg had passed through Insterburg in its retreat to the west. With a few exceptions there were no noteworthy bodies of infantry of Rennenkampf's Niemen Army on the west side of the Angerapp. Of the two Russian cavalry corps one was reported close to Angerburg, the other west of Darkehmen. Of Samsonoff's Narew Army apparently one division had reached the neighbourhood of Ortelsburg, while Johannisburg was

said to be in the enemy's possession. For the rest the
main body of this army seemed to be still concentrating
on the frontier with its western wing at Mlawa.

In the pocket-book of a dead Russian officer a note
had been found which revealed the intention of the enemy
Command. It told us that Rennenkampf's Army was
to pass the Masurian Lakes on the north and advance
against the Insterburg—Angerburg line. It was to attack
the German forces presumed to be behind the Angerapp
while the Narew Army was to cross the Lötzen—Ortelsburg line to take the Germans in flank.

The Russians were thus planning a concentric attack
against the 8th Army, but Samsonoff's Army now
already extended farther west than was originally
intended.

What indeed could we do to meet this dangerous
enemy scheme? It was dangerous less on account of the
audacity of the conception than by reason of the strength
in which it was to be carried out—at any rate strength
from the point of view of numbers. We could hope that
it would be otherwise as regards strength of will. During
the months of August and September Russia brought up
no fewer than 800,000 men and 1,700 guns against East
Prussia, for the defence of which we had only 210,000
German soldiers and 600 guns at our disposal.

Our counter-measures were simple. I will attempt
to make the broad outlines of our plan clear to the reader
even if he is not an expert.

In the first place we opposed a thin centre to Samsonoff's solid mass. I say thin, not weak. For it was
composed of men with hearts and wills of steel. Behind
them were their homes, wives and children, parents and

G

relatives and everything they had. It was the 20th Corps,
brave East and West Prussians. This thin centre might
bend under the enemy's pressure but it would not break.
While this centre was engaged two important groups on
its wings were to carry out the decisive attack.

The troops of the 1st Corps, reinforced by Landwehr
—likewise sons of the threatened region—were brought
for the battle from the right, the north-west, the troops
of the 17th Corps and the 1st Reserve Corps, with a
Landwehr brigade, from the left, the north and north-
east. These men of the 17th Corps and 1st Reserve
Corps as well as the Landwehr and Landsturm also had
behind them everything which made life worth living.

We had not merely to win a victory over Samsonoff.
We had to annihilate him. Only thus could we get a
free hand to deal with the second enemy, Rennenkampf,
who was even then plundering and burning East Prussia.
Only thus could we really and completely free our old
Prussian land and be in a position to do something else
which was expected of us—intervene in the mighty battle
for a decision which was raging between Russia and our
Austro-Hungarian Ally in Galicia and Poland. If this
first blow were not final the danger for our Homeland
would become like a lingering disease, the burnings and
murders in East Prussia would remain unavenged, and
our Allies in the south would wait for us in vain.

It was thus a case for complete measures. Everything
must be thrown in which could prove of the slightest use
in manœuvre warfare and could at all be spared. The
fortresses of Graudenz and Thorn disgorged yet more
Landwehr fit for the field. Moreover, our Landwehr
came from the trenches between the Masurian Lakes,

which were covering our new operations in the east, and handed over the defence there to a smaller and diminishing number of Landsturm. Once we had won the battle in the field we should no longer need the fortresses of Thorn and Graudenz, and should be freed from anxieties as regards the defiles between the lakes.

Our cavalry division and the Königsberg garrison with two Landwehr brigades were to remain facing Rennenkampf, who might fall upon us like an avalanche from the north-east at any time. But at the moment we could not yet say whether these forces would really be sufficient. They formed but a light veil which would easily be torn if Rennenkampf's main columns moved or his innumerable cavalry squadrons advanced, as we had to fear. But perhaps they would not move. In that case the veil would be enough to cover our weakness. We had to take risks on our flanks and rear if we were to be strong at the decisive point. We hoped we might succeed in deceiving Rennenkampf. Perhaps he would deceive himself. The strong fortress of Königsberg with its garrison and our cavalry might assume the proportions of a mighty force in the imagination of the enemy.

But even supposing Rennenkampf cradled himself in illusions to our advantage, would not his High Command urge him forward in forced marches to the south-west— in our rear? Would not Samsonoff's cry for help bring him in hot haste to the battlefield? And even if the sound of human voices echoed in vain, would not the warning thunder of the battle reach the Russian lines north of the Lakes, nay, to the enemy's Headquarters itself?

Caution with regard to Rennenkampf was therefore necessary, though we could not carry it to the extent of leaving strong forces behind, or we should find ourselves weaker on the battlefield than we ought to be.

When we considered the numbers on both sides a comparison with the probable Russian forces showed a great disparity against us, even if we counted in on our side the two Landwehr brigades which were then coming from Schleswig-Holstein, where they had been employed in coast protection (and assuming that they would arrive in time for the battle), and even if Rennenkampf did not move and indeed played no part. Moreover, it must be remembered that large bodies of Landwehr and Landsturm had to fight in the first line. Older classes against the pick of Russia's youth! We had the further disadvantage that most of our troops and, as the situation decreed, all those which had to deliver the *coup de grâce*, had just been engaged in heavy and expensive fighting. Had they not just been compelled to leave the battlefield of Gumbinnen to the Russians? The troops were not therefore marching with the proud feeling of being victors. Yet they pressed forward to the battle with stout hearts and unshaken confidence. We were told that their *moral* was good, and it therefore justified bold decisions. Where it was somewhat shaken such decisions could not fail to restore it. It had been thus before; could it be otherwise now? I had no misgivings on the score of our numerical inferiority.

He who reckons solely by the visible in war is reckoning falsely. The inherent worth of the soldier is everything. It was on that that I based my confidence. What I thought to myself was this:

The Russian may invade our Fatherland, and contact with the soil of Germany may lift up his heart, but that does not make him a German soldier, and those who lead him are not German officers. The Russian soldier had fought with the greatest obedience on the battlefields of Manchuria although he had no sympathy with the political ambitions of his rulers in the Pacific. It did not seem unlikely that in a war against the Central Powers the Russian Army would have greater enthusiasm for the war aims of the Tsar's Empire. On the other hand, I considered that, taking it all round, the Russian soldier and officer would not display higher military qualities in the European theatre than they had in the Asiatic, and believed that in comparing the two forces I was entitled to credit our side with a plus on the ground of intrinsic value instead of a minus for our numerical inferiority.

Such was our plan and such our line of reasoning before and for the battle. We compressed these ideas and intentions into a short report which we sent from Marienburg to Main Headquarters on August 23:

"Concentration of the army for an enveloping attack in the region of the 20th Corps planned for August 26."

On the evening of the 23rd I took a short walk on the western bank of the Nogat. From there the red walls of the proud castle of the Teutonic Knights, the greatest brick monument of Baltic Gothic, made a truly wonderful picture in the evening light. Thoughts of a noble chivalry of the past mingled involuntarily with conjecture as to the veiled future. The sight of the refugees flying past me from my home province deepened the sense of responsibility that possessed me. It was a melancholy reminder that war not only affects the fighting man, but proves a thousandfold scourge to humanity by the destruction of the very essentials of existence.

On August 24 I motored with my small Staff to the Headquarters of the 20th Corps, and thus entered the village which was to give its name to the battle so soon to blaze up.

Tannenberg! A word pregnant with painful recollections for German chivalry, a Slav cry of triumph, a name that is fresh in our memories after more than five hundred years of history. Before this day I had never seen the battlefield which proved so fateful to German culture in the East. A simple monument there bore silent witness to the deeds and deaths of heroes. On one of the following days we stood near this monument while Samsonoff's Russian Army was going to its doom of sheer annihilation.

On our way from Marienburg to Tannenberg the impression of the miseries into which war had plunged the unhappy inhabitants were intensified. Masses of helpless refugees, carrying their belongings, pressed past me on the road and to a certain extent hindered the movements of our troops which were hastening to meet the foe.

Among the Staff at the Corps Headquarters I found the confidence and resolution which were essential for the success of our plan. Moreover, they had a favourable opinion of the *moral* of the troops at this spot, which was at first the crucial point for us.

The day brought us no decisive information either about Rennenkampf's operations or Samsonoff's movements. Apparently it only confirmed the fact that Rennenkampf was moving forward very slowly. We

could not see the reason for this. Of the Narew Army,
we knew that its main columns were pressing forward
against the 20th Corps. Under its pressure this corps
refused its left wing. There was nothing doubtful about
this measure. Quite the contrary. The enemy, following up, would all the more effectively expose his right
flank to our left enveloping column which was marching
on Bischofsburg. On the other hand the hostile movement which was apparently in progress against our
western wing and Lautenburg attracted our attention, as
it caused us some anxiety. We had the impression that
the Russians were thinking of enveloping us in turn at
this point and coming in on the flank of our right column
as it executed the enveloping movement we projected.

August 25 gave us a rather clearer picture of Rennenkampf's movements. His columns were marching from
the Angerapp, and therefore on Königsberg. Had the
original Russian plan been abandoned? Or had the
Russian leaders been deceived by our movements and
suspected that our main force was in and around the
fortress? In any case we must now have not the slightest
hesitation in leaving but a thin screen against Rennenkampf's mighty force. On this day Samsonoff, obviously
feeling his way, was directing his main columns towards
our 20th Corps. The corps on the Russian right wing
was undoubtedly marching on Bischofsburg, and therefore
towards our 17th Corps and 1st Reserve Corps, which had
reached the district north of this village on this day.
Apparently further large Russian forces were concentrating at Mlawa.

This day marked the conclusion of the stage of
expectation and preparation. We brought our 1st Corps

round to the right wing of the 20th Corps. The general attack could begin.

August 26 was the first day of the murderous combat which raged from Lautenburg to north of Bischofsburg. The drama on which the curtain was rising, and whose stage stretched for more than sixty miles, began not with a continuous battle line but in detached groups; not in one self-contained act, but in a series of scenes.

General von François was leading his brave East Prussians on the right wing. They pushed forward against Usdau with a view to storming the key to this part of the southern battle front next day. General von Scholtz's magnificent corps gradually shook off the chains of defence and addressed themselves to the business of attack. Fierce was the fighting round Bischofsburg that this day witnessed. By the evening magnificent work had been done on our side at this point. In a series of powerful blows the wing corps of Samsonoff's right had been defeated and forced to retreat on Ortelsburg by the troops of Mackensen and Below (10th Corps and 1st Reserve Corps), as well as Landwehr. But we could not yet realize how far-reaching our victory had been. The Staff expected to have to meet a renewed and stout resistance south of this day's battlefield on the following day. Yet was their confidence high.

It was now apparent that danger was threatening from the side of Rennenkampf. It was reported that one of his corps was on the march through Angerburg. Would it not find its way to the rear of our left enveloping force? Moreover, disquieting news came to us from the flank and rear of our western wing. Strong forces of Russian cavalry were in movement away there in the south. We could not find out whether they were being followed up by infantry. The crisis of the battle now approached. One question forced itself upon us. How would the situation develop if these mighty movements and the enemy's superiority in numbers delayed the decision for days? Is it surprising that misgivings filled many a heart, that firm resolution began to yield to vacillation, and that doubts crept in where a clear vision had hitherto prevailed? Would it not be wiser to strengthen our line facing Rennenkampf again and be content with half-measures against Samsonoff? Was it not better to abandon the idea of destroying the Narew Army in order to ensure ourselves against destruction?

We overcame the inward crisis, adhered to our original intention, and turned in full strength to effect its realisation by attack. So the order was issued for our right wing to advance straight on Neidenburg, and the left enveloping wing " to take up its position at 4 A.M. and intervene with the greatest energy."

August 27 showed that the victory of the 1st Reserve Corps and 17th Corps at Bischofsburg on the previous day had had far-reaching results. The enemy had not only retired, but was actually fleeing from the battlefield. Moreover, we learned that it was only in the imagination of an airman that Rennenkampf was marching in our rear. The cold truth was that he was slowly pressing on to Königsberg. Did he, or would he, not see that Samsonoff's right flank was already threatened with utter ruin and that the danger to his left wing also was increasing from hour to hour? For it was on this day that François and Scholtz stormed the enemy's lines at and north of Usdau and defeated our southern opponent.

Now, when the enemy's centre pushed forward farther towards Allenstein—Hohenstein, it was no longer victory but destruction that lured it on. For us the situation was clear. On the evening of this day we gave orders for the complete encirclement of the enemy's central mass, his 13th and 15th Corps.

The bloody struggle continued to rage on August 28.

On the 29th a large part of the Russian Army saw itself faced with total annihilation at Hohenstein. Ortelsburg was reached from the north, Willenberg, through Neidenburg, from the west. The ring round thousands and thousands of Russians began to close. Even in this desperate situation there was plenty of Russian heroism in the cause of the Tsar, heroism which saved the honour of arms but could no longer save the battle.

Meanwhile Rennenkampf was continuing to march quietly on Königsberg. Samsonoff was lost at the very moment when his comrade was to give proof of other and better military qualities. For we were already in a position to draw troops from the battle front to cover the work of destruction in which we were engaged in the great cauldron, Neidenburg—Willenberg—Passenheim, and in which Samsonoff sought for death in his despair. Swelling columns of prisoners poured out of this cauldron. These were the growing proofs of the greatness of our victory. By a freak of fortune it was in Osterode, one of the villages which we made our Headquarters during the battle, that I received one of the two captured Russian Corps Commanders, in the same inn at which I had been quartered during a General Staff ride in 1881 when I was a young Staff officer. The other reported to me next day at a school which we had converted into an office.

As the battle proceeded ,we were able to observe what
splendid raw material, generally speaking, the Tsar had
at his disposal. I had the impression that it doubtless
contained many qualities worth training. As in 1866
and 1870, I noticed on this occasion how quickly the
German officer and soldier, with their fine feeling and
professional tact, forgot the former foe in the helpless
captive. The lust of battle in our men quickly ebbed
away and changed to deep sympathy and human feeling.
It was only against the Cossacks that our men could not
contain their rage. They ,were considered the authors of
all the bestial brutalities under which the people and
country of East Prussia had suffered so cruelly. The
Cossack apparently suffered from a bad conscience,
for ,whenever he saw himself likely to be taken
prisoner he did his best to remove the broad stripe
on his trousers which distinguished his branch of the
service.

On August 30 the enemy concentrated fresh troops
in the south and east and attempted to break our
encircling ring from ,without. From Myszaniec—that is,
from the direction of Ostrolenka—he brought up new
and strong columns to Neidenburg and Ortelsburg
against our troops, which had already completely
enveloped the Russian centre and were therefore presenting their rear to the new foe. There ,was danger ahead;
all the more so because airmen reported that enemy
columns twenty-three miles long—therefore very strong
—,were pressing forward from Mlawa. Yet we refused to
let go of our quarry. Samsonoff's main force had to be
surrounded and annihilated; François and Mackensen
sent their reserves—weak reserves, it is true—to meet the

new enemy. Against their resistance the attempt to mitigate the catastrophe to Samsonoff came to nought. While despair seized on those within the deadly ring, faint-heartedness paralysed the energies of those who might have brought their release. In this respect, too, the course of events at the Battle of Tannenberg confirmed the human and military experiences of yore.

Our ring of fire round the Russian masses, crowded closely together and swaying this way and that, became closer and narrower with every hour that passed.

Rennenkampf appears to have intended to attack the line of the Deime, east of Königsberg and between Labiau and Tapiau, this day. From the region of Landsberg and Bartenstein his masses of cavalry were approaching the battlefield of Tannenberg. However, we had already concentrated strong forces, weary but flushed with victory, for defence in the neighbourhood of Allenstein.

August 31 was the day of harvesting for such of our troops as were still engaged, a day of deliberation about the further course of operations for our leaders, and for Rennenkampf the day of the retreat to the Deime—Allenburg—Angerburg line.

As early as the 29th the course of events had enabled me to report the complete collapse of the Russian Narew Army to my All-Highest War Lord. The very same day the thanks of His Majesty, in the name of the Fatherland, had reached me on the battlefield. I transferred these thanks, in my heart as with my lips, to my Chief of Staff and our splendid troops.

On August 31 I was able to send the following report to my Emperor and King:

" I beg most humbly to report to Your Majesty that the ring round the larger part of the Russian Army was closed yesterday. The 13th, 15th and 18th Army Corps have been destroyed. We have already taken more than 60,000 prisoners, among them the Corps Commanders of the 13th and 15th Corps. The guns are still in the forests and are now being brought in. The booty is immense though it cannot yet be assessed in detail. The Corps outside our ring, the 1st and 6th, have also suffered severely and are now retreating in hot haste through Mlawa and Myszaniec."

The troops and their leaders had accomplished extraordinary feats. The divisions were now in bivouacs and the hymn of thanks of the Battle of Leuthen rose from their midst.

In our new Headquarters at Allenstein I entered the church, close by the old castle of the Teutonic Knights, while divine service was being held. As the clergyman uttered his closing words all those present, young soldiers as well as elderly Landsturm, sank to their knees under the overwhelming impression of their experiences. It was a worthy curtain to their heroic achievements.

4

The Battle of the Masurian Lakes

The sound of battle on the field of Tannenberg had hardly died down before we had begun to make our preparations for the attack on Rennenkampf's Russian Army. On August 31 we received the following telegraphic instructions from Main Headquarters:

11th Corps, Guard Reserve Corps and 8th Cavalry Division are placed at your disposal. Their transport has begun. The first task of the 8th Army is to clear East Prussia of Rennenkampf's army.

It is desired that with such troops as you can spare you should follow up the enemy you have just beaten in the direction of Warsaw, bearing in mind the Russian movements from Warsaw on Silesia.

When the situation in East Prussia has been restored you are to contemplate employing the 8th Army in the direction of Warsaw.

These orders were exactly what the situation required. They gave us a clear objective and left the ways and means to us. We considered we had reason to believe that what was left of Samsonoff's quondam army was a remnant which had already withdrawn to the shelter of the Narew or was on its way there. We had to count on its being reinforced. But that could not be for a considerable time. For the moment it appeared that all that was required was that this remnant should be watched by weak troops along the line of our southern frontier. Everything else must be assembled for the new battle. Even the arrival of the reinforcements from the West did not, in our opinion, enable us to employ forces in striking south over the line of the Narew.

It was quite clear what the word " Warsaw " meant in the second part of the order. In accordance with the plan of joint operations the armies of Austria-Hungary were to take the offensive from Galicia in the direction of Lublin, exercising their main pressure on the eastern portion of Russian Poland, while German forces in East Prussia were to hold out a hand to their allies across the Narew. It was a largely conceived, fine plan, but in the existing situation it produced grave embarrassments.

It did not take account of the fact that Austria-Hungary had sent a large army to the Serbian frontier, that 800,000 Russians had been sent against East Prussia, least of all that it had been betrayed with all its details to the Russian General Staff in peace time.

The Austro-Hungarian Army, after making a hazardous attack on superior Russian forces, was now involved in critical frontal battles, while at the moment we were not in a position to render any direct assistance, though we were holding up large hostile forces. Our Allies had to try and hold on until we had beaten Rennenkampf too. Only then could we come to their help, if not in full strength at least with our main forces.

As is known, Rennenkampf was then on the Deime—Allenburg—Gerdauen—Angerburg line. We did not know what the enemy had by way of secrets in the region south-east of the Masurian Lakes. The district of Grajevo was suspicious in any case. A good deal of movement was on foot there. Even more suspicious was the whole area behind the Niemen Army. In that quarter there was a continuous movement of trains and marching columns. Apparently that movement was to the west and south-west. Rennenkampf had doubtless received reinforcements. The Russian reserve divisions from the interior were now ready to take the field. Perhaps all that had hitherto been available were single corps which the Russian High Command believed they no longer needed against the Austrians in Poland. Would these units be sent to Rennenkampf or brought up near him, either to give him direct support or to strike at us from some unsuspected quarter?

So far as we could judge, Rennenkampf had more

than twenty divisions, yet he stood still and remained thus, while our army came up from the west and deployed for battle against him. Why did he not use the time of our greatest weakness, when the troops were exhausted and crowded together on the battlefield of Tannenberg, to fall upon us? Why did he give us time to disentangle our units, concentrate afresh, rest and bring up reinforcements? The Russian leader was known to be a fine soldier and general. When Russia was fighting in eastern Asia among all the Russian leaders it was the name of Rennenkampf that rang out over the world. Had his fame then been exaggerated? Or had the general lost his military qualities in the meantime?

Many a time has the soldier's calling exhausted strong characters, and that surprisingly quickly. The fine intellect and resolute will of one year give place to the sterile imaginings and faint heart of the next. That is perhaps the tragedy of military greatness.

We have opened and closed the book of Rennenkampf's responsibility for Tannenberg. Let us now go in thought to his headquarters at Insterburg, not to blame him but to try and understand him.

The disaster to Samsonoff showed General Rennenkampf that the main body of our 8th Army was not in Königsberg, as he supposed. But he none the less suspected that we still had strong forces in that powerful fortress. It thus seemed venturesome, too venturesome, to mask it and throw himself upon the victorious German army in the neighbourhood of Allenstein. It would be safer to hold on in the strong defensive positions between the Kurisches Haff and the Masurian Lakes. Against these lines the Germans could certainly not try their art of envelopment from the north, and only with much difficulty from the south. If they made a frontal attack he would fall upon their troops, crowded together, with strong forces held back in reserve. If they ventured on the improbable and pressed forward through the defiles between the lakes it would be possible to attack the left flank of their enveloping columns from the north while a newly-formed group was hurled at their right flank and rear from the direction of Grajevo. If all else failed, well and good—he could withdraw into Russia. Russia was large and the fortified line of the Niemen was at hand. Rennenkampf was no longer chained to East Prussia by any strategic necessity. The plan of joint operations with Samsonoff had been brought to naught, and as the army of the latter had gone to its doom even as it pressed hopefully forward, the best course was now— to be cautious.

Thus must Rennenkampf have reasoned. And critics have maintained that such *was* his reasoning. It must be admitted that no great decision could have been born of such thoughts. They did not exactly move on bold lines. Yet their translation into action could have produced many a considerable direct crisis for us and had a grave influence on the general situation in the East. The great numerical superiority of the Niemen Army would have been quite enough to cut our 8th Army to pieces, even after it had been reinforced. A premature retreat of Rennenkampf, however, would have robbed us of the fruits of our new operation and thereupon made it impossible for us to advance on Warsaw and thereby support the Austrians for a long time to come.

We had therefore to be at once cautious and bold.

H

It was this dual requirement which gave their peculiar character to the movements we now initiated. We first established our front on a broad arc from Willenburg to the outskirts of Königsberg. This took us until September 5, broadly speaking. Then our line moved forward. Four corps (the 20th, 11th, 1st Reserve and Guard Reserve) and the troops from Königsberg—comparatively a strong force—advanced against the enemy's front on the Angerburg—Deime line. Two corps (the 1st and 17th) were to push through the lake region. The 3rd Reserve Division, as the right echelon of our enveloping wing, had to follow south of the Masurian Lakes, while the 1st and 8th Cavalry Divisions had to be held in readiness behind the main columns, to range at large as soon as the lake defiles were forced. Such were the forces against Rennenkampf's flank. So the scheme differed from the movements which had led to the victory of Tannenberg. This grouping of our columns was imposed upon us by the necessity of securing ourselves against Rennenkampf's strong reserves. In this way fourteen infantry divisions were told off to attack the front, in spite of the fact that its breadth was more than ninety-five miles.

On the 6th and 7th we were approaching the Russian lines and began to see rather more clearly. There were strong Russian columns near Insterburg and Wehlau, perhaps even stronger ones north of Nordenburg. They made no movement at first, and in no way interfered with us as we deployed for battle before their lines.

The two corps on our right (1st and 17th) began to force their way through the chain of lakes on September 7, while at Bialla the 3rd Reserve Division shattered half of the Russian 20th Corps in a brilliant action. We were entering upon the crisis of our new operations. The next few days would show whether Rennenkampf intended to attempt a counter-attack and whether his resolution to do so was as great as his resources. To add to his already formidable superiority three more reserve divisions appeared to have reached the battlefield. Was the Russian commander still waiting for more? Russia had more than three million fighting men on her western front, while the Austro-Hungarian armies and ourselves had scarcely a third of that number.

The battle blazed up along the whole front on September 8. Our frontal attack made no progress, but things went better on our right wing. In that quarter two corps had broken through the enemy's lake defences and were turning north and north-east. Our objective was now the enemy's line of communications. Our cavalry appeared to have an open road in that direction.

On the 9th the battle raged further. On the front from Angerburg to the Kurisches Haff it had no appreciable result, but our bold thrust east of the lakes made headway, although the two cavalry divisions were not able to break down the unexpected resistance they encountered with the speed we could have wished. The 3rd Reserve Division defeated an enemy several times its own strength at Lyck, and thus freed us once and for all from danger in the south.

How were things going in the north? Our airmen believed they could now clearly identify two enemy corps at and west of Insterburg, as well as see another marching on Tilsit. What would be the fate of our corps, strung out fighting on a long front if a Russian avalanche of more than a hundred battalions, led by resolute wills, descended upon them? Yet it is easy to understand what our wishes and words were on the evening of this September 9: "Rennenkampf, come what may, do not abandon this front of yours we cannot force. Win your laurels with the attack of your centre." We had now full confidence that by resolutely pressing home our attack on the wing we could snatch back such laurels from the Russian leader. Unfortunately the Russian commander knew what we were thinking. He had not sufficient determination to meet our plans with force, and lowered his arms.

In the night of September 9-10 our patrols entered the enemy's trenches near Gerdauen and found them empty. "The enemy is retreating." The report seemed to us incredible. The 1st Reserve Corps immediately pressed forward against Insterburg from Gerdauen. We urged caution. It was only about midday of the 10th that we were compelled to accept the improbable and unpalatable fact. The enemy had actually begun a general retreat, even though he offered a stout resistance here and there, and indeed threw heavy columns against us in disconnected attacks. It was now our business to draw the corps and cavalry divisions on our right wing sharply north-east, and set them at the enemy's communications with Insterburg and Kovno.

On we pressed! If ever impatience was comprehensible it was comprehensible now. Rennenkampf was retiring steadily. He, too, seemed to be impatient. Yet our impatience was in striving for victory, while his brought him confusion and dissolution.

Some of the corps of the Niemen Army were marching back into Russia in three columns very close together.

The movement was effected but slowly, as it had to be covered by strong rearguards which kept back the Germans who were following up hard. September 11, in particular, was a day of bloody fighting from Goldap right to the Pregel.

In the evening of that day it was quite clear to us that only a few days more remained for us to carry out the pursuit. The development of the general situation in the Eastern theatre was having its effect. We suspected, rather than gathered from the definite reports which reached us, that the operations of our Allies in Poland and Galicia had failed! In any case, it was no good thinking of our thrust across the Niemen in Rennenkampf's rear. But if our operation at the last moment was not to prove a failure within the framework of the whole allied plan, the enemy's army must at least reach the protection of the Niemen sector so weakened and shaken that the bulk of our troops could be released for that co-operation with the Austro-Hungarian Army which had become urgently necessary.

On September 18 the 3rd Reserve Division reached Suvalki on Russian soil. Rennenkampf's southern wing escaped envelopment by our 1st Corps south of Stallupönen by the skin of its teeth. Brilliant were the feats of several of our units engaged in the pursuit. They marched and fought and marched again until the men were dropping down from fatigue. On the other hand, it was on this day that we were able to withdraw the Guard Reserve Corps from the battle-front and hold it ready for further operations.

It was on this day that our Headquarters reached Insterburg, which had been in German occupation once more since the 11th. Moving on the broad East Prussian roads past our victorious columns marching eastwards and other columns of Russian prisoners streaming west, we thus reached Rennenkampf's former Headquarters not only in imagination, but in actual fact.

This first evacuation had left behind remarkable traces of Russian semi-civilisation. The heady odours of scent, leather and cigarettes were not able to cover the odour of other things. Exactly a year later, I was returning through Insterburg after a day's hunting on a certain Sunday. At the market-place my car was turned back, as there was about to be a service of thanks to commemorate the release of the town from the Russian grip.

I had to make a détour. I had not been recognised. *Sic transit gloria mundi!*

On September 10 our troops reached Eydtkuhnen, firing in the back of the Russian horde fleeing before them. Our artillery blew great gaps in the tightly packed masses, but the herding instinct filled them up again. Unfortunately we did not reach the great main road from Wirballen to Wylkowyszki this day. The enemy knew that this would spell annihilation to many of his columns which nothing now could stop. He therefore scraped together everything he had in the way of battle-worthy units, and threw them against our exhausted troops south of the road. We had only one day more for the pursuit. By the next Rennenkampf's forces would have taken refuge in that region of forest and marsh which lies west of the Olita—Kovno—Wileny sector of the Niemen. We should not be able to follow them there.

On September 15 the fighting was over. After a pursuit of more than sixty miles, a distance we had covered within four days, the battle of the Masurian Lakes had ended on Russian soil. When the fighting concluded, the bulk of our units were fit for fresh employment elsewhere.

I have no room here to speak of the brilliant exploit performed during these days by Von der Goltz's Landwehr Division and other Landwehr formations in their battles with enemy forces many times their own strength in the region of our southern frontier, and while covering our right flank almost as far as the Vistula. By the time these actions were concluded, my command of the 8th Army had come to an end. At that point our troops had pressed forward to Ciechanov, Prassnysz and Augustovo.

CHAPTER VI

THE CAMPAIGN IN POLAND

1

I Leave the Eighth Army

AT the beginning of September we had heard from the Headquarters of the Austro-Hungarian Army that their armies in the neighbourhood of Lemberg were in serious peril and that a halt had been called to the further advance of the Austro-Hungarian 1st and 4th Armies.

Since that time we had followed events in that quarter with great anxiety and received further and worse reports. The following telegrams throw the best light on the sequence of events :

From us to Main Headquarters on September 10, 1914.

It seems to me questionable whether Rennenkampf can be decisively beaten as the Russians have begun to retreat early this morning. As regards plans for the future there is a question of concentrating an army in Silesia. Could we rely on further reinforcement from the west ? We can dispense with two corps from this front.

This was sent on September 10, the very day on which Rennenkampf had begun that retirement to the east which had so much surprised us.

Telegram from Main Headquarters to us on September 13 :

Release two corps as soon as possible and prepare them for transport to Cracow. . . .

Cracow? That sounded odd! We thought so, and said even more on the subject. In our perplexity we wired as follows to Main Headquarters on September 13 :

Pursuit ended this morning. Victory appears complete. Offensive against the Narew in a decisive direction is possible in about ten days. On the other hand Austria, anxious about Rumania, asks direct support by the concentration of the army at Cracow and in Upper Silesia. For that, four army corps and one cavalry division are available. Railway transport alone would take about twenty days. Further long marches to the Austrian left wing. Help would come too late there. Immediate decision required. In any case the army must retain its independence there.

This was on the day on which Rennenkampf was beginning to vanish into the marshes of the Niemen with the loss of not merely a few feathers, but a whole wing, and grievously stricken as well.

On September 14 Main Headquarters replied to us as follows :

In the present situation of the Austrians an operation over the Narew is no longer considered hopeful. Direct support of the Austrians is required on political grounds.

It is a question of operations from Silesia. . . .

The independence of the army will be retained even in case of joint operations with the Austrians.

So that was it!

There is a certain book, "Vom Kriege," which never grows old. Its author is Clausewitz. He knew war, and he knew men. We had to listen to him, and whenever we followed him it was to victory. To do otherwise meant disaster. He gave a warning about the encroachment of politics on the conduct of military operations. In saying this, I am far from passing a judgment upon the orders we now received. I may have criticized in thought and word in 1914, but to-day I have completed my education in the rough school of reality, the conduct of operations in a coalition war. Experience tempers criticism, indeed frequently reveals how unfounded it has been. During the war we have times without number attempted to think : " He is a lucky man who has an easier soldier's conscience than ours, and who has won the battle between his military convictions and the demands of politics as easily as we have." The political tune is a ghastly tune ! I myself during the war seldom heard in that tune those harmonies which would have struck an echo in a soldier's heart. Let us hope that if ever our Fatherland's dire necessity involves a summons to arms again, others will be more fortunate in this respect than we were !

On September 15 I had to part from General Ludendorff. He had been appointed Chief of Staff of the newly formed 9th Army. On September 17, however, His Majesty gave orders that I was to take over the command of this army while retaining my control of the 8th Army which had been left behind to protect East Prussia, but was now reduced by the loss of the 11th, 17th and 20th Corps, as well as the 1st Cavalry Division, which had been given up for the 9th Army. The separation from my Chief of Staff was therefore truly a short one. I only mention it because legend has pounced upon it and exaggerated.

In the early morning hours of September 18 I left the Headquarters of the 1st Army, at Insterburg for a two days' journey by car across Poland to the Silesian capital, Breslau. The first stage of my journey carried me over the battlefields of the last few weeks, conjuring up grateful memories of our troops. At the outset we passed through deserted, burnt-out villages, and then gradually entered a region which had not been touched by war, where we passed peasants returning eastwards to find their deserted homesteads. Genuine peasantry, the best foundation of our national strength. I accompanied them in thought to the perhaps smoke-blackened remnants of their homes, a sight from which they had been preserved for more than a hundred years, thanks to our splendid army. Then we made for the Vistula through homely villages and small towns where there seemed scarcely any traces of the splendour of historic Western culture. This was the ground Germany had colonized. Truly she had not given of her worst for it, though herself dismembered. Its greatest treasure is the capacity for work and high character of its inhabitants. A simple, loyal, reflective people. To me it seemed that here Kant's teaching of the categorical imperative had not only been preached, but was understood in the deepest sense, and had been translated into the world of action.

Almost all the German tribes have contributed to the work of culture in this region—a weary task that took centuries—and thus acquired those strong wills which have rendered priceless services to our Fatherland in its hour of need.

These and other serious thoughts of the same nature passed through my mind as we journeyed, and they never left me throughout the whole course of the desperate struggle. Germans, let me compress them into a warning:

Gird yourselves, all of you, not only with the golden band of your moral duty to mankind, but with the steel band of an equal duty to your Fatherland. Strengthen that band of steel until it becomes an iron wall in the shelter of which you will wish to live, and alone can live in the centre of a European world in flames! Believe me this conflagration will rage for a long time yet. No human voices will charm it away, no human compacts can keep it within bounds. Woe to us if the flames find even one broken fragment in that wall. It will become the battering ram of the European hordes against the last German fortress still standing. Our history has unfortunately told us so only too often!

Once again I said farewell to the Homeland with no light heart. But another farewell was even harder at this moment, the farewell to the independence we had previously enjoyed. However consoling the concluding sentence of the last telegram from Main Headquarters may have sounded, I suspected the fate which was in store for us. I knew it, not because of the pervious campaign, for then we had enjoyed military independence—a treasure of gold—in richest measure. I knew it from the history of earlier coalition wars.

2

The Advance

We had come to the conclusion that our best course was to concentrate our army in the region of Kreuznach in Central Silesia. From there we thought we should have

more room to manœuvre against the northern flank of
the Russian Army group in Poland, the exact position
of which had not been established at the moment—
" Impossible ! "

If our army were allowed, we should like to advance
with our right wing through Kielce (Central Poland)—
" Impossible ! "

We should have liked strong Austro-Hungarian forces
to have accompanied us north of the Vistula as far as
the confluence of the San—" Impossible ! "

By the time all this had been pronounced impossible
it looked as if the whole operation might be, or become,
impossible.

We therefore concentrated our troops (11th, 17th,
20th, Guard Reserve Corps, Woyrsch's Landwehr Corps,
the 35th Reserve Division and the 8th Cavalry Division)
north of Cracow in that closest touch with the left wing
of the Austro-Hungarian Army which Main Headquarters had ordered. Our own Headquarters were fixed
for a time at Beuthen, in Upper Silesia. The Austro-
Hungarian Command were sending from Cracow a
weak army of only four infantry divisions and one cavalry
division north of the Vistula. They did not think
they could spare anything more from the south side of
the river, for they themselves were bent on a decisive
attack in that quarter. This plan of our Allies was certainly bold and did credit to its authors. The only
question was whether there was any prospect that, in
spite of all the reinforcement it had received, the greatly
weakened army could carry it into execution. My doubts
were tempered by the hope that as soon as the Russians
had noticed the presence of German troops in Poland they

would throw their full weight against us and thereby
facilitate the victory of our Allies.

The picture of the situation which we drew for ourselves when the movements began was somewhat vague.
All we knew for certain was that the Russians had only
been following the retiring Austro-Hungarian armies
over the San very slowly of late. Further, there were signs
that north of the Vistula there were six or seven Russian
cavalry divisions and an unknown number of brigades of
frontier guards. A Russian army seemed to be in process of formation at Ivangorod. Apparently some of
the troops of this army had been drawn from the armies
which had previously faced us in East Prussia while
others had come fresh from Asiatic Russia. Further,
we had received reports that a great entrenched position
west of Warsaw and fronting west was in course of
construction. We were therefore marching into a situation which was quite obscure, and must be prepared
for surprises.

We entered Russian Poland and immediately realised
the full meaning of what a French general, in his description of the Napoleonic Campaign of 1806 in which he
had taken part, called a special feature of military operations in this region—mud! And it really *was* mud in
every form, not only mud in the natural sense, but mud
in the so-called human habitations and even on the
inhabitants themselves. As soon as we crossed the
frontier it was as if we had entered another world. The
question that rose involuntarily to one's lips was, how
was it possible that in the very heart of Europe the
frontier posts between Posen and Polen should form so
sharp a line of demarcation between different degrees of

culture of the same race? In what a state of physical, moral and material squalor had Russian administration left this part of the country! To what a slight degree had the civilising work of the over-refined upper social strata of Poland permeated the down-trodden lower strata! My very first impressions made me doubt whether the open political indifference of the masses could be given a higher impetus, through the influence of the clergy, for example, an impetus which might have led them voluntarily to range themselves on our side in this war.

Our movements were rendered extraordinarily difficult by the state of the roads. The enemy obtained an inkling of what we were doing and took counter-measures. He withdrew half a dozen corps from his front against the Austrians with the obvious intention of throwing them across the Vistula south of Ivangorod for a frontal attack upon us.

On October 6 we crossed the line Opatow—Radom and reached the Vistula. We here drove back such portions of the enemy's forces as were west of the river. At this point it was apparent that our northern flank was threatened from the Warsaw—Ivangorod line. In these circumstances it was impossible, for the time being, to continue our operation across the Vistula south of Ivangorod in an easterly direction. We must first deal with the enemy in the north. Everything else depended on the issue of the considerable actions which were to be expected in that quarter. A curious strategic situation was thus developing. While hostile corps from Galicia were making for Warsaw on the far side of the Vistula our own corps were moving in the same northerly direction but on this side of the river. To hold up our movement to the left the enemy threw large forces across the Vistula at and below Ivangorod. In a series of severe actions these were thrown back on their crossing-places, but we were not in a position to clear the western bank entirely of the enemy. Two days' march south of Warsaw our left wing came into touch with a superior enemy force and threw it back against the fortress. About one day's march from the *enceinte* our attack came to a standstill.

On the battlefield south of Warsaw our most important capture was a Russian Army order which fell into our hands and gave us a clear picture of the enemy's strength and intentions. From the confluence of the San to Warsaw it appeared that we had four Russian armies to cope with, that is about sixty divisions, against eighteen of ours. From Warsaw alone fourteen enemy divisions were being employed against five on our side. That meant 224 Russian battalions to 60 German. The enemy's superiority was increased by the fact that as a result of the previous fighting in East Prussia and France, as well as the long and exhausting marches of more than two hundred miles over indescribable roads, our troops had been reduced to scarcely half establishment, and in some cases even to a quarter of their original strength. And these weakened units of ours were to meet fresh arrivals at full strength—the Siberian Corps, the élite of the Tsar's Empire!

The enemy's intention was to hold us fast along the Vistula while a decisive attack from Warsaw was to spell our ruin. It was unquestionably a great plan of the Grand Duke Nicholas Nicholaivitch, indeed the greatest

I had known, and in my view it remained his greatest until he was transferred to the Caucasus.

In the autumn of 1897, after the Kaiser Manœuvres, I had met the Grand Duke on the station of Homburg, and entered into a conversation with him which turned principally on the employment of artillery. But it was here in Poland that I had seen the Russian Commander-in-Chief for the first time actually at work, for he seems to have put in only an occasional appearance in East Prussia, and then merely as a spectator. If his plans succeeded, not only our 9th Army would be in danger, but our whole Eastern Front, Silesia, and indeed the whole country would be faced with a catastrophe. Yet we must not yield to such black thoughts but find ways and means to avert the menace. We accordingly decided, while maintaining our hold of the Vistula upstream from Ivangorod, to bring up from that quarter to our left wing all the troops we could possibly release, and hurl them at the enemy south of Warsaw in the hope of defeating him before his fresh masses could put in an appearance.

Necessity lends wings! We therefore asked Austria-Hungary to send everything she could spare in the way of troops in hot haste left of the Vistula against Warsaw. The Austrian High Command showed that they fully realised the situation, but at the same time raised doubts which were hardly in keeping with the emergency. Austria-Hungary, to whose help we had rushed, was quite prepared to support us but only by the tedious method—which involved a loss of time—of taking over from the troops we had left on the line of the Vistula. This would certainly enable us to avoid the mingling of

ɪ

Austro-Hungarian and German units, but it put the whole operation in danger of miscarriage. Counter-proposals from our side led to no result, so we yielded to the wishes of Austria-Hungary in the matter.

3

The Retreat

What we had feared actually materialised. Fresh masses of troops poured forth from Warsaw and crossed the Vistula below it. Our far-flung battle-line was firmly held in front while superior enemy forces, reaching out farther and farther west, threatened to roll up our left flank. The situation could and should not be allowed to remain thus. Our whole joint plan of operations was in danger of not only floundering in the marshes—but of failing altogether. Indeed, it could be said that it had failed already, since the victory we hoped for in Galicia, south of the upper Vistula, had not materialised, although the enemy had brought great masses from there to meet the 9th Army and had therefore weakened himself against our Allies. In any case we had to take the unwelcome decision, a decision which was received very unwillingly by the troops at first, to break away clear of the threatened envelopment and find a way out of our perils by other paths. In the night of October 18-19 the battlefield of Warsaw was abandoned to the enemy. With a view to continuing the operation even now, we brought the troops fighting under Mackensen before Warsaw back to the Rawa—Lowicz line, i.e. about forty miles west of the fortress. We hoped that the enemy would hurl himself against this position, which faced east. With the troops which had been relieved by the Austrians before Ivan-gorod in the south we would then attempt a decisive blow at the main body of the Russian Army group in the bend of the Vistula. A condition precedent to the execution of this plan was that Mackensen's troops should withstand the onslaught of the Russian hordes and that the Austrian defence of the line of the Vistula should be so strong that the thrust we intended would be safe from any Russian flank movement from the east. In view of the strength of the Vistula line this appeared an easy task for our Allies. The Austrian High Command, however, made it much more difficult by their intention, good enough in itself, to attempt a great blow themselves. They decided to leave the crossings of the Vistula at and north of Ivangorod open to the enemy with a view to falling upon the enemy columns as they were in the act of crossing. It was a bold scheme which had often been discussed and executed in war-games and manœuvres in peace, and even in war carried out in brilliant fashion by Field-Marshal Blücher and his Gneisenau at the Katzbach. But it is always a hazardous operation, particularly when the general is not absolutely sure of his troops. We therefore advised against it. But in vain! Superior Russian forces pressed over the Vistula at Ivangorod. The Austrian counter-attack gained no success and was soon paralysed, and finally converted into a retreat.

Of what use was it now to us that the first Russian onslaughts on Mackensen's new front failed? The with-drawal of our Allies had uncovered the right flank of our proposed attack. We had to abandon this operation. I considered that our best course was to continue our retreat and thus break away with a view to being able to employ our army for another blow elsewhere later on. It was in our Headquarters at Radom that the idea took shape within me, at first only in outline, but yet clear enough to serve as a basis for further measures. My Chief of Staff will confirm this. His titanic energy would provide everything for their execution. Of that I was certain.

I must admit that serious doubts mingled with my resolution. What would the Homeland say when our retreat approached its frontiers? Was it remarkable that terror reigned in Silesia? Its inhabitants would think of how the Russians had laid waste East Prussia, of robbing and looting, the deportation of non-combatants, and other horrors. Fertile Silesia, with its highly developed coal mines and great industrial areas, both as vital to our military operations as daily bread itself! It is not an easy thing in war to stand with your hand on the map and say: "I am going to evacuate this region!" You must be an economist as well as a soldier. Ordinary human feelings also assert themselves. It is often these last which are the hardest to overcome.

Our retreat in the general direction of Czenstochau began on October 27. The thorough destruction of all roads and railways was to hold back the solid Russian masses until we had got quite clear and found time to initiate fresh operations. The army pressed behind the Widawka and Warta with its left wing in the neighbourhood of Sieradz. Headquarters went to Czenstochau. At first the Russians were hot on our heels, but then the distance between us began to increase. This rapid change in the most anxious situation had to be the solution for the time being.

At this point I cannot help admitting how much the punctual knowledge of the dangers that threatened us was facilitated by the incomprehensible lack of caution, I might almost say *naïveté*, with which the Russians used their wireless. By tapping the enemy wireless we were often enabled not only to learn what the situation was, but also the intentions of the enemy. In spite of this exceptionally favourable circumstance, the situation that was developing made quite heavy enough demands on the nerves of the Command on account of the great numerical superiority of the enemy. However, I knew that we had our subordinate commanders firmly in hand and had unshakable confidence that the men in the ranks would do everything that was humanly possible. It was this co-operation of all concerned that enabled us to overcome the most dangerous crisis. Yet did it not look as if our final ruin had only been postponed for a time? The enemy certainly thought so and rejoiced. Apparently he considered that we were completely beaten. This seems to have been his view of our plight, for on November 1 his wireless ran: "Having followed the enemy up for more than 120 versts it is time to hand over the pursuit to the cavalry. The infantry are tired and supply is difficult." We could therefore take breath and embark on fresh operations.

On this November 1 His Majesty the Emperor appointed me Commander-in-Chief of all the German forces in the East, and at the same time extended my sphere of command over the German eastern frontier provinces. General Ludendorff remained my Chief of Staff. The command of the 9th Army was entrusted to General von Mackensen. We were thus relieved of direct command of the army, but our influence on the whole organisation was all the more far-reaching.

We selected Posen as our Headquarters. Yet even before we took up residence there we had, at Czenstochau on November 3, come to the final decision as to our new operations, or rather I should say that our further intentions had received their final form.

4
Our Counter-attack

The consideration that formed the basis of our new plan was this : In the existing situation, if we tried to deal purely frontally ,with the attack of the Russian 4th Army, a battle against overwhelming Russian superiority would take the same course as that before Warsaw. It was not thus that Silesia would be saved from a hostile invasion. The problem of saving Silesia could only be solved by an offensive. Such an offensive against the front of a far superior enemy would simply be shattered to pieces. We had to find the way to his exposed, or merely slightly protected flank. The raising of my left hand explained what I meant at the first conference. If we felt for the enemy's northern wing in the region of Lodz we must transfer to Thorn the forces to be employed in the attack. We accordingly planned our new concentration between that fortress and Gnesen. In so doing we were putting a great distance between ourselves and the Austro-Hungarian left wing. Only comparatively weak German forces, including Woyrsch's exhausted Landwehr Corps, were to be left behind in the neighbourhood of Czenstochau. It was a condition precedent to our flanking movement by the left that the Austro-Hungarian High Command should relieve those of our forces moving north in the region of Czenstochau by four infantry divisions from the Carpathian front, which was not threatened at this time.

For our new concentration in the region of Thorn and Gnesen all the Allied forces in the East were distributed among three great groups. The first was formed by the Austro-Hungarian Army on both sides of the upper Vistula, the two others of our 8th and 9th Armies. We were not able to fill the gaps between the three groups with really good fighting troops. We had to put what were practically newly formed units into the sixty-mile gap between the Austrians and our 9th Army. The offensive capacity of these troops was pretty low to start with, and yet we had to spread them out so much along the front of very superior Russian forces that to all intents and purposes they formed but a thin screen. From the point of view of numbers, the Russians had only to walk into Silesia to sweep away their resistance with ease and certainty. Between the 9th Army at Thorn and the 8th on the eastern frontier of East Prussia we had practically nothing but frontier guards reinforced by the garrisons of Thorn and Graudenz. Facing these troops was a strong Russian group of about four army corps north of Warsaw on the northern banks of the Vistula and the Narew. If this Russian group had been sent forward through Mlawa the situation which had developed at the end of August before the Battle of Tannenberg would have been repeated. The line of retreat of the 8th Army therefore appeared to be once more seriously threatened. From the critical situation in Silesia and

East Prussia we were to be released by the offensive of
the 9th Army in the direction of Lodz against the flank
of the Russian main mass which was only weakly protected.   It is obvious that if the attack of this army did
not get home quickly the enemy masses would concentrate upon it from all sides.   The danger of this was all
the greater because we were not numerically strong
enough, nor were our troops good enough in quality, to
pin down the Russian forces in the bend of the Vistula,
as well as the enemy corps north of the middle Vistula,
by strong holding attacks, or indeed mislead them for any
considerable length of time.   In spite of all this we intended to make our troops attack everywhere, but it would
have been a dangerous error to expect too much from this.

Everything in the way of good storm troops had to
be brought up to reinforce the 9th Army.   It was to
deliver the decisive blow.   However great was the threat
to the 8th Army, it had to give up two corps to the 9th.
Under these circumstances it was no longer possible to
continue the defence of the recently freed province on the
Russian side of the frontier; our lines had to be withdrawn to the Lake region and the Angerapp.   This was
not an easy decision.   As the result of the measures of
which I have spoken the total strength of the 9th Army
was brought up to about five and a half corps and five
cavalry divisions.   Two of the latter had come from the
Western Front.   In spite of our earnest representations
Main Headquarters could not see their way to release
further units from that side.   At this moment they were
still hoping for a favourable issue to the Battle of Ypres.
The full extent and meaning of the difficulties of a war on
two fronts were revealing themselves once more.

The lack of numbers on our side had again to be made good by speed and energy.   I felt quite sure that in this respect the command and the troops would do everything that was humanly possible.   By November 10 the 9th Army was ready.   On the 11th it was off, with its left wing along the Vistula and its right north of the Warta. It was high time, for news had reached us that the enemy also intended to take the offensive.   An enemy wireless betrayed to us that the armies of the north-west front, in other words all the Russian armies from the Baltic to, and including Poland, would start for a deep invasion of Germany on November 14.   We took the initiative out of the hands of the Russian Commander-in-Chief, and when he heard of our operation on the 13th he did not dare to venture on his great blow against Silesia, but threw in all the troops he could lay hands on to meet our attack. For the time being Silesia was thus saved, and the immediate purpose of our scheme was achieved.   Would we be able to go one better and secure a great decision? The enemy's superiority was enormous at all points.   Yet I hoped for great things !

It would exceed the limits of this book if I were now to give a summary, however general, of the military events which are compressed into the designation " Battle of Lodz."   In its rapid changes from attack to defence, enveloping to being enveloped, breaking through to being broken through, this struggle reveals a most confusing picture on both sides.   A picture which in its mounting ferocity exceeded all the battles that had previously been fought on the Eastern Front !

In conjunction with the Austro-Hungarians we succeeded in stemming the floods of half Asia.

The battles of this Polish campaign, however, did not end with Lodz, but were continuously fed by both sides. More troops came to us from the West, but they were anything but fresh. Most of them were willing enough, but they were half exhausted. Some of them had come from an equally hard, perhaps harder struggle— the Battle of Ypres—than we had just fought. In spite of that, we tried with them to force back the Russian flood we had successfully dammed. And indeed for a long time it looked as if we should succeed. But in the long run, as in the battle of Lodz, it was seen that once more our forces were not sufficient for this contest with the most overwhelming superiority which faced us in every battle. We should have been able to do more if our reinforcements had not come up in driblets. We should have been able to put them in simultaneously. But the colossal block we tried to roll back to the east only moved a short stretch, then lay still, and nothing would shift it. Our energies flagged. But it was not only in battle that they were dissipated, but also in—the marshes!

The approach of winter laid its paralysing hand on the activity of friend and foe alike. The line which had already become rigid in battle was now covered with snow and ice. The question was who would be the first to shake this line from its torpor in the coming months?

CHAPTER VII

1915

1

The Question of a Decision

THE achievements of Germany and the German Army in the year 1914 will only be appreciated in all their heroic greatness when truth and justice have free play once more, when our enemies' attempt to mislead world opinion by propaganda is unmasked, and when Germany's passion for self-criticism to the point of self-mutilation has made way for a quiet, judicial examination. I have no doubt that all this will come in due course.

Yet in spite of all our achievements the mighty work that had been forced upon us was not crowned with success. Up to this point our battles had saved us for the time being, but they had not brought us final victory. The first step to such a consummation was a decision on at least one of our fronts. We had to get out of the military, political and economic ring that had been forged about us, a ring which threatened to squeeze the breath out of our bodies even in a moral sense. The reasons why victory had hitherto escaped us were debatable, and they will remain debatable. The fact remains that our High Command believed themselves compelled prematurely to draw away to the East strong forces from the West, where they were trying to secure a rapid decision. Whether an exaggerated idea of the extent of the successes hitherto obtained in the West had a great effect on that decision must remain uncertain. Whatever the cause, the result was half-measures. One objective was abandoned; the other was never reached.

In many a conversation with officers who had some knowledge of the course of events in the western theatre in August and September, 1914, I have tried to get an unbiased opinion about the transactions which proved so fateful for us in the so-called " Battle of the Marne." I do not believe that one single cause can make our great plan of campaign, unquestionably the right one, responsible. A whole series of unfavourable influences was our undoing. To these I must add (1) the watering-down of our fundamental scheme of deploying with a strong right wing; (2) the fact that through mistaken independent action on the part of subordinate commanders, our left wing, which had been made too strong, allowed itself to be firmly held; (3) ignorance of the danger to be apprehended from the strongly fortified, great railway-nexus of Paris; (4) insufficient control of the movements of the armies by the High Command; (5) perhaps also the fact that at the critical moment of the battle certain subordinate commands were not in close enough touch with a situation not in itself unfavourable. The impartial examination of history and the critics will find here a worthy field for their activities.

May I, however, here express a decided opinion that the failure of our first operation in the West brought us into a position of great peril, but in no way made the further prosecution of the war hopeless for us. If I had not been firmly convinced of this I should have deemed it my duty, even in the autumn of 1914, to make appropriate representations to higher authority, even to my All-Highest War Lord himself. Our army had displayed qualities so brilliant and so superior to those of all our enemies, that in my opinion if we had concentrated all our resources we could have secured a decision, at any rate at the outset, in one of our theatres of war, in spite of the growing numerical superiority of the enemy.

West or East? That was the great question, and on the answer to it our fate depended. Of course Main Headquarters could not allow me a deciding voice in the solution of this problem. The responsibility for that lay alone and exclusively on their shoulders. I consider, nevertheless, that I have the right and duty to bring forward my views on this subject, and express them frankly and openly.

From the general point of view, the so-called decision in the West was traditional. I might perhaps say national. In the West was the enemy whose chauvinistic agitation against us had not left us in peace even in times of peace. In the West, too, was now that other enemy who every German was convinced was the motive force working for the destruction of Germany. Compared with that, we often found Russia's greed for Constantinople comprehensible. Her longings for East and West Prussia were not taken seriously.

Thus, as regards the war in the West, the German High Command could be certain that the governing minds of the Fatherland, and indeed the feelings of the majority of the nation, were on their side. Here was a moral factor not to be despised. I should not like to say whether this played any part in the calculations of our military leaders, but I know for certain that the idea of a decision

in the West had been brought before us hundreds and
thousands of times, both verbally and in writing. Indeed, when the conduct of operations was entrusted to me
subsequently, I found those who suggested the idea of
formally sparing Russia. It was commonly believed that
it would be relatively easy for us to come to an understanding with Russia by the methods of peace.

Even to me the decisive battle in the West, a battle
which would have meant final victory, was the *ultima
ratio*, but an *ultima ratio* which could only be reached
over the body of a Russia stricken to the ground. Should
we ever be able to strike Russia to the ground? Fate
answered this question in the affirmative but only two
years later, when, as was to be made clear, it was too late.
For by that time our situation had fundamentally changed.
The numbers and resources of our other foes had in
the meantime reached giant proportions, and in the
circle of their armies Russia's place had been taken by
America, with her youthful energies and mighty
economic powers!

I believed that in the winter of 1914-5 we could answer
the question, whether we could overthrow Russia, in the
affirmative. I believe it just as much to-day. Of course
our goal was not to be reached in a single great battle,
a colossal Sedan, but only through a series of such and
similar battles. The preliminary conditions for this were
present, as had already been revealed, in the generalship
of the Russian Army commanders, though not of their
Commander-in-Chief. Tannenberg had showed it clearly.
Lodz would have shown it, perhaps on an even greater
scale, if we had not had to take the battles in Poland
against too great a numerical superiority upon our

shoulders, and so to speak stop half-way to victory for lack of numbers.

I have never underestimated the Russians. In my opinion the idea that Russia was nothing but despotism and slavery, unwieldiness, stupidity and selfishness was quite false. Strong and noble moral qualities were at work there, if only in comparatively restricted circles. Love of country, self-reliance, perseverance and broad views were not entirely unknown in the Russian Army. How otherwise could the huge masses have ever been put in motion, and the nation and troops have been willing to accept such hecatombs of human life? The Russian of 1914 and 1915 was no longer the Russian of Zorndorf, who let himself be slaughtered like sheep. But what the Russian masses lacked were those great human and spiritual qualities which among us are the common property of the nation and the army.

The previous battles with the armies of the Tsar had given our officers and men a feeling of unquestioned superiority over the enemy. This conviction, which was shared by the oldest Landsturm man with the youngest recruit, explains the fact that here in the East we could use formations, the fighting value of which would have prevented their employment on the Western Front except in emergencies. It was an enormous advantage to us that from the point of view of numbers we were so inferior to our combined enemies! Of course there were limits to the use of such troops, in view of the demands which had to be made on the endurance and strategic mobility of the units in the eastern theatre. The main blow had to be delivered, time and time again, by really effective divisions. If the numbers required to carry

through some decisive operation could not be obtained
by new formations, it was my opinion that they should
be obtained from the Western Front, even if it meant
evacuating part of the occupied territory.

These views are not the result of a process of reasoning after the event or *post hoc* criticism. It has been
urged against them that the Russians were in a position
in case of need to withdraw so far into the so-called
" vast spaces " of their Empire that our strategic impetus
must be paralysed the farther we followed them. I
think that these views were inspired far too much by
memories of 1812, and that they did not take sufficient
account of the development and transformation of the
political and economic conditions obtaining at the heart
of the Tsar's realms. I am thinking more particularly of
the railways. Napoleon's campaign drove but a comparatively small wedge into vast Russia, thinly populated,
economically primitive and, from the point of view of
domestic politics, still asleep. What a different thing a
great modern offensive would have been! What totally
different circumstances would it find now, even in
Russia?

At bottom it was these views which were the subject
of controversy between Main Headquarters, as then constituted, and my Army Headquarters. Public discussion
has introduced a good deal of legend into that controversy.
There could be no question of dramatic action, however
deeply the affair affected me personally. I leave a final
expert decision to the critics of the future, and am convinced that even these will not come to any unani-
mous conclusion. In any case, I shall never live to
see it.

2

Battles and Operations in the East

I can only deal in broad outlines with the events of the year 1915 in the East.

On our part of the Eastern Front fighting was resumed with the greatest violence. It had never completely died down. With us, however, it did not rage with quite the same fury as in the Carpathians, where the Austro-Hungarian armies in a desperate struggle had to protect the fields of Hungary from the Russian floods. The critical situation had taken even my Chief of Staff there for a time. The real reasons which led to our separation at this moment I have never known. I sought them in material considerations, and asked my Emperor to cancel the order. His Majesty graciously approved. After a short time General Ludendorff returned, full of grave experiences and holding even graver views of the condition of affairs among the Austro-Slav units.

The idea of a decision in the East must have been particularly welcome to the Austro-Hungarian General Staff. It must have recommended itself to them not only on military, but also on political grounds. They could not remain blind to the progressive deterioration of the Austro-Hungarian armies. If the war were dragged out for a long time the process would apparently make more headway in the armies of the Danube Monarchy than in that of their opponents. Further, the Austrians were fearful that the threatened loss of Przemysl would not only increase the tension of the situation on their own front, but that under the impression which the fall of this fortress must make on the nation the signs, even then

J

quite distinguishable, of the disintegration of the State and loss of confidence in a favourable termination of the war, would increase and multiply. Moreover, Austria-Hungary was already feeling herself threatened in the rear by the political attitude of Italy. A great and victorious blow in the East could fundamentally change the unhappy situation of the State.

Looking at the situation in that light, I took the side of General Conrad when he suggested to the German High Command a decisive operation in the eastern theatre. Main Headquarters considered that they could not place at my disposal the reinforcements which I considered necessary for such a decision. Of the plans proposed, therefore, only one was allotted to my sphere of command, the great blow which we delivered in East Prussia.

At the beginning of the year four army corps were placed at our disposal and transferred from home and the Western Front. They were detrained in East Prussia. Part went to reinforce the 8th Army and part to form the 10th Army under General von Eichhorn. They deployed and separated with a view to breaking out from both wings of our lightly held entrenched position from Lötzen to Gumbinnen. The 10th Russian Army of General Sievers was to suffer deep envelopment through our two strong wings which were to meet ultimately in the East on Russian soil and thus annihilate to a great extent everything the enemy had not got away.

The fundamental idea of the operation was put into the following words for our Army Commanders on January 28, while we were still at Posen:

" I intend to employ the 10th Army, with its left

wing along the line Tilsit—Wilkowischki, to envelop the enemy's northern wing, to tie him down frontally with the Königsberg Landwehr Division and the left wing of the 8th Army, and employ the right wing of the 8th Army for an attack on the Arys—Johannisburg line and south thereof."

On February 5 precise battle orders were issued from Insterburg, whither we had gone to direct the operations. From the 7th onwards they set in motion the two groups on the wings, a movement recalling in some respects our celebrated Sedan. And it was indeed a Sedan which finally befell the Russian 10th Army in the region of Augustovo. It was there that our mighty drive came to an end on February 21, and the result was that more than 100,000 Russians were sent to Germany as prisoners. An even larger number of Russians suffered another fate.

On the orders of His Majesty the whole affair was called the "Winter Battle in Masuria." I must be excused a more detailed description. What is there new I could say? The name charms like an icy wind or the stillness of death. As men look back on the course of this battle they will only stand and ask themselves: "Have earthly beings really done these things, or is it all but a fable and a phantom? Are not those marches in the winter nights, that camp in the icy snowstorm, and that last phase of the battle in the Forest of Augustovo, so terrible for the enemy, but the creations of an inspired human fancy?"

In spite of the great tactical success of the Winter Battle we failed to exploit it strategically. We had once more managed practically to destroy one of the Russian armies, but fresh enemy forces had immediately come up to take its place, drawn from other fronts to which they had not been pinned down. In such circumstances, with the resources at our disposal in the East, we could not achieve a decisive result. The superiority of the Russians was too great.

The Russian answer to the Winter Battle was an enveloping attack on our lines on the far side of the Old Prussian frontier. Mighty masses rolled up to the enemy Commander-in-Chief for use against us, overwhelming masses, each one larger than our whole force. But German resolution bore even this load. Russian blood flowed in streams in the murderous encounters north of the Narew and west of the Niemen, which lasted into the spring. Thank God it was on Russian soil! The Tsar may have had many soldiers, but even *their* number dwindled noticeably as the result of such massed sacrifices. The Russian troops which went to destruction before our lines were missing later on when the great German and Austro-Hungarian attack farther south made the whole Russian front tremble.

At this time the most violent fighting was in progress not only on the frontiers of Prussia but in the Carpathians also. It was there that the Russians tried throughout the whole winter at any price to force the frontier walls of Hungary. They knew, and were right, that if the Russian flood could sweep into Magyar lands it might decide the war and that the Danube Empire would never survive such a blow. Who could doubt that the first Russian cannon-shot in the Plains of Hungary would echo from the mountains of Upper Italy and the Transylvanian Alps? The Russian Grand Duke knew only too well for what great prize he demanded such frightful sacrifices from the Tsar's armies on the difficult battlefields in the wooded mountains.

The fearful and continuous tension of the situation in the Carpathians and its reaction on the political situation imperiously demanded some solution. The German General Staff found one. In the first days of May they broke through the Russian front in Northern Galicia and took the enemy's front on the frontiers of Hungary in flank and rear.

My Headquarters was at first only an indirect participant in the great operation which began at Gorlice. Our first duty, within the framework of this mighty enterprise, was to tie down strong enemy forces. This was done at first by attacks in the great bend of the Vistula west of Warsaw and on the East Prussian frontier in the direction of Kovno, then on a greater scale by a cavalry sweep into Lithuania and Kurland which began on April 27. The advance of three cavalry divisions, supported by the same number of infantry divisions, touched Russia's war zone at a sensitive spot. For the first time the Russians realised that by such an advance their most important railways which connected the Russian armies with the heart of the country could be seriously threatened. They threw in large forces to meet our invasion. The battles on Lithuanian soil dragged out until the summer. We found ourselves compelled to send larger forces there, to retain our hold on the occupied region and keep up our pressure on the enemy in these districts which had hitherto been untouched by war. Thus a new German army gradually came into existence. It was given the name of the " Niemen Army " from the great river of this region.

I have no space to deal with the movement of our

armies which began on May 2 in Northern Galicia and, spreading along to our lines, ended in the autumn months east of Vilna. Like an avalanche which apparently takes its rise in small beginnings, but gradually carries away everything that stands in its destructive path, this movement began and continued on a scale never seen before, and which will never again be repeated. We were tempted to intervene directly when the thrust past Lemberg had succeeded. The armies of Germany and Austria-Hungary wheeled to the north between the Bug and the Vistula. The picture that unrolled before our eyes was this: the Russian front in the southern half is stretched almost to breaking. Its northern half, held firmly on the north-west, has formed a mighty new flank in the south between the Vistula and the Pripet Marshes. If we now broke through from the north against the rear of the Russian main mass all the Russian armies would be threatened with a catastrophe.

The idea which had led to the Winter Battle presented itself once more, this time perhaps in yet broader outlines. The blow must now be delivered from East Prussia, first and most effectively from the Osowiec—Grodno line. Yet the marshes in that region prohibited our advance at that point. We knew that from the thaw in the previous winter. All that was left us was the choice between a break-through west or east of this line. A thrust right through the enemy defences, I might say into the very heart of the Russian Army, demanded the direction past and east of Grodno. We put that view forward. Main Headquarters did not shut their eyes to its advantages, but considered the western direction shorter and believed that a great success could be won on this side also. They therefore demanded an offensive across the Upper Narew. I thought that it was my duty to withdraw my objections to this plan for the time being, for the sake of the whole operation, and in any case await the result of this attack and the further course of the operation. General Ludendorff, however, inwardly adhered to our first plan; but this difference of opinion had no kind of influence on our future thoughts and actions, and in no way diminished the energy with which, in the middle of July, we translated into action the decisions of Main Headquarters, the responsible authority.

Gallwitz's army surged out against the Narew on both sides of Przasnysz. For this attack I went personally to the battlefield, not with any idea of interfering with the tactics of the Army Headquarters Staff, which I knew to be masterly, but only because I knew what outstanding importance Main Headquarters attached to the success of the break-through they had ordered at this point. I wanted to be on the spot so that in case of need I could intervene immediately if the Army Headquarters' Staff needed any further help for the execution of its difficult task from the armies under my command. I spent two days with this army, and witnessed the storming of Przasnysz, for the possession of which there had previously been violent and continuous fighting, and the battle for the district south of the town.

By July 17 Gallwitz had reached the Narew. Under the pressure of the allied armies, breaking in on every side, the Russians gradually began to give way at all points and to withdraw slowly before the menace of envelopment. Our pursuit began to lose its force in incessant frontal actions. In this way we could not gather the fruits which had been sown time and time again on bloody battlefields. We therefore returned to our earlier idea, and having regard to the course the operations were taking, wished to press forward beyond Kovno and Vilna with a view to forcing the Russian centre against the Pripet Marshes and cutting their communications with the interior of the country. However, the views of Main Headquarters required a straightforward pursuit, a pursuit in which the pursuer gets more exhausted than the pursued.

In this period fell the capture of Novo Georgievsk. In spite of its situation as a strategic bridge-head, this fortress had certainly not seriously interfered with our movements hitherto. But its possession was of importance for us at this time, because it barred the railway to Warsaw from Mlawa. Just before the capitulation on August 18 I met my Emperor outside the fortress, and later on it was in his company that I drove into the town. The barracks and other military buildings, which had been set on fire by Russian troops, were still blazing. Masses of prisoners were standing round. One thing we noticed was that before the surrender the Russians had shot their horses wholesale, obviously as a result of their conviction of the extraordinary importance which these animals had for our operations in the East. Our enemy always took the most enormous pains to destroy everything, especially supplies, which could be of the slightest use to his victorious foe.

To clear the way for a later advance on Vilna we sent our Niemen Army out eastwards as early as the middle of July. In the middle of August Kovno fell under the blows of the 10th Army. The way to Vilna was open, but once again we were not strong enough to proceed with the execution of our great strategic idea. Our forces were employed, as before, in following up frontally. Weeks passed before reinforcements could be brought up. Meanwhile the Russians were continuing their retirement to the east; they surrendered everything, even Warsaw, in the hope of at least being able to save their field armies from destruction.

It was only on September 9 that we started out against Vilna. It was possible that even now great results could be obtained in this direction. A few hundred thousand Russian troops might perhaps be our booty. If ever proud hopes were mingled with anxiety and impatience they were mingled now. Should we be too late? Were we strong enough? Yet on we went past Vilna, then south. Our cavalry soon laid hands on the vital veins of the Russians. If we could only grasp them tightly it would mean death to the main Russian armies. The enemy realised the disaster that was threatening, and did everything to avert it. A murderous conflict began at Vilna. Every hour gained by the Russians meant that many of their units streaming eastwards were saved. The tide turned, and our cavalry division had to withdraw again. The railway into the heart of the country was open to the Russians once more. We had come too late and were now exhausted!

I do not delude myself into thinking that the opposition between the views of Main Headquarters and our own will have an historical interest. Yet, in judging the plans of our High Command, we must not lose sight of the whole military situation. We ourselves then saw only a part of the whole picture. The question whether we should have made other plans and acted otherwise if we had known the whole political and military situation must be left open.

3

Lötzen

From these serious topics let me turn to a more idyllic side of our lives in the year 1915 as I pass to my memories of Lötzen. This pretty little town, lying among lakes, forests and hills, was our Headquarters when the Winter Battle in Masuria was drawing to its close. The inhabitants, freed from the Russian danger and the Russian " terror," gave us a touchingly warm reception. I have grateful memories, too, of pleasant visits to neighbouring properties, which could be reached without too great loss of time when service claims permitted it, visits which brought us hours of relaxation, recreation and good sport. There was also a certain amount of hunting. Our greatest triumph in this respect, thanks to the kindness of His Majesty, was the killing of a particularly fine elk in the Royal shoot of Niemonien by the Kürisches Haff.

In the spring, when activity on our front gradually began to die down, there was no lack of visitors of all kinds, and this was true of the summer also. German princes, politicians, scientists and professional men, as well as commercial men and administrative officials, came to us, brought by the interest which the province of East Prussia, usually so little visited, had acquired in the course of the war. Artists presented themselves with a view to immortalising General Ludendorff and myself with their brushes and chisels; but this was a distinction with which we would have preferred to dispense, in view of our scanty hours of leisure, although we much appreciated the kindness and skill of the gentlemen in question. Neutral countries also sent us guests, among others Sven Hedin, the celebrated Asiatic explorer and convinced friend of Germany, whom I learnt to know and appreciate.

Of the statesmen who came to see us at Lötzen I must give a special mention to the then Imperial Chancellor, von Bethmann Hollweg, and Grand Admiral von Tirpitz.

Even while I was at Posen in the winter of 1914-15 I had had an opportunity of welcoming the Imperial Chancellor to my Headquarters. His visit was inspired primarily by his personal kindness, and was not directly connected with any political questions. Nor do I remember that my conversation with the Imperial Chancellor touched on this subject at that time. In any case I had the impression that I was dealing with a clever and conscientious man. At this time our views about the military necessities of the moment coincided at all material points. Every word of the Chancellor's betrayed his deep sense of responsibility. I can understand that feeling, although from my soldier's point of view I considered that in his judgment of the military situation Herr von Bethmann showed too much anxiety and therefore too little confidence.

The impression I had gained in Posen was confirmed at Lötzen.

Grand Admiral von Tirpitz, who was often quoted as Bethmann Hollweg's successor about this time, was a personality of a very different stamp. On a long walk that I took with him he told me all the sorrows which vexed his flamingly patriotic, and in particular, seaman's heart. It was a bitter sorrow to him that the mighty weapon he had forged during the best years of his life should be shut up in its home harbours in time of war. It is true that the chances for a naval offensive on our side were uncommonly difficult; but, on the other hand, they did not improve with long waiting. In my opinion, the very great sensitiveness of the English to the phantom of a German invasion would have justified greater activity on the part of our Fleet, and, indeed, heavy sacrifices. I considered it possible that such a use of the Fleet might have tied up strong English forces at home, and thereby relieved the burden of our Army. It is said that the policy we pursued was intended to enable us to have a strong, intact German Fleet whenever peace negotiations came in sight. A calculation of this kind would be absolutely erroneous, for a power which one dare not use in war is a negligible factor when it comes to the peace treaty.

The desire of the Grand Admiral's heart was granted in the spring of 1916. Skagerrak gave brilliant proof of what our Fleet could really do.

Herr von Tirpitz also gave expression to his views about our U-boat operations. It was his opinion that we had begun to use this weapon at the wrong time, and then, frightened at the attitude of the President of the United States, lowered the arm which we had raised with such loud shouts of victory—likewise at the wrong time. The opinions the Grand Admiral then expressed could exercise no influence on the position I took up later with regard to this question. Almost another year and a half were to pass before the decision was to devolve on me. In that period, on the one hand the military situation had materially changed to our disadvantage, and on the other hand the efficiency of our Navy in the sphere of U-boat operations had more than doubled.

4

Kovno

In October, 1915, we transferred our Headquarters to Kovno, in the occupied territory.

To the former activities of my Chief of Staff were now added the duties of administering, reorganising and exploiting the country with a view to procuring supplies for the troops, the Homeland, and the local population. The increasing amount of work this involved would alone have been enough to take up the whole time and energies of one man. General Ludendorff regarded it as an appendix to his ordinary work, and devoted himself to it with that ruthless energy which is all his own.

It was while I was at Kovno that in the more peaceful spells during the winter of 1915-16 I found time to visit the Forest of Bialoviesa. Unfortunately, the game had suffered severely from the effects of military operations. Troops marching through and poaching peasants had cleared a good deal of it. Nevertheless, in four days of splendid deer-stalking and sleighing in January, 1916, I managed to bring down a bison and four stags. The administration of the great forest demesne was entrusted to the tried hands of the Bavarian *Forstmeister* Escherich, who was a past-master in the art of making the splendid timber supplies available for us without thereby damaging the forest permanently.

The same winter I paid a visit to the Forest of Augustovo. Unfortunately a wolf hunt which had been got up in my honour proved fruitless. The wolves seemed to have a preference for slipping away beyond range of my gun. The only traces of the battle of February, 1915, that I could see were some trenches. Apart from them, the battlefield had been completely cleared—at any rate, in those parts of the forest which I visited.

In April, 1916, I celebrated at Kovno the fiftieth anniversary of my entry into the Service.

With thanks in my heart to God and my Emperor and King, who glorified the day with a gracious message, I looked back on half a century which I had spent in war and peace in the service of Throne and Fatherland.

It was at Kovno that in the summer of 1812 a large part of the French Army had crossed the Niemen on its way east. Recollections of that epoch, and the tragic conclusion of that bold campaign, had inspired our enemies with the hope that in the vast areas of forest and marsh in the heart of Russia our own armies would suffer the same fate through hunger, cold and disease as had overtaken the proud armies of the great Corsican. This fate was prophesied for us by our enemies, perhaps less from inward conviction than with a view to tranquillizing uncritical opinion at home. It is true that our anxiety for the maintenance of our troops in the winter of 1915-16 was not small. For we knew that, in spite of all modern developments, we had to spend the worst season of the year in a relatively desolate part of the country, in many parts of which infectious diseases were rife.

CHAPTER VIII

THE CAMPAIGN OF 1916 UP TO THE END OF AUGUST

1

The Russian Attack on the German Eastern Front

IN my sphere of command the year 1915 had not made its exit with the loud flourish of trumpets of an absolutely complete triumph. There was something unsatisfactory about the final result of the operations and encounters of this year. The Russian bear had escaped our clutches, bleeding no doubt from more than one wound, but still not stricken to death. In a series of wild onslaughts he had slipped away from us. Would he be able to show that he had enough life-force left to make things difficult for us again? We found an opinion prevalent that the Russian losses in men and material had already been so enormous that we should be safe on our eastern front for a long time to come. After our previous experiences we received this opinion with caution, and indeed time was soon to show that this caution was justified.

We were not to be allowed to pass the winter in peace, for it soon appeared that the Russians were thinking of anything but leaving us alone. Things were stirring in and behind the enemy lines along our whole front and, indeed, far away to the south, although at first there was no means of knowing the intentions of the Russian High Command. I regarded the region of Smorgon, Dvinsk and Riga as special points of danger for our lines. To these led the most effective of the Russian railways. But for a long time there were no open signs of an enemy offensive at the three points I have mentioned.

Activity was uncommonly lively in the enemy's back areas. Deserters complained of the iron discipline to which the divisions drawn from the lines were subjected, for the troops were being drilled with drastic severity.

Even in quiet times the relative strengths in the different sectors were extremely unfavourable to us. We could take it for granted that on an average each of our divisional fronts (9 battalions) was faced by two or three Russian divisions (32-48 battalions). Nothing could show more eloquently than these figures the enormous difference between the demands on the fortitude of our troops as against those on the enemy. Of course this difference made itself felt to an extraordinary degree, not only in battle, but in the necessary daily duties and fatigues. To what an enormous scale had these duties mounted, thanks to the immense extension of the front! The construction of trench-lines and roads, the erection of hutments, as well as the amount of work involved in supplying the troops with war material, food, timber, etc., made the word "rest" practically a mockery to both officers and men. Yet in spite of all this the *moral* and health of the troops were remarkably good. If our Medical Services had not remained at the level they actually reached we should not, on this account alone, have been able to carry on the war so long. Some day, when all the material available has been scientifically worked through, the achievements of our Medical Services will be revealed as a glorious testimony to German industry and devotion for a great purpose. Let us hope they will then be made available for common humanity.

An unusual amount of activity began to be noticeable in the region of Lake Narocz and Postawy from the middle of February onwards. From the mass of intelligence which reached us, the enemy's preparations for an offensive at that point became more and more obvious. At first I had not believed that the Russians would really select for a great blow a point which lay far from their best railways and, further, gave their masses little room to deploy and the subordinate commanders little chance of manœuvring, thanks to the nature of the ground. Coming events revealed to me the arrival of the improbable.

As the Russian preparations proceeded, not one of us realised their enormous scale. We should never have believed that we should have to deal with the whole of the Russian forces—about 370 battalions—held ready in the region of Lake Narocz with the 70 odd battalions which we had gradually collected there. Moreover, as is known from a publication which was based on our calculations, this comparison gives only an inexact picture— firstly, because on both sides all the troops were not employed on the first day, and mainly because the Russian divisions did not attack the Germans simultaneously on a broad front, but concentrated in two powerful storming columns on the wings of von Hutier's Corps. The more northerly of these put in seven infantry and two cavalry divisions between Mosheiki and Wileity, in the Postawy sector which was manned by only four German divisions at first; while the southern, comprising eight infantry divisions and the Ural Cossacks, tried to break through

K

our barrier between Lakes Narocz and Wiszniew, which
was held by our 75th Reserve Division and the reinforced
9th Cavalry Division. So there were about 128 Russian
against 19 German battalions!

The Russian attack began on March 18. After an
artillery preparation, the violence of which had not
previously been paralleled on the Eastern Front, the
enemy columns hurled themselves at our thin lines like
an unbroken wave. Yet it was in vain that the Russian
batteries and machine-guns drove their own infantry forward against the German lines, and in vain that enemy
troops held in reserve mowed down their own first lines
when these tried to withdraw and escape destruction from
our fire. The Russian corpses were piled up in regular
heaps before our front. The strain on the defence was
certainly colossal. A thaw had set in and filled the
trenches with melted snow, dissolved the breastworks,
which had hitherto afforded some cover, into flowing mud,
and turned the whole battlefield into a bottomless morass.
In the icy water the limbs of the men in the trenches
became so swollen that they could hardly move; but there
remained enough strength and resolution in these bodies
to break the enemy onslaughts time and time again. Once
more all the Russian sacrifices were in vain, and from
March 25 onwards we could look confidently to our heroes
at Lake Narocz.

After the battle was over the German Army Order
of April 1, 1916, in the production of which we co-
operated, ran as follows:

The following order of the Russian Commander-in-Chief
on the Western front of the 4th (17th) March, No. 527, shows
what a great objective these attacks were intended to reach:

"TROOPS OF THE WESTERN FRONT,

Six months ago, fearfully weakened and with a small number of guns and but little small-arm ammunition, you arrested the advance of the enemy and took up your present positions after defeating his attempt to break through in the region of Molodetchno.

His Majesty and your Homeland now expect a fresh deed of heroism from you, the driving of the enemy from the frontiers of the Empire ! When you start upon this high task to-morrow morning, trusting in your courage, your great devotion to the Tsar and fervent love of country, I am convinced that you will do your sacred duty towards the Tsar and your Fatherland and release your brothers who sigh under the enemy's yoke. God help us in this holy task !

(*Signed*) EVERT,

ADJUTANT-GENERAL."

To anyone who knows the circumstances it is certainly extraordinary that such an enterprise should be begun at a season of the year in which its execution might be faced with the greatest difficulties from day to day through the melting of the snow. The choice of this moment is therefore due far less to the free will of the Russian High Command than to pressure put upon it by some ally in distress.

If the Russians try to explain officially that the present cessation of the attack is mainly due to the change in the weather, it is certainly only half the truth. The losses they have suffered in their heavy defeat are at least as much responsible as the soaked ground. At a conservative estimate those losses are at least 140,000 men. It would be more accurate for the enemy commander to say that the great offensive has hitherto stuck fast, not only in marsh but in marsh and blood.

As my conclusion I will take the following passage

from a German officer's description of this spring
battle :

> Not much more than a month after the Russian Tsar had
> paraded his storm troops on the Postawy front, Field-Marshal
> von Hindenburg went to the front to thank his victorious
> regiments. At Tscherniaty and Komai, Jodowze, Swirany
> and Kobylnik, only a few miles as the crow flies from the spot
> where the Tsar had held his review, the Field-Marshal spoke
> to the delegates of the troops from the front and distributed the
> iron crosses. For one moment Commander-in-Chief and
> grenade-thrower stood hand in hand, looking long and con-
> fidently into each other's eyes. The spring sun shone like
> a sun of victory over the Hindenburg front . . .

That was my share in the battle of Lake Narocz.

2

The Russian Offensive Against the Austro-Hungarian Eastern Front

" Verdun " ! The name was continually on our lips
in the East from the beginning of February in this year.
We dare only mention it under our breaths and in secret.
We pronounced the word in a tone which suggested both
doubt and hesitation. And yet the idea of capturing
Verdun was a good one. With Verdun in our hands
our position on the Western Front would be materially
strengthened. It would once and for all remove the
salient at our most sensitive point. Perhaps, too, the
capture of the fortress would open up further strategic
possibilities in the south and west.

In my opinion, therefore, the importance of this
fortress justified an attempt to take it. We had it in our

power to break off the attack at any time if it appeared impossible to carry it through, or the sacrifices it exacted seemed to be too high. Moreover, had not the boldest and most improbable actions in attacks on fortresses succeeded brilliantly time after time in this war?

After the end of February the word " Verdun " was no longer uttered secretly, but loudly and joyfully. The name " Douaumont," like a beacon of German heroism, lit up the far distances of the East and raised the spirits even of those who were now looking with anxious care towards the development of events at Lake Narocz. I must admit that the attack on Verdun was also a bitter disappointment for us, for the enterprise meant that the idea of a decision here in the East had been finally abandoned.

As time went on Verdun was spoken of in yet another tone. Doubts gradually began to prevail, though they were but seldom expressed. They could be summarised shortly in the following question : Why should we persevere with an offensive which exacted such frightful sacrifices and, as was already obvious, had no prospects of success? Instead of the purely frontal attack on the northern arc of the defence, which was supported by the permanent work of Verdun, would it not be possible to use the configuration of our lines between the Argonne Forest and St. Mihiel to cut the salient off altogether? It must be left to the future and unprejudiced examination to say whether these questions were right.

Another word followed Verdun; the word " Italy," which was mentioned for the first time after the battle of Lake Narocz had ended. This name, too, was uttered with doubt, a doubt far greater and stronger than in the case of Verdun. Indeed, not so much a doubt as an anxious foreboding. The plan of an Austro-Hungarian attack on Italy was bold, and from that point of view had therefore a military claim to success. But what made the plan seem venturesome was our opinion of the instrument with which it was to be carried out. If the best Austro-Hungarian troops were sent against Italy, troops to which not only Austria and Hungary but Germany as well looked with pride and hope, what was left against Russia? Moreover, Russia had not been so badly beaten as was suspected at the end of 1915. At Lake Narocz the immense determination of the Russian masses had again revealed itself in a fury and impetus compared with which the Austro-Hungarian units, many of them largely composed of Slav elements, had shown themselves even less effective than before.

In spite of reports of victories in Italy, our anxiety increased from day to day. It was justified only too soon by the events which now occurred south of the Pripet. On June 4 the Austro-Hungarian front in Wolhynia and the Bukovina absolutely collapsed before the first Russian onslaught. The worst crisis that the Eastern Front had ever known, worse even than those of the year 1914, now began, for this time there was no victorious German Army standing by ready to save. In the West the battle of Verdun was raging, and there were signs of the coming storm on the Somme.

The waves of this crisis reached even to our front, but not in the form of Russian attacks, fortunately for the whole situation. We could thus, at least, give a little help where the need was greatest.

Hitherto, on the German front the Russians had remained in their positions, but in the same strength as before. They had therefore obtained their first victory south of the Pripet with relatively weak forces, and not by the immense masses they usually employed. Brussiloff's plan must certainly be regarded as at the outset a reconnaissance, a reconnaissance on an immense front and carried out with great determination, but still only a reconnaissance, and not a blow with some definite objective. His task was to test the strength of the enemy's lines on a front of nearly 300 miles between the Pripet and Rumania. "Brussiloff was like a man who taps on a wall in order to find out which part of it is solid stone and which lath and plaster." So wrote a foreigner about the opening days of Brussiloff's attack. And there is no doubt that the foreigner was right.

However, the Austro-Hungarian wall revealed but few solid stones. It collapsed under the taps of Brussiloff's hammer, and through the gaps poured the Russian masses, which now began to be drawn from our front also. Where should we be able to bring them to a standstill? At first only one strong pillar remained standing in the midst of this conflagration. It was the Southern Army, under its splendid commander, General Count Bothmer. Germans, Austrians and Hungarians—all held together by good discipline.

Everything that could be spared from our part of the great Eastern Front was now sent south, and disappeared on the battlefields of Galicia.

Meanwhile the situation on the Western Front had also become worse. The French and English, in very superior numbers, had hurled themselves at our relatively weak line on both sides of the Somme and pressed the defence back. Indeed, for a moment we were faced with the menace of a complete collapse!

My All-Highest War Lord summoned me and my Chief of Staff twice to his Headquarters at Pless to confer with him over the serious situation on the Eastern Front. It was on the second occasion, at the end of July, that the decision was taken to reorganise the system of command on the Eastern Front. The German General Staff, in return for the offer of a rescuing hand to Austro-Hungary —in spite of the claims of Verdun and the Somme—had demanded a guarantee for a stricter organisation of the command on the Eastern Front. They were right! My sphere of command was accordingly extended to the region of Brody, east of Lemberg. Large Austro-Hungarian forces were placed under my command.

We visited the Headquarters Staffs of the armies newly assigned to us as soon as possible, and found among the Austro-Hungarian authorities perfect cordiality and ruthless criticism of their own weaknesses. I am bound to say that this knowledge was not always accompanied by the resolution to repair the damage that had been done; and yet, if ever an army needed one controlling and resolute will and one single impulse, it was this army, with its mixture of nationalities. Without them the best blood would run feebly in such an organism and be poured out in vain.

The extension of my sphere of command compelled me to transfer my Headquarters to the south, to Brest-Litovsk. It was there that, on the morning of August 28, I received a command from His Majesty the Emperor to go to his Headquarters as soon as possible. The only reason the Chief of the Military Cabinet gave me was this : " The position is serious ! "

I put down the receiver and thought of Verdun and Italy, Brussiloff and the Austrian Eastern Front; then of the news, " Rumania has declared war on us." Strong nerves would be required !

PART III

From Our Transfer to Main Headquarters to the Collapse of Russia

CHAPTER IX

1

Chief of the General Staff of the Field Army

AS is known, this was not the first time that my Imperial and Royal master had summoned me to conferences on the military situation and our plans. I therefore expected this time also that His Majesty merely wished to hear my views, personally and orally, about some definite question. As I anticipated being away only a short time, I took just as much kit as was absolutely necessary. On the morning of August 20 I arrived at Pless, accompanied by my Chief of Staff. On His Majesty's instructions the Chief of the Military Cabinet met us at the station. It was from his mouth that I first learned of the appointments intended for me and General Ludendorff.

In front of the castle at Pless I found my All-Highest War Lord awaiting the arrival of Her Majesty the Empress, who had come from Berlin and reached Pless shortly after I had. The Emperor immediately greeted me as Chief of the General Staff of the Field Army and General Ludendorff as my First Quartermaster-General. The Imperial Chancellor, too, had appeared from Berlin, and apparently was as much surprised as I myself at the change in the office of Chief of the General Staff, a change which His Majesty announced to him in my presence. I

163

mention this because here again legend has been at work.

The business of taking over from my predecessor was completed soon after. As we parted General von Falkenhayn gave me his hand with the words: " God help you and our Fatherland."

Neither on taking over my new office nor later did my Emperor, who always held my predecessor in high honour, tell me what were the reasons for my sudden summons to the new sphere. I never had the inclination, and then had not the time, to make inquiries for purely historical reasons. But the decision was unquestionably one of hours and not of days.

2

The Military Situation at the End of August, 1916

The military situation which gave rise to the change in our High Command was much as follows, judging by my first impressions :

The situation on the Western Front was not without anxiety. Verdun had not fallen into our hands, and the hope of wearing down the French Army in the mighty arc of fire which we had drawn round the northern and north-eastern fronts of the fortress had not been realised. The prospects of a success for our offensive at that point had become more uninviting, but the enterprise had not yet been abandoned. On the Somme the struggle had now been raging nearly two months. There we passed from one crisis to another. Our lines were permanently in a condition of the highest tension.

In the East the Russian offensive in the south-eastern

part of the Carpathians was sweeping up to their very crests. After our previous experiences it was doubtful whether this last protecting wall of Hungary could be held against the new attack with the forces now available. Moreover, the situation was extremely critical in the foot-hills of the north-western Carpathians. It is true that the Russian attacks at this point had died down somewhat, but it was too much to hope that this pause could continue for any considerable length of time.

In view of the collapse on the Galician front, the Austro-Hungarian offensive in the southern Tyrol had had to be abandoned. The Italians, in reply, had themselves passed to the offensive on the Isonzo front. These battles made a very heavy drain on the Austro-Hungarian armies, which were fighting against great superiority and under the most difficult circumstances in a manner worthy of the highest praise.

Lastly, the position in the Balkans at this moment was of importance to the whole situation and the emergencies of the times. The offensive on which, at our suggestion, the Bulgarians had embarked against Sarrail in Macedonia had had to be broken off after gaining preliminary successes. The political objective which was associated with this offensive—to keep Rumania from entering the war—had not been reached.

At the moment the initiative was everywhere in the hands of our enemies. It was to be anticipated that they would put forth their whole strength to keep up their pressure upon us. The prospects of a possibly speedy and victorious conclusion to the war must have inspired our adversaries on all fronts to exert the greatest efforts and endure the heaviest sacrifices. All of them certainly put in their last ounce to give the *coup de grâce* to the Central Powers while Rumania blew a triumphant blast!

The German and Austro-Hungarian armies had few uncommitted and available reserves at the moment. For the time being there was nothing but weak posts, largely Customs and Revenue Police, on the Transylvanian frontier which was immediately threatened. A certain number of exhausted Austro-Hungarian divisions, partly composed of remnants no longer fit to fight, were quartered in the interior of Transylvania. The new formations, which were in course of completion, were not strong enough to be regarded as capable of a serious resistance to a Rumanian invasion of the country. In this respect the situation on the southern bank of the Danube was more favourable to us. A new army, composed of Bulgarian, Turkish and German units, was being concentrated on the Bulgarian side of the Dobrudja frontier and farther up the Danube. It had about seven divisions of very different strengths.

Such were, generally speaking, all the forces we had available for the moment at the most sensitive of all the sensitive spots of our European theatre—the Rumanian frontier. The other troops we needed had to be taken from other battle fronts, from exhausted units which required rest, or obtained by forming new divisions. But it was just in this last respect that our situation was unfavourable, as was that of our Allies. The situation as regards drafts threatened to become critical in view of the perpetual and indeed increasing tension. Further, the consumption of ammunition and material in the long and immense battles on all fronts had become so enormous that the danger that our operations might be paralysed

from this cause alone was not excluded. I shall return
to the situation in Turkey later.

8
The Political Situation

My first impressions of the political situation at this
time need a short description, as well as those of the
military position. I will take that of my own Fatherland
first.

When the conduct of operations was entrusted to me
I regarded the country's *moral* as serious, though it had
not collapsed. There was no doubt that people at home
had been bitterly disappointed by the military events of
the last few months. Moreover, the privations of daily
life had materially increased. The middle classes in particular were suffering very severely from the economic
situation, which affected them exceptionally intensely.
Food had become very scarce, and the prospects of the
harvest were only moderate.

In these circumstances Rumania's declaration of war
meant a further burden on the country's resolution. Yet
our Fatherland was even now apparently quite prepared
to hold out. Of course, it was impossible to say how
long and how strongly this resolution would be maintained. In this respect the course of military events in
the immediate future would be decisive.

As regards the relations of Germany to her Allies, the
propagandist declarations of the enemy Press had it that
Germany exercised unlimited domination. It was said
that we held Austria-Hungary, Bulgaria and Turkey by
the throat, so to speak, ready to strangle them if they

L

did not do exactly what we wished. Yet there could not be a greater perversion of the truth than this assertion. I am convinced that nothing showed the weakness of Germany, in comparison with England, more clearly than the difference between the political grip each of them had on their Allies.

For instance, if official Italy had ever dared to show an open inclination for peace without British permission, England would have been in a position at any time to compel this Ally to continue the policy she had previously pursued simply through fear of starvation. Equally strong and absolutely domineering was England's attitude to France. In this respect, indeed, only Russia was more independent, but here again the political independence of the Tsar's Empire was limited by its economic and financial dependence on England. How much more unfavourable was Germany's position from this point of view! What political, economic or military weapons had we in our hands with which to repress any inclination on the part of any of our Allies to drop out? The moment these States no longer felt themselves chained to us of their own free wills, or by the menace of certain destruction, we had no power to keep them at our side. I do not hesitate to bring forward these incontestable facts as a special weakness of our whole situation.

Now to our Allies in detail.

The domestic circumstances of Austria-Hungary had changed for the worse during the summer of 1916. A few weeks before our arrival in Pless the political leaders there had made no secret to our Government of the fact that the Danube Monarchy could not stand any further burdens in the way of military and political failures. The disappointment at the failure of the offensive against Italy, which had been accompanied by far too many promises, had been very profound. The speedy collapse of the resistance on the frontiers of Galicia and Wolhynia had produced a feeling of uneasy pessimism in the great mass of the Austro-Hungarian people, and this found an echo in the Representative Assembly. Leading circles in Austria-Hungary were undoubtedly under the influence of this mood. Of course it was not the first time that pessimistic views from that quarter had found their way to us. They had too little confidence in themselves. As they did not know how to concentrate their resources, they misjudged even the extent of those resources. In saying this I am not ignoring the fact that the political difficulties of the Dual Monarchy were far greater than those of our unified German Fatherland. The food situation, too, was serious. The German-Austrian part of the country in particular suffered very severe privations. In my opinion there was no reason to doubt the fidelity of Austria-Hungary, but in any case we must make it our business to see that the country was relieved of the pressure upon it at the earliest possible moment.

The domestic situation in Bulgaria was very different —I might say more politically stable—from that of Austria-Hungary. In their war for the political unity of the Bulgarian race the nation was also fighting for the final hegemony of the Balkans. The treaties concluded with the Central Powers and Turkey, in conjunction with her previous military successes, appeared to bring Bulgaria's far-reaching ambitions within range of fulfilment. It is true that the country had entered the new war very exhausted from the last Balkan war. Moreover, nothing like the same universal enthusiasm had marked her entry into the present war as had been displayed in that of 1912. This time it was due far more to cool calculation of her statesmen than to any national impulse. It was no wonder, therefore, that the nation felt satisfied with its present acquisition of the districts in dispute and displayed no strong inclination to embark on fresh enterprises.

Whether their hesitation in declaring war on Rumania —there had been no declaration at the time of my arrival at Pless—was really an expression of that feeling I may take leave to doubt even to-day. The food situation in the country was good, measured by German standards.

Taking things all round, I considered that I was justified in hoping that our alliance with Bulgaria would stand any military test.

No less confidence did I feel with regard to Turkey. The Turkish Empire had entered the war without any ambitions for the extension of her political power. Her leading men, particularly Enver Pasha, had clearly recognised that there could be no neutrality for Turkey in the war which had broken out. It could not, in fact, be imagined that in the long run Russia and the Western Powers would continue to heed the moderating influences with regard to the use of the Straits. For Turkey her entry into the war was a question of to be or not to be, far more than for us others. Our enemies were obliging enough to proclaim this far and wide at the very start.

In this war Turkey had hitherto developed powers of resistance which astonished everyone. Her active share in operations surprised friend and foe alike ; she tied down strong hostile forces in all the Asiatic theatres. In Germany, Main Headquarters was often reproached later on with dispersion of force for the purpose of strengthening the fighting powers of Turkey. That criticism, however, does not allow for the fact that by thus supporting our Ally we enabled her permanently to keep more than a hundred thousand men of the finest enemy troops away from our Central European theatres.

4

The German High Command

The experiences of the spring and summer of 1916 had proved the necessity of a single central and completely responsible authority for our Army and those of our Allies. After negotiations with the leading statesmen, a Supreme Command was created. It was conferred on His Majesty the German Emperor. The Chief of the General Staff of the Field Army received the right to issue orders " in the name of the Supreme Command " and make agreements with the Commanders-in-Chief of the Allied Armies.

Thanks to the friendly spirit and understanding co-operation of the commanders of the Allied Armies, who had otherwise the same status as myself, I was able to confine the use of my new powers to certain particularly important military decisions. The handling of common political and economic questions was not in the province of this Supreme Command.

My principal task was to give our Allies the general outlines proposed for joint operations and concentrate their resources and activities with a view to reaching the common goal. It would have been far better for all our interests if our High Command had been able, by suppressing all private interests, and indeed disregarding all considerations which were only secondary as compared with the main decision, to insist on a decisive victory in one of the main theatres of the war. However, in accordance with the unchanging nature of a coalition war, difficulties were often to crop up for our High Command, as they had to bear in mind all kinds of susceptibilities.

It is well known that in this war Germany was much more the giver than the receiver in her relations towards her Allies. But, of course, this statement does not, and cannot, mean that Germany might just as well have fought this colossal war without Allies. Further, the view which is frequently expressed that Germany was supported by Allies who were merely a lot of cripples betrays a stupid ignorance of the truth as well as bias and exaggeration. This view ignores the fact that at many points our Allies were holding up very superior enemy forces.

As I look back over the past, my impression is confirmed that, from the standpoint of the Supreme Command, the most difficult part of our task was not the great operations, but the attempt to compromise between the conflicting interests of our various Allies. I will not attempt to discuss whether, in most of these cases, political considerations did not play a larger part than military. One of the greatest obstacles to our plans and decisions was the different quality of the Allied Armies. It was only on taking over the conduct of operations that we gradually came to know what we could expect and demand from the forces of our Allies.

It was during the campaign in Poland that I had first made the acquaintance of the Austro-Hungarian Armies, when they were working in direct co-operation with our troops. Even then they were no longer equal to the demands which we were accustomed to make on our own troops. There is no question that the main cause of the deterioration in the average efficiency of the Austro-Hungarian troops was the extraordinary shock which the Army had suffered in its purely frontal operation at the beginning of the war in Galicia and Poland, an operation which, as I have said, was in my view venturesome. It has been urged that the Austro-Hungarian offensive at that time had the result of breaking the onslaught of the Russian masses. On the other hand, it is possible that this result could have been achieved by a less risky method and at far less cost. In any case, the Russian Army recovered from the losses it then suffered, while the Austro-Hungarian Army did not. Indeed, they converted the bold and enterprising spirit of Austria-Hungary into a lasting fear of the Russian masses. All the efforts of the Austro-Hungarian High Command to make good the great harm that had been done were met by insuperable obstacles. I may be spared a more detailed recital of these. I will only put one question : How could any human agency have succeeded in breathing a fresh and revivifying impulse of common national resolution into the mixed nationalities of the Dual Monarchy after the first flower of determination, enthusiasm and self-confidence had been blighted? In particular, how was the Officer Corps which had suffered so heavily in the first invasion to be brought to its old level again? Let us not forget that Austria-Hungary never had the moral forces at her disposal on which Germany was able to draw so often and so long.

It is quite an error to suppose that the whole Austrian Army was affected at all points and to the same degree by the progressive deterioration of the troops. The Danube Monarchy had excellent units at its disposal right up to the end. It is true that in many quarters there was a strong leaning to unjustified pessimism in critical situations. In particular, the higher Austro-Hungarian commanders were subject to this weakness. This alone could explain the fact that even after splendid achievements in attack the determination of our Allies suddenly collapsed and, indeed, gave place to the reverse.

The natural result of the phenomena on which I have touched was that an element of great uncertainty was introduced into the calculations of our Supreme Command. We were never certain that some sudden collapse of part of the forces of our Allies would not face us unexpectedly with a quite new situation, and so throw out all our plans. The troops of every army have their weak moments, for these are part of human nature itself. The general must allow for them as for a given factor, the dimensions of which it is impossible to ascertain. With really good troops such moments are usually quickly overcome, and even in the greatest collapses at least a nucleus of determination and spirit generally survives. But woe betide if this last nucleus too gives way! Disaster, rank disaster, overtakes not only the troops immediately affected, but also those tougher units on their wings or sandwiched in among them; the latter are caught by the catastrophe in flank and rear, and often suffer a worse fate than the poorer troops. This was frequently the tragic end of troops of ours which were sent to stiffen up the Austro-Hungarian front. Was it any wonder that, owing to this cause, the opinion of our troops about their Austro-Hungarian comrades was not always confident and complimentary!

Taking it all round, however, we must not underestimate the achievements of Austria-Hungary in this mighty contest and give way to those bitter feelings which have many a time been the result of disappointed hopes. The Danube Monarchy remained a loyal Ally to us. We have passed through wonderful times together, and will take care not to drift apart, in spirit, in our common misfortune.

The internal framework of the Bulgarian Army was quite different from that of the Austro-Hungarian. It was self-contained from the national point of view. Until the autumn of 1916 the Bulgarian Army had suffered relatively little in the great war. However, in estimating its value we could not forget that quite a short time before it had been engaged in another murderous war in which the flower of the Officer Corps, and, indeed, the whole of the educated classes of the country, had been destroyed. The reconstruction of the Army was quite as difficult in Bulgaria as in Austria-Hungary. Moreover, the condition of the Balkan countries, virtually still primitive, hindered the introduction and employment of many means that are absolutely necessary both for fighting and transport in modern war. This made itself felt all the more as on the Macedonian front we were faced by first-class French and English troops. For this reason alone it could not be at all surprising that we had to help Bulgaria not only with material, but also with German troops.

The state of affairs in the Turkish Army was otherwise than in the Austro-Hungarian and Bulgarian. Our German Military Mission had scarcely had time to make its presence felt before the war, let alone effect a real improvement in the shaky condition of the Turkish Army. Yet they had succeeded in mobilising a large number of Turkish units. Unfortunately, the Army had suffered extraordinarily high losses in the Dardanelles and their first offensive in Armenia. Yet the Turkish Army seemed equal to the task which Main Headquarters first set it—the defence of the Turkish territorial possessions. Indeed, it was to prove possible gradually to employ a considerable number of Turkish units in the European theatre. Our military help to Turkey was practically limited to the delivery of war material and the loan of a large number of officers. In agreement with the Turkish General Staff, the German formations which had been sent to the Asiatic theatres up to the autumn of 1916 were gradually brought back, after the Turks had proved themselves capable of taking over and using the material left behind by these formations.

We sent material even to the Senussi on the north coast of Africa. These we supplied principally with rifles and small arm ammunition, with the help of our U-boats. Though these deliveries were but small, they had an extraordinarily rousing effect on the war spirit among the Mohammedan tribes. Hitherto we have not been able to appreciate the practical advantages of their operations to our cause. Perhaps they were greater than we believed at the time.

We tried to assist our brothers-in-arms even beyond the north coast of Africa. Thus we took up the idea, which had been mooted by Enver Pasha in 1917, of sending financial help to the tribes of the Yemen which had remained faithful to their Padishah in Constantinople. As the land route thither was closed to us by rebellious nomadic tribes of the Arabian desert, and the coasts of the Red Sea were out of reach owing to the insufficient radius of action of our U-boats, the only way left to us was that of the air. However, much to my regret, we did not possess at that time any airship which could with certainty have overcome the meteorological difficulties of a cruise over the Great Desert. We were, therefore, unable to carry out the plan.

In this connection I may mention, by way of anticipation, that in 1917 I followed with the greatest interest the attempt to send our Protective Force in East Africa arms and medical stores by way of the air.

As is well known, the Zeppelin had to return when over the Sudan, as in the meantime the Protective Force had been driven farther south, and transferred the scene of its operations to Portuguese East Africa. I need hardly say with what proud feelings I followed in thought the deeds, the almost superhuman achievements, of this splendid force during the war. They raised a deathless monument to German heroism on African soil.

Looking back on the achievements of our Allies, I must admit that in the service of our great common cause they subjected their own powers to the greatest strain that their individual political, economic, military and ethical resources permitted. Of course, none of them attained the ideal, and if it was we who more nearly approached that ideal than the others, it was only due to that mighty inward strength—a strength we did not ourselves realise at first—which we had been acquiring in the course of the last decades. This inward strength was to be found in all classes of our Fatherland. It did not slumber, but was always at work, and increased and multiplied even as it worked. It is only when a State is healthy in itself, and an incorruptible life-force courses so strongly through it that at the critical moment the unhealthy elements are swept along by it, that such feats are possible as those which we performed, feats which went far beyond our obligations to our Allies.

That these things could be is mainly due, as can historically be proved, to the Hohenzollerns, and among them our Emperor William II, in the last epoch of German greatness. True to the traditions of his House, this Sovereign saw in the Army the best school for the nation, and worked untiringly for its further development. Thus Germany's Army stood out as the first in the world; an imposing guardian of the works of peace before the war, and in the war the very manifestation of our might.

5

Pless

The Upper Silesian town of Pless had occasionally been selected for headquarters by Main Headquarters at previous periods of the war. The reason for its selection was the fact that it was close to the town of Teschen, in Austrian Silesia, in which the Austrian High Command had its Headquarters. The advantages that accrued from the possibility of quick personal conferences between the two Headquarters were now the main reason why we stayed there.

It was only natural that the German General Headquarters should form a meeting-place for German and allied princes who wished to have direct discussion with my Imperial Master on political and military questions. The first Sovereign whose personal acquaintance I had the honour of making was the Tsar Ferdinand of Bulgaria. He gave me the impression of a superb diplomatist. His political outlook extended far beyond the frontiers of the Balkans. He was a past-master in the art of explaining the position of his country and keeping it in the foreground when great questions of world-politics were being decided. It was his view that in this war the future of Bulgaria was to be decided by the final elimination of Russian influence and the gathering-in of all men of the Bulgarian race under a single leadership. The Tsar never spoke to me of any of his other political ambitions. I was particularly struck by the way in which the Bulgarian Sovereign conducted the political education of his eldest son. The Crown Prince Boris was to a certain extent the private secretary of his royal father, and seemed to me to be initiated into the most secret political intentions of the Tsar. This gifted prince, with his lofty habit of mind, played the important part entrusted to him most tactfully, modestly keeping himself in the background. Parental discipline was apparently pretty strict.

To all intents and purposes the Tsar conducted the foreign policy of his country in person. I am not able to say how far he also controlled the complicated internal affairs of the State. I believe, however, that he knew how to make his will felt in the parliamentary anarchy of Bulgaria which frequently distracted the country. It may be also that he did this by autocratic methods. His task in that respect was no doubt very difficult. Like all the Balkan nations, the Bulgarians had stepped out of servitude into complete political freedom. They had not, therefore, had the training and hard work which accompany the slow transition from one stage to the other. I am afraid that these nationalities, often the possessors of such splendid natural endowments, have still many decades to suffer from the consequences of not having experienced that educative interregnum.

However that may be, the Bulgarian King was at that time one of the most distinguished statesmen. He always proved himself a faithful Ally to us.

It was while we were in residence at Pless that the Emperor Francis Joseph died. Both for the Danube Monarchy and ourselves his death was a loss, the full and impressive import of which was only to be appreciated later. There was no doubt that with his death the ideal bond of union between the various nationalities of the Dual Monarchy was lost. With the venerable white-haired Emperor a large part of the national conscience of the conglomerate Empire sank for ever into the grave.

The difficulties with which the young Emperor was faced were not to be compared, from the point of view of numbers and complication, with those attending a change of throne in an Empire composed of one nationality only. The new Sovereign tried to make good the loss of the moral cement which the Emperor Francis Joseph's death involved, by making concessions to the various nationalities. Even in dealing with elements which were intent on the destruction of the State he believed in the moral effects of political toleration. The method was a total failure. These elements had long made their pact with our common enemies and were far from anxious to break off relations with them.

The impressions I had gained of General Conrad von Hötzendorf as soldier and commander were confirmed in the frequent and active personal intercourse with him which our residence in Pless involved. General Conrad was a gifted personality, a glowing Austrian patriot, and a whole-hearted adherent of our common cause. There was no doubt that it was from the deepest conviction that he proved so obdurate to political influences which strove to break him of that attachment. The general was very broad in his strategic ideas. He knew how to distinguish the central issues of great questions from the desert of secondary matters which had little effect on the decision. He had a peculiarly intimate knowledge of affairs in the Balkans and Italy.

The general was perfectly familiar with the great difficulties which stood in the way of a strong national impulse in the Austro-Hungarian Army and all the defects to which this gave rise. Yet on occasion his great plans were based on an overestimate of what could possibly be expected of the army with which he was entrusted.

I also came to know the military leaders of Turkey and Bulgaria in the course of the autumn and winter at Pless.

In his dealings with me, Enver Pasha displayed an unusually firm and free grasp of the elements of strategy in the present war and the methods required. The devotion of this Turk to our common task, great and heavy as it was, was unlimited. I shall never forget the impression made upon me by the Turkish Generalissimo

at our first conference at the beginning of September,
1916. At my request he was then describing the military
situation in Turkey. With remarkable lucidity, decision
and frankness he gave us an exhaustive picture, and,
turning to me, concluded with these words : " Turkey's
position in Asia is in some respects very critical. We
must expect to be thrown back yet farther in Armenia.
It is not altogether improbable that the fighting in Irak
will soon be renewed. Moreover, I am convinced that
before long the English will be in a position to attack
us in superior force in Syria. But, whatever may happen
in Asia, this war will be decided in Europe, and for that
reason I put all my available divisions at your disposal."

Nothing more practical and unselfish has ever been
said by one ally to another. Nor was it a matter of words
only.

Although Enver Pasha took long views about war,
generally speaking he had not received a really thorough
military training, or what I might call a General Staff
training. This was a drawback which apparently applied
to all the Turkish Commanders and their Staffs. In this
respect it looked as if it was a question of some natural
defect with the Oriental. The Turkish Army appeared
to possess only a few officers who were able to master the
technical, inside problems of command, a knowledge of
which was essential to the execution of well-conceived
plans. They seemed not to realise that the General Staff
must necessarily look after the details, even in the
execution of great operations. The result was that the
wealth of Oriental imagination was often quite wasted
owing to a lack of a sense of military reality.

Our Bulgarian colleague, General Jekoff, was a very

different character from the fertile-minded Turk. He was a man of remarkable powers of observation, not by any means blind to great conceptions, but essentially restricted in his outlook to the sphere of the Balkans. I am not in a position to judge whether in the last respect he was held in leading-strings by his Government. Whether that were so or not, he sincerely believed in the direction which Bulgarian foreign policy was taking. Certainly his views had nothing in common with her domestic policy.

General Jekoff loved his men and was beloved of them. In this connection I remember a remarkable expression he used when doubts were raised as to whether the Bulgarian soldier would not refuse to fight against the Russian : "When I tell my Bulgarians to fight they will fight, no matter against whom." For the rest, the general was not unaware of those defects of his soldiers which sprang from their national character. I shall return to this point later.

In addition to the leading military personalities of our Allies I came into touch with their political leaders at Pless. I will confine myself here to a reference to the Turkish Grand Vizier, Talaat Pasha, and the Bulgarian Minister-President, Radoslavoff.

Talaat Pasha impressed me as a gifted statesman. He was in no doubt as to the magnitude of his problem and the poverty of his country's resources. If he did not succeed in eradicating the self-seeking and national indolence which hung like a millstone round his country's neck, it was mainly due to the enormous difficulties to be overcome. It was quite impossible to improve in a few months what had been neglected for centuries and

M

ruined long before the war by the mixture of nationalities and the inward moral exhaustion of many circles in the State. He himself reached the highest position in his country with clean hands, and held it with clean hands. Talaat was an excellent representative of the ancient Turkish chivalry. Absolutely loyal from the political point of view, he met us first in 1916, and said good-bye to us in the autumn of 1918.

The weaknesses of Turkey's statesmanship, as well as her conduct of military operations, lay in their great dependence on the domestic situation. Members of the so-called Committee Government, self-seeking politically and financially, interfered in military affairs, and frequently tied the hands of the generals so that these were unable to improve recognised defects with the resources available. Of course a few really splendid men did everything within their power. But the authority of the State no longer extended into every part of the Empire. Constantinople, the heart of the Empire, beat too feebly and sent no healthy, invigorating and life-giving blood to the distant provinces. It is true that new ideas had sprung up during the war and grew in quite Oriental profusion with the laurels of the victories at the Dardanelles and on the Tigris. The public began to think of the religious and political unification of all Islam. In spite of the obvious failure that had attended the proclamation of a Holy War, they began to count on the uprising of Mohammedan believers, in Northern Africa for example. The course of events was to show that these examples of religious fanaticism were only the effect of local peculiarities, and that the hope that they would extend to the distant areas of Central Asia was an illusion—not merely an illusion, but a fatal military peril.

The Bulgarian, Radoslavoff, was more earthly in his political thought than the Turkish statesman with his large views. I venture to doubt whether Radoslavoff ever really appreciated in all its greatness the audacity of the step which brought Bulgaria to our side in 1915. I ought, perhaps, to say the greatness with which the Tsar endowed it. In his foreign policy Radoslavoff was always absolutely loyal to us.

The wild fury of Bulgarian domestic party controversy did not cease, even during the Great War, and was also widespread in the army. Russophile sentiments were a cause of dissension, but the contest between political parties went on among the troops and their leaders also. For this Radoslavoff was partly responsible.

CHAPTER X

LIFE AT HEADQUARTERS

ENCOURAGED by the interest which has been taken in many quarters in my daily life during the Great War, I will now attempt to describe the course of an ordinary day at our Headquarters. I must ask all those who have no liking for such trivialities in the middle of great world-events to skip the next few pages. These details are not essential to a proper understanding of the mighty epoch.

It was impossible to think of a regular routine for our Army Headquarters, with each hour mapped out, during the war of movement in East Prussia and Poland in the autumn of 1914. It was only when our Headquarters was transferred to Posen, in November, 1914, that greater regularity began to be observed in our official and—if such a thing exists in war—unofficial life. Later on our longer stay at Lötzen was particularly favourable for the organisation of a strictly regulated routine.

My appointment as Chief of the General Staff of the Field Army made no material difference to the methods of business we had established and found satisfactory, although in many respects more important and pressing activities took up our time.

I usually began the day's business at about nine o'clock —that is, after the morning reports had come in—by visiting General Ludendorff in order to discuss with him any changes in the situation and issue the necessary instructions. As a rule this did not mean a long conference. The military situation was always present to both our minds and we knew each other's thoughts. The decisions were, therefore, usually a matter of a few sentences; indeed, very often a few words were all that was required to establish that mutual understanding which served the general as a basis for his further working-out of the plans.

After this conference I used to go for a walk for about an hour, accompanied by my Adjutant. Occasionally I asked visitors at Headquarters to join me in my morning walk, in the course of which I heard their sorrows as well as their suggestions, and chastened many an anxious soul before he hurled himself upon my First Quartermaster-General to pour out his heart about his wishes, hopes and schemes to that authority whose business it was to go into further details.

After my return to the office I had further conferences with General Ludendorff, and then received the personal reports of my departmental heads in my own office.

Apart altogether from official duties, I had to deal with a mass of personal correspondence. There was quite a large number of people who considered themselves compelled to open their hearts to me in writing about every conceivable occurrence, or acquaint me with their views. It was perfectly impossible for me to read them all myself. I had to employ the services of a special officer for the purpose. Poetry as well as prose figured in this correspondence. Enthusiasm and the reverse were displayed in every possible degree. It was often very difficult to see any connection between the requests made to me and my official position. To take only two of hundreds of examples, it has never been clear to me what I, as Chief of the General Staff, had to do with the removal of refuse in a provincial town—no doubt very necessary in itself, or with the loss of the certificate of baptism of a German lady from Chile. Yet in most cases the writers called on me to help. There is no doubt that written requests of this kind were a proof of a touching, in many cases somewhat naïve, confidence in my personal influence. I was only too glad to help, at least with my signature, when time and circumstances permitted. But as a rule I considered it my duty to refrain from intervening personally.

About midday I was regularly summoned to make my report to His Majesty the Emperor. At this conference General Ludendorff described the situation. When more important decisions had to be taken I made the report myself, and requested the Emperor's approval of our plans whenever that was necessary. The Emperor's great trust in us made a special Royal approval unnecessary except in vital questions. For the rest His Majesty usually satisfied himself with hearing our reasons when new operations were proposed. I never remember any differences of opinion which were not composed by my War Lord before the conference was over. The Emperor's wonderful memory for situations was of the greatest help to us at these reports. His Majesty not only made the most careful study of the map, but was in the habit of making sketches himself. The time of our daily report to the Kaiser was frequently also employed in conferences with representatives of the Government.

After the conclusion of the report to the Kaiser my

immediate Staff joined me at the luncheon table. The time spent on the meal was cut down to what was absolutely necessary. I attached importance to my officers having time to get a little recreation afterwards or getting away from work in some other way. To my continual personal regret, I could not consent to an extension of the meal-time, even when we had guests with us. Regard for the maintenance of the efficiency of my colleagues had to come before social graces. For the majority of these officers a sixteen-hour day was the rule. And this in a war lasting years! Thus we at Main Headquarters were compelled to use our human material to the extreme limit of capacity just as much as the men in the trenches.

The afternoon passed in much the same way as the morning. The longest break for all of us was dinner, which began at eight. After the meal we used to sit round in groups in neighbouring rooms until General Ludendorff gave the signal to break up, at half-past nine punctually. Conversation in our circle was usually very lively. It was perfectly free and absolutely frank, and covered all topics and occurrences that concerned us directly or were of general interest. Nor was there any lack of high spirits. I considered it a duty to my colleagues to encourage this side. It was a pleasure to see that our visitors were obviously surprised by our quiet confidence on the one hand and the spontaneity of our conversation on the other.

After our evening gathering broke up we went back together to the office. The final reports of the day had arrived and the situation on the different fronts been marked on the map. One of the more junior Staff Officers explained it. It depended upon the events in the various theatres whether I had to have a further conference with General Ludendorff or could dispense with his services for the time being. The officers of my immediate Staff now resumed work. Frequently it was at this stage that the last data required for the drawing-up and issue of final orders were given, and it was from now onwards that the innumerable requests, suggestions and proposals of the armies and other services streamed in. The day's work thus never ended before midnight. The reports of the heads of departments to General Ludendorff lasted pretty regularly into the early hours of the next day. There would have to be quite an exceptional lull at the front for my First Quartermaster-General to leave his office before midnight, although he was always back again by eight o'clock next morning. We were all delighted when General Ludendorff could allow himself to knock off a little earlier, although it was only a matter of hours.

Our whole life and work and all our thoughts and feelings were shared in common. Even now the memories of this time fill me with grateful satisfaction. Generally speaking, we remained a restricted circle. In view of the official routine, changes of personnel were naturally infrequent. It was occasionally possible to meet the urgent requests of the officers for at least temporary employment at the front. Moreover, occasions arose in which it was necessary to send officers to particularly important parts of our own fronts or those of our Allies. But, generally speaking, the continuity of the very highly-organised and complicated system required that at least the senior officers should remain permanently at their posts at Main Headquarters.

The hand of death was also felt in our midst. As

early as 1916, when I was Commander-in-Chief in the East, I had lost Major Kammerar as the result of a chill. He was my personal Adjutant, very dear to me, and universally esteemed. In October, 1918, Captain von Linsingen succumbed to an attack of influenza, which at this time was claiming many victims at Main Headquarters. In spite of the urgent representations of the doctor and his comrades, Captain von Linsingen considered that he could not leave his post at that extremely critical time, and he carried on until he *had* to put his work down, physically exhausted and shaken with fever, too late to be saved. In him we lost a comrade who represented the highest in spirit as in character. His young wife did not arrive in time to close his eyes. Many of those who were temporarily attached to my Staff subsequently fell at the front.

This picture of our life would be incomplete if I said nothing of the visitors who came to us from all parts and at all times. I am not thinking now of our routine dealings with the many professional people who came into official touch with us, but rather of others who were brought to us by many other interests. I gladly opened my door and my heart to them so long as they treated me with the same frankness.

We had a large number of guests, and, in fact, had few days without them. Not only Germany and her Allies, but neutrals also sent us a considerable contingent. Our circle at table often gave me the impression of the most motley mixture of races, and it sometimes happened that a Christian Minister sat down side by side with a Mohammedan believer. People of all social classes and parties received a warm welcome. I was glad to give them my few hours of leisure. Of the statesmen I have a preference for Count Tisza, who visited me at Pless in the winter of 1916-17. His whole being spoke of his unbroken strength of will and the glowing fervour of his patriotism. Other politicians of all shades of opinion from our own and Allied lands came on flying visits to me. Sometimes there was something strange to me in their ways of thought, but I appreciated their ardour in our great common cause. I remember so many words of glowing patriotism as we parted.

In my circle I pressed the hard and horny hands of artisans and working men, and their frank looks and straightforward words were a real pleasure to me. Representatives of our great industries and men of science introduced us to new discoveries and ideas and waxed enthusiastic over future economic plans. They certainly complained of the narrow-minded bureaucracy at home and the scanty resources put at their disposal for the exploitation of their ideas. On the other hand, bureaucrats grieved over the greed for gold of inventors for what they feared would turn out to be fantasies or mere airy schemes. I well remember the interesting questions of an official very high up in the Treasury service who wanted to know the cost of a shell of every calibre of gun, so that he could calculate the enormous cost of a battle. He spared me the result of his calculations, knowing, no doubt, that I would not limit the consumption of ammunition on that ground.

Other things besides necessities, cares and ordinary duties found their way to us. Vulgar curiosity also sought admission. I have often laughed to myself over the different speeches with which an attempt at some sort of justification was made. Whether the result of such visits always came up to expectation I would not like to affirm in all cases. By way of contrast, many a splendid regimental officer, bearing the marks of hard fighting and a hard life, was a really welcome guest at our table. A few tales of trench life were far more eloquent than long written reports. The reality of what I myself had gone through in earlier years was brought vividly before my eyes. In this most terrible of all conflicts everything had indeed reached the level of the grotesque in comparison with previous wars! The few hours' battle of past times had become the Titanic action lasting months, and human endurance seemed to have no limits.

Count Zeppelin was another of our guests at Pless, and affected us all with the touching simplicity of his manner. Even at that time he considered his airships an antiquated weapon. In his opinion it was the aeroplane which would control the air in future. The Count died soon after his visit, and thus never lived to see the disaster to his Fatherland. Happy man! Two other lords of the air who had gained laurels accepted my invitation—two invincible young heroes : Captain Bölcke and Captain von Richthofen. We liked the merry and modest ways of both of them. Honour to their memories. I had U-boat commanders also among my guests, among them Captain König, the commander of the commercial submarine *Deutschland*.

Thus no class and no clan were kept away from us, and I believe that we really often felt the common pulse of the Army and our Homeland, our Allies and ourselves.

CHAPTER XI

1

The Rumanian Campaign

OUR political situation with regard to Rumania during the campaigning year of 1915-16 had made exceptionally high demands not only on our statesmen but on our Army leaders as well. It is a piece of cheap wisdom to criticise the authorities and individuals then responsible after the entry of Rumania into the circle of our enemies and in view of our inadequate military preparations to meet the new foe. Such judgments, usually based on voluntary assertions and passed without knowledge of the real circumstances, remind me of an expression of Fichte in his " Reden an die Deutsche Nation," in which he speaks of that brand of writer who always knows exactly what was going to happen after a success has been achieved.

There can hardly be any doubt that if the Entente had been in our position they would have eliminated the Rumanian danger, or perhaps it would be better to say the Rumanian military menace, by 1915 at the latest by the employment of methods such as they used against Greece. As was to be revealed later, Rumania was driven into the whirlpool of war by an ultimatum from the Entente in the summer of 1916. In that ultimatum Rumania was required either to intervene immediately or to renounce her schemes of aggrandisement for ever. However, a solution of that kind would have been politically too high-handed to have found adherents among us without the very gravest necessity. We thought we ought to deal properly with Rumania, though certainly hoping that she would dig her own grave. That is exactly what happened, but after what crises and sacrifices!

Rumania's entry into the war on the side of our enemies was drawing very nigh when the Austrian Eastern Front collapsed. It is not impossible that the danger could have been averted even then if effect could have been given to the German plan of a great counter-attack against the Russian southern wing which had reached the Carpathians. This operation was not carried out simply owing to the series of collapses on the Austro-Hungarian front. The forces to have been used for attack were swallowed up in the defence.

In view of the course the fighting on the Eastern Front was taking in the middle of August, the German General Staff, in conjunction with General Jekoff, had adopted the emergency measure of delivering a great blow against the Entente forces at Salonica with the Bulgarian wing armies. The idea was a thoroughly sound one both from the military and political point of view. If the enterprise succeeded, we could expect that Rumania would be cowed and there would be an end to her hopes—hopes she must even then have been cherishing—of co-operating with Sarrail. Rumania would probably be compelled to remain inactive if strong Bulgarian forces were released for employment elsewhere after a victory over Sarrail. The German General Staff, indeed, found itself placed to a certain extent in a military quandary through this very attack of the Bulgarians. As they were compelled to concentrate troops in Northern Bulgaria to exercise a restraining influence on war fever in Rumania, which was growing stronger every day, forces which might have been employed for the attack on Sarrail on the Macedonian front had to be sent to the Danube for political reasons. The action of Main Headquarters was explained on the one hand by their confidence in the offensive capacity of the Bulgarian Army and on the other by a certain under-estimate of the enemy's strength at Salonica. In particular we were absolutely deceived about the value of the newly-formed Serbian units, six infantry divisions, which had made their appearance there.

As regards the Bulgarian attack in Macedonia, the army on the left wing reached the Struma, but, on the other hand, that on the right wing could not get through in the direction of Vodena. The enterprise was hung up at this point for reasons the discussion of which would carry us too far afield. On this occasion the Bulgarian infantry fought splendidly in attack, but were handled with more energy than skill. They gained glory, but victory had slipped from their grasp. This conclusion of the attack in Macedonia faced Main Headquarters with a new and difficult problem. The Rumanian war fever was continually on the increase. It was to be expected that the pause in the Bulgarian operation in Macedonia would rouse the war-like passions of political circles in Bucharest. Should the German General Staff now break off the Bulgarian attack finally with a view to bringing to northern Bulgaria strong Bulgarian forces from the Macedonian front, which had now been materially shortened, or should they venture to transfer to Macedonia the forces they had assembled on the Danube with a view to renewing the attempt to cut the Rumanian Gordian knot with the sword? Rumania's declaration of war solved the problem for Main Headquarters.

Thus had the general situation developed south of the Danube. Not less difficult was the situation north of the Transylvanian Alps. For while Rumania was openly arming, the battles on the German Western Front, as well as those on the Austrian Eastern and South-Western Fronts, were using up all the troops which Main Headquarters seemed to have available as reserves or could possibly still be drawn from parts of the front which were not being attacked. It seemed impossible to release any troops for use against Rumania.

The result was that the Rumanian Declaration of War found us practically defenceless against the new enemy. I have devoted myself expressly to the development of this situation because I wish to make clear how the great crisis arose with which we found ourselves faced on and after that day. It can hardly be denied that such a crisis existed in view of the subsequent victorious course of the campaign.

But although the Quadruple Alliance had only made inadequate preparations to meet the Rumanian danger, it goes without saying that their responsible military leaders had come to a decision in good time about the appropriate measures for this eventuality. For this purpose a conference of the Commanders-in-Chief of Germany, Austria-Hungary and Bulgaria had been held at Pless on July 28, 1916. It resulted in the adoption of a plan of campaign in which the following words figured in the decisive Cipher 2 :

" If Rumania joins the Entente, the most rapid
advance in the greatest possible strength, to keep the war
certainly from Bulgarian soil, and as far as possible from
Austro-Hungarian, and invade Rumania. For this
purpose

" (a) Demonstration of German and Austrian
troops from the north, with a view to tying down
strong Rumanian forces.

" (b) Rapid advance of Bulgarian troops over the
frontier of the Dobrudja against the Danube crossings at Silistria and Tutrakan, with a view to protecting the right flank of the main force.

" (c) Prepare the main force to cross the Danube
at Nikopoli, with a view to attack on Bucharest."

The share of the Turks in a Rumanian campaign was
arranged at a conference held with Enver Pasha at Buda-
Pesth shortly afterwards. Enver undertook to prepare
two Turkish divisions for speedy employment in the
Balkan Peninsula.

While my predecessor still held the reins no changes
were made in this plan of campaign against Rumania.
However, the different Commanders - in - Chief met
several times to exchange ideas about it. Moreover,
Field-Marshal von Mackensen, who had been appointed
to command the troops concentrated south of the Danube,
was also heard on the subject. On these occasions two
currents of thought were clearly distinguishable. General
Conrad favoured the idea of a speedy and relentless
advance on Bucharest, while General Jekoff wished to
open the campaign in the Dobrudja. When war broke
out the forces south of the Danube were still much too
weak to carry out simultaneously the double task, i.e.

effect a crossing of the Danube and attack Silistria and Tutrakan, which had been set them on this front.

On August 28 my predecessor issued orders to Field-Marshal von Mackensen to attack as soon as possible. The direction and the objective were left to his discretion.

Such was the military situation with regard to Rumania when I took over the conduct of operations on August 29.

It is certain that so relatively small a state as Rumania had never before been given a rôle so important, and, indeed, so decisive for the history of the world at so favourable a moment. Never before had two great Powers like Germany and Austria found themselves so much at the mercy of the military resources of a country which had scarcely one-twentieth of the population of the two great states. Judging by the military situation, it was to be expected that Rumania had only to advance where she wished to decide the world-war in favour of those Powers which had been hurling themselves at us in vain for years. Thus everything seemed to depend on whether Rumania was ready to make any sort of use of her momentary advantage.

Nowhere was this fact appreciated more clearly, felt more keenly, and regarded with more apprehension than in Bulgaria. Her Government hesitated to declare war. Can they be reproached on that account? Whatever may be the answer, when Bulgaria decided in our favour, on September 1, the nation placed themselves at our side with all their resources, and inspired by all the hatred which dated from the Rumanian attack in their rear in the year 1913 when the country was engaged in a desperate

N

struggle with Serbia and Greece. The murderous day of Tutrakan gave us the first proofs of the warlike ardour of our Ally.

In view of our defective preparations, the plan of campaign which had been adopted had lost its original significance. In the first place the enemy had complete freedom of action. Thanks to the state of his preparations and numerical strength, which, unknown to us, had been materially increased by Russian help, it was to be feared that our own forces would be inadequate to limit the Rumanian High Command's freedom of movement to any appreciable degree at the outset. Great objectives and easy victories seemed to beckon to the Rumanians where-ever they chose to begin operations—whether across the Alps against Transylvania, or from the Dobrudja against Bulgaria. I was particularly afraid of a Russo-Rumanian offensive towards the south. Bulgarians themselves had expressed doubts whether their soldiers would fight against the Russians. General Jekoff's firm confidence in that respect—I mentioned this earlier on—was by no means universally shared in Bulgaria. No one could doubt that our enemy would rely on Russophile sentiment in at least a large part of the Bulgarian Army. Quite apart from that, it would have been easy for the Rumanians to hold out a hand to Sarrail's army by an attack on the south. What would our position be if the enemy once again succeeded in interrupting our communications with Turkey—the situation which had existed before we embarked on the campaign against Serbia—or, worse still, forcing Bulgaria out of the alliance? Turkey, isolated and simultaneously threatened from Armenia and Thrace, and Austria-Hungary, left with practically no hope, would never have survived a change in the situation so unfavourable to us.

The immediate advance of Mackensen, which my predecessor had ordered, was entirely in keeping with the needs of the hour. On the other hand, there could be no question of a crossing of the Danube with the forces available in northern Bulgaria. It would be enough for our purposes if we robbed the enemy of the initiative in the Dobrudja, and so upset his plan of campaign. But if we were to attain the last object really effectively we must not limit the Field-Marshal's attack to the capture of Tutrakan and Silistria. It would be much better, by exploiting to the full the success in the southern Dobrudja, to try and make the Rumanian High Command anxious about the rear of their main force which was on the Transylvanian frontier. In that we absolutely succeeded. In view of the Field-Marshal's progress to within a menacing distance of the Constanza—Cernavoda line, the Rumanian Commander-in-Chief found himself compelled to send reinforcements to the Dobrudja from the forces engaged in his operations against Transylvania. At the same time, by bringing up other fresh troops, he tried to take Mackensen's offensive in the rear from Rahovo, downstream from Rustchuk. A fine plan on paper! Whether it was a Rumanian inspiration or that of one of her Allies is still unknown, even to-day. After the experiences which the Rumanians had had of us before the day of this Rahovo interlude, I regarded the enterprise as more than bold, and not only thought to myself but said openly : " These troops will all be caught ! " This desire, clothed in appropriate orders, was fulfilled by the Germans and Bulgarians in the best possible style. Of the dozen

Rumanian battalions which reached the southern bank of the Danube at Rahovo, not a single man saw his home again during the war.

Disaster now overtook Rumania because her army did not march, her military leaders had no understanding, and at long last we succeeded in concentrating sufficient forces in Transylvania before it was too late.

Sufficient! Unquestionably sufficient for this enemy! We might possibly be called rash to the point of madness if the relative strengths were alone considered. However, we took the offensive against the Rumanian Army, and on September 29 General von Falkenhayn destroyed the Rumanian western wing at Hermannstadt.

After the battle of Hermannstadt the general threw his army eastward. Disregarding the danger of the Rumanian numerical superiority and their favourable position north of the Upper Aluta, he swept his main columns south of this river, along the foot of the mountains, towards Kronstadt. The Rumanians hesitated, lost confidence in their numerical superiority, as in their own capabilities, made no attempt to exploit the situation which was still favourable to them, and halted on the whole front. Even as they did so they took the first steps in retreat. General von Falkenhayn had now secured the initiative completely, overcame the enemy's resistance south of the Geisterwald, and marched on. The Rumanians were now in full retreat at all points from Transylvania, not without suffering another bloody defeat at Kronstadt on October 8. They thus retired to the protecting wall of their country. Our next task was to get over this wall. At first we had great hopes of strategically exploiting our previous tactical successes by

forcing our way directly to Bucharest from Kronstadt.
Though the rugged mountains and the enemy superiority
set our few weak divisions a very heavy task, the advantages of a break-through from this direction were much
too obvious for us to neglect the attempt.   It did not
succeed, though our troops fought stoutly for every peak,
every cliff, and every boulder.   Our advance was completely held up when a severe early winter laid a mantle
of snow on the mountains and turned the roads into icy
streams.   In spite of unspeakable privations and sufferings, our troops held all the ground they had gained,
ready to press on when time and opportunity should
allow.

Our previous experiences showed us that we must find
another road into the Wallachian Plain than that which
led from Kronstadt across the broadest part of the Transylvanian Alps.   General von Falkenhayn proposed an
irruption through the Szurduk Pass, farther west.   Of
course, this direction was less effective from a strategic
point of view, but under existing circumstances it was
the only one possible from a tactical and technical point
of view.   We thus invaded Rumania through this pass
on November 11.

Meanwhile General von Mackensen had been ready,
south of the Danube, to join hands with the invasion
from the north.   On October 21 he had thoroughly beaten
the Russo-Rumanian army south of the Constanza—
Cernavoda line.   On the 22nd Constanza had fallen into
the hands of the Bulgarian 3rd Army.   The enemy retired
north at top speed.   However, we broke off our pursuit
as soon as a line of defence had been reached north of
the railway which could be held with comparatively small

forces. All the troops that could possibly be spared were sent to Sistova. Alluring was the prospect of occupying the whole of the Dobrudja, and then forcing our way to the rear of the Rumanian main armies in the region north of the Danube. The only question was—how were we to get the necessary bridging material to the northern Dobrudja? There were no railways there, and the Rumanian batteries on the northern bank of the Danube prevented us from using the river. We had to thank the gods that these batteries had not destroyed our one available heavy bridging-train at Sistova long before, although it had been within range of the enemy guns for months, and owed its escape solely to what we regarded as an inexplicable omission on their part. We were thus able to contemplate the crossing of the river, at any rate at that point.

In the grey morning hours of November 23 Field-Marshal von Mackensen gained a footing on the northern bank of the Danube. The direct co-operation between him and General von Falkenhayn, for which we had been working, was achieved. It was crowned by the destruction of the Rumanian main force on the battlefield of the Argesch. The curtain came down on the last act on December 3. Bucharest fell into our hands without resistance.

In the evening of that day I concluded my general report on the military situation with the words, " A splendid day." When I stepped out into the winter night later on, the church tower of the town of Pless was already pealing forth for the great new victory. For a long time I had been thinking of nothing else but the wonderful achievements of our brave Army and hoping that these feats would bring us nearer to the conclusion of the terrible struggle and its great sacrifices.

It must be admitted that we had imagined the capture of the Rumanian capital as a rather more military affair. We had thought Bucharest was a powerful fortress, brought up our heaviest siege artillery to reduce it, and now the famous *place d'armes* had turned out to be no more than an open town. There were no longer any guns on the mighty walls of the forts, and the armoured cupolas had been replaced by wooden roofs. Our spying in peace time, of which the enemy had so much to say, had not even managed to discover that the fortress of Bucharest had been dismantled before the Rumanian campaign began.

The fate of Rumania had been brought to a dramatic conclusion. The whole world must see, and Rumania saw it well enough, that the old rhyme of the German pikeman was more than a mere empty sound :

" Wer Unglück will im Kriege han,
Der binde mit dem Deutschen an." *

In quoting this verse I do not wish in any way to depreciate the value of the help which Austria-Hungary, Turkey and Bulgaria gave in this great and splendid enterprise. Our Allies were all in their places and co-operated loyally in the heroic task. Rumania, who had had the fate of the world in her hands, must have been thankful that the remnants of her army were saved from destruction by Russian help. Her dream that, as in 1878 on the battlefield of Plevna, Russia would press her hand for services rendered in dutiful gratitude,

* " If anyone wants a disastrous war, let him pick a quarrel with the German."

though with bitter feelings at heart, had been cruelly reversed. Times had changed.

At the end of October, 1916, I had given my All-Highest War Lord my opinion that by the end of the year we should have concluded the Rumanian campaign. On December 81 I was able to report to His Majesty that our troops had reached the Sereth and that the Bulgarians were on the southern side of the Danube delta. We had reached our goal.

2

The Fighting on the Macedonian Front

The difficulties of our military situation had been materially increased in the autumn of 1916 by the course of the fighting on the Macedonian front.

Sarrail's army would have lost its very *raison d'être* if it had not taken the offensive itself at the time of the Rumanian declaration of war. We expected it to attack in the valley of the Vardar. If it had done so, and reached the neighbourhood of Gradsko, it would have seized the central point of the most important Bulgarian communications and made it impossible for the Bulgarians to remain in the district of Monastir. Sarrail chose to make a direct attack on Monastir, perhaps compelled by special political considerations. As the result of his offensive the Bulgarian Army on the right wing was driven from its position, south of Florina, which it had won in the August offensive. In the further course of the fighting it lost Monastir, but then managed to hold fast. These events had compelled us to send reinforcements to the Bulgarians from our own battlefronts, reinforcements which had nearly all been earmarked for the

Rumanian campaign. If the amount of help we sent—about twenty battalions and many heavy and field batteries—was not very large compared with our whole resources, this sacrifice was imposed on us at an extremely critical moment in which every man and gun had to be economised.

Like ourselves, Turkey willingly sent help to her Bulgarian Ally in her hard struggle. In addition to the reinforcements promised for the Rumanian campaign, Enver Pasha sent a whole Turkish Army Corps to relieve Bulgarian troops on the Struma front. This reinforcement was not accepted very willingly by the Bulgarians. They were afraid that it would form the basis for unpleasant political claims on the part of Turkey. However, Enver Pasha assured us expressly that he would prevent any such claims being formulated. It was quite comprehensible that Bulgaria should prefer German reinforcements to Turkish, but it was incomprehensible that Sofia would not see that Germany was in no position at this moment to increase the burden on her forces.

In my opinion the loss of Monastir had no military importance. In a military sense it would have been a great advantage if the Bulgarian right wing had been voluntarily withdrawn to the extraordinarily strong positions at Prilep, as this would have materially facilitated the work of supply to the Bulgarian Army and correspondingly hampered that of the enemy. It was just the enormous difficulties the Bulgarians had had with their communications which had greatly contributed to the crises which had supervened time after time in the recent battles. The troops had had to go hungry all day, and occasionally suffered from lack of ammunition. Putting our own interests on one side, we had done everything in our power to enable the Bulgarians to overcome these difficulties. The length of the communications to the rear, and the nature of this rugged and barren mountain region made the solution of this problem uncommonly difficult.

In the battles for Monastir the Bulgarians had had their first experience of heavy fighting on the defensive. Although the previous reports of our officers about the condition of the Bulgarian Army had spoken brilliantly of the splendid spirit displayed by the men in attack, these now began to speak of a certain reluctance to face long and continuous hostile artillery fire. This may seem a surprising assertion, but it is confirmed by the experience of all peoples, on the enemy's side as well as ours, who enter upon war with their so-called natural, primitive courage. It looks as if the nerve-racking effects of modern offensive weapons demand for an unshakable defence something more than this primitive courage, something which can only come from a higher training of the will. In the bulk of our German raw material there seems to be the right mixture of moral and physical powers which, combined with our military training of the will, enable our men successfully to resist the fearful effects of a modern battle. The Commander-in-Chief of the Bulgarian Army realised this sensitiveness of his men to which I have referred. With soldierly frankness he told us of his concern on this point, though he was far from being of an anxious temperament.

8
The Asiatic Theatres

In view of the position which the German Chief of the General Staff now occupied within the framework of the combined operations, we were compelled to take an active interest in the course of events in the Asiatic theatres also. When Enver Pasha visited our Headquarters at the beginning of 1916 our estimate of the situation in Asia was as follows :

The Russian offensive in Armenia, after reaching the line Trebizond—Erzingan had come to a standstill. The Turkish offensive, which in the summer of this year had begun in the south from the direction of Diabekr against the left flank of this Russian advance, had made no progress owing to the extraordinary difficulties of the country and the wholly inadequate supply system. It was to be expected that in view of the early approach of winter in the Armenian mountain-plateau the Russians would soon suspend their further attacks for good.

The fighting value of the two Turkish armies in the Caucasus had sunk to an extremely low level, and some divisions were divisions in name only. Privations, heavy losses, and desertion had had devastating effects on the establishments. Enver Pasha was extremely anxious about the coming winter. His troops were without the necessary clothing. Moreover, this region, barren and for the most part unpopulated and desolate, made the supply of the armies extraordinarily difficult. Owing to the shortage of draught and pack animals the requirements of the Turkish soldier in the way of food and military material in the dreary roadless mountains had to be satisfied by carrier-columns, and involved several days'

march.   Wives and children picked up a meagre pittance
in this way, but often found death too.

The situation in Irak at this time was better.   For the
moment the English had not yet made sufficient progress
with their communications to be able to embark on an
offensive to revenge Kut-el-Amara.   We had no doubt
that they would take their revenge, but we were not in a
position to judge whether the Turkish forces in Irak were
strong enough to offer a victorious resistance to the
English attack.   In spite of the very optimistic view of the
Turkish General Staff we warned them that they ought
to reinforce the troops there.   Unfortunately, Turkey
allowed herself to be led by political and pan-Islam
ambitions to send a whole Army Corps into Persia.

The third Asiatic theatre, Southern Palestine, gave
cause for immediate anxiety.   The second Turkish attempt
on the Suez Canal had been defeated in August, 1916, in
the heart of the northern part of the Sinai peninsula.
Following on this occurrence, the Turkish troops had
gradually been withdrawn from this region and were now
in the neighbourhood of Gaza, on the southern frontier
of Palestine.   The question if and when they would be
attacked here seemed to depend largely on the time which
it would take the English to complete their railway from
Egypt behind their front.   The threatened attack on
Palestine seemed far more dangerous for the military and
political stability of Turkey than an attack in Mesopotamia,
which was so far away.   We must expect that the loss of
Jerusalem—quite apart from the loss of the whole of
Southern Arabia which it would presumably involve—
would lay a burden on Turkish statesmanship which it
would not be able to carry.

Unfortunately, the strategic conditions in Southern Syria were not materially better for the Turkish operations than those in Mesopotamia. In both theatres the Turks, in striking contrast to their enemy, suffered from such extraordinary difficulties in their communications that a material increase of their forces beyond the existing figure meant hunger and even thirst for everyone. In Syria, too, the situation as regards food supply was occasionally desperate. To add to the bad harvest and involuntary or voluntary failures of the responsible authorities, the attitude of the Arab population was pretty generally hostile.

In the course of the war many well-meant representations were made to me in the hope of convincing me that Mesopotamia and Syria ought to be defended with stronger forces, indeed that we ought to pass to the offensive in both theatres. There was a great deal of interest in many German circles in these regions. Without saying as much, the thoughts of these gentlemen were probably straying beyond Mesopotamia to Persia, Afghanistan and India, and beyond Syria to Egypt. With their fingers on the map men dreamed that by these routes we could reach the spinal cord of British world power, our greatest peril. Perhaps, too, such ideas were an unconscious return to earlier Napoleonic schemes. But we lacked the first elements—sufficient really effective lines of supply—required for the execution of such far-reaching plans.

4

The Eastern and Western Fronts to the End of 1916

While we were occupied in overthrowing Rumania the Russians had continued their operations in the Carpathians and Galicia. On the Russian side there had been no intention of giving the new Ally direct assistance in her attack on Transylvania, but the continuation of the previous Russian attacks on the Galician front was to facilitate the Rumanian operations. On the other hand, the Russians gave Rumania direct help in the Dobrudja, and indeed from the outset. The reasons for this were as much political as military. Russia no doubt placed high hopes in the Russophile sentiment in the Bulgarian Army. With this idea in view, when the battles in the Southern Dobrudja began Russian officers and men tried to fraternise with the Bulgarians, and were bitterly dèceived when the Bulgarians replied by firing at them. Another reason was that the occupation of Transylvania by Rumania aroused no political jealousy in Russia, but Russia could not suffer the new Ally to bring Bulgaria to her knees by her own efforts and then possibly force her way to Constantinople or at least open the way there. For the capture of the Turkish capital had been the historic and religious preserve of Russia for centuries.

I need not discuss whether it was good policy on the part of Russia to give the Rumanians no direct support, even by sending Russian troops for a nucleus, and allow her to conduct the operations in Transylvania single-handed. In any case the efficiency of the Rumanian Army and its leadership were overrated, and there was an erroneous idea that the forces of the Central Powers on the Eastern Front had been completely pinned down by the Russian attacks and were absolutely exhausted.

It is true that these attacks did not entirely attain their purpose, but time and time again they produced considerable crises for us.   Occasionally the situation was so bad that we were apprehensive that our defence lines would be thrown back from the crest of the Carpathians.   Yet the maintenance of these lines was for us a condition precedent to our deployment and first operations against the new enemy.   In Galicia, too, we had to keep back the Russians at any price.   The evacuation of further stretches in that district would have been of small military importance for our general situation in itself if we had not had, immediately behind our lines in Galicia, the oil-fields which were of such immense value to us and indeed absolutely indispensable for our military operations.   For this cause troops destined for the attack against Rumania had to be deflected to this part of the front when it showed signs of collapse.

But even though we survived the critical situation and brought our campaign against Rumania to a successful conclusion, it cannot be said that the Russian relief attacks had completely failed to achieve their great strategic purpose.   It is certainly true that Rumania's Allies were not responsible for her downfall.   On the contrary, the Entente did everything that their situation and resources permitted, not only in direct association with the Rumanian Army but indirectly through Sarrail's attacks in Macedonia, the Italian offensive on the Isonzo, and lastly the continuation of the Anglo-French onslaught in the West.

As has already been said, we anticipated at the start that, with the entry of Rumania into the war, the enemy would renew his attacks on the Western Front also with all his might—English stubbornness and French *élan*. That is exactly what happened.

Our rôle as supreme directors of these battles was
simple.   For lack of men we could not contemplate the
idea of a relief attack either at Verdun or the Somme,
however strong were my own inclinations for such a
measure.   Very soon after I took over my new post I
found myself compelled by the general situation to ask His
Majesty the Emperor to order the offensive at Verdun to
be broken off.   The battles there exhausted our forces
like an open wound.   Moreover, it was obvious that in
any case the enterprise had become hopeless, and that for
us' to persevere with it would cost us greater losses than
those we were able to inflict on the enemy.   Our forward
zone was at all points exposed to the flanking fire of
superior hostile artillery.   Our communications with the
battle-line were extremely difficult.   The battlefield was
a regular hell and regarded as such by the troops.   When
I look back now, I do not hesitate to say that on purely
military grounds it would have been far better for us to
have improved our situation at Verdun by the voluntary
evacuation of the ground we had captured.   In August,
1916, however, I considered I could not adopt that course.
To a large extent the flower of our best fighting troops had
been sacrificed in the enterprise.   The public at home
still anticipated a glorious issue to the offensive.   It would
be only too easy to produce the impression that all these
sacrifices had been incurred in vain.   Such an impression
I was anxious to avoid in the existing state of public
opinion, nervous enough as it already was.

We were disappointed in our hopes that with the
breaking-off of our offensive at Verdun the enemy would
more or less confine himself to purely trench warfare
there.   At the end of October the French opened a

largely-conceived and boldly-executed counter-attack on the eastern bank of the Meuse, and overran our lines. We lost Douaumont, and had no longer the strength to recover that field of honour of German heroism.

For this attack the French commander had abandoned the former practice of an artillery preparation extending over days or even weeks. By increasing the rate of fire of the artillery and trench-mortars to the extreme limit of capacity of material and men, only a short period of preparation had preceded the attack, which had then been launched immediately against the physically exhausted and morally shaken defenders. We had already had experience of this enemy method of preparation for the attack in the course of the long attrition battles, but as the herald to a great infantry attack it was a novelty to us, and it was perhaps just this feature which doubtless produced so important a success. Taking it all round, on this occasion the enemy hoisted us with our own petard. We could only hope that in the coming year he would not repeat the experiment on a greater scale and with equal success.

It was not until December that the actions at Verdun died down. From the end of August the Somme battle too had taken on the character of an extremely fierce and purely frontal contest of the forces on both sides. The task of Main Headquarters was essentially limited to feeding the armies with the reinforcements necessary to enable them to maintain their resistance. Among us battles of this kind were known as "battles of material." From the point of view of the attacker they might also be called "battering-ram tactics," for the commanders had no higher ideal. The mechanical, material elements of

o

the battle were put in the foreground, while real generalship was far too much in the background.

If our western adversaries failed to obtain any decisive results in the battles from 1915 to 1917 it must mainly be ascribed to a certain unimaginativeness in their generalship. The necessary superiority in men, war material and ammunition was certainly not lacking, nor can it be suggested that the quality of the enemy troops would not have been high enough to satisfy the demands of a more vigorous and ingenious leadership. Moreover, in view of the highly-developed railway and road system, and the enormous amount of transport at their disposal, our enemies in the West had free scope for far greater strategic subtlety. However, the enemy commander did not make full use of these possibilities, and our long resistance was to be attributed, apart from other things, to a certain barrenness of the soil in which the enemy's plans took root. But notwithstanding all this, the demands which had to be made on our commanders and troops on this battlefield remained enormous.

At the beginning of September I visited the Western Front with my First Quartermaster-General. We had to familiarise ourselves with the conditions there if we were to render any effective help. On the way there His Imperial and Royal Highness the German Crown Prince joined us and honoured me at Montmédy by parading a Storm Company at the station. This reception was thoroughly in keeping with the chivalrous habit of mind of this exalted Prince whom I was to meet frequently henceforth. His merry, frank manner and sound military judgment have always given me pleasure and confidence. At Cambrai, on orders from His Majesty the Emperor, I met two other tried Army Commanders, the Crown Princes of Bavaria and Würtemberg, and the Prussian Staffs which had been lent to them, and held quite a long conference with the Chiefs of Staff on the Western Front. Their statements showed that rapid and ruthless action was urgently necessary if our terrible inferiority in aircraft, arms and munitions were at all to be made good. General Ludendorff's immense capacity for work overcame this serious crisis. To my great joy officers from the front told me subsequently that the results of the conference at Cambrai had soon made themselves felt among the troops.

The extent of the demands which were being made on the army in the West was brought before my eyes quite vividly for the first time during this visit to France. I will not hesitate to admit that it was only now that I fully realised all that the Western Armies had done hitherto. What a thankless task it was for the commanders and troops, on whom pure defence was imposed and who had to renounce the vision of a tangible victory! Victory in the defensive battle does not release the defender, even when he is victorious, from the permanent oppressive atmosphere of the battlefield, I might perhaps say the spectacle of all its misery. The soldier has to renounce that mighty spiritual exaltation which accompanies a victorious advance, an exaltation of such overwhelming force that a man must have experienced it to realise its true meaning. How many of our brave men have never known this, the purest of a soldier's joys. They hardly ever saw anything but trenches and shell-holes in and around which they fought with the enemy for weeks and even months. What a strain on the nerves!

How little to brace them! What a strong sense of duty
and what self-sacrificing devotion must have been required
to endure such conditions for years and silently to
renounce all hopes of greater battle fortune! I admit
frankly that these impressions gripped me deeply. I
could now understand how everyone, officers and men
alike, longed to get away from such an atmosphere, and
how all hearts were filled with the hope that now at last,
after these exhausting battles, a stronger offensive spirit
would mean more vigorous operations on the Western
Front also.

But for all that, our leaders and their men were to
wait a long time yet before those hopes could be fulfilled.
Many of our best and finest fighting men had to pour out
their heart's blood in destroyed trenches before that stage
was reached! It was only when the arrival of the wet
season began to make the ground impossible that things
became quieter in the battle area of the Somme. The
millions of shell-holes filled with water or became mere
cemeteries. Neither of the contending parties knew the
exaltation of victory. Over everyone hovered the fearful
spectre of this battlefield which for desolation and horror
seemed to be even worse than that of Verdun.

CHAPTER XII

1

Foreign Policy

I HAD always felt it my duty to take an interest in the great historical past of our Fatherland. The life histories of its great sons were to me of equal importance with books of devotion. Under no circumstances, not even war, would I neglect these sources of instruction and inward inspiration. And yet it would be perfectly accurate to say that mine is a non-political temperament. It was against my inclination to take any interest in current politics. Perhaps my liking for political criticism is too weak, and possibly my soldierly instincts are too strong. The latter are certainly responsible for my dislike of everything diplomatic. This dislike can be called prejudice or want of understanding. I would not have disavowed the fact, even here, if I had not had to give expression to it so often and so loudly during the war. I had the feeling that the business of diplomacy made unfamiliar demands on us Germans. No doubt this is indeed one of the principal reasons for our backwardness in matters of foreign politics. This backwardness must of course have played a larger part the more we seemed to be becoming a world people as the result of the immense development of our trade and industry and the spread of the German spirit beyond the frontiers of the Fatherland. I never found among German statesmen that sense of political power, silent but self-contained, which was characteristic of the English.

When holding my high posts of command in the East, and even after I was appointed Chief of the General Staff of the Field Army, I had never felt either necessity or inclination to mix myself up in current political questions more than was absolutely necessary. Of course I believed that in a coalition war, with its innumerable and complicated problems that affect the conduct of operations, it was impossible for the military leaders to have absolutely no say in political affairs. Nevertheless, I recognised that the standard which Bismarck had laid down for the relations between military and political leadership in war was thoroughly sound as applied to our case also. Moltke himself was adopting the Bismarckian point of view when he said : " The commander in his operations has to keep military victory as the goal before his eyes. But what statesmanship does with his victories or defeats is not his province. It is that of the statesman." On the other hand, I should never have been able to account to my conscience if I had not brought forward my own views in all cases in which I was convinced that the efforts of others were leading us on doubtful paths, if I had not applied driving power where I thought I detected inaction or aversion to action, and if I had not made the very strongest representations when the conduct of operations and the future military security of my country were affected or endangered by political measures.

It will be allowed that the border-line between politics and the conduct of operations cannot be drawn with exact precision. The statesman and the soldier must have co-operated previously in peace time, as their different spheres unconditionally demand mutual understanding. In war, in which their threads are inextricably intertwined, they have to be mutually complementary the whole time. This complicated relation can never be regulated by definite rules. Even in Bismarck's incisive phraseology the boundaries seem to overlap on both sides. It is not only the problem at issue which decides in these questions, but also the character and temperament of the men engaged in their solution.

I grant that I have covered many expressions of opinion on political questions with my name and responsibility even when they were only loosely connected with our military situation at the time. In such cases I thrust my views on no one. But whenever anyone asked what I thought, or some question cropped up which awaited, but did not find, a decision or the definition of the German point of view, I saw no reason why I should hold my peace.

One of the first political questions in which I was concerned, shortly after I assumed control of operations, was the future of Poland. In view of the great importance of this question during and after the war I think I ought to treat more fully of the manner in which it was handled.

Until of late I have never had any personal animosity against the Polish people. On the other hand, I should have been entirely lacking in patriotic instincts and the knowledge of historical evolution if I had ignored the serious dangers which the restoration of Poland involved for my country. I never had the slightest doubt that we could not expect a word of thanks from Poland for freeing her from the Russian knout with our sword and blood, as we had received little recognition for the economic and moral advancement of the Prussian Poles among us. No feeling of gratitude—so far as such a thing exists in politics —would deter a restored, free Poland from seeing *irridenta* in our frontier provinces.

From whatever side a solution of the Polish problem was sought, Prussia—Germany—was bound to be the unhappy party who had to pay the bill. Austro-Hungarian statesmanship appeared to see no dangers to her own existence in the creation of a free, united Poland. Indeed influential circles in Vienna and Buda-Pesth seemed to think that it would be possible to bind Catholic Poland permanently to the Dual Monarchy. In view of the thoroughly Germanophobe attitude of the Poles, this policy of Austria was pregnant with danger for us. It could not be ignored that it meant that the strength of our alliance would in future be put to a test which could not be borne in the long run. In no circumstances could Main Headquarters, anxious about our future military situation on the Eastern frontier, leave this political point of view out of sight.

In my view all these political and military considerations showed Germany that she should touch the Polish question as little as possible, or at any rate deal with it in a very dilatory fashion, to use an expression employed in such cases. Unfortunately this was not done on the German side. The reasons why we did not act with the caution that was required are unknown to me. However that may be, the fact is that in the middle of August, 1916, a compact was made at Vienna between the statesmen of Germany and Austria-Hungary, a compact which provided for the speediest possible announcement of an independent Kingdom of Poland with an hereditary

Constitutional Monarchy. Both the contracting parties
had tried to make this agreement more palatable to us
Germans by undertaking not to make over any part of
their ancient Polish districts to the new Polish State, and
by guaranteeing that Germany should have the right to
command the future army of United Poland. I considered both concessions Utopian.

The political situation behind our Eastern Front would
have been completely changed by this public announcement. For that reason my predecessor had immediately,
and rightly, raised his voice against it. His Majesty the
Emperor decided in favour of General von Falkenhayn.
However, it was now clear to everyone who knew the
conditions in the Danube Monarchy that the compact
made in Vienna would not remain a secret. It might
be kept an official secret for a short time still, but could
not be got rid of altogether. As a matter of fact, it was
known everywhere by the end of August. So when I
went to Main Headquarters I was faced with a *fait
accompli*. Shortly afterwards the Governor-General of
Warsaw, who was not officially responsible to me, asked
me on behalf of our Government to announce the Polish
Kingdom as an act which could no longer be postponed.
He gave me the choice between difficulties in the country
and the certain prospect of a reinforcement of our armies
by Polish troops, a reinforcement which would amount to
five trained divisions in the spring of 1917 and one million
men on the introduction of universal military service.
However unfavourable was the opinion I had formed in
1914 and 1915 of the prospects of any Polish contribution
to the war against Russia, the Governor-General thought
he knew better. He knew how the domestic situation of

the conquered country had developed since 1915, and was convinced that the priests would help us with our recruiting.

In our military situation, how could I have taken the responsibility of declining this reinforcement which was promised so definitely? But if I decided to accept it no time must be lost if we were to put fully-trained troops into the front lines by the time the next spring battles began. A victorious Germany would be able to settle the Polish question after the peace. At this point, greatly to my surprise, we met with objections on the part of the Government. It was about this time that the Government thought that they had discovered threads leading to a separate peace with Russia, and therefore considered it bad policy to compromise the steps they had taken by proclaiming an independent Poland. Political and military views were thus in conflict.

The conclusion of the whole business was that the hopes of a separate peace with Russia broke down, that the manifesto was published in the early days of November, and that the recruiting of Polish volunteers, to which it referred, was entirely without results. Our recruiting appeals not only received no support from the Catholic priesthood, but were openly resisted by them.

As soon as the manifesto was published, the opposition between the interests of Austria and those of Germany in the Polish problem was at once revealed. Our Allies were aiming more and more openly at the union of Congress Poland with Galicia, the whole being subject to their own suzerainty. As a reply to these efforts, and failing the ability of our Government to bring them to naught, I considered that the least we could ask for was a corresponding ratification of our Eastern frontier from the purely military point of view.

Of course, the fact was that all these questions could only be decided by the result of the war. I therefore sincerely regretted that they took up so much of our time during the operations. But I cannot sufficiently insist that the friction between our Allies and ourselves in political matters never had the slightest influence on our military co-operation.

The rôle that was played by Poland in our relations with Austria-Hungary was played by the Dobrudja in our political and military dealings with Bulgaria. At bottom the Dobrudja question amounted to whether Bulgaria was to secure possession of the Cernavoda—Constanza railway by her acquisition of the whole province. If she did so, she would control the last and, after the Orient Railway, the most important land route between Central Europe and the near Orient. Of course Bulgaria realised that the favourable moment to wring concessions from us in this direction was during the war. Turkey, on the other hand, as the country most immediately affected, asked for our political support against these Bulgarian plans. We gave her that support. Thus began diplomatic guerilla warfare in military guise, and lasted nearly a year. Put shortly the position was as follows :

The alliance concluded between us and Bulgaria provided, in case of war with Rumania, for a return to our Ally of that part of the southern Dobrudja which had been lost in 1912, as well as for frontier adjustments in that region ; but it said nothing about the assignment of the whole Rumanian province to Bulgaria. In accordance with this compact, as soon as the Rumanian campaign was virtually over, we had handed over the original Bulgarian portions of the southern Dobrudja to be administered by the Bulgarian Government, but established a German administration in the central Dobrudja in agreement with all our Allies. As the result of a special economic agreement this German administration worked almost exclusively on behalf of Bulgaria. The northern Dobrudja, being in the military zone, was controlled by the 3rd Bulgarian Army there. As far as one could see, the matter seemed to have been arranged entirely satisfactorily. However, the satisfaction did not last for long.

The gauntlet was thrown down to us by the Bulgarian Minister-President. Even before the Rumanian campaign was over he had mooted to his Ministers the idea of the cession of the whole of the Dobrudja to Bulgaria, and represented the German General Staff as the obstacle in the way of these ambitions. The result was a strong political agitation against us. At first King Ferdinand had not agreed with the proceedings of his Government, but at length he felt himself compelled to yield to the general excitement. In the same way, at the outset the Bulgarian General Staff had not let themselves be drawn into the affair. They fully realised the danger of a new element of unrest being added to the political currents within their army which themselves flowed strongly and diversely. However, before long even General Jekoff felt that he could resist the pressure of the Minister-President no longer. The Bulgarian Government lost control of the movement they had started, and the result was a general political outcry against the German

General Staff, an outcry which was mainly the work of irresponsible agitators and had no respect for the relations between brothers-in-arms. The obstinacy with which certain circles in Bulgaria pursued this goal of their ambitions would have been better devoted to attaining our common aims in the war.

This incident betrayed the consequences of a defective side of our compact with Bulgaria. When that compact was made, we had given the Bulgarians the most far-reaching assurances possible with regard to the aggrandisement of the country and the unification of the Bulgarian race. We should have been able to give effect to those assurances only if we had won a complete victory. Bulgaria, however, was not satisfied with these assurances. She was continually advancing fresh claims without stopping to consider whether such a small State would be able, later on, to manage her new acquisitions politically and economically.

Moreover, there was a direct military danger for us in these excessive ambitions. I have already said what a great military advantage it would have been to us to withdraw our line of defence on the western wing of the Macedonian front to the neighbourhood of Prilep. At the very suggestion of such a proceeding from our side, however, all political circles in Bulgaria joined in raising the most serious objections. They immediately feared that they would thus abandon all political claims to areas evacuated for military reasons. They preferred to risk a whole army rather than be responsible to their fellow-countrymen for the abandonment of what they called the " old Bulgarian town of Ochrida." We shall see, later on, what our far-reaching concessions to Bulgaria were to involve.

The perplexities of all these innumerable political problems and counter-problems meant hours of thankless work for me, and considerably increased my aversion to politics.

The purport of our compact with Turkey was quite different from that with Bulgaria. As regards the Turkish Government we had only pledged ourselves before the war to maintain Turkey's territorial integrity. Now the Turks had lost an important part of their possessions in Asia during the first two years of the war. A very heavy burden had thus been laid on our treaty obligations. It did not seem impossible that these unhappy failures would have a harmful reaction on the conduct of operations. The Turkish Government could base claims in this direction which we should possibly not be in a position to disregard owing to political reasons. In these circumstances Enver Pasha's lofty conception of our common purpose and its decisive issues was of the very greatest value. Moreover, for the time being, the political views of the other Turkish statesmen seemed to offer a guarantee that Turkey's previous losses would not involve an excessive overdraft on our military account. We were thus certain that in case peace negotiations were opened, the Turkish Government would not tie us down to the strict letter of our compact, but would accept the recognition of a more or less formal suzerainty over a large part of the lost territory so long as we succeeded in finding a formula which would preserve the prestige of the present Government.

It was thus a very important task, both for our statesmen and our military commanders, to support the existing Ottoman Government; it would not be easy to find a substitute for Enver or Talaat Pasha, who were completely and absolutely loyal to us.   Of course, this does not mean that we attempted to check political currents in Turkey which had an adverse influence on the military task of the nation within the framework of the combined operations. I am referring here to my previous remarks about the Pan-Islam movement.   From the military point of view it always tended to deflect Turkey into wrong paths. After the collapse of Russia, Pan-Islam sought its conquests in the direction of the Caucasus.   Indeed, it cast its eye beyond them to the Transcaspian region, and finally lost itself in the distant areas of Central Asia, inspired by the fantastic ambition of uniting all men of its own culture and faith under the Ottoman sway.

It was obvious that we could not lend military support to such Oriental political dreams, but that we must demand the abandonment of these far-reaching schemes for the sake of existing military realities. Unfortunately, all our efforts failed.

How much more difficult than our efforts to exercise influence on the problems of Turkish foreign policy must be those to obtain some influence on her domestic affairs. And yet we could not refrain from making at least an attempt to acquire such influence. It was not only her primitive economic condition that impelled us. Ordinary human feelings worked in the same direction.

The surprising revival of Ottoman military power and the renascence of her ancient heroism in this fight for existence also showed up the darkest side of Turkish domination.   I mean her attitude to the Armenian portions of her Empire.   The Armenian question embodied one of Turkey's most difficult problems.   It affected both

the Pan-Turkish and the Pan-Islam ideals. The whole
world took a deep interest during the war in the methods
with which the fanatical Turk attempted to solve it.
Attempts have been made to associate us Germans with
the horrible occurrences in the whole Turkish Empire,
and, towards the end of the war, even in Armenian Trans-
caucasia. I therefore feel it my duty to touch on this
question here, and indeed have no reason to pass over the
part we played in silence. We never hesitated, both
verbally and in writing, to exercise a deterrent influence
on the savage and licentious methods of warfare which
were traditional in the East, thanks to racial hatreds and
religious animosities. We received soothing assurances
from men high up in the Turkish Government, but were
not in a position to overcome the passive resistance which
was opposed to our intervention. For example, the Turks
insisted that the Armenian question was essentially their
own domestic concern, and were very sensitive when we
referred to it. Even our officers who happened to be on
the spot frequently failed in their efforts to secure some
moderation in the acts of hatred and vengeance. The
awakening of the beast in a man fighting a life and death
battle, and inspired by political and religious fanaticism,
forms one of the blackest chapters in the history of all
times and nations.

Moreover, observers of neutral nationalities were
agreed in their opinion that from the point of view of
massacre, the contending parties, stirred as they were to
their inmost depths, were just as bad as each other. This
would be the natural result of the moral notions peculiar
to races of this region, notions which seemed to be sanc-
tified by the practice of the vendetta which still prevailed,

or had only been out of date for a short time. The harm which was done by these massacres is quite immeasurable. It made itself felt, not only in the human and political sphere, but even in economic and military affairs. The number of the best Turkish troops who came to a miserable death by privation in the Caucasian mountain winters during the war, as the result of this policy of massacre of the Armenians, will certainly never be known. The consequence of this wholesale slaughter by every imaginable kind of privation was that another chapter was added to the tragic history of the brave Anatolian soldier, the very backbone of the Ottoman Empire. Is it the last?

2

The Peace Question

It was in the very middle of our preparations for the Rumanian campaign that the peace question came to my notice. So far as I know, it was first brought up by the Austro-Hungarian Foreign Minister, Baron Burian. Those who know me and my views on war will require no further assurance that my natural human feelings welcomed such a step. For the rest, the only motive behind the part I played in this question was the interests of my Emperor and country. I considered it my duty in this matter to strive for such a solution that neither the Army nor the Homeland should suffer any injury. Main Headquarters had to co-operate in settling the wording of our peace offer. It was a difficult and thankless task to avoid creating an impression of weakness at home and abroad while giving all provocative expressions a wide berth. I was able to see with what a devout sense of duty

P

to God and man my All-Highest War Lord devoted himself to the solution of this peace problem, and I do not think that he regarded a complete failure of this step as probable. On the other hand, my own confidence in its success was quite small from the outset. Our adversaries had vied with one another in putting forward excessive claims, and it appeared to me out of the question that any of the enemy Governments could and would voluntarily go back on the promises which they had made to each other and their peoples. However, this view did not in any way affect my honest intention to co-operate in this work for the good of humanity.

On December 12 our readiness to conclude peace was announced to our enemies. Our answer from enemy propaganda, as well as the hostile camps, was only scorn and a rebuff.

Hot on the heels of our own peace step came a similar effort on the part of the President of the United States. Main Headquarters was informed by the Imperial Chancellor of the suggestions which the President had made through the medium of our ambassador in the United States. I myself considered that President Wilson was not exactly suited to the rôle of an unprejudiced intermediary as I could not overcome my feeling that the President had strong leanings towards our enemies, and more particularly England. That was indeed a perfectly natural consequence of his Anglo-Saxon origin. Like millions of my countrymen, I could not consider Wilson's previous attitude as neutral, although, possibly, it did not contravene the strict letter of neutrality. In all questions of breaches of International Law the President treated England with all possible consideration. In so doing, he had received some very severe rebuffs. On the other hand, in the question of submarine warfare, which was our only reply to England's arbitrary actions, Wilson had shown the greatest touchiness and immediately taken to threats of war. Germany signified her assent to the principle of Wilson's proposals. The reply of our enemies to Wilson was a recital of their demands, which to all intents and purposes comprised the permanent economic and political paralysis of Germany, the dismemberment of Austria-Hungary and the destruction of the Ottoman State. To anyone who judged the military situation at that time dispassionately, it must have been obvious that the enemy's war aims had no prospect of acceptance except by a hopelessly defeated foe, and that we had no reason to regard ourselves in that position. In any case, as things were then, I should have regarded it as a crime to my country and a betrayal of our Allies if I had taken any other course but absolutely refuse to consider enemy demands of that kind. In view of the military situation at the moment, my convictions and my conscience impelled me to regard no peace as a good peace which did not so secure our position in the world as to make us safe against the same kind of political oppression which had led to the present war, and enable us to offer our Allies the support they required against any kind of menace. For me as a soldier it was a secondary matter along what political and geographical lines this purpose was achieved; the main thing was that it should be achieved. Further, I considered that there was no doubt that the German people and its Allies would be strong enough to reject the unexampled enemy demands in arms, cost what it might. As a matter of fact, public opinion in our country

was absolutely hostile to the enemy's claims. Nor was
there at this time any indication of a tendency to give way
on the part of Turkey or Bulgaria. I considered that the
vacillation of Austria-Hungary would be overcome. The
main thing was that the Austro-Hungarian public should
keep before their eyes the fate which the enemy's terms
meted out to the Danube Monarchy, and should give a
wide berth to the delusion that, for the time being,
negotiations with the enemy on fairer lines was possible.
We had already discovered, in dealing with Austria-
Hungary, that she was capable of far more than she
herself believed. Her Government must find itself faced
with blunt necessity, and would then find itself equal to
even greater efforts. For all these reasons it was my
opinion that it was a mistake to deal with Austria-
Hungary with soft words. Such words do not strengthen
and encourage confidence and resolution. This is true of
politicians and soldiers alike. All in good time. But
when things go hard, firm demands, combined with real
resolution on the part of the strong, carry the weak along
quicker and farther than soft words about better times
in the days to come.

In contrast to our view, President Wilson's message
of January 22 to the American Senate saw in our enemies'
declaration of war aims of January 10 a more suitable
basis for peace efforts than our diplomatic Note, which
merely expounded the principles on which we agreed to
the continuation of his steps for peace. This behaviour
on the part of the President shook my confidence in his
impartiality even further. I should not have refused my
approval of the lofty and to a certain extent praiseworthy
humanitarian note in his message if I had not searched it

in vain for any rejection of the attempt of our enemies to hold us up as men of a lower order. Moreover, the sentence about the restoration of a single free and independent Poland aroused my distrust. It seemed to me to be aimed directly at Austria-Hungary and ourselves, to compel the Danube Monarchy to renounce Galicia, and would mean the loss of territory or suzerainty for Germany as well. In view of that, how could anyone speak of the impartiality towards the Central Powers of Wilson's mediation? For us, the message was a Declaration of War rather than a peace proposal. If we had once committed ourselves into the hands of the President we should have found ourselves on a steep slope which threatened in the long run to bring us to a peace which would have meant the renunciation of our whole political, economic and military position. It seemed to me not impossible that after the first step of consent we should gradually find ourselves politically farther and farther in the depths and end up by being compelled to capitulate in the military sense.

In October, 1918, I learned from certain publications that immediately after his message to the Senate of January 22, 1917, President Wilson had informed the German Ambassador in Washington of his willingness to take official steps for peace. The news had reached Berlin on January 28. Until the autumn of 1918 I had never heard of this step of Wilson which apparently went pretty far to meet us. I do not know, even to-day, whether mistakes or a chain of adverse circumstances were responsible. In my view, war with America was inevitable at the end of January, 1917. At that time Wilson knew of our intention to start unrestricted U-boat war-

fare on February 1. There can be no doubt that, thanks
to the English practice of intercepting and deciphering
our telegrams on this subject to the German Ambassador
in Washington, Wilson was as well informed about this
matter as about the contents of all our other cables. The
message to the Senate of January 22, and the offer of
mediation which accompanied it, were thus branded for
what they were at the outset. Disaster was on its way. It
could therefore no longer be averted by our declaration of
January 29 that we were prepared to stop U-boat warfare
out of hand if the President were successful in his efforts
to establish a basis for peace negotiations. The events
of 1918 and 1919 appear to me to confirm the opinions I
then held at all points, opinions which were entirely shared
by my First Quartermaster-General.

3
Home Politics

When I was on the Active List I had kept away from
current questions of domestic politics. Even after my
retirement they had interested me solely as a silent
onlooker. I was never able to understand how it was
that here and there the welfare of the Fatherland had to
be sacrificed to mere petty party interests, and from the
point of view of political conviction felt myself most at
home in the shade of that tree which was firmly rooted
in the ethico-political soil of the epoch of our great and
venerable Emperor. That epoch, with what I regarded
as its wonderful glories, seemed to have become part
of me, and I adhered firmly to its ideals and principles.
The course of events in the present war have hardly been

of a kind to make me particularly enthusiastic about the developments of later times. A powerful, self-contained State in Bismarck's sense was the world in which I preferred my thoughts to move. Discipline and hard work within the Fatherland seemed to me better than cosmopolitan imaginings. Moreover, I fail to see that any citizen has rights on whom equal duties are not imposed.

In war I thought only of war. In my view of the seriousness of our situation all obstacles which prevented us from waging it with all our might should be ruthlessly removed. Our enemies were doing so and we had to learn from their example. Unfortunately, we did not do so, but pursued the phantom of international justice instead of putting our own national feeling and national strength before everything else in this fight for existence.

During the war Main Headquarters had to take an active interest in several internal problems, especially in the economic sphere. We did not seek these problems; they thrust themselves on our attention much more than we wished. The close relations between the Army and industry made it impossible for us to draw a hard-and-fast line between industrial questions at home and the conduct of operations such as we had drawn between the war zones and the Homeland.

I take full responsibility for the form of the great industrial programme which bears my name. The one principle which I laid down for its working-out was that the needs of our fighting troops must be supplied at any cost. I should have regarded any other foundation as a crime against our Army and my country. It is true that our demands meant that the figures would reach gigantic proportions compared with what had gone before, but I

did not venture to judge whether they could be attained.
The programme has been reproached, since the war ended,
with having been dictated by despair. The inventor of
that phrase has been woefully misled about the point of
view under the influence of which this programme came
into existence.

I had devoted myself wholeheartedly to the introduction of the Auxiliary Service Law. It was my wish that
in the crisis facing our Fatherland, not only every man
fit to fight, but every man fit to work, and even women,
should place themselves or be placed at the disposal of
our great cause. I was convinced that by a law of this
kind, moral as well as personal forces would be released
which we could throw into the scales of war. The final
form of the law certainly produced somewhat modest
results which indeed differed materially from those we
had had in view. Disillusioned as I was, I almost regretted that we had not tried to achieve our purpose by
utilising existing legislation, as had been proposed in other
quarters. The idea of presenting the acceptance of the
law as a powerful and impressive manifesto by the whole
German people had made me overlook the influence of
the currents of domestic politics. In the long run, the
law was passed, not through the pressure of public opinion,
but on the grounds of industrial necessities.

The reproach has been levelled at Main Headquarters
that in the Auxiliary Service Law and the demands of
the so-called "Hindenburg Programme," they produced
measures, ill-considered in a social, financial and economic
sense, the consequences of which can clearly be traced in
our social revolution and even further. I must leave the
decision of this question to some future inquiry which will

not be influenced by the present currents of party politics. One thing, however, I must refer to. The absence of an Industrial General Staff, trained for war, made itself very severely felt in the course of the struggle. Experience showed that such a Staff could not be procured by magic during the war. Though our military and financial mobilisation, if I may use the term, was brilliantly carried out, there was no industrial mobilisation at all. What proved essential in this last respect, and therefore had to be introduced, exceeded all previous calculation. As a result of our virtually complete loss of foreign imports and the enormous consumption of material and ammunition as the result of the long duration of the war, we saw ourselves faced with quite new problems which human fancy had hardly ventured even to contemplate in peace time. As a result of the colossal problems which affected both the Army and the nation very intimately, the closest co-operation of all the State authorities revealed itself as an absolute necessity if affairs were to be conducted with a minimum of friction. Indeed, it was really vital to create a common central authority, to which all demands should be made and from which all supplies should flow. Some such authority alone would have been able to take far-seeing economic and military decisions; it would have had to act with an open mind and be assisted by economic experts who were in a position to foresee the consequences of their decisions. There was no such authority. I need not try to explain that only an unusually gifted intelligence and exceptional organising powers could have been equal to such a task. Even if all these preliminary requirements had been fulfilled, there would still have been considerable friction.

In questions of domestic politics the more I endeavoured to avoid getting mixed up in party wrangles, or even being appropriated by one of the existing parties, the greater was my pleasure to lend my support in social questions of a general nature. In particular, I thought it my duty to take a special interest in the question of soldiers' settlements. It was the ethical side of these schemes which more than anything else appealed to me. For I know nothing more agreeable and satisfying than the sight of a little nucleus of culture in the home of a happy man. How many of our brave heroes at the front must have hoped and longed for such a thing in quiet hours? My desire is that large numbers of my loyal comrades may realise those hopes after all their sufferings and strivings!

CHAPTER XIII

PREPARATIONS FOR THE COMING CAMPAIGN

1

Our Tasks

WHEN the results of the fighting in the year 1916 could be more or less realised, we had to get some clear idea of how the war was to develop in the year 1917. We had not the slightest doubt about what our enemies would do in the coming year. We had to anticipate a general hostile offensive, as soon as their preparations and the weather permitted it. It was to be assumed that, warned by the experiences of the past year, our enemies would endeavour to co-ordinate their attacks on all fronts, if we left them time and opportunity to do so.

Nothing could commend itself more strongly, or be more in accordance with our desires and feelings, than to anticipate this general offensive, and in so doing blow the enemy's plans sky high and secure the initiative at the outset. I can certainly claim that with this end in view, I had neglected nothing in the past campaigning year, as soon as the necessary resources, on a scale at all adequate, had been put at my disposal. Now, however, we had to be careful that this ambition did not cloud our views of the tactical situation.

There was no doubt that, at the end of 1916, the position as regards relative numbers between us and our enemies had developed even more to our disadvantage than had been the case at the beginning of the year. Rumania had joined our enemies, and in spite of her heavy defeat remained a serious factor with which we had still to reckon. Behind the Russian lines the Rumanian Army found shelter and time for reorganisation, a process for which she could rely on the co-operation of the Entente in the fullest measure.

It was a fateful thing for us that throughout the whole war our High Command never succeeded in forcing even one of our smaller opponents, with the exception of Montenegro, to desert the ranks of our enemies. In 1914 the Belgian Army had escaped from Antwerp and was now facing us, though practically inactive, and thus imposing on us a certain wastage which was not unimportant. Our experiences with the Serbian Army in 1915 had been only superficially better for us. It had avoided our enveloping movements, though its condition was very pitiful. In the summer of 1916 it reappeared, once more in fighting trim, in the Macedonian theatre, and its units were being continually reinforced and increased from all kinds of countries, of late more particularly by Austro-Hungarian deserters of Slav nationality.

In all three cases—Belgium, Serbia and Rumania—the fate of the hostile army had hung by a thread. The reasons for their escape were no doubt various, but the effect was always the same. Faced with facts such as these, it is only too easy to ascribe a large rôle to luck in war. The use of such an expression degrades war from its high place to the level of a game of chance. I have never regarded it as such. In its course and in its results, even when the latter turned to our disadvantage,

I have always and everywhere seen the plain consequences of pitiless logic. He who helps himself, and can help himself, secures victory, and he who fails, or is forced to fail, loses.

For the campaign of 1917 we were in considerable doubt as to whether our main danger would come from the West or the East. From the standpoint of numerical superiority only, the danger appeared greater on the Eastern Front. We had to anticipate that in the winter of 1916-17, as in previous years, Russia would succeed in making good her losses and renewing the offensive powers of her armies. No intelligence came through to us which revealed any particularly striking indications of the disintegration of the Russian Army. Besides, experience had taught me to accept reports of this kind with extreme caution, whenever and from whatever source they originated.

Faced with this Russian superiority, we could not regard the condition of the Austro-Hungarian Army without anxiety. Reports which we received did not reveal much confidence that the favourable issue of the Rumanian campaign, and the relatively favourable if still tense situation on the Italian front, had had a really uplifting and far-reaching influence on the *moral* of the Austro-Hungarian troops. We had further to anticipate that attacks by the Russians might once again mean the collapse of the Austrian lines. It was in any case impossible to withdraw direct German support from the Austrian front. On the contrary, we had to be ready to send further reinforcements to our Allies' front in case of emergency.

It was equally uncertain how things would shape on

the Macedonian front. In the course of the last battle a German Army Group Headquarters had taken over the command of the right and centre Bulgarian armies—in short, the front from Ochrida to Lake Doiran. Further, two other German commanders from the battles of 1915 and 1916 exercised authority on this front. German officers were occupied in giving the Bulgarian armies the benefit of their wealth of experience on all our fronts. The result of this work would only be revealed when fighting was resumed. For the time being, it seemed advisable not to pitch our hopes too high. In any case, we had to be ready to send help to the Macedonian front also.

On our Western Front we had to expect that in the coming spring our enemies would reappear in the arena in full strength, in spite of the heavy losses they undoubtedly had suffered in the past year. I use the expression " full strength " in the conditional sense only, for though the troops could be brought up to their old level numerically in the course of a few months, it was not the same with their quality. In this respect the enemy was subject to the same hard laws as ourselves.

The tactical situation on the most important part of this front was much as follows. In a fierce and obstinate conflict on the Somme, which lasted five months, the enemy had pressed us back to a depth of about six miles on a stretch of nearly twenty-five miles. Let these figures be kept in mind for future comparison!

This success which had been bought at the price of hundreds of thousands of lives was truly small when compared with the length of our whole front. However, the salient in our lines affected the neighbouring fronts north and south. It was urgently necessary that the position should be improved, otherwise we ran a risk of being enveloped in this salient by enemy attacks there combined with secondary attacks north and south of it. An enveloping attack of our own against the enemy at the point where he had broken through was the most obvious remedy, but in view of our general situation it was almost the most doubtful. Could we venture to devote all our resources to a great attack in the Somme region, alive with enemy troops, while running the risk of a breakthrough on some other part of the Western Front or the Eastern Front? Once again it was seen that when our leaders, with great plans in mind, cast their gaze to one side, they could not close their eyes to what was going on elsewhere. In this respect the year 1916 spoke a language which made itself heard.

If an improvement in the configuration of the front bequeathed by the Somme battle could not be effected by an attack, it only remained to adopt the necessary alternative and withdraw our lines. We therefore decided to adopt that expedient, and transferred our line of defence, which had been pushed in at Péronne at one point and bulged out to west of Bapaume, Roye and Noyon at others, to the chord position Arras—St. Quentin—Soissons. This new line is known as the Siegfried Line.

So it was a case of retreat on the Western Front instead of attack! It was a dreadful disappointment for the army in the West; worse, perhaps, for the public at home; and worst—as we had good reason to fear—for our Allies. Loud rejoicings among our enemies! Could more suitable material for propaganda be imagined? The brilliant, if somewhat belated, visible result of the bloody battle, the collapse of German resistance, the impetuous unceasing pursuit, the paroxysms about our methods of warfare! We could hear all the stops being drawn out beforehand. What a hail of propagandist literature would now descend on and behind our lines!

Our great retirement began on March 16, 1917. The enemy followed us into the open, generally speaking, with considerable caution. Where this caution was inclined to give place to greater haste our rearguards knew how to cool down the enemy zeal.

The measure we took not only gave us more favourable local conditions on the Western Front, but improved our whole situation. The shortening of our lines in the West made it possible for us to build up strong reserves. We were attracted by the idea of throwing at least a part of those reserves upon the enemy at the very moment when he was following our retreat to the Siegfried position across the open country, where we felt ourselves absolutely superior to him. However, we renounced the idea and kept our powder dry for the future.

The situation which we created for ourselves by the spring of 1917 may perhaps be described as a great strategic " stand to," a stage in which we abandoned the initiative to the enemy for the time being, but from which we could emerge at any time to attack any of the enemy's weak points. In view of the enormously increased scale of everything, historical comparisons cannot be drawn from earlier wars.

In connection with these dispositions I must mention two plans to which we had to devote our attention in the winter of 1916-17. These were proposals for attacks in

Italy and Macedonia. In the former case the initiative was taken by General Conrad von Hötzendorff during that winter. He promised himself a far-reaching effect on our entire military and political situation as a result of a great victory over Italy. I could not share that view. As I have already said, I was always of opinion that Italy was far too much under the heel of England, economically and therefore politically, for that country to be forced to make a separate peace, even after a great defeat. What General Conrad mainly had in mind in his proposal was the favourable effect of a successful campaign against Italy on public opinion in Austria-Hungary. He relied on the great relief of the military strain which such a victory would mean for Austria-Hungary. I could readily enough admit the justice of these points of view. Without strong German help—it was a matter of about twelve German divisions—General Conrad considered he could never again undertake an attack on the Italians from the Southern Tyrol. On the other hand, I did not think I could take the responsibility of allowing so many German troops to be locked up for an unlimited time in an enterprise which, in my opinion, lay too far from our Eastern and Western fronts, which were the most important and the most imperilled.

The same considerations applied to the question of an attack on the Entente troops in Macedonia. Bulgaria was toying with this plan, and very naturally from her own point of view, for if we had won a decisive victory it would have compelled the Entente to evacuate this region. By that means Bulgaria would have been practically completely relieved, in a political as well as a military sense. Further, the enterprise was dear to the

Q

heart of the nation and its Government, for the Bulgarians were always casting greedy eyes at the fine harbour of Salonica which had been so great a bone of contention. I admit that this last point of view had no weight with me, and in my opinion at that time the military relief of Bulgaria would have been of no advantage to our general situation. If we had compelled the Entente forces to withdraw from Macedonia we should have had them on our necks again on the Western Front. I always regarded it as at least doubtful whether we should have been allowed to employ the Bulgarian troops thus released outside the Balkans. The employment of Bulgarian divisions during the Rumanian campaign north of the Danube, outside the areas in which Bulgaria was directly interested, had previously led to unpleasant friction with these units. I therefore considered that the Bulgarian forces were rendering the greatest service to our joint operations when they were occupied in holding down the Entente armies in Macedonia. Of course this did not mean that I would not have warmly welcomed an independent Bulgarian offensive in Macedonia at any time. In that case its objective would have had to be very much more modest than the expulsion of the Entente from the Balkans or the capture of Salonica. But the Bulgarians considered that they could not embark on an offensive operation without substantial German help—at least six divisions—and in that they were no doubt right.

At the time in which the question of an offensive in Macedonia was being mooted—that is the winter of 1916-17—news of the development of the political situation in Greece sounded like an enticing siren's song. However, I was absolutely deaf to the siren voices. I very much doubted whether the Hellenic people were very enthusiastic for war, particularly a war in which they would find themselves shoulder to shoulder with the Bulgarians. Generally speaking, there would have been a recurrence of the events of 1913, and the two victorious partners, after their common victory, would have once more taken each other prosaically by the hair instead of poetically by the arm.

From all I have said it must be perfectly clear that the strain on the German armies was so great, as a result of the general situation, that we could not allow it to be increased by further undertakings except such as were imperatively required for military and political reasons. Even the most splendid plans, which might offer certain prospects of great military victories, could not be allowed to turn us aside from our most important and immediate military task. This task was the fighting in the East and West, and indeed on both fronts, against overwhelming enemy superiority.

When I think of the later consequences of my attitude of objection to operations in Italy and Macedonia, and ask myself whether I should, and could, have decided otherwise, I am compelled to answer that question even now in the negative. I think I can claim that the subsequent course of events in Central Europe has proved that we acted for the best. We dare not, and could not, run the risk of a collapse of our Western or Eastern front in the hope of winning cheap laurels in the plains of Northern Italy or on the Vardar.

Turkey could be given no special instructions for 1917. Her task was to defend her territorial possessions and keep the armies facing her away from us. If she succeeded in

accomplishing this she would be doing all that was required
of her within the framework of our combined operations.

With a view to preserving the efficiency of the troops
thus employed, in the autumn of 1916 we had suggested
to the Turkish General Staff that they should withdraw
the bulk of their two Caucasus armies from the sparsely
populated and barren Armenian plateau with a view to
making it easier for the troops to get through the winter.
The necessary orders were issued too late, and as a result
large numbers of troops were killed off by hunger and
cold, as we had foreseen. It is possible that no epic, no
book of heroes, will ever tell their tragic end. So let my
modest record be their epitaph.

2

The U-boat Warfare

Think of seventy million human beings living in semi-
starvation, thousands of them slowly succumbing to its
effects! Think of all the babes in arms who perished
because their mothers starved! Think of all the children
who were left sick and weakly for life! And this was not
in distant India or China, where a stony-hearted, pitiless
Nature had refused her blessed rain, but here, in the very
centre of Europe, the home of culture and humanity! A
semi-starvation which was the work of the decrees and
power of men who were wont to glory in their civilisation!
Where is the civilisation in that? Do these men stand
any higher than those others who shocked the whole
civilised world by their savagery against non-combatants
in the highlands of Armenia and there came to a miserable
end in thousands as a punishment of Fate? No other

voice than that of vengeance, certainly not that of pity,
has ever spoken to the rough Anatolian peasant.

What was the object of these decrees of the champions
of " civilisation "? Their plan was clear. They had seen
that their military power would never enable them to
realise their tyrannical ambitions, that their methods of
warfare were useless against their adversary with his
nerves of steel. They would therefore destroy those
nerves. If it could not be done in battle, man to man, it
might be done from behind, by finding a way through the
Homeland. They would let the wives and children
starve! " With God's help," *that* would have its effect
on the husbands and fathers at the front, perhaps not at
once, but certainly by degrees! Perhaps it would compel
those husbands and fathers to throw down their arms, for
otherwise the menace of death would hover over their
wives and children; the death—of civilisation. There
were men who reasoned thus, and indeed prayed
thus.

" Our enemies are hurling American shells at us.
Why do we not sink the ships in which they come? Have
we not the means to do so? A question of right? Where
and when has our enemy ever thought about right? "

With these and similar words on their lips, the nation
and the Army had turned to their leaders, not for the
first time on August 29, 1916, but long before. The
desire to employ the U-boat weapon in full force with a
view to a speedy delivery of our homeland from its
sufferings and the relief of the Army in the terrible contest, was in existence before I took over the conduct of
operations. In this pitiless battle against our non-combatants at home, it was a question of an eye for an eye

and a tooth for a tooth. Everything else seemed callousness towards our own flesh and blood.

But though we had the weapon and the will to use it, we must not lose sight of the consequences which might flow from the ruthless employment of this destructive instrument. If we need not have any regard for the stony-hearted enemy, we must have regard for the interests of maritime nations which had hitherto remained neutral. As a result of the employment of this weapon, the nation must not be faced with greater dangers and anxieties than those from which we proposed to deliver it. There was thus a considerable amount of hesitation, a hesitation comprehensible enough, to which ordinary human feelings also contributed.

Such was the situation when I appeared at Main Headquarters. To all the serious crises on land was now added a troublesome and fateful problem at sea. At first sight the decision of this question was the province of the Civil Government and the Naval Staff. Yet the General Staff was also seriously concerned. It was perfectly obvious that on purely military grounds we should desire the commencement of the U-boat campaign. The advantages which it would bring to our operations on land was plain to every eye. It would have been an immense relief to us if the enemy's manufacture of war material, or its transport over sea, could be materially hampered. It would be equally valuable if we succeeded at any rate in partially paralysing their over-seas operations. What an immense relief that would mean not only to Bulgaria and Turkey, but to ourselves! And it would not have cost us a drop of German blood! Further, there would be a chance of restricting the imports of raw material and food into the Entente countries to an intolerable degree, and placing England, if not her Allies, before the fateful alternative either of holding out the hand of reconciliation to us or losing her place in world trade. The U-boat campaign seemed likely to have a decisive effect on the course of the war; indeed, at the beginning of 1917 it appeared to be the only means we could employ to secure a victorious conclusion to the war if we were compelled to fight on.

The connection between the U-boat campaign and the whole military and political situation appears from a memorandum which we addressed to the Government at the end of September, 1916. This memorandum was to serve as the basis for instructions to our ambassador in Washington. It ran as follows:

" Count Bernstorff should be told, for his personal information, that the intention of the Entente to break through on the Eastern and Western fronts has hitherto miscarried, and will miscarry in the future, as will their operations from Salonica and the Dobrudja. On the other hand, the campaign of the Central Powers against Rumania is making victorious progress. However, it is still doubtful whether we shall achieve successes this year which will end the war. We must therefore reckon that the war will continue for a considerable time longer.

" On the other hand, in view of England's economic situation, the Imperial Admiralty promises us that by the ruthless employment of an increased number of U-boats we shall obtain a speedy victory, which will compel our principal enemy, England, to turn to thoughts of peace in a few months. For that reason, the German General Staff is bound to adopt unrestricted U-boat warfare as one of its war measures, because among other things it will relieve the situation on the Somme front by diminishing the imports of munitions and bring the futility of the Entente's efforts at this point plainly before their eyes. Finally, we could not remain idle spectators while England, realising all the difficulties with which she has to contend, makes the fullest possible use of neutral Powers in order to improve her military and economic situation to our disadvantage. For all these reasons we must recover the freedom of action which we reserved in the Note of May 4.

" Of course the situation would be completely altered if President Wilson, in pursuance of the intention he has indicated, presents a proposal of mediation to the Powers. Such a proposal must, in any case, be without definite suggestions of a territorial nature, since questions of that kind must be one of the objects of the peace negotiations. Any action of this kind must be taken soon. If Wilson wished to wait until after his election, or even shortly before it, he would find that the moment for such a step had practically gone. Nor must the negotiations aim primarily at the conclusion of an armistice. They must be conducted mainly by the contending parties and lead directly to a preliminary peace within a short time. Any considerable delay would make Germany's military position worse, and mean that the Powers would make further preparations to continue the war next year, so that there would be an end to the idea of peace for a long time to come.

" Count Bernstorff should discuss the affair with Colonel House—the intermediary between himself and the President— and ascertain the intentions of Mr. Wilson. Any action of the President in the direction of peace, which had better seem spontaneous on his part, would receive our very serious consideration, and this in itself would mean a victory for Wilson in his election campaign."

The most difficult question was and remained: " Within what time would U-boat warfare produce decisive results? " On this question the Naval Staff could, of course, make no definite promises. But even what they alleged was an estimate based on the most conservative calculations was so favourable to us, that I considered that we were entitled to face the risk of finding that we had brought another adversary into the field as the result of employing the new weapon.

But even though the Navy was very insistent, political and military considerations demanded that the commencement of the unrestricted U-boat campaign should be postponed over the autumn of 1916. In the critical military situation in which we found ourselves at that time we dared not bring a new opponent into the field. In any case, we had to wait until the Rumanian campaign had ended victoriously. If it did so, we should find ourselves strong enough to prevent any neutral States on our frontiers from joining the ranks of our enemies, to whatever extent England might intensify her economic pressure upon them.

To considerations of a political nature were added others of a military nature. We did not wish to resort to the intensified use of the U-boat weapon until our peace step had proved a complete failure.

When this peace measure collapsed, however, military considerations alone had any weight with me. The development of the military situation, especially in Rumania, in my opinion now permitted the most drastic use of this very effective weapon.

On January 9, 1917, our All-Highest War-Lord decided in favour of the proposals of the Naval and General Staffs and against the Imperial Chancellor, von Bethmann. Not one of us was in doubt about the seriousness of the step.

In any case, the adoption of unrestricted U-boat warfare, with its alluring prospects, increased the moral resolution of both the army and nation to continue the war on land for a long time to come.

In view of the fateful conclusion of the war, it has been suggested that the declaration of the unrestricted U-boat campaign was a last desperate throw. That judgment is intended to be a condemnation of our decision on political, military and even ethical grounds. It ignores the fact that practically all critical decisions, certainly not military decisions only, always involve a heavy risk. Indeed, the greatness of an action is mainly to be appreciated and measured by the question whether much was at stake. When a commander on the battlefield throws in his last reserves he is only doing what his country rightly demands of him. He accepts full responsibility and finds the courage to take the last decisive step without which victory cannot be won. A commander who cannot or will not dare to stake his last resources for the sake of victory is committing a crime towards his own people. If his blow fails, he is certain to have the curses and scorn of the weaklings and cowards upon his head! That is always the fate of soldiers. To act only on absolutely safe calculations, or win laurels which are not dependent on the courage to take responsibility, is to banish the very elements of greatness. The whole object of our German military training was to breed that courage. We need only point to the outstanding examples in our own history, as well as the greatest achievements of our most dangerous enemies. Could there be a better example of the bold employment of the last resources than when the

Great King staked everything at Leuthen and thereby saved his country and its future? Have we not approved Napoleon's decision to send in his last battalions at Waterloo, even though, as Clausewitz says, he then slunk from the battlefield as poor as a beggar? If the Corsican had not had a Blücher against him he would have won, and world history would certainly have taken another course. On the other side, take our much-belauded "Marshal Vorwärts." Did he not stake everything in that decisive conflict? Let us hear what one of our most violent opponents had to say on this subject before the war: "The finest manœuvre which I have ever known is the action of old Blücher, who, thrown to the ground and lying under the feet of the horses, sprang up, turned furiously on his beaten men, stopped their flight and led them from the defeat of Ligny to the triumph of Waterloo."

I cannot close this section without questioning the view that has been put forward that with the entry of America into the ranks of our enemies our cause was finally lost. But let us first take a glance at the predicament in which we put our enemies, both by our U-boat operations and, at times, by our great successes on land in the spring of 1917. We shall then be in a position to realise that we were several times within an ace of wearing the victor's laurels ourselves, and will perhaps appreciate that other than military reasons are responsible for the fact that the war did not end victoriously, or at least tolerably, for us.

8

Kreuznach

After the victorious conclusion of the Rumanian campaign and the relief it brought to our situation in the East, the centre of gravity of our next operations must be sought in the West. In any case it was here that we must anticipate an early commencement of the fighting in the next campaigning year. We wanted to be close to the battlefield. If we established our Headquarters in the West it would be easier and take less time to get into direct personal touch with the Headquarters of the Army Groups and Armies. A further reason was that the Emperor Charles wished to be near the political authorities of his country, and was, moreover, unwilling to dispense with direct personal intercourse with his Commander-in-Chief. Accordingly, in the early months of 1917 the Headquarters of the Austro-Hungarian Army was transferred to Baden near Vienna. The result was that there was no longer any reason why His Majesty our Emperor and Main Headquarters should remain at Pless. In February we moved our Headquarters to Kreuznach.

On leaving Pless I considered it a special duty to thank the prince and his officials for the great hospitality they had shown us in housing all our officers, as well as in private life. Moreover, I myself had particularly grateful memories of plenty of splendid hunting over the estates of Pless and its neighbour Neudeck, on the few free evenings we had.

The district in which we now settled was associated in my mind with memories of my previous activities as Chief of Staff in the Rhine Province. I had made the

acquaintance of the town of Kreuznach itself at that time.
Its inhabitants now vied with one another in giving us
proofs of quiet hospitality. Among other ways this
hospitality was shown in the fact that our quarters and
common dining-room were decorated with fresh-cut
flowers every day by young ladies.

I accepted all this as an act of homage to the whole
army, of which I was one of the oldest representatives in
the war. Shortly after our departure from Pless, General
Conrad left the Austro-Hungarian Headquarters to take
over the command on the South Tyrolese front. I have
never known the cause of his transfer. I gather it was
due to personal reasons, as there were no professional
reasons so far as I knew. I have loyal and brotherly
memories of him. His successor was General von Arz.
He had a practical head and sound views, was a splendid
soldier and therefore as valuable a colleague as his predecessor. He always got to the root of things and despised
appearances. I believe that he shared my aversion to
intervention in political questions. In my opinion General
von Arz displayed admirable perseverance and did everything that could be done, in view of the difficult internal
situation of the Danube Monarchy to which I have previously referred. He never had any doubt about the
magnitude of his task. He deserves all the more gratitude
for having faced it with such manly confidence.

At the beginning of October my stay in Kreuznach
brought me the celebration of my seventieth birthday.

His Majesty my Emperor, King and master, was
gracious enough to be the first to give me his personal
congratulations at my house. To me this was the very
consecration of the day! Then the youth of Kreuznach

greeted me in the bright autumn sunshine as I went to
the office. My colleagues awaited me before the doors of
our common workroom, and in the adjacent garden were
representatives of the town and its neighbourhood,
recruits, sick and wounded, convalescing at the various
establishments of this health resort, and finally veterans
who had fought with me in days long past. The end of
the day brought a little military interlude. For some
reason I have never been able to fathom, it was rumoured
that a great enemy bombing attack on our Headquarters
would probably take place this day. It is possible, too,
that, as so often happened, some enemy aeroplane was
this evening finding its way from the Saar to the Rhine
or *vice versâ*. It was hardly surprising that imagination
was rather more vivid than usual, and that at night more
was seen and heard between the earth and the shining
moon than was actually there. But however that may be,
about midnight our anti-aircraft defences opened a mighty
barrage. Thanks to the high rate of fire, the available
ammunition supplies were speedily exhausted, so that I
could sleep in peace with the thought that I should be
disturbed no more. When I reported next day my All-
Highest War Lord showed me a large vase filled with
fragments of German shells which had been collected in
the garden of his quarters. We had thus been running
risks that night after all!

For the rest, some of the Kreuznach folk had taken
the nocturnal shooting for a final military salute in honour
of my birthday.

CHAPTER XIV

THE HOSTILE OFFENSIVE IN THE FIRST HALF OF 1917

1

In the West

AS soon as the best season of the year began, we awaited the opening of the expected general enemy offensive with the greatest anxiety. We had made strategic preparations to meet it by re-grouping our armies, but in the course of the winter we had also taken tactical measures to deal with what would in any case be the greatest of all the efforts of our enemies.

Not the least important of these measures were the changes we introduced into our previous system of defence. They were based on our experiences in the earlier battles. In future our defensive positions were no longer to consist of single lines and strong points but of a network of lines and groups of strong points. In the deep zones thus formed we did not intend to dispose our troops on a rigid and continuous front but in a complex system of nuclei and distributed in breadth and depth. The defender had to keep his forces mobile to avoid the destructive effects of the enemy fire during the period of artillery preparation, as well as voluntarily to abandon any parts of the line which could no longer be held, and then to recover by a counter-attack all the points which were essential to the maintenance of the whole position. These principles applied in detail as in general.

We thus met the devastating effects of the enemy artillery and trench-mortar fire and their surprise infantry attacks with more and more deeply distributed defensive lines and the mobility of our forces. At the same time we developed the principle of saving men in the forward lines by increasing the number of our machine-guns and so economising troops.

So far-reaching a change in our defensive system undoubtedly involved an element of risk. This element lay primarily in the fact that in the very middle of the war we demanded a break with tactical practices and experiences with which our subordinate commanders and the men had become familiar, and to which many of them naturally ascribed some particular virtue. A change from one tactical method to another provoked a mild crisis even in peace time. On the one hand it involved a certain amount of exaggeration of the new features, and on the other a very stubborn adhesion to the old. Even the most carefully worded instructions left room for misunderstandings. Voluntary interpreters had the time of their lives, and the force of inertia in human thought and action was frequently not to be overcome without a tremendous effort.

But it was not for these reasons only that our tactical innovations were a risky step. It was much more difficult to give ourselves an affirmative answer to the question whether, in the middle of war, our army, constituted as it was now, was in a position to adopt the new measures and translate them into the reality of the battlefield.

We could be in no doubt that the military machine with which we were now working was not to be compared with those of 1914 and 1915, or indeed with that of the opening months of 1916. A vast number of our most splendid fighting men had been buried in our cemeteries or sent home with shattered limbs or diseased bodies. It is true that we still had a proud nucleus of our 1914 men, and around them had gathered a mass of young and enthusiastic newcomers prepared for any sacrifice. But an army requires more than that; bodily strength and resolution have to be trained and taught by experience. An army with the moral and intellectual powers and the great traditions of the German Army of 1914 retains its intrinsic worth for many years in war, so long as it receives physical and moral reinforcement from the Homeland. But its general average sinks, and indeed, in the natural course of things is bound to sink, even though its value compared with that of the enemy, who has been just as long in the field, remains relatively at the old level.

Our new defensive system made heavy demands on the moral resolution and capacity of the troops because it abandoned the firm external rigidity of the serried lines of defence, and thereby made the independent action, even of the smallest bodies of troops, the supreme consideration. Tactical co-operation was no longer obtained by defences that were continuous to the eye, but consisted of the invisible moral bond between the men engaged in such tactical co-operation. It is no exaggeration to say that in these circumstances the adoption of the new principles was the greatest evidence of the confidence which we placed in the moral and mental powers of our Army, down to its smallest unit. The immediate future was to prove whether that confidence was misplaced.

The first storm in the West broke just after the

R

beginning of spring. On April 9 the English attack at Arras gave the signal for the opening of the enemy's great spring offensive. The attack was prepared for days with the whole fury of masses of enemy artillery and trench-mortars. There was nothing of the surprise tactics which Nivelle had employed in the October of the previous year. Did not the English believe in these tactics, or did they feel themselves too inexperienced to adopt them? For the moment the reason was immaterial. The fact alone was sufficient and spoke a fearful language. The English attack swept over our first, second and third lines. Groups of strong points were overwhelmed or silenced after a heroic resistance. Masses of artillery were lost. Our defensive system had apparently failed!

A serious crisis now supervened, one of those situations in which everything appears to be beyond control. "Crises must be avoided," says the layman. The only reply the soldier can make is this: "Then we had better keep out of war from the start, for crises are inevitable." They are of the very nature of war and distinguish it as the domain of peril and the unknown. The art of war is to overcome crises, not to avoid them. He who recoils from the menace of a crisis is binding his own arms, becomes a plaything in the hands of a bolder adversary, and soon goes in a crisis to destruction.

I do not mean to suggest that the crisis on April 9 could not have been avoided after all the preparations which we had been in a position to make. It is certain that we should not have had a crisis on such a scale if we had replied to the enemy break-through with a prompt counter-attack with reserves brought up for the purpose. Of course, after such infernal artillery preparation as preceded this attack, serious local disasters were only to be expected.

The evening report of this April 9 revealed rather a dark picture. Many shadows—little light. In such cases more light must be sought. A ray appeared, though a tiny flickering ray. The English did not seem to have known how to exploit the success they had gained to the full. This was a piece of luck for us, as so often before. After the report I pressed the hand of my First Quarter-master-General with the words : " We have lived through more critical times than to-day together." To-day ! It was his birthday ! My confidence was unshaken. I knew that reinforcements were marching to the battlefield and that trains were hastening that way. The crisis was over. Within me it was certainly over. But the battle raged on.

Another battle picture. After the first weeks of April the French guns were thundering at Soissons, and from there far away eastwards to the neighbourhood of Rheims. Hundreds of hostile trench-mortars were scattering death. Here Nivelle commanded, the reward of the fame he had won at Verdun. Apparently he, too, had not drawn the inferences we expected from his recent experiences at Verdun. The French artillery raged for days, nay weeks. Our defensive zone was to be converted into a waste of rubble and corpses. All that was lucky enough to escape physical destruction was at any rate to be morally broken. There seemed little doubt that such a consummation would be attained in this fearful conflagration. At length Nivelle supposed our troops to be annihilated, or at any rate sufficiently cowed. On April 16 he sent forward his battalions, pretty confident of victory. Or perhaps it would be better to say that he commissioned his men to gather in the fruits which had ripened in the tropical heat! Then the incredible happened. From the shattered trenches and shell-holes rose German manhood, possessed of German strength and resolution, and scattered death and desolation among the advancing ranks and the masses behind them which were already flinching under the storm of our artillery fire and tending to herd together. The German resistance might be overcome at the points where destruction had been fiercest, but in this battle of giants what did the loss of small sectors mean compared with the triumphant resistance of the whole front?

In the very first day it was clear that the French had suffered a downright defeat. The bloody reverse proved the bitterest, indeed the most overwhelming disappointment to the French leaders and their men.

The battles of Arras, Soissons and Rheims raged on for weeks. It revealed only one tactical variation from the conflict on the Somme in the previous year, a variation I must not forget to mention. After the first few days our adversaries won not a single success worth mentioning, and after a few weeks they sank back exhausted on the battlefield and resumed trench warfare. So our defence measures had proved themselves brilliantly, after all.

Now for a third picture. The scene was changed to the heights of Wytschaete and Messines, north-west of Lille and opposite Kemmel Hill. It was June 7, a moment at which the failure of the battles I have just mentioned was already obvious. The position on the Wytschaete hills, the key to the salient at that point, was very unfavourable for a modern defence. The com-

paratively restricted back area did not permit the employment of a sufficiently deep defensive zone. Our forward
trenches lay on the western slope and were a magnificent
target for hostile artillery. The wet soil sank in summer
and winter; below ground were mines innumerable, for
this method of warfare had been employed earlier on in
extremely bitter fighting for the possession of the most
important points. Yet it was long since any sounds of
underground burrowing had been heard. Our trenches
on the heights of St. Eloi as well as at the corner-stone
of Wytschaete and Messines were exposed to hostile
artillery fire not only from the west but from north and
south as well.

The English prepared their attack in the usual way.
The defenders suffered heavily, more heavily than ever
before. Our anxious question whether it would not be
better voluntarily to evacuate the heights had received the
manly answer : " We shall hold, so we will stand fast."
But when the fateful June 7 dawned the ground rose from
beneath the feet of the defenders, their most vital strong-
points collapsed, and through the smoke and falling
débris of the mines the English storm troops pressed
forward over the last remnants of the German defence.
Violent attempts on our part to restore the situation by
counter-attacks failed under the murderous, hostile artillery fire which from all sides converted the back-area of
the lost position into a veritable inferno. Nevertheless,
we again succeeded in bringing the enemy to a halt before
he had effected a complete breach in our lines. Our
losses in men and war material were heavy. It would
have been better to have evacuated the ground voluntarily.

In my judgment the general result of the great enemy

offensive in the West had not been unsatisfactory hitherto. We had never been defeated. Even our worst perils had been surmounted. Though gaining a good deal of ground, our enemies had never succeeded in reaching more distant goals, much less in passing from the break-through battle to open warfare. Once more we were to exploit our successes in the West on other fronts.

2

In the Near and Far East

Even before the wild dance had begun on our Western Front, Sarrail had renewed his attacks in Macedonia with his centre of gravity at Monastir. These events, too, commanded our full attention. Once more our enemy had far-reaching objectives. Simultaneously with this onslaught on the Bulgarian front, our enemy had instigated a rising in Serbia with a view to menacing our communications with the Balkan peninsula. The rising was suppressed at its critical point, Nish, before it had extended over the whole of Old Serbia, an eventuality which was much feared by Government circles in Bulgaria. The fighting on the Macedonian front was marked by great bitterness, but the Bulgarian Army succeeded in maintaining its position practically intact without our having to send further German reinforcements. A very satisfactory result for us! Our Allies had fought very well. They had plainly realised that the work we had done in their ranks had been brilliantly justified. I felt convinced that the Bulgarian Army would remain equal to its task in future, and this opinion was confirmed when the Entente renewed their attacks in May. Once more their onslaught along the whole front from Monastir to Lake Doiran was an utter failure.

The front on the Armenian plateau had remained inactive. Occasional small raids during the winter seemed to be inspired far more by anxiety to secure booty than by any revival of the offensive spirit on either side. Under the influence of their great supply difficulties, the Russians had withdrawn the bulk of their troops from the wildest and most desolate parts of the mountains to more fertile districts in the interior. The complete pause in the Russian activity was certainly surprising. The Turks sent us no news which could in any way explain it.

On the Irak front the English attacked in February, and were in possession of Bagdad by March 11. They owed this success to their skilful envelopment of the strong Turkish positions.

In Southern Palestine the English attacked at Gaza in great superiority, but purely frontally and with little tactical skill. Their onslaught collapsed completely in front of the Turkish lines. It was only the failure of a Turkish column which had been sent out to envelop their wing that saved the English from utter defeat.

I shall have to deal later with the effect of these events in Asia on our general military situation.

8

On the Eastern Front

Even before the French and English opened their general offensive in the West the foundations of the Russian front were already trembling. Under our mighty blows the framework of the Russian State had begun to go to pieces.

Hitherto the unwieldy Russian Colossus had hung over the whole European and Asiatic world like a nightmare. The interior of the mass now began to swell and stretch. Great cracks appeared on its surface, and through the gaps we soon had glimpses of the fires of political passion and the workings of infernal primitive forces. Tsardom was tottering! Would some new power arise which could extinguish those passions in the icy prisons of Siberia, and suffocate those powers of barbarism in living graves?

Russia in revolution! How often had men with a real or pretended knowledge of the country announced that this event was at hand? I had ceased to believe in it. Now that it had materialised, it aroused in me no feeling of political satisfaction, but rather a sense of military relief. But even the latter was slow in coming. I asked myself whether the fall of the Tsar was a victory of the Peace or the War Party. Had the grave-diggers of Tsardom only worked in order to bring to nought, with the last crowned head, the well-known anxiety for peace of Russian upper circles and the peace longings of great masses of the people?

So long as the behaviour of the Russian Army provided no clear answer to this question our situation with regard to Russia was, and remained, indefinite. The process of disintegration had undoubtedly begun in the Russian State. If a dictatorship, with powers to be employed as ruthlessly as those which had just been overthrown, did not arise, this process would continue, though perhaps slower than normally in the mighty and ponderous

Russian Colossus with its unwieldy movements. From the outset our plan was to leave this process alone. We must, however, take care that it left us alone, and did not perhaps destroy us too. In a situation like this we should remember the lesson of the cannonade of Valmy, which more than a hundred years before had welded together again the cracked and broken structure of French national power and started that great blood-red flood which swept over all Europe. Of course Russia of 1917 no longer had at her disposal the immense untapped sources of man-power which France then had. The Tsar's best and finest men were at the front, or lay in graves innumerable before and behind our lines.

For me personally to wait quietly while the process of Russian disintegration developed was a great sacrifice. If for political reasons I was not allowed to consider an offensive in the East, all my soldierly feelings urged me towards an attack in the West. Could any notion be more obvious than that of bringing all our effective fighting troops from the East to the West and then taking the offensive? I was thinking of the failure of the English attack at Arras and the severe defeat of France between Soissons and Rheims. America was still far away. If she came after the strength of France was broken, she would come too late!

However, the Entente too recognised the peril with which they were menaced, and worked with all their might to prevent the collapse of Russian power, and with it the great relief that collapse would mean to our Eastern Front. Russia must remain in the war, at least until the new armies of America were on French soil; otherwise the military and moral defeat of France was certain. For this reason the Entente sent politicians, agitators and officers to Russia in the hope of bolstering up the shattered Russian front. Nor did these Missions forget to take money with them, for in many parts of Russia money is more effective than political argument.

Once more we were robbed of the brightest prospect of victory by these counter-measures. The Russian front was kept in being, not through its own strength, but mainly through the work of the agitators whom our enemies sent there, and who achieved their purpose, even against the will of the Russian masses.

Ought we not to have attacked when the first cracks of the Russian edifice began to be revealed? May it not be that political considerations robbed us of the finest fruits of all our great victories?

Our relations to the Russian Army on the Eastern Front at first took the form of an ever more obvious approach to an armistice, although there was nothing in writing. By degrees the Russian infantry everywhere declared that they would fight no more. Yet with the apathy of the masses they remained in their trenches. If the relations between the two sides led to too obviously amicable an intercourse, the Russian artillery intervened every now and then. This arm of the service was still in the hands of its leaders, not out of any natural conservative instinct, but because it counted fewer independent heads than its sister arm. The agitators of the Entente and the officers still had great influence with the Russian batteries. It was true that the Russian infantry grumbled about the way in which this long-desired armistice was thus disturbed, and indeed occasionally turned on their artillery sister and openly rejoiced when our shells fell among the gun-pits. But the general situation I have described remained unchanged for months.

The Russian disinclination to fight was most patent on the northern wing. From there it extended to the south. The Rumanians were apparently unaffected by it. After May it appeared that the commanders had got the reins in their hands again, even in the north. Friendly relations between the two trench lines gradually stopped. There was a return to the old method of intercourse, weapon in hand. Before long there was no doubt that in the areas behind the Russian front the work of discipline was being carried on at top pressure. In this way parts, at any rate, of the Russian Army were once more made capable of resistance, and indeed capable of attack. The war current had set strongly, and Russia advanced to a great offensive under Kerensky.

Kerensky, not Brussiloff? The latter had been swept from his high post by the streams of blood of his own countrymen which had flowed in Galicia and Wolhynia in 1916, just as Nivelle had been swept away in France in the spring of this year. Even in Russia, with her immense resources in man-power, the authorities seemed to have become sensitive about sacrifices in mass. In the great war ledger the page on which the Russian losses were written has been torn out. No one knows the figures. Five or eight millions? We, too, have no idea. All we know is that sometimes in our battles with the Russians we had to remove the mounds of enemy corpses from before our trenches in order to get a clear field of fire against fresh assaulting waves. Imagination may try to reconstruct the figure of their losses, but an accurate calculation will remain for ever a vain thing.

It was difficult to say whether Kerensky adopted the idea of an offensive of his own free will, or was induced or compelled to do so by the Entente. In either case it was entirely to the interest of the Entente that Russia should be driven into an offensive once more. In the West they had already offered up in vain a good half of their best fighting troops; perhaps more than half. What other alternative had they but to send in what they had left, as American help was still far away? It was in these very months that the U-boat warfare was encroaching on the margin of existence of our bitterest and most irreconcilable foe to such a degree that it appeared questionable whether shipping would be available for the American reinforcements in the coming year. German troops must therefore be held down fast in the East, and for that reason Kerensky must send Russia's last armies to the attack. It was a venturesome game, and for Russia most venturesome of all! Yet the calculation on which it was based was an accurate one, for if the game succeeded, not only would the Entente be saved, but a dictatorship in Russia could be created and maintained. Without such a dictatorship Russia would lapse into chaos.

It must be admitted that the prospects of Kerensky's offensive against the German front were hardly more inviting than on previous occasions. Good German divisions might have been sent to the West, but those that were left were sound enough to hold up a Russian onslaught. Our enemy had not the inward resolution to turn his attack into the long drawn out storms of 1917. A large number of Russian apostles of freedom were roving the back areas of the army for loot, or streaming homewards. Even good elements were leaving the front, inspired by anxiety for their relatives and possessions in view of the internal catastrophe which was threatening. But, on the other hand, the situation on the Austro-Hungarian front gave cause for anxiety. It was to be feared that once more, as in 1916, the Russian onslaught would find weak spots. In the spring of this year a representative of our Ally had given us a very grave description of the state of things on this part of the front, and told us his general impression that "the great majority of the Austro-Slav troops would offer even less resistance to a Russian attack than they had in 1916." The fact was that the process of political disintegration was affecting them simultaneously with the Russian troops. The same authority gave us Kerensky's plan which had been told him by deserters. It was this : local attacks against the Germans in order to tie them down, while the main blow was dealt at the Austro-Hungarian wall. And that is exactly what happened.

The Russians attacked the German lines at Riga, Dvinsk and Smorgon and were driven off. The wall in Galicia proved to be stone only where Austro-Hungarian troops were stiffened by German. On the other hand the Austro-Slav wall near Stanislau collapsed under Kerensky's simple tap. But Kerensky's troops were not like Brussiloff's. A year had passed since that last offensive—a year of heavy losses and deep demoralisation for the Russian Army. So notwithstanding fairly favourable prospects, the Russian offensive did not get right through at Stanislau. The Russian grain was now ripe for reaping. The reaper too was ready. It was just the time at which the real harvest was beginning in the fields of our German Homeland. The middle of July!

CHAPTER XV

COUNTER-ATTACK! No troops, no leader in the field can ever have received such news with more joyous satisfaction than I felt when I realised that the time for such a measure had at length arrived.

I have previously described our situation before the spring of 1917 as a stage of strategic " stand to." Of course, this does not mean that our reserves were closely concentrated like the masses of Napoleon when he awaited the attack of his foes who were closing in on him from all sides in the autumn of 1813. The immense distances which we had to cover forbade a system of that kind. On the other hand, the capacity of our railways made it possible to collect widely distributed reserves and carry them quickly to a point selected for an offensive.

The defensive battles in the West had been a heavy drain on our available reserves. A comparison of numbers and the difficulties of this front made a counter-offensive there with what was left out of the question. On the other hand these reserves seemed sufficient to enable us to turn the situation in the East once and for all in our favour, and thereby precipitate the political collapse of our adversary on that side. Russia's foundations had become rotten. The last manifestations of force of the now Republican Army were only the result of an artificially produced wave, a wave which no longer welled up

from the depths of the nation. But in a great struggle
of nations, when the national army is once in process of
decay, complete collapse is inevitable. Such being my
conviction, it was my opinion we could now achieve
decisive results in Russia even with moderate resources.

It is easy to understand that there were voices which
even now warned us against employing our available
reserves in an offensive. It must be admitted that this
was not so easy a question to decide as may appear now,
when we look back upon the course of events. At the time
we made the decision we had to face a good many anxieties
and risks. It was even then clear that the English attack
of June 7 at Wytschaete and Messines was but the prelude to a much greater military drama which, carrying on
the work then begun, would have its background in the
great stretch of Flanders on the north. We had also to
anticipate that France, too, would resume her attack as
soon as her army had recovered from the serious disaster
of the spring offensive.

It was undoubtedly a risk to take troops from the
West—it was a question of six divisions—but a risk
similar to that we had taken in 1916 in our attack on
Rumania. On that occasion, of course, it had been a case
of imperious necessity. Now we did it of our own free
will. But in both cases the venture had been based on
our unshakable confidence in our troops. Dissentient
voices were raised against our plan on other grounds
besides that of the general military situation. As a result
of the enemy's experiences with our defence, some among
us doubted the possibility of a really great offensive victory. I remember how, just before the opening of our
counter-offensive on the Galician front, we were warned

that with the troops we had concentrated we could not hope for more than a local success—that means the production of a salient in the enemy lines such as our opponents had so often created in their offensives at the first rush. Was that our goal? Then had we not better renounce the whole operation?

Among opinions on this side there was another that was quite plausible : we ought to keep our land forces principally on the defensive and otherwise wait until our U-boats had fulfilled our hopes. There was something very alluring in this idea. According to such reports as we had then received, the result of the U-boat warfare had already exceeded all expectations. Its effects must therefore soon make themselves felt. Yet I was not able to give my consent to that proposal. The military and political situation in the East now demanded something more than that we should stand still for months and simply look on. We feared that if our counter-blow did not follow hard on the heels of Kerensky's attack, the war party in Russia would once more get the upper hand. There is no need for me to describe the reaction such an event would have on our country and our Allies.

While Kerensky strove in vain to get the mass of his still effective troops to break through the Austro-Hungarian lines—which had meanwhile been propped up by German troops—we concentrated a strong force southwest of Brody, that is on the flank of the Russian breakthrough, and on July 19 attacked in a south-easterly direction towards Tarnopol. Our operation struck a part of the Russian line which had little capacity for resistance, and, indeed, had been exhausted in the previous attack. The Russian troops were quickly scattered to the

winds, and Kerensky's whole offensive collapsed at a blow.
Nothing but a hasty retreat of the Russian troops on the
north, and more particularly on the south, of our point
of irruption saved the Russian Army from a catastrophe.
Our whole Eastern Front in Galicia and right south into
the Carpathians was soon in movement, pursuing the
retreating enemy. By the end of August almost the
whole of Galicia and the Bukovina were clear of the foe.
It was told that in these following-up actions the Austro-
Hungarian field artillery had particularly distinguished
itself. With exemplary boldness it had gone on ahead of
its own infantry and hard on the heels of the Russians.
I had learned to admire this splendid arm at Königgrätz
in 1866, and therefore rejoiced doubly at this fresh proof
of its fame on our side.

Our offensive came to a standstill on the frontier of
Moldavia. No one regretted it more than I did. We
were in the most favourable strategic position imaginable
to effect the occupation of this last part of Rumania by
continuing our advance. Judging by the political situation in Russia at the moment, the Rumanian Army would
unquestionably have dissolved if we had compelled it to
abandon the country altogether. How could a Rumanian
king and a royal Rumanian Army have remained in
existence on revolutionary Russian soil? However, thanks
to the destruction of the stations by the retreating
Russians, our communications had become so difficult
that with a heavy heart we had to renounce the further
prosecution of the operations at this point. A later
attempt on our part to shatter the Rumanian Army in
Moldavia was unsuccessful. We adhered to our decision
not to let go of Russia until she had been finally eliminated

s

in a military sense, even though the commencement of
the drama in Flanders was claiming our attention and,
indeed, filling us with increasing anxiety. If we could
not destroy the Russian Army in Wolhynia and
Moldavia we must do so at some other part of the front.
Riga seemed a peculiarly favourable point, a militarily
and politically sensitive point, at which Russia could be
hit. At Riga the Russian northern wing formed a mighty
flank position, more than forty miles deep and only twenty
wide along the coast to the western bank of the Dvina.
It was a position which threatened our whole front, both
strategically and tactically. This situation had irritated
us in previous years when I was Commander-in-Chief
in the East. Both in 1915 and 1916 we had planned to
break through this salient somewhere near its base, and
thereby deal a great blow at its defenders.

On paper this seems a simple enough operation,
but it was not so simple in practice. The spear-head
must be driven northwards across the broad Dvina above
Riga. It is true that in the course of the war great rivers
had certainly not lived up to their imposing reputation
as obstacles. Had not General von Mackensen crossed
the mighty Danube in full view of the enemy? We could
therefore face the prospect of crossing the smaller Dvina
with a light heart; but the great drawback to the operation lay in the fact that the strongly-held Russian trenches
lay on the far bank, so that the Dvina formed a kind of
moat.

However, on September 1 our bold attack succeeded,
as the Russians abandoned their trenches on the bank
during our artillery preparation. Moreover, the occupants
of the great flanking salient west of the river withdrew,

marching day and night, through Riga to the east, thus for the most part evading capture.

Our attack at Riga aroused the liveliest fears in Russia for the safety of Petersburg. The capital of the country was in a panic. It felt itself directly threatened by our attack on Riga. Petersburg, still the intellectual centre of Russia, fell into a condition of extreme nervous anxiety which made calm and practical thinking impossible. Otherwise the citizens would merely have taken compasses and measured the distances which still separated our victorious troops at Riga from the Russian capital. It was not only in Russia, but also in our own country, that imagination became very vivid about this affair and forgot space and time. Even among us there were great illusions about an advance on Petersburg. It goes without saying that no one would have been more pleased to carry out such an advance than I. I well understood the anxiety of our troops and their leaders to continue our invasion, at least as far as Lake Peipus. But we had to renounce all these ideas, alluring though they undoubtedly were. They would have tied down too many of our troops—and for too long—in a region with which our future plans were not concerned. Our thoughts had now returned from the Gulf of Riga to the coast of the Adriatic. But of that more anon.

But if we could not continue our advance to Petersburg and thereby keep the nerve-centre of Russia at the highest tension until collapse was inevitable, there was still another way by which we could attain that end— the way of the sea. At our instigation our Fleet accepted our suggestion with loyal devotion. Thus originated the decision to capture the island of Oesel lying at the entrance to the Gulf of Riga. From that point we should directly threaten the Russian naval harbour of Reval and intensify our pressure on nervous Petersburg without employing any large forces.

The operation against Oesel stands out in this war as the one completely successful enterprise on either side in which an army and a fleet co-operated. The execution of our plans was rendered so doubtful by bad weather at the outset that we were already thinking of disembarking the troops on board. The arrival of better weather then enabled us to proceed with the venture. From that point everything went like clockwork. The Navy answered to the high demands which we had to make on it in every direction. We succeeded in possessing ourselves of Oesel and the neighbouring islands. In Petersburg nerves were more shaken than ever. The structure of the Russian front became ever looser. It became clearer with every day that passed that Russia was too shaken by internal agitation to be capable of any military demonstration within a measurable time. Everything that still held fast in this turmoil was gradually being swept away by the red flood. The pillars of the State were crumbling stone by stone.

Under our last blows the Colossus not only trembled, but split asunder and fell. But we turned to a new task.

CHAPTER XVI

THE ATTACK ON ITALY

ALTHOUGH the situation in Flanders this autumn was extremely serious, we decided on an offensive against Italy. In view of my previous attitude of aversion to such an enterprise, it may cause surprise that I should now obtain the consent of my All-Highest War Lord to the employment of German troops for an operation from which I promised myself little effect on our general situation. On the contrary, I must maintain that I had not changed my views on this question. In August, 1917, I still considered that even if we won a wholesale success we should not succeed in forcing Italy out of her alliance with our enemies. I believed that it was as inadvisable to draw German troops from our imperilled Western Front, mainly for the glory of a successful campaign against Italy, in the autumn of 1917 as it had been when the year opened. The reasons why I now approved our co-operation in such an operation were to be ascribed to other considerations. Our Austro-Hungarian allies had told us that they no longer felt themselves strong enough to resist a twelfth Italian attack on the Isonzo front. This news was equally significant to us from the military and political point of view. What was at stake was not only the loss of the line of the Isonzo, but, in fact, the entire collapse of the Austro-Hungarian resistance. The Danube Monarchy was far more sensitive to defeat on the Italian front than to any reverse in the Galician theatre. No one in Austria had ever fought with much enthusiasm for Galicia. "He who loses the war will keep Galicia anyhow," was an Austro-Hungarian joke that was often heard during the campaign. On the other hand, the interest of the Danube Monarchy in the Italian theatre was always particularly strong. In Galicia—that is, against Russia—Austria-Hungary was fighting only with her head, whereas against Italy she was fighting with her whole soul. It was very significant that in the war against Italy all the races of the Dual Monarchy co-operated with practically equal devotion. Czecho-Slovak troops which had failed against Russia did excellent work against Italy. The war on this side formed to a certain extent a military bond of unity for the whole Monarchy. What would happen if even this bond were severed?

The danger of such an eventuality at the time at which I am writing was great. To begin with, at the end of August Cadorna had gained a considerable amount of ground in the eleventh Isonzo battle. All previous losses of ground had been misfortunes we could survive. Our multifarious experiences had taught us that they were a natural consequence of the destructive effect of offensive weapons against even the strongest defences. But by now the Austro-Hungarian line of defence had been brought as far back as it could be. If the Italians resumed their artillery preparation and won further ground, Austria-Hungary would not be able to maintain any line in front of Trieste. The threat to Trieste was therefore absolutely critical. But woe betide if that city fell. Like Sebastopol in the Crimean War, Trieste seemed to be the bone of contention between Italy and

Austria. For the Danube Monarchy Trieste was not only
the symbol of greatness, but of the very highest practical
value. The economic independence of the country in the
future largely depended on its possession. Trieste
must therefore be saved, with German help if not
otherwise.

If we succeeded in bringing as much relief to our
Allies by a joint and far-reaching victory on the South-
western front as we had just done on her Eastern front,
as far as we could see Austria-Hungary would be in a
position to continue the war by our side. The great
battles on the Isonzo front had already been a heavy
drain on Austria-Hungary's armies. The bulk of her
best troops had been facing Cadorna and lost very heavily
on the Isonzo. Austro-Hungarian heroism had won the
greatest human triumphs in those battles, for the defenders
on the Isonzo had for years been opposed by a threefold
Italian superiority, and, moreover, held positions which
for desolation and horror were quite equal to our battlefields on the Western Front, and, indeed, in many
respects worse. Nor must we forget what immense
demands Alpine warfare in the Southern Tyrol had made
on the troops engaged in defence there. At many points
this warfare was carried on even in the region of eternal
ice and snow.

For an operation against Italy the most obvious idea
was to break out from the Southern Tyrol. From there
the bulk of the Italian armies could be destroyed or dissolved in the great cauldron of Venetia. On no other of
our fronts did the strategic contour of the opposing lines
offer such favourable prospects for a mighty victory.
Compared with this, every other operation must appear

practically an open confession of strategic failure. And yet we had to renounce the idea!

In judging our new plan of campaign we must not leave out of sight the intimate connection between our fighting on the Western Front and the war against Italy. Bearing in mind our position in the West, we could spare for the Italian campaign not more than half the number of divisions which General Conrad had considered essential for a really decisive attack from the Southern Tyrol in the winter of 1916-17. We were quite unable to put stronger forces at the disposal of our Ally, even though, as actually happened, we considered it possible that our foes on the Western Front might find themselves compelled by their Ally's serious defeat to send a few divisions to Italy, divisions which they could spare in view of their great numerical superiority. Another objection to an operation from the Southern Tyrol was the consideration that an early winter might set in before our concentration there was complete. All those reasons compelled us to satisfy ourselves with a more modest objective and to attempt to break through the Italian front on the obviously weak northern wing of the Isonzo Army, and then deal an annihilating blow at the main Italian army in the south before it could retire behind the defences of the Tagliamento. Our attack began in the region of Tolmino on October 24. Cadorna had great difficulty in getting his southern armies, which were threatened with destruction, into safety behind the Piave, and then only by leaving thousands of prisoners and a vast amount of war material behind. It was only there that the Italians, associated with and supported by French and English divisions which had been rushed up, found themselves strong enough to renew their resistance. The left wing of the new front clung desperately to the last peaks of the Venetian Alps. We failed in our attempt to capture these heights, which commanded the whole plain of Upper Italy, and therefore to ensure the collapse of the enemy resistance in the Piave front also. I had to convince myself that our strength was insufficient for the execution of this task. The operation had run itself to a standstill. In face of that fact even the greatest resolution on the part of the commanders and troops on the spot had to lower its arms.

However great was my joy at the victory we had gained in Italy, I could not entirely resist a certain feeling of dissatisfaction. At the last the great victory had not been consummated. It is true that our splendid men returned from this campaign with feelings of justifiable pride. Yet the elation of the rank and file is not always shared by their leaders!

CHAPTER XVII

FURTHER HOSTILE ATTACKS IN THE SECOND HALF OF 1917

1
In the West

WHILE we were delivering the final blows against Russia and bringing Italy to the very brink of military collapse, England and France were continuing their attacks on the Western Front. There lay the greatest danger of the whole year's campaign for us.

The Flanders battle flamed up at the end of July. I had a certain feeling of satisfaction when this new battle began, in spite of the extraordinary difficulties it involved for our situation on the Western Front and the danger that any considerable English successes might easily prejudice our operations in the other theatres. As we anticipated, England was now making her supreme effort in a great and decisive attack upon us even before the assistance coming from the United States could in any way make itself felt. I thought I could detect the effects of the U-boat campaign, which were compelling England to obtain a military decision this year and at any cost.

From the point of view, not of scale, but of the obstinacy which the English displayed and the difficulties of the ground for the defenders, the battles which now began in Flanders put all our battles on the Somme in 1916 completely in the shade. The fighting was now over the marshes and mud of Flanders instead of the hard chalk of the Artois. These actions, too, developed into one of the long-drawn-out battles with which we were already so familiar, and in their general character represented an intensification of the sombre scenes peculiar to such battles. It is obvious that these actions kept us in great and continual anxiety. In fact, I may say that with such a cloud hanging over our heads we were seldom able to rejoice wholeheartedly over our victories in Russia and Italy.

It was with a feeling of absolute longing that we waited for the beginning of the wet season. As previous experience had taught us, great stretches of the Flemish flats would then become impassable, and even in firmer places the new shell-holes would fill so quickly with ground water that men seeking shelter in them would find themselves faced with the alternative : " Shall we drown or get out of this hole? "   This battle, too, must finally stick in the mud, even though English stubbornness kept it up longer than otherwise.

The flames of battle did not die down until December. As on the Somme, neither of the two adversaries could raise the shout of victory in Flanders.

As the Flanders battle was drawing to a close, a fierce conflict unexpectedly blazed up at a part of the line which had hitherto been relatively inactive. On November 20 we were suddenly surprised by the English near Cambrai. The attack at this point was against a portion of the Siegfried Line which was certainly very strong from the point of view of technical construction, but was held by few troops and those exhausted in previous battles. With the help of their tanks, the enemy broke through our series of obstacles and positions which had been entirely undamaged. English cavalry appeared on the outskirts of Cambrai. At the end of the year, therefore, a breach in our line appeared to be a certainty. At this point a catastrophe was averted by German divisions which had arrived from the East, and were more or less worn out by fighting and the long journey. Moreover, after a murderous defensive action lasting several days we succeeded in quickly bringing up comparatively fresh troops, taking the enemy's salient in flank by a counter-attack, and almost completely restoring the original situation at very heavy cost to the enemy. Not only the Army Headquarters Staff on the spot, but the troops themselves and our railways had performed one of the most brilliant feats of the war.

The first considerable attack on our side in the West since the conduct of operations was entrusted to me had come to a victorious conclusion. Its effect on me personally was as strong and invigorating as on our troops and their leaders. I felt it as a release from a burden which our defensive strategy on the Western Front had placed upon my shoulders. For us, however, the success of our counter-attack involved far more than mere satisfaction. The element of surprise which had led to our success contained a lesson for the future.

With the Battle of Cambrai the English High Command had departed from what I might call the routine methods which hitherto they had always followed. Higher strategy seemed to have come into its own on this occasion. The pinning down of our main forces in Flanders and on the French front was to be used to facilitate a great surprise blow at Cambrai. It must be admitted that the subordinate commanders on the English side had not been equal to the demands and possibilities of the situation. By neglecting to exploit a brilliant initial success they had let victory be snatched from them, and indeed by troops which were far inferior to their own, both in numbers and quality. From this point of view our foe at Cambrai deserved his thorough defeat. Moreover, his High Command seemed to have failed to concentrate the resources required to secure the execution of their plans and their exploitation in case of success. Strong bodies of cavalry assembled behind the triumphant leading infantry divisions failed, even on this occasion, to overcome the last line of resistance, weak though it was, which barred the way to the flanks and rear of their opponents. The English cavalry squadrons were not able to conquer the German defence, even with the help of their tanks, and proved unequal to decorating their standards with that victory for which they had striven so honourably and so often.

The English attack at Cambrai for the first time revealed the possibilities of a great surprise attack with tanks. We had had previous experience of this weapon in the spring offensive, when it had not made any particular impression. However, the fact that the tanks had now been raised to such a pitch of technical perfection that they could cross our undamaged trenches and obstacles did not fail to have a marked effect on our troops. The physical effects of fire from machine-guns and light ordnance with which the steel Colossus was provided were far less destructive than the moral effect of its comparative invulnerability. The infantryman felt that he could do practically nothing against its armoured sides. As soon as the machine broke through our trench-lines, the defender felt himself threatened in the rear and left his post. I had no doubt that though our men had had to put up with quite enough already in the defence, they would get on level terms even with this new hostile weapon, and that our technical skill would soon provide the means of fighting tanks, and, moreover, in that mobile form which was so necessary.

As was to be expected, the French did not stand idly by and watch the attacks of their English Ally in the summer and autumn. In the second half of August they attacked us at Verdun and on October 22 north-east of Soissons. In both cases they captured a considerable portion of the trench systems of the armies at those points and caused them important losses. But, speaking generally, the French High Command confined themselves to local attacks in the second half of the year. They were undoubtedly compelled to do so by the appalling losses they had suffered in the spring, losses which made it seem inadvisable to subject their troops to any similar disastrous experiences.

2

The Balkans

Hostile attacks on the Bulgarian front in Macedonia during the later summer months of 1917 had made no difference to the general situation in that theatre. Apparently Sarrail had no considerable objective in these operations. On the contrary, he seemed to have imposed remarkable limits on himself, so much so that from the point of view of the whole war his troops might hardly have been there at all.

It was at this time that Bulgaria watched the Greek

mobilisation with ever-increasing anxiety. The news we ourselves received from Greece left it doubtful whether Venizelos would succeed in creating an effective force. For a long time even the so-called Venizelist Divisions were nothing more than a collection of supers who preferred the rôle of hero in the Macedonian theatre to the actual battles of heroes. The real, sound heart of the Greek people was always averse to supporting a domestic policy of open disloyalty. Bulgaria's anxieties were based, perhaps, on memories of the events of 1913.

8
Asia

I will now turn to the course of events in Asiatic Turkey. To omit them would, in my opinion, be a crime against our brave and loyal Ally. Moreover, such an omission would mean an unfinished picture of the mighty drama, the scenes of which extended from the Northern seas to the shores of the Indian Ocean. Here again I will concern myself less with the description of events than with a discussion of their interdependence.

The fancies of our armchair strategists did not confine themselves merely to plans of campaign in Central Europe, but were frequently lost in the distances of the Far East. The products of these imaginings frequently came into my own hands. As a rule, in their letters the authors confined themselves to " general principles," in order " not to take up too much of my precious time," and were kind enough to think that the rest could be left to me. But in most cases we were urged to lose no time ! One such strategist among our young hopefuls wrote to me one day : " You *must* see that this war will be decided at Kiliz. So send all our armies there." The first business was to find out where Kiliz was. It was at length discovered in the temperate zone north of Aleppo.

However novel this young man's idea may seem, it contained a large element of sound strategic instinct. Perhaps not the course of the whole war, but certainly the fate of our Ottoman Ally, would have been settled out of hand if England had secured a decision in that region, or even seriously attempted it. Possession of the country south of the Taurus would have been lost to Turkey at a blow if the English had succeeded in landing in the Gulf of Alexandretta, and from there striking east. In so doing they would have severed the main artery of all Trans-Taurian Turkey, through which fresh blood and other revitalising forces flowed to the Syrian, Mesopotamian and a part of the Caucasian armies. The quantity of blood and the virtue of the forces were small enough, it is true, but they would enable the Ottoman armies to prolong their resistance for a long time yet to the enemy operations and offensives, which were insufficiently prepared and in many cases feebly and inefficiently carried out.

The protection of the Gulf of Alexandretta was entrusted to a Turkish army which contained scarcely a single unit fit to fight. Every man who could be of use in the fighting line was gradually transferred to Syria or Mesopotamia. Moreover, coast protection by artillery at this point was more a figment of the Oriental imagination than a military reality. Enver Pasha exactly described the situation to me in the words : " My only hope is that the enemy has not discovered our weakness at this critical spot."

Was there really any probability that the enemy would not discover this critical weakness at the Gulf of Alexandretta? I did not think so. Nowhere did the hostile Intelligence Service find fewer obstacles and greater possibilities of assistance among the medley of nationalities than in Syria and Asia Minor. It seemed impossible that the English High Command should not know the true state of the coast defences in this theatre. Moreover, England had no reason to fear that in pushing east from the Gulf of Alexandretta she would be treading on a hornets' nest. There were no hornets. If ever there was a prospect of a brilliant strategic feat, it was here. Such a campaign would have made an enormous impression on the whole world, and unquestionably have had a far-reaching effect on our Turkish Ally.

Why did England never make use of her opportunity here? Perhaps her experiences in the Dardanelles had sunk too deeply into her soul. Perhaps there was too great anxiety about our U-boats for anyone on the enemy's side to venture on such an enterprise.

Some day history will perhaps clear up this question also. I say "perhaps," for it is not likely that England will ever clear it up herself. We obtained an insight into the main current of British thought by an expression let fall by a high English naval officer at the time of the Fashoda affair. In reply to a question as to his prospective idea of the rôle to be played by the English fleet in the Mediterranean in case of an Anglo-French war, he said: " I have the strictest instructions not to stake England's Trafalgar fame."

The fame of Trafalgar is great and well deserved. It is that kind of metaphorical jewel which goes to make

T

a nation's most priceless treasure. England knew how to preserve this jewel and to keep it ever in the brightest light before the admiring eyes of the whole world. It is true that many shadows have been cast over that jewel in the Great War. The Dardanelles is one example. And further shadows were to follow in the battles against the German Navy, the strongest and blackest being Skagerrak. England will never forgive us the eclipse of the fame of Trafalgar!

England renounced the idea of a bold thrust into the heart of her Turkish adversary and proceeded with her costly and tedious efforts to bring about the collapse of Turkish dominion south of the Taurus by gradually driving back the Ottoman armies. The capture of Bagdad at the beginning of the year was the first great and promising step towards the realisation of this war aim. On the other hand the attack at Gaza in the spring had failed, and the English had to begin all over again. But for the time being further military operations were paralysed under the leaden weight of the summer heat.

The loss of Bagdad was painful for us and, as we well believed, still more painful for all thinking Turkey. How often had the name of the old city of the Caliphs been mentioned in Germany in previous years? How many dreams had been associated with it, dreams which it would have been better to cherish in silence rather than shout all over the world in the impolitic German way?

The general military situation was not further affected by events in Mesopotamia, but the loss of Bagdad was a sore point for German foreign policy. We had guaranteed the Turkish Government the territorial integrity of the Empire, and now felt that, in spite of the generous

interpretation of this contract, our political account was
heavily overdrawn by this new great loss.

Enver Pasha's request for German help in order to
recover Bagdad was therefore welcomed by all of us, not
the least because the Turkish High Command had always
shown itself willing to assist us in the European theatre.
At Enver's suggestion the conduct of the new campaign
was to be put in German hands, not because the assistance
of German troops was contemplated on any considerable
scale, but because the Turkish Generalissimo considered
it essential that the military prestige of Germany should
preside over the enterprise.   But the success of the scheme
was inconceivable unless we managed to overcome the
enormous difficulties of supply due to the appalling length
of the lines of communication.   A Turkish commander
would have come to grief over this essential preliminary.

On the suggestion of the Turks, His Majesty the
Emperor entrusted the conduct of this extraordinarily
difficult operation to General von Falkenhayn.   In May,
1917, the general, to familiarise himself with the elements
of his problem, visited Mesopotamia and Syria, as well as
Constantinople.   The visit to Syria was necessary because
General von Falkenhayn could not possibly operate against
Bagdad unless he had an absolute guarantee that the
Turkish front in Syria would hold.   For there could be
no doubt that the Bagdad enterprise would soon be
betrayed to England, and that such news must provoke
an English attack on Syria.

General von Falkenhayn came to the conclusion that
the operation was possible. We therefore met the
demands he made upon us.   We restored to Turkey all
the Ottoman troops which we were still employing in the

European theatre. The Ottoman Corps in Galicia left the German Army just as Kerensky's troops were withdrawing eastwards before our counter-offensive. It returned homewards accompanied by expressions of the liveliest gratitude on our part. The Turk had once more revived his ancient military fame in our ranks and proved himself a thoroughly effective instrument of war in our hands. I must, of course, admit that Enver Pasha had given up the very best troops he had available for the Eastern Front and Rumania. The quality of this corps could therefore not be taken as a standard of the efficiency and capacity of the whole Turkish Army. The unsparing work which our Army Headquarters Staff had devoted to the education and training of the Turkish troops, and more particularly their attention to their feeding and health, had borne fruit in fullest measure. How many of these rough children of nature had found friendship and fellow-feeling for the first time—and indeed for the last—under German protection.

I had hoped that the Ottoman Corps would form a particularly valuable element in the force earmarked for the expedition against Bagdad. Unfortunately these expectations were not fulfilled. No sooner were these troops out of range of our influence than they went to pieces again, thus proving what little effect our example had had on the Turkish officer. In comparison with the great mass of insufficiently trained and ineffective elements only a few individuals proved particularly brilliant exceptions. The Turkish Army would have required complete reorganisation if it was really to become capable of the achievements which the sacrifices of the country required. The defects of its present condition were revealed most strikingly in an extremely high rate of wastage. This phenomenon was characteristic of every army which was insufficiently trained and had not been properly prepared for war. A really thorough training of the army saves the man power of a nation in case of war. What enormous proportions the rate of wastage reached in Turkey during the war appears from a piece of intelligence which reached me to the effect that in a single province of Anatolia the villages had been drained of every male inhabitant except boys and old men. This is credible enough when we remember that the defence of the Dardanelles cost the Turks about 200,000 men. How many of them succumbed to hunger and disease is unknown.

Apart from a number of officers who were lent for special employment, the German reinforcements for the Bagdad enterprise comprised the so-called " Asiatic Corps." There has been a certain amount of criticism in our country on the ground that we placed so splendid a corps at the disposal of the Turks for a distant objective instead of using these precious troops in Central Europe. However, the corps consisted of only three infantry battalions and a few batteries. The name " Asiatic Corps " was chosen in order to mislead the enemy. We have never known whether it really did so. With regard to this help it was less a question of the material reinforcement of our Allies than of giving them moral and intellectual support —that is, resolution and experience. The peculiar character of the help we rendered was hit off exactly in an expression of the Tsar Ferdinand when, after the autumn battles of 1916 in Macedonia, he warned us against withdrawing all the German troops from the Bulgarian front : " My Bulgarians like to see spiked helmets, for the sight gives them confidence and a sense of security. They have everything else themselves.'' This again confirmed the experience which Scharnhorst once put into words when he said that the stronger will of the trained man is the more important for the whole operation than brute force.

The operations against Bagdad never materialised. Before the summer months were over it appeared that the English had completed all their preparations to attack the Turkish forces at Gaza before the wet season set in. General von Falkenhayn, who was permanently stationed in the East, became more and more convinced that the Syrian front would not prove equal to the strain of an English attack, which would doubtless be made in great superiority. Turkish divisions which had been earmarked for the operations against Bagdad had to be diverted to the south. The result of this was that the chance of a successful enterprise in Mesopotamia had vanished. At Enver Pasha's suggestion I accordingly agreed that all available reserves should be sent to Syria with the idea of taking the offensive ourselves before the English attacked. The German command hoped to improve the capacity of the railway and the administration of the Turkish districts to such an extent that a substantially larger number of troops could be supplied in this theatre and provided with all the war material required.

Thanks to both political and military causes of friction, General von Falkenhayn lost a lot of precious time. At the beginning of November the English succeeded in taking the offensive at Beersheba and Gaza. The Turkish armies were driven north, and Jerusalem was lost at the beginning of December. It was not until the middle of this month that the Turkish lines were re-established north of the line Jaffa—Jerusalem—Jericho.

Although we had feared that these Turkish defeats, and especially the loss of Jerusalem, would have a regrettable political reaction on the position of the existing government in Constantinople, nothing of the kind happened—at least, not to outward appearance. A remarkable atmosphere of indifference took the place of the agitation we feared.

I myself had no doubt that Turkey would never recover possession of Jerusalem and the holy places. This view was shared, though tacitly, at the Golden Horn also. Ottoman eyes were now turned in deeper longing than ever to other regions of Asia, seeking compensation for the lost provinces. Unfortunately, this was premature from the military point of view.

CHAPTER XVIII

A GLANCE AT THE INTERNAL SITUATION OF THE STATES AND NATIONS AT THE END OF 1917

THE reader need not fear that, overcoming my aversion to politics, I am about to plunge into the whirlpool of party strife; but if I am not to leave too many gaps in the picture which I am trying to give I cannot very well omit the remarks that follow. Is there anyone, indeed, who could succeed in giving a complete description of the times of which I write? A whole series of further questions suggest themselves after the "Why?" and "How?" There will always be gaps, as so many lips which could have given priceless information are now dumb. Nor can I fill in all the details of my picture. I can only put in a stroke here and there. It is more a character sketch than a finished painting. Arbitrarily, perhaps, I will take the East first.

"Turkey is a cipher." These words can be found in a memorandum dating from pre-war times, and it is a German memorandum, and therefore not inspired by political hatred of Turkey. A peculiar cipher, by which the Dardanelles were defended and the victory of Kut-el-Amara gained; a cipher which marched on Egypt and brought the Russian attack in the mountains of Armenia to a standstill! For us it was a valuable cipher, which, as I said before, was now tying down hundreds of thousands of enemy troops, picked troops which were nibbling at the Turkish frontier provinces, and indeed nibbling them away, but without succeeding in devouring the whole body!

What gave this cipher its inward strength? A puzzle even to those who were now living in or had lived long in the land of the Ottoman. The masses seemed apathetic and indifferent, while a great part of the upper classes were selfish and dead to all higher national demands. As far as one could see the State was composed only of classes which were separated by deep gulfs and had no national common life. And yet this State remained in existence and gave proofs of its power. The authority of Constantinople seemed to end at the Taurus. Beyond Asia Minor Turkey seemed to have no real influence, and yet Turkish armies were maintaining themselves in distant Mesopotamia and Syria. The Arabs in those regions hated the Turks, and the Turks the Arabs. And yet Arab battalions were still fighting under Turkish standards, and did not desert in masses to the enemy, even though he not only promised them mountains of gold but actually scattered with prodigal hand the gold they so much coveted. Behind the Anglo-Indian Army, which as it thought was bringing the long-desired freedom to the Arab tribes, downtrodden and oppressed by the Turks, these very tribes rose and turned against their so-called deliverers. There must be some force here which acted as a bond of unity, and indeed a force which was not the resultant of pressure from outside but of a cohesive influence, a feeling of community of interest within. It could not be solely the authority of those in power in Turkey which supplied this centralising force. The Arabs could easily have escaped that authority. They had only to raise their arms and walk out of their trenches towards

the enemy or rise in revolt behind the Turkish Army.
And yet they did not do so. Was it their faith, the relic
of their ancient faith, which was the unifying influence
here? Some said it was, and on good grounds, while
others denied it on equally good grounds. Here was a
point at which our knowledge of Ottoman psychology
seemed to have reached its limits. We must leave the
conflict of opinions undecided.

Thus, in spite of the heaviest afflictions, the State
could not be altogether moribund. Moreover, we heard
of splendid officials who, side by side with others who
entirely forgot their duty, proved themselves men of great
ideas and immense energy. I came to know one of them,
Ismail Hakki, at Kreuznach. He was a man with many
of the drawbacks of his race, who yet possessed a powerful
and fertile intellect. It was a great pity that he had not
sprung from a healthier soil. It was said that he never
wrote anything down, but did everything in his head; and
yet he had thousands of things to think about and was
inspired by national views which went far beyond the
horizon of the war! His principal sphere of work, and
that in which he revealed his greatest powers, was the
food supply of the army and Constantinople. If Ismail
Hakki had been dismissed, the Turkish Army would have
suffered a shortage of everything; its privations would
have even been greater than was inevitable at this stage,
and Constantinople would probably have starved. Practically the whole country was going hungry, and this not
because food was lacking, but because administration and
transport were at a standstill and there was no means of
adjusting supply to demand. No one knew how the
inhabitants of the larger towns managed to exist at all.

We supplied Constantinople with bread, sent corn from the Dobrudja and Rumania, and gave what help we could, in spite of our own shortage. Of course, what we delivered to Constantinople would not have gone far with our millions of mouths. If we had stopped these deliveries we should have lost Turkey, for a starving Constantinople would have revolted, no matter what autocracy might do. Was there really an autocracy in that country? I have already spoken of the Committee. But there were other influences there working against the strong men; influences which sprang from political and possibly commercial hatreds, such hatreds as create factions. Beneath the externally peaceful surface strong currents were in motion. We could often see the whirlpools when they attempted to suck the present leaders down into the depths.

The Army too suffered from these currents, and, as I have said above, the High Command had to allow for them in their calculations and frequently to give way to them to the prejudice of the general situation. If they had not done so the Army, the numerical strength of which was already being frittered away, would have been dissolved internally also. Privations and want of food were to a large extent playing havoc with the troops. The length of the war was also having a serious effect on their establishment, for with the previous wars in the Yemen and Balkans many Turkish soldiers seemed never to have stopped fighting. The longing for their homes, wives and children—such longings are not unknown even to Islam—drove thousands of men to desertion. Of the complete divisions which were entrained at Haidar-Pasha only fragments ever reached Syria or Mesopotamia. Men may go on arguing whether the number of Turkish deserters in Asia Minor was 300,000 or 500,000. In any case it was nearly as large as the total number of fighting troops in the Turkish Army. It was not an encouraging picture, and yet—Turkey still held on and loyally did her duty without a word of complaint.

Bulgaria also was suffering from scarcity. Scarcity of food in a land which usually produces more than it needs! The harvest had been only moderate, but it could have sufficed if the country had been administered like our own and available supplies could have been properly distributed between districts that had too much and those that had not enough. In reply to a suggestion to this effect a Bulgarian answered : " We don't understand such things ! " A simple excuse, or rather self-accusation. The Bulgarians simply folded their hands because they had never learnt to use them. We know that as Bulgaria had passed straight from Turkish slavery to complete political freedom, she had never known the educative influence of a strong organising authority. If I may be allowed to speak as a Prussian, she had never had a King Frederic William I, who raised the pillars of iron on which our State securely rested for so long. Bulgaria did not know what good administration was. But she had plenty of parties. Most of them were bitterly hostile to the Government, not on the ground of its foreign policy, which promised a great future, national unity and the hegemony of the Balkans, but on account of domestic issues around which the contest went on the more fiercely. No methods, however dangerous, were despised. Neither their Allies nor their own army were sacred. It was a dangerous game! The Dobrudja was always a favourite subject for party agitation. The Government had conjured up menacing spectres in order to put pressure on Turkey and ourselves, and now found they could not get rid of these spectres which threatened to destroy everything, and for party purposes preached hatred of the Allies and their representatives. In the autumn of 1917 it seemed to us best, for the time being, to give way on this Dobrudja question and leave its final solution until after the war. On our part it was a retreat inspired by policy, not by conviction. It was remarkable that as soon as we gave way all interest in the matter vanished in Bulgaria. The word " Dobrudja " had lost its power to excite party passions. Thus ended what had, at any rate, been a bloodless battle so far as we were concerned, but the struggle for power between the political parties continued and ruthlessly thrust a disruptive wedge into the framework of the Army, and, indeed, deeper than in peace time.

The troops showed themselves susceptible to these disintegrating influences, for they were badly supplied and already beginning to suffer from scarcity. The lack of organising energy and ability was revealed at every end and turn. We made many proposals in the direction of far-reaching improvements. The Bulgarians recognised that these proposals were timely, but they had not the energy and disliked the bother of putting them into effect. They confined themselves to grumbling about the Germans who were occupying their country (as a matter of fact, a country which had been conquered by joint operations!) who by the terms of the compact were to be supplied by the Bulgarians themselves because they were fighting on the Macedonian frontier, not for the protection of Germany, but primarily for the protection of Bulgaria. According to the Bulgarians, the Germans ought to feed

their own men, and as a matter of fact and for the sake
of peace they did so, and sent cattle as well as hay from
the homeland to Macedonia. It must be admitted that
these unending disputes went on in the lines of communication area behind the common front, and not among the
fighting troops, for these still had some self-respect. With
the idea of preventing disputes we suggested the exchange
of our German troops in Macedonia for Bulgarian
divisions which were in Rumania. We were thus offering
the Bulgarians two, or rather three, men for one; but
there were immediately loud cries in Sofia about a breach
of faith. We therefore confined ourselves to withdrawing
only some of our troops and sending a few of our battalions to take over from the Bulgarians in Rumania.
Thus the Bulgarian divisions left the northern bank of
the Danube, to which they had originally crossed only
with extreme reluctance.

Thus the Bulgarian picture also was not without its
shadows. But we could rely on her continued loyalty—
at any rate, so long as we could and would meet her great
political claims. When, however, as a result of expressions
in the German Press and speeches in the German Parliament in the summer of 1917, both Sofia and the Bulgarian
Army began to have doubts as to whether we would really
keep our promises, they listened, holding their breath,
and, what is worse, began to suspect us. The parties now
began to clamour for the resignation of Radoslavoff. His
foreign policy was recognised to be far-seeing and all of
them still approved it, but it appeared that he was not
the man to hold his own with the Allies. Moreover, his
home policy was disliked in many quarters. New men
ought to be put at the helm, for in the opinion of Bulgaria

the old had already been in power too long. They might have feathered their own nests. Moreover, everyone who had any connection whatever with Radoslavoff, from the highest official down to the village mayor, would have to depart with the Government, for that alone was consistent with the parliamentary, the so-called " free " system. And this was to be done at once, even in the middle of a war!

I have little to say about Austria-Hungary. Her internal difficulties had not become less. I have already said that the attempt to reconcile the Czech elements, which were intent on the destruction of the State, by the method of toleration had utterly failed. Efforts were now being made to create a bond of unity for the different races of the Empire, or at any rate their most influential circles, by putting forward the power and authority of the Church and giving prominence to religious feeling. But neither did these efforts achieve the hoped-for result. They merely widened the lines of cleavage and provoked mistrust where had previously been devotion. The mutual aversion of the different races was intensified by inequalities in the distribution of food. Vienna was starving while Buda-Pesth had something to spare. German-Bohemia was almost dying from exhaustion while the Czechs lacked practically nothing. As ill-luck would have it, the harvest was a partial failure. This intensified the crisis and would continue to do so. As in Turkey, Austria-Hungary was not without the technical resources required to adjust matters between districts which had too much and those which had not enough. But there was no centralising power and no all-pervading State authority. Thus the old evil of domestic feuds, with all its destructive consequences, was extended to the domain of food supply. It was hardly surprising that the longing for peace grew and that confidence in a favourable conclusion of the war began to fail. The collapse of Russia made things worse rather than better. The elimination of the danger from that side seemed to have made men indifferent rather than strengthened their resolution. Even the victory in Italy was welcome only to certain classes and circles of the nation. The masses had lost all their pride, for starvation was undoubtedly at work here and there. Moreover, much that still stood for something before the death of the old Emperor had lost its ethical significance. Thousands of Czech and other agitators trampled the honour of the State under foot. It was certain that far stronger nerves than those possessed by the governing authorities would have been required to offer further resistance to the pressure of the masses, which to a certain extent were anxious for peace at any price.

And now to our own country.

In the course of the military events of which I have been writing far-reaching and fateful changes had been taking place in the domestic circumstances of our own Fatherland. The resignation of the Imperial Chancellor, von Bethmann, showed how critical the situation had become. Although I said originally that we were at one in our views of the situation created by the war, as time went on I was bound to recognise with regret that this was no longer the case. The conduct of military operations had been entrusted to me, and for my task I needed all the resources of the Fatherland. To dissipate these resources by internal friction at a time of extreme tension, instead of concentrating them, could only lead

to a diminution of our political and military power. With
that in mind I could not take the responsibility of standing by and saying nothing when I saw that the sense of
unity which was so essential at the front was being
destroyed at home. Convinced as I was that, compared
with our enemies, we were falling back in this respect
and taking the opposite course to theirs, I, unfortunately,
soon saw myself at loggerheads with our Government.
Our co-operation thereby suffered. For that reason I
considered it my duty to ask my All-Highest War Lord
for permission to resign, however hard such a step must
be for me as a soldier. His Majesty did not approve my
request. Simultaneously the Chancellor had requested to
be allowed to resign as a result of a declaration of the
party leaders in the Reichstag. His wish was granted.

The outward consequences of this retirement were
regrettable. There was an end to the appearance of party
peace which had hitherto been maintained. A Majority
Party with a definite tendency towards the Left came
into existence. The omissions which were alleged to have
distinguished our political development of earlier times
were now exploited, even in the middle of a war and under
the pressure of the extremely difficult situation in which
the Fatherland found itself, to force further concessions
from the Government in the direction of a so-called parliamentary system. ' Along such paths our inward unity
was bound to be lost. The reins of government gradually
fell into the hands of the extreme parties.

Dr. Michaelis was appointed to succeed Bethmann
Hollweg. Within a very short time my relations with
him were on a footing of mutual confidence. He had
entered upon his difficult office undismayed, but he

U

did not hold it for long. Circumstances were to prove too strong for him, stronger than his own good intentions.

The atmosphere of parliamentary faction was never again improved. The Majority Parties inclined more and more to the Left, and as far as deeds were concerned, and in spite of many fine words, began to represent the elements which were intent on the destruction of the ancient political order in the State. It became ever clearer that in the strife of party interests and party dogmas our homeland was forgetting the real seriousness of our situation, or refusing any longer to realise it. Our enemies publicly rejoiced at this and knew how to add fuel to the party flames. In these circumstances efforts were made to find an Imperial Chancellor who would be able to compose party differences by virtue of his parliamentary past. The choice fell on Count Hertling. I had met him at Pless in the company of the King of Bavaria. I still have happy recollections of the kindness which he showed when offering me his congratulations on the Grand Cross of the Iron Cross which His Majesty had just awarded me. To me it was both touching and encouraging to see how gladly the old Count dedicated the strength of his last years to the service of his Fatherland. His unshakable confidence in our cause and his hopes for our future survived the most critical situations. He handled the parliamentary parties with skill, but, compared with the seriousness of our position, was unable to effect anything really vital. Unhappily, his relations with Main Headquarters suffered from the existence of misunderstandings which were a legacy from earlier times, and this occasionally prejudiced co-operation. My respect for the

Count was thereby in no way diminished. As is known, he died shortly after he resigned his thankless office.

Even apart from the misfortunes to which I have already referred, everything was far from comfortable in the homeland at the end of 1917. Nothing else could have been expected, for the war and privation were a heavy burden on a large portion of the nation and adversely affected its *moral*. A year of empty, or at any rate unsatisfied, stomachs prejudiced all higher impulses and tended to make men indifferent. Under the effects of insufficient physical nourishment the thoughts of the great mass among us were no better than elsewhere, even though the authority of the State and the moral resolution of the nation permeated our whole life to a greater degree. In such circumstances that life was bound to suffer, especially as no fresh intellectual and moral forces came into existence to revive it. We too lacked a stimulant of that kind. We met with the dangerous view that nothing more could be done against the indifference of the masses even in circles in which other opinions usually prevailed. The representatives of this view simply folded their hands and let things slide. They looked on while parties exploited the exhaustion of the nation as fertile soil for the growth of ideas which aimed at the dissolution of state order, and scattered their destructive seed which took root and flourished more and more. They would not use their hands to pluck up those weeds.

Indifference had the same effect as slothfulness. It prepared the soil for discontent. It infected not only the people at home, but also the soldiers who returned among them.

The soldiers who returned home from the front were in

a position to exercise an inspiring and stimulating influence on the public. Most of them did so. But they could also have a depressing influence, and unfortunately many of them proved it, though they were not the best from our ranks. These men wanted no more war; they had a bad effect on the already poisoned soil, themselves absorbed the worst elements of that soil, and carried the demoralisation of the homeland back with them into the field.

There is much that is gloomy in this picture. Not all of it was an actual consequence of the war, or at any rate need have been such a consequence. War does not only stimulate, it demoralises. And this war had a more demoralising influence than any previous war. It destroyed not only bodies but souls.

The enemy intensified the process of demoralisation, not only by his blockade and the semi-starvation it involved, but by another method, known as " Propaganda in the Enemy's Camp." This was a new weapon, or rather a weapon which had never been employed on such a scale and so ruthlessly in the past. The enemy used it in Germany as in Turkey, Austria-Hungary and Bulgaria. The shower of inflammatory pamphlets fell not only behind our fronts in East and West, but also behind the Turkish fronts in Irak and Syria.

This method of propaganda is known as " Enlightening the Enemy," but it ought to be called " Concealing the Truth," or even " Poisoning the Enemy's Character." It is the result of the adversary's conviction that he is no longer strong enough to defeat his enemy in open and honourable fight and conquer his moral resolution merely by the victory of his triumphant sword.

And now let us try and secure a peep into the heart of the States hostile to us. I say "try" advisedly. For during a war there could be no question of anything more. Not only our economic intercourse, but every other kind of intercourse with foreign countries was cut off by the blockade. The fact that to a certain extent we had neutral States on our frontiers hardly affects this statement at all. Our spy service produced only miserable results. In this sphere even German gold succumbed in the struggle between our enemies and ourselves.

We knew that on the far side of the Western Front a Government was in power which was personally inspired by thoughts of hatred and revenge, and incessantly whipped up the inmost passions of the nation. Whenever Clemenceau spoke the burden of his words was: "Woe to our ancient conqueror." France was bleeding from a thousand wounds. If we had not known it, the public declarations of her Dictator would have told us so. But France was going to fight on. There was not a word, not a suggestion, of concession. The moment a crack appeared in the structure of the State—which was held together with iron chains—the Government intervened, and intervened ruthlessly. It achieved its purpose. The majority of the nation may have longed for peace, but if any public expression was given to such a feeling in the land of republican freedom, it was cold-bloodedly stamped into the ground, and the nation received a further dose of liberal phrases. Even before the outbreak of war, in the so-called anti-militarist France the words "Humanity" and "Pacifism" were branded as "dangerous narcotics with which the doctrinaire advocates of peace wished to corrupt the manliness of the nation. Pacifism has proved this at all times. Its proper name is cowardice, and it means the exaggerated self-love of the individual who takes care to avoid every personal risk which does not bring him direct advantage." These were the words of men in " peace-loving France." Was it surprising that the ideals of " France at War " were just as ruthless, and that every man who ever dared to speak of peace was branded as a traitor to his country?

We could not doubt that even at the end of 1917 the French nation was better fed than the German. In the first place Paris received special attention. As far as possible it was spared from scarcity and consoled by every conceivable kind of pleasure. It seemed to us doubtful whether the Gaul would endure the privations of daily life with the same devotion and for so long as his German adversary. But, in any case, we might be certain that even a starving France would have to go on fighting for as long as England wished, even if she thereby succumbed altogether.

The French prisoners certainly told us of the miseries of war and the scarcity which was making itself felt at home. But their own appearance did not indicate any shortage. All of them were longing for the end of the war, but no one thought that it would come so long as " the others wanted to go on fighting."

How was it with England?

The Motherland found her economic and world position faced with an immense peril. But no one there ventured to say so. There was only one way out: Victory! In the course of the last year England had survived a " fit of weakness." For a time it had looked as if the national resolution had begun to crumble and England's war aims to become more modest. The voice of Lord Lansdowne was heard. However, it died away under the oppressive weight of an autocratic power which held out the prospect of an approaching end of the war. After the economic and political *moral* of the nation had sunk to a low level in the summer, the public had once more scented the air of approaching victory, though until the end of 1917 we did not know why. As we found out later, that air had its origin in the political sink of corruption in Central Europe. Thoughts of approaching victory once more restored the unity of the whole nation. It was once again willing to bear the loss of its pleasures and found it easier to give up its old habits and political freedom in the hope of realising its anticipation that after the successful conclusion of this war every individual Englishman would be richer. The political self-discipline of the Englishman reinforced his commercial selfishness. And so here, too, nothing was said about peace so long as the war did not cost too much. English prisoners at the end of 1917 spoke in the same tone as those of the end of 1914. No one had any stomach for fighting. Yet no one asked any questions in that country. The State demanded, and its demands were satisfied.

The condition of affairs in Italy appeared to be otherwise than in France and England. In the campaign of the previous autumn many thousands of Italian soldiers had laid down their arms without any urgent military necessity, not from a lack of courage, but from disgust at what seemed to them senseless slaughter. They looked happy enough on their journey into our country and greeted the familiar workshops with German songs. But even if the enthusiasm for the war, both in the army and

in the country itself, had dwindled to nothing, the nation
was not wholly paralysed. They knew that they would
otherwise starve and freeze. The will of Italy had still
to bow to that of the foreigner. That was her bitter fate
from the start, and she only found it tolerable thanks to
the prospects of great and alluring booty.

From the United States even fewer voices reached us
than from Europe. What we ascertained confirmed our
suspicions. Her brilliant, if pitiless, war industry had
entered the service of patriotism and had not failed it.
Under the compulsion of military necessity a ruthless
autocracy was at work, and rightly, even in this land at
the portals of which the Statue of Liberty flashes its
blinding light across the seas. They understood war.
Weaker voices had to be silent until the hard task had
been done. Only then might the spirit of freedom make
itself heard again for the good of humanity. For the
time being it must be silenced for the good of the State.
All creeds and races felt themselves at one in this battle
for an ideal, and in cases where conviction or the call of
the blood did not speak in favour of the poor Anglo-Saxon
on the verge of ruin, gold was thrown into the scale of
understanding.

I need say no more about Russia. We could look into
her heart as into an open furnace. She would be utterly
consumed, perhaps, but in any case she lay prostrate on
the ground, and her Rumanian Ally had been involved
in her fall.

Such was our view of the situation at the end of 1917.

Many a man in those days asked himself the significant
question : " How is it that our enemies abate nothing of
their ruthless political demands upon us, in spite of their

many military failures in the year 1917, the disappearance
of Russia as a factor from the war, the unquestionably
far-reaching effects of the U-boat warfare, and the
corresponding uncertainty as to whether the great
American reinforcements could ever be brought to the
European theatre? How could Wilson, with the approval
of the enemy Governments, in January, 1918, propose
conditions for a peace such as might be dictated to a
completely beaten adversary, but which could not be put
before a foe who had hitherto been victorious and whose
armies were practically everywhere on enemy soil?

This was my answer then, and it is still my answer :

While we were defeating our enemy's armies their
Governments and peoples directed their gaze steadfastly
at the development of the domestic situation of our
Fatherland and those of our Allies. The weaknesses
which I have already described could not be concealed
from them. It was those weaknesses which reinforced
what seemed to us such incomprehensible hopes and
resolution.

It was not only the enemy's Intelligence Service,
though it worked under the most favourable circumstances
imaginable, which gave the enemy the glance he so much
desired at our home situation. Our people and their
political representatives did nothing whatever to conceal
our domestic troubles from the enemy's eyes. The
German proved that he was not yet politically educated
to the point of exercising self-control. He had to give
utterance to his thoughts, however disastrous the effect
might be at the moment. He thought he could only
satisfy his vanity by publishing what he knew and felt
to the whole world. Thanks to the vague cosmopolitan

sentiments by which he was largely swayed, he regarded
it as a secondary matter whether this behaviour on his
part advantaged or injured the Fatherland. He was convinced that what he had said was right and clever, was
himself perfectly satisfied in the matter, and assumed that
his audience would be so too. The affair was then closed
so far as he was concerned.

This failing has done us even more injury in the
great conflict for our national existence than military
misfortunes. To the lack of the political discipline which
is second nature with the Englishman and that patriotism
free from cosmopolitan crazes which distinguishes the
French, I attribute in the last resource the German
" Peace Resolution," which received the approval of the
Reichstag on July 19, 1917, the very day on which the
military power of Russia palpably received its death blow.
I know well enough that beneath the objective reasons
which were then put forward as paramount for this
Resolution the great disappointment at the course of
military events and the visible results of our U-boat
campaign played a large part. Different views may be
held about the justification for such doubts about our
position. As is known, I considered it fairly favourable;
but I was convinced that the method of approaching such
a step from the parliamentary side was a hopeless mistake.
We shouted our longings for peace into the ears of our
enemies at the very moment when a proper political
attitude on the part of the Germans would perhaps have
made them only too glad to be able to detect even the
slightest inclination to peace in the pulse of our people.
The phraseology in which we tried to clothe the step was
much too threadbare to have deceived anyone in the enemy

camp. Among us Clemenceau's battle cry, " I make war! " found the echo, " We seek peace! "

I therefore opposed this Peace Resolution not from the standpoint of human feeling, but from that of soldierly instinct. I foresaw what it would cost us and expressed it thus: " Another year of war at least! " Another year of war in the serious situation in which both we and our Allies found ourselves!

PART IV

The Fight for a Decision in the West

CHAPTER XIX

THE QUESTION OF AN OFFENSIVE IN THE WEST

1

Our Intentions and Prospects for 1918

IN view of the serious situation which I have described in the last few pages I shall be asked the very natural question for what reason I considered we had prospects of bringing the war to a favourable conclusion by a last great offensive.

For my answer I will get away from political considerations, and speak solely from the standpoint of the soldier as I turn in the first place to the situation of our Allies.

In view of the military helplessness of Russia and Rumania, as well as the heavy defeat of Italy, I considered that the burden on Austria-Hungary had been relieved to such an extent that it would not be difficult for the Danube Monarchy to carry on the war on her own fronts by herself. I believed that Bulgaria was in every sense capable of dealing with the armies of the Entente in Macedonia, all the more so as the Bulgarian forces which had been employed against Russia and Rumania could very shortly be entirely released for Macedonia. Turkey, too, had been immensely relieved in Asia Minor by the collapse of Russia. So far as I could see the result was that she had sufficient troops at her disposal materially to reinforce her armies in Mesopotamia and Syria.

In my view the further resistance of our Allies depended, apart from their own resolution, mainly upon the effective employment of the resources available, which were in any case sufficient for their task. I asked nothing more than that they should hold out. We ourselves would secure a decision in the West. For the purposes of such a decision our armies in the East were now available, or we could, at any rate, hope to have them available by the time the best season began. With the help of these armies we ought to be able to secure a preponderance of numbers in the West. For the first time in the whole war the Germans would have the advantage of numbers on one of their fronts! Of course it could not be as great as that with which England and France had battered our Western Front in vain for more than three years. In particular, even the advent of our forces from the East did not suffice to cancel out the immense superiority of our enemies in artillery and aircraft. But in any case we were now in a position to concentrate an immense force to overwhelm the enemy's lines at some point of the Western Front without thereby taking too heavy a risk on other parts of that front.

Even with the advantage of numbers on our side, it was not a simple matter to decide on an offensive in the West. It was always doubtful whether we should win a great victory. The course and results of the previous attacks of our enemies seemed to offer little encouragement. What had our enemies achieved in the long run with all their numerical superiority and their millions of shells and trench-mortar bombs, not to mention the hecatombs of corpses? Local gains of ground a few miles in depth were the fruits of months of effort. Of course we too had suffered heavy losses in the defence, but it was to be assumed that those of the attacker had been materially higher. A decision was not to be reached merely by these so-called " battles of material." We had neither the resources nor the time for battles of that kind, for the moment was coming nearer when America would begin to come on the scene fully equipped. If before that time our U-boats had not succeeded in making the transport of large masses of troops with their supplies highly questionable, our position would become serious.

The question that pressed for an answer was this : What was there that entitled us to hope for one or more real victories such as our enemies had always failed to secure hitherto? It is easy to give an answer but difficult to explain it. The answer is the word " confidence." Not confidence in our lucky star or vague hopes, still less confidence in numbers and the outward show of strength. It was that confidence with which the commander sends his troops forward into the enemy fire, convinced that they will face the worst and do the seemingly impossible. It was the same confidence which inspired me in 1916 and 1917 when we had subjected our Western Front to an almost superhuman test in order to be able to carry out great attacks elsewhere; the same confidence which had enabled us to keep superior enemy forces in check in all the theatres of war, and even to overthrow them.

Moreover, if the necessary numbers were in existence, it seemed to me that the necessary resolution was everywhere present likewise. I seemed to feel the longing of the troops to get away from the misery and oppression of pure defence. I knew that the German " rabbit "—which one of our bitterest enemies had held up to the derision

v

of the English as "driven from the open into its holes"
—would become the German soldier in his steel helmet
who would rise from his trenches in great and overwhelming anger to put an end by attack to the years of torment
he had suffered in defence.

Moreover, I thought that the summons to attack would
have even greater and more far-reaching consequences.
I hoped that with our first great victories the public at
home would rise above their sullen brooding and ponder-
ing over the times, the apparent hopelessness of our
struggle and impossibility of ending the war otherwise
than by submission to the sentence of tyrannical powers.
Let the sword flash on high and all hearts would rise with
it. It had always been thus; could it be otherwise now?
My hopes soared even beyond the frontiers of our homeland. Under the mighty impression of great German
military victories, I saw the revival of the fighting spirit
in hard-pressed Austria-Hungary, the rekindling of all the
political and national hopes of Bulgaria and the strengthening of the will to hold out even in far-away Turkey.

What a renunciation of my unshakable confidence in
the success of our cause it would have meant if in the face
of my Fatherland and my conscience I had suggested to
my Emperor that we ought to lay down our arms. "Lay
down our arms?" Yes, that is what it meant! We
must not delude ourselves into the belief that our enemies
would not put their claims as high as that. If we once
started on the slippery path of surrender, if we once re-
laxed our efforts to put forth all our strength, no other
alternative could be seen unless we first paralysed both
the enemy's arm and his will. These had been our
prospects in 1917, and later events were to show that

they were our prospects now. We never had any choice except between fighting for victory or a defeat involving extinction. Did our enemies ever say anything else? No other voice ever reached my ear. If any voice in favour of peace ever made itself heard, it did not get through the atmosphere which separated me from the enemy statesmen. I believed that we had both the strength and the military spirit required to seek a decision in one last great passage of arms.

We had now to make up our minds how and where we should seek it. The " how " might in general be summed up in the words, " we must avoid a deadlock in a so-called battle of material." We must aim at a great and if possible surprise blow. If we did not succeed in breaking the enemy resistance at one stroke, this first blow must be followed by others at different points of the enemy lines until our goal was reached.

Of course from the start the ideal objective for my purposes was a complete break-through the enemy lines, a break-through to unlock the gate to open warfare. This gate was to be found in the line Arras—Cambrai—St. Quentin—La Fère. The choice of this front for attack was not influenced by political considerations. We had no idea of attacking there merely because we had the English against us at this point. It is true that I still regarded England as the main pillar of the enemy resistance, but at the same time it was clear to me that in France the desire to injure us to the point of annihilation was no less strong than in England.

Moreover, from the military point of view it was of little importance whether we attacked the French or English first. The Englishman was undoubtedly a less skilful opponent than his brother-in-arms. He did not understand how to control rapid changes in the situation. His methods were too rigid. He had displayed these defects in attack, and I had no reason to think it would be otherwise in defence. Phenomena of that kind are regarded as inevitable by those who have much knowledge of military training. They are due to the lack of appropriate training in peace time. Even a war that lasts years cannot wholly make good the effects of insufficient preparation. But what the Englishman lacked in skill he made up, at any rate partially, by his obstinacy in sticking to his task and his objective; and this was true both of attack and defence. The English troops were of varying value. The élite consisted of men from the Colonies— a fact which is undoubtedly to be attributed to the circumstance that the colonial population is mainly agrarian.

The average Frenchman was a more skilful fighter than his English comrade. On the other hand, he was not so obstinate in his defence. Both our leaders and their men regarded the French artillery as their most dangerous opponent, while the prestige of the French infantryman was not very high. But in this respect also the French units varied with the part of the country from which they were recruited. In spite of the apparent lack of close co-operation on the Anglo-French front, it was certainly to be anticipated that either of the Allies would hasten to the help of the other in case of need. I considered it obvious that in this respect the French would act more promptly and ruthlessly than the English, in view of the political dependence of France on the goodwill of England and our previous experiences in the war.

At the time of our decision to attack, the English army was massed, and had been since the battles in Flanders, mainly on the northern wing of its front which extended from the sea to south of St. Quentin. Another and somewhat weaker group appeared to have remained in the neighbourhood of Cambrai after the battle there. Apart from that, the English forces were apparently distributed pretty evenly. The least strongly held part of their line was that south of the Cambrai group. The English salient in our lines near this town had been somewhat flattened as the result of our counter-attack on November 30, 1917, but it was marked enough to permit of the application of tactical pincers—to use a phrase in vogue—from north and east. By so doing we should be able to cut off the English troops there. Of course it was always doubtful whether the English would keep their forces distributed in the way to which I have referred until our attack began. This depended very largely on whether we should be able to conceal our intentions. A fateful question! All our experience negatived such a possibility, much more a probability. We ourselves had known of the enemy's preparations in all his attempts to break through our Western Front, and generally long before the battles themselves began. We had been able to prevent the extension of the enemy's attacks to the wings practically every time. His months of preparation had never escaped the eagle eye of our scouting planes. Moreover, our ground reconnaissance had developed an extreme sensitiveness to any changes on the enemy's side. The enemy had patently renounced the element of surprise in his great attacks, in view of the apparent impossibility of concealing his extensive preparations and the concentration of troops. We, on the other hand, believed that quite special importance must be attached to surprise. Our efforts in that direction naturally meant that to a certain extent thorough technical preparation had to be sacrificed. To what extent it must be sacrificed was left to the tactical instinct of our subordinate commanders and their troops.

Our great offensive involved tactical training as well as technical preparation. As for defence in the previous year, new principles were now laid down for attack and issued to the troops in comprehensive pamphlets. In our confidence in the offensive spirit of the troops, the centre of gravity of the attack was to be found in thin lines of infantry, the effectiveness of which was intensified by the wholesale employment of machine-guns and by the fact that they were directly accompanied by field-artillery and battle-planes. Of course, the offensive powers of these infantry waves were entirely dependent on the existence of a strong offensive spirit. We were completely renouncing the mass tactics in which the individual soldier finds the driving force in the protection given him by the bodies of the men around him, a form of tactics with which we had become extremely familiar from the practice of the enemy in the East and with which we had had to deal occasionally even in the West.

When the enemy Press announced German mass attacks in 1918 they were using the expression primarily with a view to satisfying the craving for sensation, but also to make the battle pictures more vivid to the minds of their readers and simplify the explanation of events. Where on earth should we have found the men for such mass tactics and such holocausts? Besides, we had had quite enough of watching other armies sink down hopelessly before our lines because our reapers with that scythe of the modern battlefield, the machine-gun, were able to devote themselves to the bloody harvest with greater zeal, the thicker the human corn stood.

What I have said, which is more concerned with the spirit of our battle preparations than their technicalities, must suffice for a general indication of our offensive principles. Of course the German infantryman would still bear the brunt of the battle. His sister arms had the not less glorious and costly task of facilitating his work. The decisive importance of the approaching passage of arms in the West was truly and fully realised by us. We regarded it as an obvious duty to concentrate for our bloody task all effective troops that could in any way be spared from the other theatres of war. Our existing situation and the further developments in the political and economic sphere introduced all kinds of difficulties into the execution of our plans and repeatedly made my personal intervention necessary. I will deal generally with this important question and begin with the East.

On December 15 an armistice had been concluded on the Russian front. In view of the progressive disruption of the Russian Army, we had previously made a beginning with the transport of a large number of our troops from that theatre. Yet some divisions, effective and suitable for manœuvre warfare, had had to remain in Russia and Rumania until we had finally settled with these two countries. Of course it would have entirely corresponded to our military desires if peace bells could have rung in the year 1918 in the East. The place of these bells was taken by the wild, inflammatory speeches of revolutionary doctrinaires with which the conference room in Brest-Litovsk resounded. The great masses of all countries were summoned by these political agitators to shake off the burden of slavery by establishing a reign of terror. Peace on earth was to be ensured by the wholesale massacre of the bourgeoisie. The Russian negotiators, especially Trotsky, degraded the conference table, at which the reconciliation of two mighty opponents was to be effected, to the level of a muddle-headed tubthumper's street corner.

In these circumstances it was hardly surprising that the peace negotiations made no progress. It seemed to me that Lenin and Trotsky behaved more like the victors than the vanquished, while trying to sow the seeds of political dissolution in the rear as well as the ranks of our army. As events were shaping, peace seemed likely to be worse than an armistice. The representatives of our Government indulged in a good deal of false optimism in their dealing with the peace question. Main Headquarters can at any rate claim that it recognised the danger and gave warning of it.

However great may have been the difficulties under which our German Commission at Brest-Litovsk laboured, it was unquestionably my duty to insist that for the sake of our proposed operations in the West peace should be attained in the East at the earliest possible moment. However, affairs only came to a head when on February 10 Trotsky refused to sign the Peace Treaty, but for the rest declared the state of war at an end. In this attitude of Trotsky, which simply flouted all international principles, I could see nothing but an attempt to keep the situation in the East in a state of perpetual suspense. I cannot say whether this attempt revealed the influence of the Entente. In any case the situation which supervened was intolerable from a military point of view. The Imperial Chancellor, Count von Hertling, agreed with this view of the General Staff. On February 13 His Majesty decided that hostilities should be resumed in the East on the 18th.

Our operations met with practically no resistance anywhere. The Russian Government realised the peril with which it was threatened. On March 3 the Treaty of Peace between the Quadruple Alliance and Great Russia was signed at Brest-Litovsk. The military power of Russia was thus out of the war in the legal sense also. Great tracts of country and many peoples were separated from the former united Russian organism, and even in the heart of Russia there was a deep cleavage between Great Russia and the Ukraine. The separation of the border states from the old Empire as a result of the peace conditions was in my view mainly a military advantage. It meant that—if I may use the term—a broad forward zone was created against Russia on the far side of our frontiers. From the political point of view I welcomed the liberation of the Baltic Provinces, because it was to be assumed that from henceforth the German elements there would be able to develop in greater freedom, and the process of German colonisation in that region would be extended.

I need hardly give any assurance that to negotiate with a Russian terrorist Government was extremely disagreeable to a man of my political views. However, we had been compelled to come to some final agreement with the authorities that now held sway in Great Russia. In any case Russia was in a state of the greatest ferment at this time, and personally I did not believe that the reign of terror would last for long.

In spite of the conclusion of peace it was even now impossible for us to transfer all our effective troops from the East. We could not simply abandon the occupied territories to Fate. It was absolutely necessary for us to leave behind strong German forces in the East, if only to maintain a barrier between the Bolshevist armies and the lands we had liberated. Moreover, our operations in the Ukraine were not yet at an end. We had to penetrate into that country to restore order there. Only when that had been done had we any prospect of securing food from the Ukraine, mainly for Austria-Hungary, but also for our own homeland, as well as raw materials for our war industries and war materials for our armies. In these enterprises political considerations played no part so far as Main Headquarters were concerned.

Of very different import was the military assistance which in the spring of that year we sent to Finland in her war of liberation from Russian domination. The Bolshevik Government had not fulfilled the promise it had made us to evacuate this country. We also hoped that by assisting Finland we should get her on our side, and thus make it extremely difficult for the Entente to exercise military influence on the further development of events in Great Russia from the vantage points of Murmansk and Archangel. Further, we were thus gaining a foothold at a point which immediately menaced Petersburg, and this would have great importance if Bolshevik Russia attempted to attack our Eastern Front again. The part played by the small force that was required—it was only a matter of about a division—was a very profitable investment.   My frank sympathies with the Finnish nation in its struggle for liberty were, in my opinion, easily reconciled with the demands of the military situation.

The troops which we had left in Rumania were practically wholly available when the Government of that country saw itself compelled to come to terms with us as the result of the conclusion of peace with Russia.   The rest of our fighting troops which still remained in the East formed the source from which our Western armies could to a certain extent be reinforced in the future.

The transport of the German divisions which we had employed in the campaign against Italy could be begun at once in the course of the winter.   I considered that Austria-Hungary was unquestionably in a position to deal with the situation in Upper Italy by herself.

One important question was whether we could approach Austria-Hungary with the request to place part of her available forces in the East and Italy at our disposal for the approaching decisive battle.   As the result of reports I received, however, I came to the conclusion that these forces would be better employed in Italy than in the mighty conflict in the West.   If by an impressive threat to the whole country Austria-Hungary succeeded in tying down the whole Italian Army, and perhaps also the English and French troops in the line in the North, or if she kept these away from the decisive front by a successful attack, the corresponding relief which we in the West would enjoy would perhaps be greater than the advantage of direct assistance.   We confined ourselves to securing the transfer of some Austro-Hungarian artillery. For the rest I had no doubt that General von Arz would uphold our requests for greater Austro-Hungarian assistance at any time and to the best of his ability.

About this time the Austro-Hungarian Foreign Minister had announced in a speech that the resources of the Danube Monarchy would be employed for the defence of Strasburg as readily as for that of Trieste. This loyal declaration had my full approval. It was only later that I came to know that these expressions of Count Czernin had aroused the most violent opposition among non-German circles in the Danube Monarchy. This political agitation had, therefore, no influence on my decisions as to the amount of Austro-Hungarian help we should require on our future battlefields in the West.

I regarded it as elementary that we should make an attempt to recover for our Western offensive all the effective troops which we had hitherto employed in Bulgaria and Asiatic Turkey. I have already shown how violent was the political opposition to such a step in Bulgaria. General Jekoff was too sensible a soldier not to realise the justice of our demands, but apparently he shared his Sovereign's opinion that the German spiked helmet was indispensable in Macedonia. Thus the transfer of the German troops from the Macedonian front was a very slow process. It was with great reluctance, and after repeated representations on our part, that General Jekoff decided to relieve them by Bulgarian troops from the Dobrudja. The serious reports about the *moral* and attitude of the Bulgarian troops on the Macedonian front which we received from our German commanders on that front finally compelled us to leave behind the rest of the

German infantry, three battalions and some of our numerous artillery units.

Efforts in the same direction had a similar result in Turkey. In the autumn of 1917 our Asiatic Corps had been transferred to Syria with the Turkish divisions which had originally been earmarked for the campaign against Bagdad. The uncertain position on that front compelled us at the beginning of 1918 to increase that corps to double its size. Most of the troops thus required were taken from our forces in Macedonia. Before these reinforcements reached their new destination we thought that a material improvement in the position on the Syrian front had taken place, and therefore negotiated with Enver Pasha for the return of all German troops in that theatre. Enver approved. Urgent military and political representation on the part of the German commander in Syria, as well as the German Government which had been influenced by that commander, compelled us to cancel the recall.

To sum up, I am entitled to claim that on our side nothing was neglected to concentrate all the fighting forces of Germany for the decision in the West. If we did not manage to get hold of every man the reason must be sought in circumstances of the most varied character, but certainly not in any ignorance of the importance of this question to us. In the winter of 1917-8 we had at last attained the object of three years' strivings and longings. No longer threatened in the rear, we could turn to the great decision in the West and must now address ourselves to this passage of arms. We should perhaps have been spared the trouble if we had only overthrown the Russians once and for all in 1915.

I have already shown how much more difficult our task had become by 1918. France was still a mighty opponent, though she might have bled more than we ourselves. At her side was an English army of many millions, fully equipped, well trained and hardened to war. We had a new enemy, economically the most powerful in the world, an enemy possessing everything required for the hostile operations, reviving the hopes of all our foes and saving them from collapse while preparing mighty forces. It was the United States of America and her advent was perilously near. Would she appear in time to snatch the victor's laurels from our brows? That, and that only, was the decisive question! I believed I could answer it in the negative.

The result of our great offensive in the West has given rise to the question whether we should not have been better advised virtually to adopt the defensive on the Western Front in the year 1918, supporting the armies previously employed there with strong reserves, while we concentrated all our other military and political efforts on the business of restoring order and creating economic stability in the East and assisting our Allies in the execution of their military tasks. It would be an error to assume that I had not fully considered such an idea before I adopted the plan of an offensive. I rejected it after mature reflection. Sentiment had no weight with me. How were we to bring the war to a conclusion on such lines? Even though, at the end of 1917, I considered that there was nothing to make me doubt the ability of us Germans to continue our resistance through the coming year, I could not conceal from myself the regrettable decay of the powers of resistance of our Allies. We must devote all our resources to secure a victorious conclusion of the war. That was the more or less express demand of all our Allies. It cannot be urged against us that even our opponents had come to the extreme limits of their material and moral efforts. If we did not attack they might prolong the war for years, and if any among them had been unwilling to go on he would simply have been compelled to do so by the others.

A slow death from exhaustion, unless our enemies succumbed to it first, would unquestionably have been our fate. Even when I consider the present misfortunes of my Fatherland, I feel an unshakable conviction that the proud consciousness that it devoted its last breath to the preservation of its honour and its existence will do more towards the work of reconstruction than if the war had taken the course of slow paralysis to end in exhaustion. Our country would not thus have escaped its present fate, and the uplifting memories of its incomparable heroism would have been lacking. When I seek for a parallel in history I find that the glory of Preussisch-Eylau shone like a star in the darkness of the years 1807-12, though it could not avert the fate of Old Prussia. Its lustre helped so many on the path of reconstruction and enlightenment. Can the German heart have changed? My Prussian heart beats to that refrain.

2

Spa and Avesnes

Approving our suggestion, His Majesty gave orders that our headquarters were to be transferred to Spa, and the removal was carried out on March 8. The change had been necessitated by the coming operations in the West. From our new headquarters we could reach the most important parts of our Western Front in far shorter time than we could have done from Kreuznach. As we wished to be in the closest possible touch with coming events we also selected Avesnes as a kind of advanced headquarters of Main Headquarters. We arrived there on March 19 with the greater part of the General Staff, and found ourselves in the very centre of the headquarters of the Army Groups and armies which were to play the principal parts in the forthcoming battle for a decision.

As regards outward appearance the town was dominated by its mighty but cumbersome old church. The ruins of its old fortifications were a reminder that Avesnes had played a part in military history in days gone by. As far as I remember, units of the Prussian Army had occupied the fortress after the Battle of Waterloo in 1815 and from there had marched on Paris. The district was not touched by the war of 1870-1.

The town is a quiet place embedded in the heart of great woods. Even our presence added little to its activity. I found myself, after an interval of forty-one years, among the French population, and this time on a longer visit. Compared with 1870-1 the different types I saw in the streets seemed to me so unchanged that I could easily have forgotten that there ever had been such an interval. Now, as then, the inhabitants sat before their doors, the men usually lost in thought, the women bustling round and monopolising the conversation, and the children playing and singing on the playground as if the world were quite at peace. Lucky children!

For the rest, our long sojourn at Avesnes confirmed

the general experience that the French population submitted with dignity to the hard fate which the long war meant for them. We were never compelled to take any measures to maintain order or secure our own protection. We were able to confine ourselves to securing quiet for our work.

His Majesty did not take up residence in Avesnes, but lived in his special train during the period of the great events which followed. The train was moved about according to the military situation. This residence of several weeks in the restricted quarters on the train may serve as an example of the simple ways of our War Lord. At such a time he lived entirely with his army. Regard for danger, even from enemy airmen, was quite beyond the range of our Emperor's thoughts.

Our stay at Avesnes during the next few months gave me more frequent opportunities than I had previously enjoyed to come into direct personal touch with the commanders of our Army Groups and armies as well as officers of other higher Staffs. I was particularly glad of the chance of seeing regimental officers. Their experiences and stories, which were usually told in touchingly simple language, were of extreme interest to me, not only from the military but from the purely human point of view.

It was a quite peculiar and special pleasure to be able to pay an occasional visit to the Masurian Regiment which bore my name, the Guards Regiment in which I had served as a young officer through two wars, and the Oldenburg Infantry which I had once commanded. Of course there was little left of the original regiment, but I found the old soldierly spirit in the new men. I was seeing most of the officers and men for the first time—and in many cases the last also. Honour to their memory!

w

CHAPTER XX

1

The "Great Battle" in France

SHORTLY before we left Spa His Majesty issued the Order for the first great battle. I will quote the material portion of this order in full to save a detailed description of our plans. By way of explanation I may remark that the preparations for the great battle are indicated by the rubric "Michael," and that the day and hour of the attack were only inserted when we knew for certain that our preparations were complete.

MAIN HEADQUARTERS
10-3-18

BY HIS MAJESTY'S ORDERS :

1. The Michael attack will take place on the 21.3. The first attack on the enemy's lines is fixed for 9.40 A.M.

2. The first great tactical objective of the Crown Prince Rupprecht's Army Group is to cut off the English in the Cambrai salient and reach the line Croisilles (south-east of Arras)—Bapaume—Péronne. If the attack of the right wing (17th Army) proceeds favourably this army is to press on beyond Croisilles.

   The further task of this Army Group is to push forward in the general direction Arras—Albert, keep its left wing on the Somme at Péronne and intensifying its pressure on the right wing, compel the retirement of the English front facing the 6th Army also, and release further German troops from trench warfare for the general advance. . . .

8. The German Crown Prince's Army Group will first gain the
   line of the Somme south of the Omignon stream (this
   flows into the Somme south of Péronne) and the Crozat
   Canal (west of La Fère).   By pushing on rapidly the 18th
   Army (right wing of the Crown Prince's Army Group)
   is to secure the crossings of the Somme and the Canal. . . .

The tension in which we had left Spa in the evening
of March 18 had increased as we arrived at our new
headquarters at Avesnes.   The beautiful bright weather
of early spring which we had been enjoying had changed.
Violent rain-storms swept over the country.   They did
full justice to the nickname which the French had given
to Avesnes and its neighbourhood.   In themselves clouds
and rain were by no means unwelcome to us in these
days.   They would probably shroud our final preparations.
But had we really any grounds for hoping that the enemy
had not got wind of what we were about?   Here and
there the hostile artillery had been particularly wide-
awake and lively.   But the firing had then died down.
From time to time enemy airmen at night had tried to
observe the most important of our roads with the help
of light-balls and turned their machine-guns on all suspected movements.   But all this supplied no definite data
on which to answer the question : " Can our surprise
succeed ? "

The reinforcements earmarked for the attack entered
the assembly trenches in the final few nights; the last
trench-mortars and batteries were brought up.   The
enemy did not interfere to any appreciable extent !   At
different points parties volunteered to drag heavy guns
right up to our wire and there conceal them in shell-holes.
We believed that we ought to be venturesome if we could

thereby guarantee that the attacking infantry should have artillery support in their passage through the whole enemy defensive system. No hostile counter-measures hindered this preparatory work.

The weather was stormy and rainy almost the whole day on March 20. The prospects for the 21st were uncertain. Local mist was probable. But at midday we decided definitely that the battle should begin in the morning of the following day.

The early morning hours of March 21 found the whole of Northern France, from the coast to the Aisne, shrouded in mist. The higher the sun mounted into the sky the thicker the fog became. At times it limited the range of vision to a few yards. Even the sound waves seemed to be absorbed in the grey veil. In Avesnes we could only hear a distant indefinite roll of thunder coming from the battlefield, on which thousands of guns of every calibre had been belching forth fury since the early hours of the morning.

Unseeing and itself unseen, our artillery had proceeded with its work. It was only our conscientious preparation which offered any guarantee that our batteries were being really effective. The enemy's reply was local, fitful and of varying violence. It looked as if he were groping about for an unseen enemy rather than systematically fighting a troublesome foe.

It was therefore still uncertain whether the English were not fully prepared with their defence and expecting our attack. The veil which hid everything did not lift. About 10 A.M. our brave infantry advanced into the very heart of it. At first we received only vague reports, recitals of objectives reached, contradictions of previous reports, recalls. It was only gradually that the atmosphere of uncertainty cleared and we were in a position to realise that we had broken through the enemy's first line at all points. About midday the mist began to dissolve and the sun to triumph.

By the evening hours we were able to piece together a definite picture of what had been accomplished. The armies on the right wing and the centre of our battle front were to all intents and purposes held up in front of the enemy's second position. The army on the left had made immense progress beyond St. Quentin. There was no doubt that the right wing was faced with the stoutest opposition. The English had suspected the danger which was threatening them from the north and brought up all their available reserves to meet it. On the other hand the left wing had had relatively the easiest task, apparently as the result of a wholesale surprise. In the north our losses had been larger than we expected; otherwise they were in accordance with anticipation.

The results of the day seemed to me satisfactory. Such was also the opinion of the General Staff officers who had followed the troops and were now returning from the battlefield. Yet only the second day could show whether our attack would now share the fate of all those which the enemy had made upon us for years, the fate of finding itself held up after the first victorious break-through.

The evening of the second day saw our right wing in possession of the second enemy position. Our centre had even captured the third enemy line, while the army on the left wing was in full career and now miles away to the west. Hundreds of enemy guns, enormous masses of ammunition and other booty of all kinds were lying behind our lines. Long columns of prisoners were marching eastwards. The destruction of the English troops in the Cambrai salient could not be achieved, however, as, contrary to our expectations, our right wing had not pushed on far and quickly enough.

The third day of the battle made no change in the previous impressions of the course of events; the heaviest fighting was on our right wing, where the English defended themselves with the greatest obstinacy and were still maintaining themselves in their third line. On the other hand we had gained more ground in our centre and also on the left wing. This day the Somme had been reached south of Péronne, and indeed crossed at one point.

It was this day, March 23, that the first shells fell into the enemy's capital.

In view of the brilliant sweep of our attack to the west, a sweep which put into the shade everything that had been seen on the Western Front for years, it seemed to me that an advance on Amiens was feasible. Amiens was the nodal point of the most important railway connections between the two war zones of Central and Northern France (the latter being mainly the English sphere of operations) which had the line of the Somme as a definite boundary. The town was thus of very great strategic importance. If it fell into our hands, or even if we succeeded in getting the town and its neighbourhood under effective artillery fire, the enemy's field of operations would be cleft in twain and the tactical breakthrough would be converted into a strategical wedge, with England on one side and France on the other. It was possible that the strategic and political interests of the two countries might drift apart as the result of such a success. We will call these interests by the names of Calais and Paris. So forward against Amiens!

We did indeed go forward, and with giant strides. And yet it was not quick enough for active imaginations and glowing wishes. For we had to fear that the enemy also would realise the peril in which he now stood, and would do everything in his power to avert it. English reserves from the northern wing, French troops drawn from the whole of Central France were hastening to Amiens and its neighbourhood. It was also to be expected that the French High Command would take our advance in flank from the south.

The evening of the fourth day saw Bapaume in our hands. Péronne and the line of the Somme south of it was already well behind our leading divisions. We were once more treading the old Somme battlefield. For many of our men it was rich in proud, if serious memories, and for all who saw it for the first time it spoke straight to the heart with its millions of shell-holes, its confused medley of crumbling and overgrown trenches, the majestic silence of its desolate wastes and its thousands of graves.

Whole sections of the English front had been utterly routed and were retiring, apparently out of hand, in the direction of Amiens. It was the progress of the army on our right wing which was first held up. To get the battle going again at this point we attacked the hills east of Arras. The attempt only partially succeeded, and the action was broken off. Meanwhile our centre had captured Albert. On the seventh day our left wing, guarding against French attacks from the south, pressed forward through Roye to Montdidier.

The decision was therefore to be sought more and more in the direction of Amiens. But here also we found the resistance stiffening, and our advance became slower and slower. The hopes and wishes which had soared beyond Amiens had to be recalled. Facts must be treated as facts. Human achievements are never more than patchwork. Favourable opportunities had been neglected or had not always been exploited with the same energy, even where a splendid goal was beckoning. We ought to have shouted into the ear of every single man : " Press on to Amiens. Put in your last ounce. Perhaps Amiens means decisive victory. Capture Villers-Brétonneux whatever happens, so that from its heights we can command Amiens with masses of our heavy artillery ! " It was in vain ; our strength was exhausted.

The enemy fully realised what the loss of Villers-Brétonneux would mean to him. He threw against our advancing columns all the troops he could lay hands on. The French appeared, and with their massed attacks and skilful artillery saved the situation for their Allies and themselves.

With us human nature was urgently voicing its claims. We had to take breath. The infantry needed rest and the artillery ammunition. It was lucky for us that we were able to live to a certain extent on the supplies of the beaten foe ; otherwise we should not even have been able to cross the Somme, for the shattered roads in the wide shell-hole area of the first enemy position could only have been made available after days of work. Even now we did not give up all hope of capturing Villers-Brétonneux. On

April 4, we made another attempt to drive the enemy from the village.   The first reports of the progress of our attack on that day were very promising, but the next day brought a reverse and disillusionment at this point.

Amiens remained in the hands of the enemy, and was subjected to a long-range bombardment which certainly disturbed this traffic artery of our foe but could not cut it.

The " Great Battle " in France was over!

2
The Battle on the Lys

Among the battle proposals for the opening of the 1918 campaign we had contemplated and worked out an attack on the English positions in Flanders.   The fundamental idea behind this plan was that we should attack the great easterly bulge of the English northern wing on both sides of Armentières, and by pressing forward in the general direction of Hazebrouck cause the whole line to collapse.   The prospects which opened for us if we made good progress in such an operation were very alluring, but the execution of the attack was faced with most serious obstacles.   In the first place, it was clear that we were dealing with the strongest English group at this point.   This group, concentrated in a comparatively confined area, was quite in a position to bring our attack to a standstill after it had made but little progress.   Such an enterprise would therefore face us with the very danger we were most anxious to avoid.   To that must be added the difficulties of the ground on either side of Armentières over which we had to attack.   In the first place, there were the low-lying meadows of the Lys, several miles broad, and then the river itself to be crossed. In winter this low-lying area was to a large extent flooded, and in spring it was often nothing but a marsh for weeks on end—a real horror for the troops holding the trenches at this point. North of the Lys the ground gradually rose, and then mounted sharply to the great group of hills which had its mighty pillars at Kemmel and Cassel.

It was perfectly hopeless to think of carrying out such an attack before the valley of the Lys was to some extent passable. In normal circumstances of weather, we could only expect the ground to become dry enough by the middle of April. But we thought we could not wait until then to begin the decisive conflict in the West. We had to keep the prospects of American intervention steadily before our eyes. Notwithstanding these objections to the attack, we had the scheme worked out, at any rate in theory. In this working out we provided for the eventuality that our operation at St. Quentin would compel the enemy's leaders to withdraw large reserves from the group in Flanders to meet our break-through there.

This eventuality had materialised by the end of March. As soon as we saw that our attack to the west must come to a standstill, we decided to begin our operations on the Lys front. An inquiry addressed to the Army Group of the Crown Prince Rupprecht elicited the reply that, thanks to the dry spring weather, the attack across the valley of the Lys was already feasible. The enterprise was now taken in hand by the Army Headquarters Staff and the troops with amazing energy.

On April 9, the anniversary of the great crisis at Arras, our storm troops rose from their muddy trenches on the Lys front from Armentières to La Bassée. Of course they were not disposed in great waves, but mostly in small detachments and diminutive columns which waded through the morass which had been upheaved by shells and mines, and either picked their way towards the enemy lines between deep shell-holes filled with water or took the few firm causeways.   Under the protection of our artillery and trench-mortar fire, they succeeded in getting forward quickly in spite of all the natural and artificial obstacles, although apparently neither the English nor the Portuguese, who had been sandwiched in among them, believed it possible.   Most of the Portuguese troops left the battlefield in wild flight, and once and for all retired from the fighting in favour of their Allies.   It must be admitted that our exploitation of the surprise and the Portuguese failure met with the most serious obstacles in the nature of the ground.   It was only with the greatest difficulty that a few ammunition wagons were brought forward behind the infantry.   Yet the Lys was reached by the evening and even crossed at one point.   Here again the decision was to be expected only in the course of the next few days.   Our prospects seemed favourable. On April 10 Estaires fell into our hands and we gained more ground north-west of Armentières.   On the same day our front of attack was extended to the region of Wytschaete.   We again stormed the battered ruins of the much-fought-for Messines.

The next day brought us more successes and fresh hopes.   Armentières was evacuated by the enemy and we captured Merville.   From the south we approached the first terrace of the great group of hills from which our opponent could see our whole attack and command it with his artillery.   From now on progress became slower. It soon came to a stop on our left wing, while our attack in the direction of Hazebrouck was slowly becoming paralysed. In our centre we captured Bailleul and set foot on the hills from the south. Wytschaete fell into our hands, but then this first blow was exhausted.

The difficulties of communication across the Lys valley which had to be overcome by our troops attacking from the south had been like a chain round our necks. Ammunition could only be brought up in quite inadequate quantities, and it was only thanks to the booty the enemy had left behind on the battlefield that we were able to keep our troops properly fed.

Our infantry had suffered extremely heavily in their fight with the enemy machine-gun nests, and their complete exhaustion threatened unless we paused in our attack for a time. On the other hand, the situation urgently exacted an early decision. We had arrived at one of those crises in which the continuation of the attack is extremely difficult, but when the defence seems to be wavering. The release from such a situation can only come from a further attack and not by merely holding on.

We had to capture Mount Kemmel. It had lain like a great hump before our eyes for years. It was only to be expected that the enemy had made it the key to his positions in Flanders. The photographs of our airmen revealed but a portion of the complicated enemy defence system at this point. We might hope, however, that the external appearance of the hill was more impressive than its real tactical value. We had had experiences of this kind before with other tactical objectives. Picked troops which had displayed their resolution and revealed their powers at the Roten-Turm Pass, and in the fighting in the mountains of Transylvania, Serbian Albania and the Alps of Upper Italy, might once more make possible the seemingly impossible. A condition precedent to the success of our further attacks in Flanders was that the French High Command should be compelled to leave the burden of the defence in that region to their English Allies. We therefore first renewed our attacks at Villers-Brétonneux on April 24, hoping that the French commander's anxiety about Amiens would take precedence of the necessity to help the hard-pressed English friends in Flanders. Unfortunately this new attack failed. On the other hand, on April 25 the English defence on Mount Kemmel collapsed at the first blow. The loss of this pillar of the defence shook the whole enemy front in Flanders. Our adversary began to withdraw from the Ypres salient which he had pushed out in months of fighting in 1917. Yet to the last Flemish city he clung as if to a jewel which he was unwilling to lose for political reasons.

But the decision in Flanders was not to be sought at Ypres, but by attacking in the direction of Cassel. If we managed to make progress in that quarter, the whole Anglo-Belgian front in Flanders would have to be withdrawn to the west. Just as our thoughts had soared beyond Amiens in the previous month, our hopes now soared to the Channel Coast. I seemed to feel how all England followed the course of the battle in Flanders with bated breath. After that giant bastion, Mount Kemmel, had fallen, we had no reason to flinch from the difficulties of further attacks. It is true that we had received reports about the failure of certain of our units. Mistakes and omissions had occurred on the battlefield.

Yet such mistakes and omissions are inherent in human nature. He who makes the fewest will remain master of the battlefield. We were now the master and intended to remain so. Victories such as we had gained at Kemmel not only elate the troops who actually win them, but revitalise the spirits of whole armies. Therefore on! We must have Cassel at least! From that vantage point the long-range fire of our heaviest guns could reach Boulogne and Calais. Both towns were crammed full with English supplies, and were also the principal points of debarkation of the English armies. The English army had failed in the most surprising fashion in the fight for Kemmel. If we succeeded in getting it to ourselves at this point, we should have a certain prospect of a great victory. If no French help arrived, England would probably be lost in Flanders. Yet in England's dire need this help was once more at hand. French troops came up with bitter anger against the friend who had surrendered Kemmel, and attempted to recover this key position from us. It was in vain. But our own last great onslaught on the new Anglo-French line at the end of April made no headway.

On May 1 we adopted the defensive in Flanders, or rather, as we then hoped, passed to the defensive for the time being.

8

The Battle of Soissons—Rheims

After the conclusion of the battles in Flanders, we still adhered to the plans we had chosen for the attainment of our great goal. Of course we intended to proceed with our task of " shaking the hostile edifice by closely connected partial blows in such a way that sooner or later the whole structure would collapse.'' Thus were our plans described in a memorandum drawn up at that time. Twice had England been saved by France at a moment of extreme crisis. Perhaps the third time we should succeed in gaining a decisive victory over this adversary. The attack on the English northern wing remained as before the *leit motiv* of our operations. I believed that the war would be decided if this attack were successfully carried through. If we reached the Channel Coast we should lay hands directly on England's vital arteries. In so doing we should not only be in the most favourable position conceivable for interrupting her maritime communications, but our heaviest artillery would be able to get a portion of the South Coast of Britain under fire. The mysterious marvel of technical science, which was even now sending its shells into the French capital from the region of Laon, could be employed against England also. The marvel need only be a little greater to get the heart of the English commercial and political world within its range from the coast near Calais. That would be a serious prospect for Great Britain, not only for the moment, but for her whole future! These triumphs of the art of Krupp can now be constructed anywhere. Whether they are to be regarded as a guarantee of peace or an incitement to war the future must decide. England, with her far-seeing views and extreme sensitiveness to the peril threatening her in the future, has already thought this all out. Perhaps, in secret, France too has already drawn the appropriate inference. It is obvious that between friends utterance could not be given to such thoughts. Yet each of them feels the weapon in the pocket of the other!

In May, 1918, it was our immediate business to attempt to separate the two friends in Flanders once more. England was easier to beat when France was far away. If we faced the French with a crisis on their own front, they would withdraw the divisions which were now in line on the English front in Flanders. The greatest possible haste was necessary, or the reinforced enemy might snatch the initiative from us. A dangerous enemy irruption into our defensive fronts, which were not very strong, would have thrown out our calculations and perhaps upset them altogether. The sensitive point of the French front was the direction of Paris. At the time the political atmosphere of Paris seemed to be heavily charged. Our shells and attacks from the air had hitherto not produced the explosion, but we had reason to hope that there would be an explosion if we advanced our lines nearer to the city. From the information at our disposal the French defences in the region of Soissons were particularly lightly held, yet here the ground was extremely unfavourable for attack.

When I paid my first visit to Laon at the beginning of the year 1917, I walked on the terrace of the Préfecture which is in the southern part of this peculiarly sited hill-town. The whole region around me was exposed to full view on this splendid spring morning. Bounded by two groups of hills on the west and east, the landscape stretched away to the south and there ended in a mighty wall, the Chemin des Dames. One hundred and three years before, after days of violent fighting south of the Marne, Prussian and Russian forces under the command of Blücher had crossed the heights of the Chemin des Dames from the south, and after the murderous action at

Craonne had been drawn up for battle against the great Corsican in the immediate neighbourhood of Laon. In the night of March 9-10, 1814, the battle on the eastern slopes of the steep hills of Laon had been decided in favour of the Allies.

It was on the heights of the Chemin des Dames that the French spring offensive of 1917 had been brought to naught. Fighting had raged on this position for weeks with varying fortune, and then silence had reigned. In October, 1917, however, the right shoulder of this ridge, north-east of Soissons, had been stormed by the enemy and we were forced to evacuate the Chemin des Dames and establish our defences behind the Ailette.

Our troops had now to attack once more over the slopes of the Chemin des Dames. The success of this enterprise depended even more on surprise than had been the case with our previous offensives. If we failed in this respect, our attack would break down on the northern face of the high ridge. However, our surprise completely succeeded.

I will venture to give the peculiar explanation which was put forward to account for our success. An officer who had taken part in the preparations on the Ailette expressed the opinion that the croaking of the frogs in the streams and damp meadows had been so loud that it was impossible to hear the sounds made by the approach of our bridging trains. Others may think what they like about this piece of news, but I can at any rate give the assurance that I had not been previously irritating my informant with chestnuts from my sporting experiences! Another and more illuminating explanation to account for the success with which we concealed the preparations

x

for our attack was given by a captured enemy officer. According to his story, on the day before our attack began a Prussian non-commissioned officer was brought in who had been captured in a raid. In reply to the question whether he could tell anything about a German attack he spoke as follows: " There will be a tremendous German bombardment in the early morning hours of May 27. However, it will only be a feint, for the German infantry attack which will follow it will only be carried out by a few volunteer detachments. The *moral* of the German troops has been so shaken by their fearful losses at St. Quentin and in Flanders that the infantry has openly resisted the orders for a general attack." The officer said quite frankly that this report had seemed to him entirely credible, so that on May 27 he had awaited the development of events with perfect unconcern. Perhaps these reminiscences of mine will come to the knowledge of that brave German soldier. I press his hand in thought and thank him on behalf of the whole army, to which he rendered so priceless a service, and in the name of the many hundreds, perhaps thousands, of his brave comrades whose lives he saved by his presence of mind. The deception of the enemy officer would not, perhaps, have been so complete if hostile propaganda, with its silly exaggeration of our previous losses, had not prepared the ground for belief in the story of the Prussian non-commissioned officer. Thus propagandist lies and exaggerations prove a boomerang from time to time.

The battle began on May 27, and everything went brilliantly. At the outset we were bound to anticipate that our attack would come to a halt on the Aisne—Vesle line and would be unable to get beyond that sector. We were therefore not a little surprised when we received a report about midday on the opening day that smoke from German shrapnel could already be seen on the southern bank of the Aisne and that our infantry would cross the same day.

The centre of our complete tactical break-through reached the Marne from Château-Thierry to Dormans in a few days. Our wings wheeled towards Villers-Cotterêts on the west, and on the east against Rheims and the hilly region south of that city. Our booty was colossal, for the whole area of concentration of the French spring offensive of 1917 was in our hands with its immense supplies of all kinds. The construction of new roads and hutments for thousands of men, as well as much else, furnished a proof of the immense scale on which the French had then prepared their attack in many months of strenuous labour. We had made short work of the affair! It was during these days that I paid a visit to the battlefields of Laon. Since the winter of 1917 life there had certainly lost its almost peaceful character. A few days after our huge guns had opened fire on Paris from the forests of Crépy, west of Laon, enemy batteries in the valley of the Aisne had begun to fire upon the unfortunate town. I do not mean to suggest that the enemy raged against his own flesh and blood without sound military reasons. They believed that the ammunition required for our batteries which were thus annoying Paris had to pass through Laon, and it was a very natural mistake. As they fired at the station a large number of big shells fell into the town, which was still thickly populated, and, moreover, enemy airmen dropped bombs at all hours of the day. Those of the afflicted inhabitants who could not tear themselves from their homes, threatened with destruction as they were, had to live in cellars or dug-outs, and offered a picture of wholesale misery such as we had had to witness for the same reason at other points behind our Western Front without being able to do anything. On the very first day of the attack the enemy long-range guns in the valley of the Aisne had been captured, and with that the bombardment of Laon had come to an end. A member of one of their guns' crews was taken through the town as a prisoner. He requested to be allowed to visit the quarter which had been bombarded, as he was interested to see where the shots from his gun had fallen. What an extraordinary revelation of the depths to which a heart hardened in war can sink!

I must readily admit that the war did not always have that effect, even with our enemies. They too knew what it was to feel the throbbing of a human heart after a hand-to-hand struggle. Of the examples of which I heard I will give just one. It was on March 21 in St. Quentin, which was still under heavy English fire. German columns were blocking the bombarded streets which were being shelled. Enemy prisoners coming from the battle and carrying our wounded were forced to halt. They laid their burdens down. A severely wounded German private, far nearer death than life, raised his stiffening arm and groaned to his bearer who was bending over him : " Mutter, Mutter." The English ear understood the German sound. The Tommy knelt down by the side of the grenadier, stroked his cold hand, and said : " Mother, yes ; Mother is here ! "

I myself saw the workings of deep human feeling on these battlefields. In company with a German general

I was walking on the heights west of Craonne just after these had been stormed. He bent over all the unburied enemy dead and covered their faces, a tribute to the majesty of death. He looked after the living also, supplied such of the wounded as had remained behind, because they were too weak to move, from his own stock, and arranged for their comfortable transport. I had had an opportunity earlier on to observe the real humanity of this German. In the March of this year in his company I was driving past some columns of enemy prisoners on which his serious gaze was fixed in deep thought. When we reached the head of one of these columns he had a halt called and spoke to the assembled enemy officers a few words of praise of the bravery of their troops, consoling them with the reflection that the bitterest fate—that of capture—was often the lot of those who had showed the greatest courage. His words seemed to produce a great effect, especially on a very tall young officer who, in intense emotion, had been hanging his head as if from shame. The thin form now straightened itself like a young fir tree freed from the weight of snow, and its grateful glance met the eyes—of my Emperor!

With a view to broadening our front of attack we had extended the right wing of our attack west to the Oise even while the battle in the Marne salient was still in progress. The attack was only partially successful. Another which we made from the Montdidier—Noyon line in the direction of Compiègne on June 9 only got half-way to that town. Moreover, our efforts in the direction of Villers-Cotterêts yielded no better results. We were thus led to the conclusion that in the Compiègne

—Villers-Cotterêts region we had the main enemy resistance before us, to break which we had not the resources at our disposal.

By way of conclusion, let me sum up my description of the Soissons—Rheims battle with the comment that the fighting had carried us much farther than had originally been intended. Once more unexpected successes had filled us with fresh hopes and given us fresh objectives. That we had not completely attained these objectives was due to the gradual exhaustion of the troops we employed. It was not in keeping with our general intentions that we should employ more divisions in the operation in the region of the Marne. Our gaze was still directed steadfastly at Flanders.

4

Retrospect and Prospects at the End of June, 1918

From the military point of view, what we had accomplished in the three great battles completely put in the shade everything that had been done in offensive operations in the West since August, 1914. The greatness of the German victories was clearly shown by the extent of the ground gained, the amount of booty, and the bloody losses inflicted on the enemy. We had shaken the structure of the enemy resistance to its very foundation. Our troops had shown themselves in every respect equal to the great demands we had made upon them. In weeks of offensive fighting the German soldier had proved that the old spirit had not been paralysed in the years of defence, but that it had risen to the heights of the moral elation of 1914 as soon as the word "Forward" was given. The impetuosity of our infantry had not failed to produce its effect on the foe. "What an admirable and gallant infantry you have!" said an enemy officer to one of my General Staff officers. In close co-operation with the infantry their sister arms had stood in the front in all situations. A single common impulse had permeated the whole organism, down to the last private on the last ammunition wagon. Had they not all pressed forward to play their part, lend their aid and share the emotions of the great event? How often had we not heard the shouts of triumph, the songs of victory and the fervent prayers of gratitude? I myself had once more enjoyed on these battlefields that spirit which charmed me like a breath from my far-away youth. The span of a man's life separated me from those days, but my man's heart and my German soldier's instincts had remained unchanged. Our brave boys in the old blue coat had spoken and sung in the camps of Königgrätz and Sedan exactly as our field-greys were now speaking and singing in the great battles for our Fatherland and our existence, our Emperor and our Empire.

Unfortunately everything we had done had not hitherto been enough to wound our adversaries to death in a military and political sense. There was no sign of surrender on the enemy's part. On the contrary, each military defeat seemed only to strengthen the enemy's lust for our destruction. This impression was in no wise diminished by the fact that here and there the voice of moderation was heard in the hostile camp. The dictatorial authority of the political organisms against which we were fighting was on the whole in no way injured. They held the wills and the resources of their nations together as if with iron bands, and by more or less autocratic methods suppressed the capacity for harm of all who dared to think differently from the tyrants in power. To me there was something very impressive in the working of these autocratic powers. They kept their own hopes alive and turned the attention of their peoples mainly to the gradual relaxation of our efforts. In their opinion, these efforts were gradually bound to collapse. Hunger in the German homeland, the fighting at the front, the poison of propaganda, bribery, pamphlets from the air, internal dissensions had hitherto failed to bring us to destruction. Now another factor was at work : the help of America. We had made the acquaintance of her first trained troops at Château-Thierry. They had attacked us there, and had proved themselves clumsily but firmly led. They had taken our weak units by surprise, thanks to their numerical superiority.

With the appearance of the Americans on the battlefield the hopes which the French and English had so long cherished were at length fulfilled. Was it remarkable that the enemy statesmen were now less inclined than ever for a peaceful compromise with us? The destruction of our political and economic existence had long been decided upon, even though they tried to conceal this intention under threadbare and sophistical professions of moderation. They used such phrases only when it served their propagandist ends, either of making the necessary bloodshed tolerable to their own peoples or of destroying the resolution of our nation. Thus for us the end of the war was not in sight.

In the middle of June the general military situation had materially changed for the worse for the Quadruple Alliance. After a promising beginning the Austro-

Hungarian offensive in Italy had failed. Although our adversaries there were not strong enough to turn the failure of the Austro-Hungarian enterprise to greater advantage, the collapse of the offensive was accompanied by consequences which were worse than if it had never been attempted. Our Ally's misfortune was also a disaster for us. The enemy knew as well as we did that with this attack Austria-Hungary had thrown her last weight into the scales of war. From now onwards the Danube Monarchy ceased to be a danger for Italy. We must certainly anticipate that Italy would now be unable to refuse the urgent solicitations of her Allies and would herself send troops to the decisive theatre in the West, not only to prove the existence of a political united front, but to play a really effective part in the coming battle. If we were not to take this fresh burden on our own shoulders, we must make efforts to get Austro-Hungarian divisions sent to our Western Front. For us, this was the main motive for our request for immediate direct reinforcements from Austria-Hungary. We did not expect any great effect from these reinforcements, at any rate at first. The fate of the whole Quadruple Alliance hung more than ever on the strength of Germany.

The question was whether our resources would be sufficient to secure a victorious conclusion of the war. I have already spoken of the brilliant achievements of our troops; before I can answer that question I must turn to another and less pleasing side.

With all my affection for our soldiers and gratitude for what they had done, I could not entirely close my eyes to those defects in the structure of our army which had been revealed in the course of the long war. The lack

of a sufficient number of well-trained commanders of the
lower ranks had made itself very much felt in our great
offensive battles. Battle discipline had occasionally gone
to pieces. It was natural enough in itself that a private,
finding himself in the middle of plentiful supplies in an
enemy depôt, should thoroughly enjoy food and other
delicacies which he had not tasted for a very long time.
But he should never have been allowed to do so at the
wrong time, and thereby neglect his duties. Quite apart
from the damaging effect of such behaviour on the spirit
of the troops, there was also the danger that favourable
situations would not be exploited, and indeed would be
allowed to turn to our disadvantage.

The battles had made further great gaps in our ranks,
gaps that could not be filled up. Many an infantry regiment needed reconstruction from top to bottom.
Generally speaking the material available was no longer
of the same value as the old. The weaknesses of the
situation at home were frequently mirrored in the *moral*
of the recruits who came to us in the field. It is true that
public opinion at home had been greatly revitalised in
many quarters by the influence of our military victories.
The news from the front was followed with the greatest
anxiety, and the public hoped for a rapid and successful
conclusion of the fearful conflict. Hunger, the loss of
life and the feeling of apprehension seemed not to have
been in vain, and much was forgotten or endured with
manly stoicism as long as a happy end of the colossal trial
seemed to be approaching. Thus the victories of the army
made good many of the omissions of our political leadership. But the starting-point for the process of demoralisation which was to destroy our whole national organism was

provided by the unpatriotic passions of a certain section of the German people who were permeated by political notions which had degenerated as the result of self-interest and self-seeking. These were men whose shaken nerves and moral depravity prompted them to regard the victory of the enemy as the herald of peace and happiness for the Fatherland, men who could see nothing but good in the camp of the enemy and nothing but evil in our own. Trotsky had certainly not wasted his words on the desert air of Brest-Litovsk. His political heresies had swarmed over our frontier posts and found numerous admirers among all classes and from the most varying motives. Enemy propaganda continued its work in public and private. It invaded every department of our activities. Thus the diminution of the will to resist in our people and army threatened to join with the enemy's lust for our destruction to compass our ruin. Military victory seemed to provide the only way out of so critical a situation. To reach a successful end by that means was not only my unshakable resolve but also my sure hope. For such a triumph it was essential that we should not lose the initiative. That meant we must remain on the offensive. We should find ourselves under the hammer the minute we let it slip from our hands.

We could fight on so long as the homeland gave us the physical and moral forces which were still at her disposal ; so long as she retained her courage and her confidence in final victory and so long as our Allies did not fail us. Such were my thoughts and sentiments as I turned to the development of our further plans.

CHAPTER XXI

1

The Plan of the Rheims Battle

THE situation in the Marne salient after the June action came to an end gave me the impression of an imperfect and uncompleted task. Although we occupied this salient from the middle of June, we could not remain there permanently. The lines of communication in the mighty semicircle were defective. They were just good enough for a state of relative inactivity, but threatened serious complications if a great battle lasting any length of time should flame up. We had only one railway, of very slight capacity, at our disposal as the principal line of supply of our great mass of troops to an area which was relatively confined. Moreover, the deep salient obviously invited our enemy to attack it from all sides.

A real improvement of our supply system as well as our tactical situation was only possible if we captured Rheims. In the battles of May and June we had not managed to get possession of the town. We had then exercised our main pressure principally to the west of it. The capture of Rheims must now be the object of a special operation, but the operation thus required fitted into the general framework of our plans.

I have already emphasised that after we broke off the

Lys battle we did not abandon our goal of dealing the English a decisive blow in Flanders. Our offensive at Soissons had been in keeping with that idea, for it had compelled the enemy High Command to withdraw the French reinforcements from the English front in Flanders.

In the interval we had proceeded with our preparations for the new Flanders battle. While the work was proceeding on the future fronts of attack the divisions earmarked for the execution of our plans were billeted in Belgium and Northern France for the purpose of rest and training.

I had no fear of any offensive counter-measures on the part of the English. Even though the larger portion of the English Army had now had several months in which to recover the fighting qualities which had been so seriously affected, it appeared improbable that the English would venture on an offensive in view of the dangers threatening them in Flanders.

Our former experiences enabled me to hope that we should soon settle with the English main armies in Flanders when once we had succeeded in keeping the French away from that battlefield for all time. The resumption of the attack at Rheims would therefore serve our greater and further purpose of seeking a decision against the English main armies.

The situation on the French front at the beginning of July was more or less as follows : General Foch kept the bulk of his reserves in the region of Compiègne and Villers-Cotterêts. From a strategical point of view this position was very favourable. They were prepared to meet any further attack of ours in the direction of these two towns, but they were also in a position, thanks to their extraordinarily good railway communications, to be transferred rapidly from their present concentration area to any part of the French and English front. It seemed to me highly improbable that Foch would attempt a great offensive before strong American reinforcements arrived, unless he found himself driven to such a step by a particularly inviting situation or urgent necessity.

There were apparently no large bodies of enemy troops south of the Marne. On the other hand, there was unquestionably a strong hostile group at Rheims and in the hills south of it, a group which comprised English and Italian units as well as French. On the rest of the French front the situation was not materially different from what it had been at the time of our spring offensive. The position on these fronts was not essentially changed by the perpetual replacement of worn-out divisions by troops from other parts of the line. We were not absolutely clear about the arrival of the American reinforcements, but it was obvious that the American masses would now be poured out uninterruptedly on the soil of France. Our U-boats were unable to hinder or limit these movements, just as they had previously failed to reduce the shipping available to the enemy to a figure which made this mass transport impossible. In view of the urgent necessity of rapid and comprehensive military assistance for France and England, the enemy put on one side considerations of the food supply and economic necessities of their countries. We had to find some way of dealing with this situation. If we worked the intended attack on Rheims in close strategic co-operation with our plans in Flanders we had still to decide the question what

extension we should wish and have to give to the operation
at Rheims. We had originally intended to be satisfied
with the capture of the town. The possession of Rheims
would be settled by the occupation of the hilly district
between Epernay and Rheims. The main purpose of our
attack was the capture of these hills. To facilitate our
advance at that point—and that meant to eliminate the
danger of a hostile flank attack from the south bank of
the Marne—a considerable force was to cross to the south
side of this river on both sides of Dormans, and then
also press on to Epernay. The crossing of the river in
the teeth of an opponent prepared to dispute it was
certainly a bold operation. However, in view of our
successive experiences in crossing various rivers and
streams, we did not regard such an attempt as too
hazardous in this case. Our principal difficulty was not
in mastering the river sector, but in proceeding with the
action on the far side of the obstacle. Artillery and all
war material and supplies for the troops engaged could
only be brought up by temporary bridges, which naturally
offered easy targets for the long-range guns and bombing
squadrons of the enemy. After we had originally decided
to limit our operation practically to the capture of Rheims,
our plan was extended in the course of various conferences
by adding an attack eastwards and right into Champagne.
On the one hand our motive was an intention to cut off
the Rheims salient from the south-east also. On the other
we believed that, in view of our recent experiences, we
might perhaps reach Châlons-sur-Marne, attracted as we
were by the prospect of great captures of prisoners and
war material, if an operation on such a scale succeeded.
We therefore decided to face the risk of weakening our

forces at decisive points for the sake of securing a broad front of attack.

Of course it was of great importance to us that our new operation should begin soon. Thanks to the arrival of American reinforcements, time was working not for but against us. To find a proper balance between the requirements of preparation and the demands of the general situation was our special problem, and certainly not the easiest element in our decision. Quite apart from purely tactical preparations, such as bringing up and assembling everything required for the attack to the appropriate front, and in spite of the claims of the general situation, we could not ignore the difficulties which the proper rest and recuperation of our troops would put in the way of fresh operations. Thus in the case in question we could not fix the date of the attack for earlier than July 15.

2

The Rheims Battle

In the early hours of July 15 our thousand-stringed artillery began to play its battle tune on the new front of attack. It was equally active on our side of the Marne. At the outset the reply of the enemy was not particularly violent, though it gradually became more so. We had noticed nothing which seemed to indicate that the enemy front had been reinforced or special counter-measures taken. Our infantry succeeded in crossing to the southern bank of the Marne. Enemy machine-gun nests were destroyed; we mounted the heights on the far side of the river and captured a number of guns. The news of this first advance reached us very soon in Avesnes.

It relieved our natural anxiety and increased our hopes.

As on the Marne, the battle flamed up in a wide circle round Rheims without actually touching the town itself and its immediate neighbourhood. The town was to fall into our hands by being cut off from both sides. In Champagne and away to the Argonne the first enemy defensive system had been destroyed by the fire of our artillery and trench mortars. Behind the enemy's front lines there was a great maze of trenches which were the legacy of earlier battles. No one could say whether we should find them occupied, wholly or partially. In any case they offered the enemy innumerable strong points, and very little work would have been required to make them serviceable again and suitable to play a part in some new defensive scheme. On the other hand our opponents here in Champagne appeared to be quite unprepared to resist, judging by first impressions. The reply of their artillery was not very strong. It was apparently loosely and remarkably deeply distributed.

After concentrating our heaviest fire on the first enemy lines, as in previous offensive battles, these tightly-packed storm clouds began their devastating march across the hostile defences. Our infantry followed. The first enemy lines were stormed, practically without resistance, along the whole front. The attack was continued, but as soon as our barrage lifted from the second objective, in order to make way for the infantry, an unexpected and violent resistance on the part of the enemy was encountered. The enemy's artillery fire began to swell mightily. Our troops nevertheless attempted to struggle on. In vain! The infantry guns were brought up. They arrived partly

Y

horse-drawn and partly man-handled, for horses were of little use in this wilderness of shell-holes. Scarcely were the guns in position before they lay in fragments on the ground. The enemy had obviously used his second position as his principal line of defence. Our most effective artillery preparation had, therefore, been practically without result. A new system of defence against the destructive effects of our massed artillery had been introduced and employed by the enemy—thanks to a German traitor, as the enemy subsequently announced in triumph to the whole world!

The situation in Champagne remained unchanged until the evening of the first day.

Our operations south-west of Rheims and on both sides of the Marne took a more favourable course. South of the river our infantry pressed forward for nearly a league, exercising its main pressure in the direction of Epernay. By the evening we had got a third of the way, after very severe fighting. North of the river also our attack had made progress in the " Mountain of the Forest of Rheims," greater than the chalk cliffs of the Chemin des Dames, a medley of heights cleft by deep gullies and for the most part crowned with dense forest. The whole district was eminently suited for the most obstinate defence, for it made it extremely difficult for the attacker to concentrate the full fury of his artillery on definite targets. Yet our infantry made progress. For the first time they had met Italian troops on the Western Front, troops who apparently fought with little enthusiasm on French soil.

By the evening of July 15 we had captured about fifty guns on the whole front of attack. Fourteen thousand prisoners were reported. The results certainly did not correspond to our high hopes. But we expected more on the following day. In Champagne the morning of July 16 passed without our troops making definite progress at any point. We were faced with the difficult alternative either of breaking off the attack at this point or renewing our attempts at a decision with our forces, which were not very numerous. We ran the risk of seeing our troops bleed to death in vain, or in the most favourable case suffer such heavy losses that they would hardly be in a condition thoroughly to exploit the advantages they had gained. Our goal at Châlons had, therefore, vanished into the dim distance. For these reasons I approved the suggestion that we should dig in at this point. On the other hand we adhered to our plan of continuing our attacks south of the Marne and in the Rheims hills. During the day we were gradually forced to the defensive on the far side of the river. The enemy counter-attacked us with strong forces. In the direction of Epernay, however, we gained more ground on both sides of the river. By the evening we were half-way to the town—that is, about six miles off. In the Rheims hills we were approaching the Epernay— Rheims road in spite of desperate counter-attacks on the part of the enemy. The fate of Rheims seemed to hang by a thread. Even if all the rest of our plan could now be regarded as a failure, Rheims at least would fall. The town was an important military objective for us, and therefore justified the effort. If we captured it, perhaps a very great impression might be made on the enemy.

On July 17 the battle died down in Champagne. South of the Marne the situation began to change ever more to our disadvantage. It is true that we held the ground we had gained against severe enemy attacks; but our lines were so near to the river, and therefore had so little depth, that a reverse might prove fatal. Moreover, our temporary bridges across the Marne were increasingly in danger from the long-range fire of hostile artillery and French bombing squadrons. We had, therefore, to withdraw to the northern bank as we could not gain any more ground on the southern. Hard though it was for me, I ordered the withdrawal of our troops to the north bank of the Marne. The movement was carried out in the night of July 20-21.

In the Rheims hills the enemy attacks continued with extreme desperation on July 17. They were beaten off. But for us also further progress was impossible for the time being. It required a fresh and thorough preparation.

We seemed to have very little left of all we had striven for. The operation had apparently failed and, so far as the French front was concerned, nothing definite had been gained. But it was not impossible that it might prove very valuable for our attack on the Flanders front. The battles had not been in vain if the only result we achieved was to keep the French forces away from the English defences.

With this thought in mind, General Ludendorff went to visit the Army Group of Crown Prince Rupprecht on the evening of July 17 in order to discuss the proposed attack on the English northern wing in greater detail.

For the execution of our plans in the region of Rheims it was essential that the western flank of the great Marne salient between Soissons and Château-Thierry should stand

firm. It was to be assumed that our offensive would provoke counter-measures on the part of the French reserves
concentrated in the neighbourhood of Compiègne and
Villers-Cotterêts. If General Foch were in a position to
embark on active operations at all, he would have to
abandon his previous attitude of passivity as soon as our
plan of attack across the Marne and at Rheims was
revealed. I have already said that the French commander
knew of our plans in time and had plenty of opportunity
to make preparations to meet them.

In the case of a French attack from the general direction of Villers-Cotterêts the task of our troops in line
between the Aisne and the Marne was therefore not a
simple one. We had disposed a number of divisions
behind our forward lines and believed consequently that
we could proceed in full confidence to the great attack on
Rheims which I have described. It is true that the troops
between Soissons and Château-Thierry were not all fresh,
but they had fought so brilliantly in the previous battles
that I regarded them now as fully equal to their task. The
main consideration, in my view, was that every part of
our defences there should keep the probability of a strong
enemy attack continuously in mind. Whether there were
omissions in this respect on the Soissons—Château-Thierry
front will probably always remain a subject of debate. In
view of later information, I myself believe that the initial
successes which were gained in our operations on the
Marne and near Rheims from July 15 to 17 made some
of our troops on the Soissons—Château-Thierry front
inclined to ignore the seriousness of the position on their
own front. During those days these troops could hear the
thunder of the guns on the battlefield. They knew of our

crossing of the Marne and the success it promised. Exaggerated accounts of our victories reached them, as happened so often, through irregular channels. There was talk of the capture of Rheims and of great victories in Champagne. However, on their own front everything was quiet for these three days, unnaturally quiet to an expert observer, but agreeably quiet to anyone who liked to enjoy the sensation and had no intimate knowledge of the situation. Phenomena observed in the direction of Villers-Cotterêts, which still had our full attention on July 15, were deemed less worthy of notice on the 17th. Messages which were transmitted immediately to all our telephone stations when our operation began seemed to get held up at some intermediate station on the third day. Thus touch with the situation was to some extent lost and the first feeling of anxiety had passed off.

On the morning of July 18 some of our troops, who were not in line at the time, went out on harvest work in the cornfields. Suddenly a violent hail of shells descended upon the back areas. Harassing fire? Our own artillery replied but feebly, apparently because a pretty thick haze veiled everything. The *tat-tat* of machine guns began on a broad front and showed that it was a question of more than harassing fire. Before the situation was definitely ascertained enemy tanks appeared in the high corn. The enemy was undoubtedly attacking on the whole front from the Aisne to the Marne. Our first lines had already been broken through in places. The sector between the Ourcq and Soissons appeared to be the greatest danger point. While what was left of our decimated and isolated troops in the front lines were fighting with the fury of despair, our reserves farther back attempted to form and hold a new line of resistance until the divisions in support could be brought up for a counter-attack. Many a heroic deed was done. In parts of the line which were temporarily recovered, our troops found German machine-gun nests in which every single man of the guns' crews lay dead surrounded by whole circles of fallen opponents. Yet even heroism such as this could no longer save the situation; it could only prevent an utter catastrophe. The enemy had penetrated particularly deeply towards Soissons and farther south; that is, at our most sensitive point, the western pillar of the Marne salient south of the Aisne. The enemy pressed down from here on the rest of our line of defence as far as Château-Thierry. What was worse, he was approaching the single line of railway communicating with the Marne salient at the point where it turns south from the valley of the Aisne east of Soissons into the centre of our great semicircle.

The position was thus serious for us from the very first moment. It threatened to become a real catastrophe unless we succeeded in restoring the original situation or, at any rate, preventing it from getting any worse. It was my desire and intention to take the enemy irruption in flank from the north across the Aisne near Soissons and destroy him where he stood. However, the necessary concentration would have taken too much time, and so I had to accept the counter-proposal that we should first completely secure the part of our front which had been attacked, in order to be masters of our own decisions once more. All the reserves which were available were therefore employed to that end. Unfortunately the crisis was not overcome but only postponed. The enemy broke through at other points and aggravated our situation in the Marne salient. How did it help us that, generally speaking, the enemy onslaught south of the Ourcq was a failure, and more particularly that the strong but unskilfully led American attacks collapsed before our weak lines, especially at Château-Thierry? We could not and must not allow the situation to hang in the balance for any length of time. It would have been madness. We therefore withdrew our left wing from Château-Thierry and at first retired a short distance eastwards while still keeping our flank on the Marne.

In conformity with our decision of July 17 we had withdrawn from the southern bank of this river in good time after very severe fighting. The splendid behaviour of our troops—thanks to which all the French attacks had failed—had enabled us successfully to overcome the critical situation at that point. The retirement had been carried out even more successfully than we expected. It was only on July 21 that, after powerful artillery preparation, the enemy attacked our evacuated lines—tanks in front and strong columns behind. Our troops watched this little piece of by-play from the northern bank of the Marne.

Owing to the hostile artillery fire from every side the conduct of operations in the salient, which was still very deep, was extremely difficult. The enemy artillery had the critical section of our railway east of Soissons under fire. A regular hail of enemy aeroplane-bombs descended upon it day and night. We were compelled to detrain the arriving reinforcements and reliefs in the neighbourhood of Laon and far away from the salient. They then proceeded to the battlefield by forced marches which took days. Often enough they reached their destination only just in time to take over the line from their exhausted comrades and save a complete collapse.

The situation could not be allowed to remain thus for long. The battle threatened to consume all our reserves. We must evacuate the salient and say good-bye to the Marne. It was a grievous decision, not from the purely military standpoint but from that of professional pride. How the enemy would rejoice if the word " Marne " were to mean a revolution in the military situation for the second time ! Paris, and indeed all France, would breathe again. What would be the effect of this news on the whole world? We realised how many eyes and hearts would follow us with envy, hatred—and hope.

But at such a time military considerations could alone prevail. Their warning rang out loud and clear : get out of this situation ! There was no reason for precipitate action. General Foch might hurl all his armies at us from all sides, but a really deep break-through was a rare occurrence. We could thus retire step by step, save our precious war material from the clutches of the enemy, and withdraw in good order to the new line of defence which nature offered us in the Aisne—Vesle sector. The movement was completed in the first days of August. It was a masterpiece on the part of both commanders and men. It was not the power of the enemy's arms which forced us out of the Marne salient, but the hopelessness of our situation as the result of the difficult communications in the rear of our troops fighting on three sides. General Foch had thoroughly realised those difficulties. He had a great goal in sight. The magnificent behaviour of our men prevented him from reaching it. After the first surprise they had fought brilliantly. They had done everything that human beings could have done. The result was that our infantry left the battlefield in no way with the feeling of having been vanquished. Their sense of pride was partially due to their observation of the fact that their enemies' attacks had largely failed when they had been carried out without the protection or the moral support of tanks.

Where there were no tanks our enemy had sent black waves against us. Waves of black Africans! Woe to us when these waves reached our lines and massacred, or worse, tortured our defenceless men! It is not at the blacks who performed such atrocities that indignant humanity will point an accusing finger, but at those who brought these hordes to the soil of Europe to take part in the so-called struggle for Honour, Freedom and Justice. The blacks were led to the slaughter in thousands.

Though Englishmen, Americans, Italians, French and all their subject races swarmed round our infantry, when it came to fighting, man against man, our soldier felt and proved himself the lord of the battlefield. Even the feeling of helplessness against the enemy's tanks had to some extent been overcome. Our men had often made audacious attempts to lay low this troublesome foe and had been lustily supported by our own artillery. Once more the French artillery had been responsible for the worst crises with which our men had been faced. The employment for hours, and even days, of this destructive weapon, which was boldly brought out into the open and disdained even the cover of shell-holes, had shattered the lines of our infantry and put their nerves to the hardest test. The approach of the enemy storm troops had often been regarded as a release from the menace of inevitable destruction.

Our troops had had to perform prodigies, not only in the fighting itself, but also in unremitting preparation, marching, and the endurance of privations. Their losses had been great and the strain on their nerves even greater. I had several conversations with soldiers who had taken part in the recent fighting. Their homely and straightforward replies and stories were more eloquent than volumes about their experiences and the mighty moral resolution which imbued them. How could one ever doubt such splendid men! They were tired, of course, needed physical rest and mental relief. We were only too anxious to give them all that, but it was questionable whether the enemy would leave us time to do so.

Although the fighting in the Marne salient had saved us from the annihilation our enemy had intended, we could have no illusion about the far-reaching effects of this battle and our retreat.

From the purely military point of view it was of the greatest and most fateful importance that we had lost the initiative to the enemy, and were at first not strong enough to recover it ourselves. We had been compelled to draw upon a large part of the reserves which we intended to use for the attack in Flanders. This meant the end of our hopes of dealing our long-planned decisive blow at the English Army. The enemy High Command was thus relieved of the influence which this threatened offensive had had on their dispositions. Moreover, the English armies, thanks to the battle in the Marne salient, were relieved from the moral spell which we had woven about them for months. It was to be expected that resolute generalship on the part of the enemy would exploit this change in the situation, which they could not fail to realise, to the full extent of their available forces. Their prospects were very favourable, as, generally speaking, our defensive fronts were not strong and had to be held by troops which were not fully effective. Moreover, these fronts had been considerably extended since the spring and were thus strategically more sensitive.

Of course, it was to be assumed that the enemy also had suffered very heavily in the recent fighting. Between July 15 and August 4, 74 hostile divisions, including 60 French, had been suffering losses while the English armies had been practically spared for months. In these circumstances the steady arrival of American reinforcements must be particularly valuable for the enemy. Even if these reinforcements were not yet quite up to the level of modern requirements in a purely military sense, mere numerical superiority had a far greater effect at this stage when our units had suffered so heavily.

The effect of our failure on the country and our Allies was even greater, judging by our first impressions. How many hopes, cherished during the last few months, had probably collapsed at one blow! How many calculations had been scattered to the winds!

But if we could only master the situation at the front once more we could certainly rely on the restoration of the political balance.

PART V

Beyond Our Powers

CHAPTER XXII

ON THE DEFENSIVE

August 8

OUR troops had taken up their new line on the Aisne. The last waves of the enemy attack flowed in and flowed out. In places there was desultory fighting from time to time.

Several of our divisions which had been exhausted in the recent fighting and required rest, were in billets behind our lines. Among other areas they were quartered in the region of Avesnes. I was thus able to see how quickly our soldiers recovered. When they had a day or two of good sleep, regular meals and rest, they seemed quickly to forget all they had suffered, even their mental torture. Of course, for this purpose the rest had to be real rest, undisturbed by enemy shells and bombs, and if possible somewhere where the thunder of the guns could not be heard. But how seldom and how few of our troops had a rest of that kind in the long years of fighting! Swept from one theatre of war to another, from battlefield to battlefield, they were practically subjected to an uninterrupted physical and moral strain. Herein lay the principal difference between the achievements of our men and those of all our opponents.

The roar of battle in the Marne salient had reached us at Avesnes like the rolling thunder of a heavy storm, now sharp and clear, now sullen. For the moment it had practically died down.

On the morning of August 8 this comparative peace was abruptly interrupted. In the south-west the noise of battle could clearly be heard. The first reports, which came from Army Headquarters in the neighbourhood of Péronne, were serious. The enemy, employing large squadrons of tanks, had broken into our lines on both sides of the Amiens—St. Quentin road. Further details could not be given.

The veil of uncertainty was lifted during the next few hours, though our telephone lines had been broken in many places. There was no doubt that the enemy had penetrated deeply into our positions and that batteries had been lost. We issued an order that they were to be recovered and that the situation must everywhere be restored by an immediate counter-attack. We sent officers to ascertain precisely how matters stood, to secure perfect harmony between our plans and the dispositions of the various Staffs on the shaken front. What had happened?

In a very thick haze a strong English tank attack had met with immediate success. In their career the tanks had met no special obstacles, natural or—unfortunately—artificial. The troops on this front had certainly been thinking too much about continuing the offensive and not enough of defence.

In any case, it would have cost us heavy losses to dig trenches and construct obstacles when we were in direct contact with the enemy, for as soon as the hostile observers noticed any movement, even if it were a matter of a few individuals, their artillery immediately opened fire. It seemed our best plan to lie quietly in the high corn, without cover against enemy shells it is true, but at the same time safe from enemy telescopes. In this way we were spared losses for the time being but ran the risk of suffering even greater losses if the enemy attacked. It was not only that little work had been done on the first line; even less had been done on the support and rear lines. There was nothing available but isolated sections of trenches and scattered strong points. On these so-called quiet fronts the troops were not numerous enough for trench-digging on any large scale.

On this August 8 we had to act as we had so often acted in equally menacing situations. Initial successes of the enemy were no new experience for us. We had seen them in 1916 and 1917, at Verdun, Arras, Wytschaete, and Cambrai. We had only quite recently experienced and mastered another at Soissons. But in the present case the situation was particularly serious. The great tank attack of the enemy had penetrated to a surprising depth. The tanks, which were faster than hitherto, had surprised Divisional Staffs in their headquarters and torn up the telephone lines which communicated with the battle front. The Higher Command-posts were thus isolated, and orders could not reach the front line. That was peculiarly unfortunate on this occasion, because the thick mist made supervision and control very difficult. Of course our anti-tank guns fired in the direction from which the sound of motors and the rattle of chains seemed to come, but they were frequently surprised by the sight of these steel colossi suddenly emerging from some totally different quarter. The wildest rumours began to spread in our lines. It was said that masses of

z

English cavalry were already far in rear of the foremost German infantry lines. Some of the men lost their nerve, left positions from which they had only just beaten off strong enemy attacks and tried to get in touch with the rear again. Imagination conjured up all kinds of phantoms and translated them into real dangers.

Everything that occurred, and was destined to prove our first great disaster, is comprehensible enough from the human point of view. In situations such as these the old war-hardened soldier does not lose his self-possession. He does not imagine; he thinks! Unfortunately these old soldiers were in a fast vanishing minority, and, moreover, their influence did not always and everywhere prevail. Other influences made themselves felt. Ill-humour and disappointment that the war seemed to have no end, in spite of all our victories, had ruined the character of many of our brave men. Dangers and hardships in the field, battle and turmoil, on top of which came the complaints from home about many real and some imaginary privations! All this gradually had a demoralising effect, especially as no end seemed to be in sight. In the shower of pamphlets which was scattered by enemy airmen our adversaries said and wrote that they did not think so badly of us; that we must only be reasonable and perhaps here and there renounce something we had conquered. Then everything would soon be right again and we could live together in peace, in perpetual international peace. As regards peace within our own borders, new men and new governments would see to that. What a blessing peace would be after all the fighting! There was, therefore, no point in continuing the struggle.

Such was the purport of what our men read and said.

The soldier thought it could not be all enemy lies, allowed it to poison his mind and proceeded to poison the minds of others.

On this August 8 our order to counter-attack could no longer be carried out. We had not the men, and more particularly the guns, to prepare such an attack, for most of the batteries had been lost on the part of the front which was broken through. Fresh infantry and new artillery units must first be brought up—by rail and motor transport. The enemy realised the outstanding importance which our railways had in this situation. His heavy and heaviest guns fired far into our back areas. Various railway junctions, such as Péronne, received a perfect hail of bombs from enemy aircraft, which swarmed over the town and station in numbers never seen before. But if our foe exploited the difficulties of the situation in our rear, as luck would have it he did not realise the scale of his initial tactical success. He did not thrust forward to the Somme this day, although we should not have been able to put any troops worth mentioning in his way.

A relatively quiet afternoon and an even more quiet night followed the fateful morning of August 8. During these hours our first reinforcements were on their way.

The position was already too unfavourable for us to be able to expect that the counter-attack we had originally ordered would enable us to regain the old battle front. Our counter-thrust would have involved longer preparation and required stronger reserves than we had at our disposal on August 9. In any case we must not act precipitately. On the battle front itself impatience made men reluctant to wait. They thought that favourable opportunities were being allowed to slip, and proceeded to rush at unsurmountable difficulties. Thus some of the precious fresh infantry units we had brought up were wasted on local successes without advantaging the general situation.

The attack on August 8 had been carried out by the right wing of the English armies. The French troops in touch with them on the south had only taken a small part in the battle. We had to expect, however, that the great British success would now set the French lines also in motion. If the French pushed forward rapidly in the direction of Nesle our position in the great salient projecting far out to the south-west would become critical. We therefore ordered the evacuation of our first lines south-west of Roye, and retired to the neighbourhood of that town.

2

The Consequences of August 8 and Further Battles in the West up to the End of September

I had no illusions about the political effects of our defeat on August 8. Our battles from July 15 to August 4 could be regarded, both abroad and at home, as the consequence of an unsuccessful but bold stroke, such as may happen in any war. On the other hand the failure of August 8 was revealed to all eyes as the consequences of an open weakness. To fail in an attack was a very different matter from being vanquished on the defence. The amount of booty which our enemy could publish to the world spoke a clear language. Both the public at home and our Allies could only listen in great anxiety. All the more urgent was it that we should keep our presence of mind and face the situation without illusions, but also without exaggerated pessimism.

The military situation had certainly become serious. Of course the position on the part of our front which had been attacked could be restored, the lost war material made good and fresh reserves brought up. But all this did not exhaust the effects of our defeat. We could only expect that, encouraged by his great victory, our enemy would now open similar attacks at other points. He had now found out that, in comparison with 1917, our present defence lines had many defects. In the first place, from a technical point of view. Generally speaking, our troops had done little work on the trenches we had won in the spring of 1918. In the sector east of Amiens, as on other parts of the front, too much had been said about continuing our offensive and too little about the requirements of defence. Moreover, the behaviour of very many of our troops in the battle must have convinced the enemy that on our defensive fronts the stubborn resolution of 1917 was no longer present at all points. Further, the enemy had learned a good deal from us since the spring. In the last operation he had employed against us those tactics with which we had soundly beaten him time after time. He had fallen upon us suddenly, and not after months of preparation, and had no longer tried to force a decision by driving a wedge into our defences. He had surprised us in an attack on a broad front. He was able to venture on such tactics now because he realised the weaknesses of our lines. If the enemy repeated these attacks with the same fury, in view of the present constitution of our Army, there was at any rate some prospect of our powers of resistance being gradually paralysed. On the other hand, the fact that the enemy had once more failed to extract all possible advantages from his great initial successes gave me the hope that we should overcome further crises.

This line of reasoning enabled me, when I was summoned on August 13 to a political conference at Spa with the members of the Government to discuss the military situation, to affirm that this was certainly serious, but that it must not be forgotten that we were still standing deep in the enemy's country. I emphasised this point of view to my Emperor also on the following day, when I summarised affairs after a pretty lengthy conference. I agreed with the views of the Imperial Chancellor, Count Hertling, that no official steps in the direction of peace should be taken on our side until there had been some improvement in the existing military situation. This fact alone shows to what an extent we had had to renounce our former political goals.

In the middle of August I did not consider that the time had come for us to despair of a successful conclusion of the war. In spite of certain distressing but isolated occurrences in the last battle, I certainly hoped that the Army would be in a position to continue to hold out. I also believed that our public at home would be strong enough to survive even the present crisis. I fully realised what the homeland had already borne in the way of sacrifices and privations and what they would possibly still have to bear. Had not France, on whose soil the war had now been raging for four years, had to suffer and endure far more? Had that country ever been cast down by failure during the whole of that time? Did she despair when our shells fell into her capital? I believed that our own public would keep this in mind even in this serious crisis, and stand firm if only we at the front continued to stand firm too.. As long as we did so I felt sure that it would have its effect on our Allies. Their military tasks, at any rate those of Austria-Hungary and Bulgaria, were simple enough.

In this process of reasoning, mere anxiety to uphold the honour of our arms played no predominant part. In the four years of war our Army had laid the foundations of that honour so deeply that the enemy could never remove them, come what might. The main motive for my decisions and proposals was regard for the welfare of my country and that alone. If we could not by victory on the battlefield force our enemies to a peace which gave us everything which once and for all secured Germany's future, we could at any rate make certain that the strength and resolution of our enemies would be paralysed during the campaign. It was to be assumed that even this would mean a tolerable political existence for the State.

After the battle in the Marne salient came to an end, General Foch had certainly realised that the success he had gained would be wasted if our troops were given time to recover. I felt convinced that the enemy High Command now believed that it must stake everything on one card.

On August 20 the French attacked between the Oise and the Aisne in the direction of Chauny. In three days of fighting they threw us back on that town. On August 21 and the following days the English extended their front of attack of August 8 to the north as far as north-west of Bapaume. The enemy broke through at several points and compelled us gradually to withdraw our line in this quarter. On August 26 the English hurled themselves at our line in the direction of Cambrai. They broke through, but were finally held. On September 2 a fresh hostile attack overran our lines once and for all on the great Arras—Cambrai road and compelled us to bring the whole front back to the Siegfried Line. For the sake of economising men we simultaneously evacuated the salient north of the Lys which bulged out beyond Mount Kemmel and Merville. All these were disagreeable decisions which had been carried out by the end of the first week of September. These movements did not ease the situation, as we had hoped. The enemy pressed forward at all points and the crisis continued.

On September 12 fighting flamed up on the hitherto inactive front south-east of Verdun and at Pont-à-Mousson. At this point we were holding lines which had solidified after our attacks in the autumn of 1914. They were a tactical abortion which invited the enemy to attempt a great blow. It is not easy to understand why the French left us alone for years in this great triangle which projected into their front. If they had made a mighty thrust along the line of the base a serious crisis for us would have been inevitable. It may possibly be made a matter of reproach to us that we had not evacuated this position long before, certainly as soon as our attack on Verdun was broken off. The only point was that it was the very conformation of our lines at this point which had had the most serious effect on the enemy's freedom of movement at Verdun and barred the valley of the Meuse, so important to him, south of the fortress. It was only at the beginning of September, when there seemed to be a certain liveliness on the part of the enemy between the Meuse and the Moselle, that we decided to evacuate this salient and withdraw to the

lines we had long prepared along its base. Before the
movement had been carried out in its entirety the French
and Americans attacked and inflicted a serious defeat
upon us.

Generally speaking, however, we managed more or
less to hold up the enemy attacks upon our front. The
extension of the enemy's attacks to Champagne on
September 26 affected the general situation from the coast
to the Argonne but little at first. On the other hand,
the Americans this day penetrated our line between the
Argonne and the Meuse. This was the first occasion on
which the power of America, expressed through an independent army, made itself decisively felt on the battlefields of the last phase.

Although as a result of the enemy irruptions our
Western Front had to be repeatedly withdrawn, it had
not been broken through. It was shaking, but it did
not fall. But at this moment a great gap was torn in
our common front. Bulgaria collapsed.

CHAPTER XXIII

1

The Collapse of Bulgaria

IN the year 1918 there had been no material change in the domestic situation in Bulgaria. It was still serious, but on the other hand the country's foreign policy seemed to be in no way prejudiced by it. It is true that from time to time news reached us of unauthorised negotiations of certain Bulgarians with the Entente in neutral Switzerland. Moreover, there was no reason to doubt that the American Consulate-General in Sofia was a hotbed of schemes aiming at our ruin. We made a vain attempt to secure the removal of the Americans. Policy demands the use of the velvet glove even in the iron realities of war.

The furious strife between the political parties of Bulgaria continued. The Army, too, was compromised ever more deeply. Radoslavoff's enemies had at length managed to secure his overthrow in the spring. The new men assured us of their loyal adherence to the Alliance, and that was the decisive consideration to us. Meanwhile pacifism was making great headway among the Bulgarian people. The question of food supply was becoming more difficult. The Army in particular suffered from this cause, or, I should perhaps say, was allowed to suffer from it. At times the soldiers practically starved, and moreover were so badly clad that for a time even the most essential things were lacking. Mutinies occurred, though these were generally kept quiet from us. The Army was permeated with foreign elements. Men from the occupied territories were forced into it to keep the units up to establishment. The result was that desertion occurred on an amazing scale. Was it surprising that in these circumstances the *moral* of the troops deteriorated? It apparently touched its lowest point in the spring. At that time, at the suggestion of the German Headquarters Staff of the Army Group, the Bulgarian General Staff had planned an attack in Albania, west of Lake Ochrida. It was hoped that if this operation succeeded it would effectively close the Santa Quaranti—Koritza road, which was so important for the enemy, and further have a favourable reaction on the *moral* of the Army and the nation. In the end it proved impossible to proceed with this undertaking, as Bulgarian officers declared that the troops would refuse to attack. An even more serious condition of affairs was revealed when, in May, the Bulgarian troops offered no resistance to the attack of the Greeks and French in the centre of the Macedonian front, and abandoned their positions practically without fighting. Most of the divisions told off for the counter-attack mutinied.

In the course of the summer the internal condition of the Army seemed to have improved. We gave such help as we could, sent food supplies as well as clothing from our own stock. Moreover, our victories on the Western Front at this time aroused intense enthusiasm in the Bulgarian Army. It was none the less clear to us that this better spirit would soon vanish again if we ourselves suffered any reverses. Even the more favourable reports which reached us at the end of July could leave us in no doubt about that.

As regards the comparative strength of the opponents on the Macedonian front, there seemed to have been no material change in the course of 1918. After the conclusion of peace with Rumania, Bulgaria was in a position to concentrate all her forces on one front. Compared with this reinforcement the withdrawal of a few German battalions from Macedonia did not really affect the question of numbers. One English division had been transferred to Syria, the French troops had sent their youngest classes back home, while the so-called " Royal Greek Divisions," which had just been mobilised, showed little stomach for fighting. It was apparently for this reason that the defence of the Struma sector had been entrusted to these troops. If we could accept the reports of deserters, most of these men were quite ready to join us if German troops were put in line on the Struma front. We therefore sent out to Macedonia a few battalions which could not be used on the decisive fronts in the West. They arrived at their destination at the very moment when the war was decided, so far as Bulgaria was concerned.

In the evening of September 15 we received the first reports of the commencement of the attack of the Entente armies in Macedonia. There was something very striking about this date. Had not Bulgarian soldiers declared in the spring that they would abandon their lines on this day if the war were not previously concluded?

On the other hand it was not less extraordinary that the enemy should select for his attack a sector in the very centre of the rugged mountains in which his advance would have been faced with critical difficulties if the Bulgarian troops and their subordinate commanders had shown any inclination to resist. For this reason we thought we could await the development of this battle with confidence, and continue to expect the serious and decisive effort of the enemy in the valley of the Vardar. At that point and in the neighbourhood of Lake Doiran, preparations to attack on the part of the English had been observed for some considerable time. Here again we thought that there could be no danger, in view of the extraordinary strength of the defences, so long as the Bulgarians took the necessary measures. The Bulgarian High Command certainly had the numbers required at their disposal.

The first reports of the course of the battle on September 15 gave no cause for alarm. The first lines had undoubtedly been lost, but there was nothing unusual in that. The main thing was that the enemy had not succeeded in getting right through on the first day. Later reports were more serious. The Bulgarians had been forced back farther north than had at first been thought. The troops which had first taken part in the battle had apparently made little resistance and shown even less resolution. The reserves which came up, or ought to have come up, displayed little inclination to face the enemy's fire. Apparently they preferred to abandon the battlefield to the enemy, and this at a point which was perilously close to Gradsko, the most important centre of all the communications in the Macedonian theatre.

If Gradsko fell, or the enemy were able to reach it with his guns, the Bulgarian right wing army in the neighbourhood of Monastir would be deprived of its most important line of communication, and in the long run it would be impossible to keep it supplied in its present position. Moreover, the Bulgarian army on both sides of the Vardar valley in the centre would find its railway connection with the homeland severed. It seemed incredible that the Bulgarian commanders should not realise the peril that was threatening them and bring up every man they had to avert an appalling catastrophe to their main armies.

In contrast to the behaviour of the Bulgarian army south of Gradsko, the Bulgarian troops between the Vardar and Lake Doiran had been fighting very strenuously since September 18. It was in vain that the English strove to force their way through at this point. Bulgarian courage and obstinacy had never been displayed to better advantage. But how could heroism at Lake Doiran help, if faint-heartedness held the field at Gradsko —indeed perhaps something worse than faint-heartedness?

Vain were the attempts of the German Staff to save the situation in the centre of the Bulgarian Army with German troops. What could the small and weak German nucleus do when the Bulgarians were running away on the right and left? Entire Bulgarian regiments streamed past the German battalions which were marching to meet the enemy, and openly refused to fight. It was an extraordinary scene. Still more extraordinary were the declarations of the Bulgarian troops. They were off home to their wives and children, for they wanted to see their houses and farms again and look after their fields. Most of them bore their officers no ill-will. If the officers liked to come back home with them they were welcome, but if they wanted to remain on the field of honour they would have to remain alone. The Bulgarians were ready enough to assist any German who got into difficulties while marching to meet the enemy. They helped to get . the German guns over bad bits of road. But for the rest they left the fighting to the Germans. Along these lines Macedonia was certainly lost to Bulgaria. But the Bulgarian peasant told himself that he had quite enough land at home. So he continued on his homeward way and left anxiety and fighting for Macedonia, and the rest of the Great Power business, to others.

Faced with facts such as these, the German Staff, which exercised command from Lake Ochrida to Lake Doiran, found themselves in a desperate position. Anything they could lay hands on in the way of German troops, units on the lines of communication, Landsturm and recruits, were scraped together to bolster up the Bulgarian centre and save Gradsko. The prospects of success became smaller every minute. In view of the speed in retreat shown by the Bulgarian centre, the only possibility of safety was to withdraw the wings of the army. Such a movement would in itself be of small tactical disadvantage, for in Macedonia great defensive positions lay one behind the other, and the farther north the enemy got the more difficult became his communications. It is true that the communications of the Bulgarians also became much worse when the valley of the Vardar was abandoned. However, it seemed likely that this measure would enable us to save the bulk of the army.

The Bulgarian leaders raised the most serious objections to the decision of the German Headquarters Staff of the Army Group. They believed that their troops would still hold on in their present lines and, indeed, fight. They were also convinced that their armies would dissolve altogether if an order to retreat were issued.

It was a truly desperate position, desperate for all concerned. The Bulgarians complained that there were not enough German troops, and because we had previously withdrawn some of the German troops in this theatre. But in any case what could a few more German battalions have done in this general collapse? How many German divisions should we have had to send to defend the Macedonian front? Germany could not seek a decision in the West and send divisions to Macedonia at the same time. The Bulgarians would not realise that Germany's resources were not inexhaustible. The Bulgarians themselves were far from exhausted. What really was exhausted was their own will to fight.

We at Main Headquarters were also faced with fateful problems. We had to try and save whatever could be saved in Bulgaria. We had to send reinforcements, and indeed at once, however hard it was for us. It was on September 18 that the full meaning of this necessity became clear. Just think how fearfully the battle was raging on our Western Front at this time. Only a few days before, the Americans had gained their great success between the Meuse and the Moselle and we were faced with an extension of the attack. The first reinforcements which we could make available were the troops—a mixed brigade—which had been earmarked for Trans-Caucasia and were even then in process of transport across the Black Sea. They were recalled by wireless and ordered to return by Varna and Sofia. But these troops would not be enough. A few more divisions could certainly be spared from our Eastern Front.   We had intended to bring them to a quiet part of the Western Front.   But what kind of troops were they?   Not a man was under thirty-five, and all the General Service men had already been brought to the West.   Could anything very striking be expected of them?   They might have the best intentions in the world, but in this climate and destitute of suitable equipment for fighting in a mountainous country there were limits to their usefulness on the Macedonian front.   Yet it had to be, for not only the Bulgarian Army but the Bulgarian Government and the Tsar must have German backing in this very critical situation.

We also sent reinforcements from the West.   Our Alpine Corps, which had just been engaged in very severe fighting, was entrained for Nish.   Austria-Hungary also joined in the attempt to help Bulgaria and made several divisions available.   We had thus to renounce the prospect of further Austro-Hungarian reinforcements on our Western Front.

Until these German and Austrian reinforcements arrived the attempt had to be made to save the main Bulgarian armies at any rate.   With that end in view, and in spite of Bulgarian opposition, the German Army Group Headquarters issued the order for retreat to the Bulgarian armies on the right wing and in the centre. Their lines on the Belashitza, north of Lake Doiran, were to form the pivot for the entire movement.   During the whole of this time the Bulgarian army on the left wing had not been attacked.   Its lines on the Belashitza and behind the Struma were extremely strong.   A few machine guns and batteries would have been quite enough for their defence.   Yet confusion overtook this army

2 A

also. Courage and hard thinking went to a discount. Its commander considered his position untenable and begged the Tsar to conclude an armistice at once. The Tsar replied : '' Go and die in your present lines.'' The remark shows that the Tsar was still master of the situation and that I had made no mistake about him.

The Crown Prince Boris also showed himself equal to the situation. He hastened to the front to save everything that could be saved. But where everyone was losing his head and his resolution what could one individual do, even if he had the love of many and the respect of all?

On September 20 the centre army began its retreat in accordance with orders. This led to utter dissolution. Confusion was worse confounded by unskilful dispositions. The Staffs failed, the Army Staff worst of all. There was only one man, the Commander-in-Chief, who retained a clear vision and was inspired by firm resolution.

The right wing army had a difficult task. Its main line of retreat was through Prilep on Veles. As the enemy was already quite close to Gradsko, this line of retreat was very seriously threatened. Another road farther west led from the region of the lakes and Monastir through the rugged mountains of Albania to Kalkandelen. At Uskub it met the road through Veles. This tract through the Albanian mountains was safe but very difficult, and it was doubtful whether a large body of troops would find the necessary supplies in that region. In spite of these drawbacks large numbers of troops had to use it. Even larger bodies had to take this route when the enemy captured Gradsko and then pressed forward against the Prilep—Gradsko road from the south-east. Gradsko had fallen as early as September 21. From being a wretched little village it had become a regular hutted town and its appearance and size reminded one of a brand new American settlement. An immense quantity of supplies, sufficient for a whole campaign, was stored here. Judging by the depots there was nothing to account for the fact that the Bulgarian Army at the front had had to go short. The whole lot was now either destroyed by the Bulgarians or captured by the enemy. It was not only at Gradsko but at many other points that Bulgaria had large depots. Hitherto we had heard nothing about them, as they were guarded by a miserly bureaucracy which in Bulgaria, as in other lands, forms the crust of the national organism in spite of the most liberal laws and a free parliament.

Bulgaria could therefore continue the war as long as she did not, or would not, herself regard it as lost. Our plan, which met with the approval of the Bulgarian High Command, was as follows : The centre army was to fall back to the frontier of Old Bulgaria. The army on the right wing was to be concentrated at Uskub or farther north ; it would be reinforced by the approaching German and Austrian divisions. These troops would be quite enough to restore the situation at Uskub ; indeed if the Bulgarian units were not hopelessly ineffective, we might anticipate that from Uskub we should be able to embark on an offensive towards the south. It seemed impossible that without rest the enemy would be able to bring his strong columns forward to Uskub and the frontier of Old Bulgaria. How would he cope with his supply difficulties as we had utterly destroyed the railway and roads? Moreover, we hoped that the energy and sense of responsibility of the Bulgarian troops would revive when they stood on their own soil.

The proposed operation was only possible on the assumption that Uskub could be held until the Bulgarian troops from Kalkandelen arrived. This seemed to be an easy task, as the enemy was coming up from Gradsko with relatively weak forces.

While all these events were in progress, Sofia was remarkably quiet. On their arrival our battalions, which were intended to calm the inhabitants and protect and support the Government, found nothing of the atmosphere of agitation they feared. Life was certainly somewhat peculiar owing to the mobs of soldiers who had deserted their units and were pouring homewards through the town. The men handed in their arms at the depots, took leave of their comrades and officers, while some of them promised to return as soon as they had had time to look after their fields. It was indeed an odd picture and a remarkable revelation of mentality. Or was the whole thing a question of collusion? We had certainly no reason to think that it was so in the case of the men. It is true that this process of dissolution had not proceeded peacefully at all points, but the rumours of horrible outrages turned out to be exaggerated, generally speaking.

There was no change at the front. The retirement of the Bulgarian masses continued uninterruptedly. It was impossible to stop their career, even though the forces of the pursuing enemy were but weak. It was in vain that we tried to get individual bodies—there was no longer any question of proper formations—to form a front against the enemy and offer a real resistance, at least in places. The moment the enemy approached the Bulgarians fired a few rounds and then left their lines. German troops were no longer able to provide a nucleus for the Bulgarian resistance.   Equally impossible was it for German and Bulgarian officers, rifle in hand, to produce by their example any effect on the uncontrollable and indifferent mob.

Thus the enemy approached Uskub before fresh German and Austro-Hungarian troops could arrive there. On September 29 strong bodies of the right wing of the Bulgarian Army emerged from the mountain region and reached Kalkandelen.   They had only to make for Uskub by a good road.   We were told that the troops were thoroughly keen and fit to fight.   The worst of the crisis, therefore, seemed to have been overcome.   In a military sense that may have been true, but morally the cause was lost once and for all.   That was soon to be proved beyond doubt.   Weak Serbian units captured Uskub.   The troops at Kalkandelen lost heart.   They capitulated.   In the evening of September 29 Bulgaria concluded an armistice.

2

The Overthrow of Turkish Power in Asia

The opening of 1918 marked a great revival of the war fever in Turkey.   Even before the end of winter, in the highlands of Armenia Turkey opened an attack on the Russian armies there.   Russian power in this region turned out to be simply a phantom.   The bulk of the armies had already dissolved.   The only resistance the Turks met with in their advance was offered by Armenian bands.   The difficulties which the nature of this mountainous country placed in the way of the Turks at this season proved more formidable than this Armenian opposition.   The fact that the advance proceeded success-

fully was one of those remarkable manifestations of
temporary vigour characteristic of the Ottoman Empire.
The Turks crossed the frontier of Turkish Armenia into
the region of Trans-Caucasia urged on by various motives;
Pan-Islam dreams, thoughts of revenge, hopes of compensation for the territory they had lost, and anticipation
of booty. There was yet another reason, the search for
man-power. The Empire, and more particularly the
portion inhabited by the splendid Anatolian, was absolutely exhausted from the point of view of man-power.
In Trans-Caucasian Adzerbaidjan and among the Mohammedans of the Caucasus new and great sources seemed to
be available. Russia had not drawn on these Mohammedans for regular military service, and now they were to
fight under the Crescent. The number of the prospective
volunteers, as communicated to us, revealed all the wealth
of Oriental imagination. Further, if the Turkish reports
were to be believed, we had to assume that the Mohammedan peoples of Russia had for long had no more intense
longing than to form one great and self-contained
Mohammedan nation in the Turkish Empire. But we
must not lose sight of the fact that Turkey found fresh
resources at her disposal in these regions, and that England
would find herself compelled to devote special attention
to the development of these events. On the other hand
it is just as well occasionally to have some regard for sober
reality. We therefore attempted to calm the billows
of Ottoman hopes and expectations, unfortunately not
with the success that we could have wished. It was agreed,
from the point of view of the whole war, that Turkey's
principal task lay far more in Syria and Mesopotamia than
in the Caucasus and on the Caspian. But what was the

good of promises and good intentions in Constantinople when the commanders in the outlying theatres went their own way !

We sent troops to Georgia with a view to securing at least a share of the abundant supplies of raw material in Trans-Caucasia to be used in our joint war. We hoped to help the Georgian Government with the re-establishment of a proper economic system. However, the Pan-Islam fanatics and profiteers in Constantinople would not rest until Baku was in Turkish hands, and this at a time when the ancient structure of Turkish dominion in Asia was about to collapse.

The idea of exercising a paramount influence in Persia led Turkey even farther east. The Turks intended to use Persia as a starting-point for a flank attack on the English operations in Mesopotamia, a plan which was good enough in itself, but required time for its realisation. It was certainly doubtful whether we should be allowed that time. But it was always possible that the first Turkish movement in Northern Persia would tie down English troops and therefore save Mesopotamia for Turkey. England appeared to be anxious to influence the course of events in Russia through the Caspian Sea and Baku as much as from the White Sea and Archangel. From that point of view the execution of the Turkish plans in Persia and Trans-Caucasia was in our interests also. The only thing was that defence in Mesopotamia and especially in Syria must not be neglected. The formation of an effective Turkish reserve army in the neighbourhood of Aleppo would have been far more useful than great operations in Persia, in view of the strategic possibilities open to the English south of the Taurus.

Judging by the map, the situation in Mesopotamia had remained unchanged since the autumn of 1917 ; but, as a matter of fact, the Turkish armies south of Mosul had suffered a real catastrophe, and that not in battle. As in the Armenian highlands in the winter of 1916-17, Turkish soldiers succumbed in large numbers on the plains of Mesopotamia in the winter of 1917-18. There was talk of 17,000 men who were starving there or had died as the result of privations. We cannot say whether the figures are accurate. " He who starves dies a hero's death," as a Turk once assured us, not from cynicism, but from honest inward conviction. Only fragments of the Turkish army in Mesopotamia survived the winter. It is very doubtful whether they could ever have been brought up to effective strength again. The question was, "Why did not the English attack in Mesopotamia, or, rather, why did they not simply advance?" Were these shades of the ancient power of Turkey enough to keep their enemy to his programme of a colonial war? The English Staff may put forward all kinds of reasons for the circumspection of their operations, but the strength of their opponents cannot be one of them.

While the Turkish armies were celebrating triumphs in the mountains of Armenia, the Syrian front had not remained inactive. There had been several frontal attacks on the part of the English which had led to no material change in the situation. In the spring of 1918 the English general seemed at length to have grown tired of this unending monotony. He adopted another line of action, and broke out through Jericho into the country east of the Jordan. He supposed that the Arabian tribes in this region were only waiting for the arrival of their liberators from the Turkish yoke to fall on the rear of the Ottoman armies. The enterprise failed pretty ingloriously against the resistance of weak German and Turkish forces, thanks to splendid Turkish generalship. For the summer the position in Syria was thus saved, for during this season inactivity was usually general in these sun-baked regions. It was all the more certain that in the autumn the English would renew their attacks somewhere or other. We believed that the interval would be long enough to enable us to secure this front by bringing up fresh Turkish forces.

The internal difficulties of Turkey continued during the year 1918. The death of the Sultan had at first no visible effect. At home matters began gradually to improve. The new Sultan was apparently a man of action. He displayed a firm resolve to rid himself of the ancient tutelage of the Committee and to set his face against the serious abuses in the State. He selected the men around him from the circles which had old-Turkish leanings.

I had made the acquaintance of the new Padishah at Kreuznach when he was still the presumptive heir, and had had the honour of receiving him as my guest. In view of the difficulties of direct intercourse, as the Sultan spoke no language but Turkish, we conversed through the medium of an interpreter, and our remarks were practically confined to the exchange of formal addresses. The reply of the heir to my speech was of a very friendly and loyal character. His attitude after he ascended the throne was thoroughly in keeping with it.

One of the Sultan's first resolutions was to exercise personal influence on the organisation of the Army. He was also anxious to visit the armies in the distant provinces. I am not in a position to say whether such visits would have resulted in material improvements.

The land was completely exhausted by the war. It could hardly give the Army anything more. The result was that even during the summer the efforts to improve the situation on the Syrian front were a failure. It is difficult to estimate how much more could have been done in that quarter in view of the positively pitiable communications. The supply of the Army was still in a bad way. The troops were not actually starving, but they were practically continuously short of food, physically exhausted, and morally numb.

As I have said earlier on, we had had to renounce the idea of withdrawing the German troops from the Syrian front. The German commander there considered that the position could not be regarded as secure unless German help was at hand. It must be admitted that we did not regard the offensive spirit of the Anglo-Indian Army as very high, especially judging by the evidence we got from Mohammedan Indian deserters. Moreover, the previous achievements of English generalship had been so unimpressive that we felt we were justified in hoping that with the small force at our disposal it would, at any rate, be possible to delude the enemy into thinking that we were still capable of offering further resistance. How long we could keep up the illusion mainly depended on whether the enemy would ever bring himself to embark on a resolute and wholesale operation, and thereby bring down the whole structure of Turkish resistance, with its weak German supports, about our ears.

On September 19 the English opened a surprise

attack on the right wing of the Turkish armies in the coast plain. They broke through the lines there practically without opposition. The rapid advance of the Indo-Australian cavalry squadrons sealed the fate of the two Turkish armies on the Syrian front.

It was just at this time that Turkey was robbed of her former land defences in Europe by the collapse of Bulgaria. Constantinople was thus immediately rendered defenceless on the land side. Of recent times the Turkish troops at the Dardanelles had become steadily worse. The armies in the outlying provinces had drained them of all men who were of any fighting value. Thrace was unprotected except for some weak coast-defence garrisons which were scarcely fit to fight. The fortifications of the far-famed Chataldja lines consisted of collapsed trenches which had been left by the Turkish troops after the battles of 1912-13. The rest of the Turkish army existed only in imagination or was engaged in the execution of plans which were will-o'-the-wisps. Those who are wise after the event may shake their heads over all this, but at bottom it only revealed the firm purpose to employ all the available troops at the decisive outposts. It would indeed have been disastrous if these outer walls had collapsed and the enemy floods had poured into the very heart of the country.

That heart was now threatened by such a flood. As soon as the first reports of the threatening collapse of Bulgaria arrived certain formations were hastily scraped together and sent from Constantinople to man the Chataldja lines. No resistance worth mentioning, however, could have been expected of such troops. For moral rather than practical reasons we ordered the immediate

transfer of German Landwehr units from the south of
Russia to Constantinople. Turkey also decided to send all
the divisions which had been recalled from Trans-Caucasia
to Thrace. A considerable time would elapse before any
appreciable force could reach Constantinople. Everything which had been published hitherto leaves it
uncertain why the enemy did not use this interval to
occupy the capital. Once more Turkey found herself
saved from a direct catastrophe. But at the end of
September such an eventuality seemed only a matter of
days.

3

Military and Political Issues in Austria-Hungary

After the failure of the attack of the Austro-
Hungarian armies on Italy, it became ever clearer that
the Danube Monarchy had employed her last and best
resources in that enterprise. It no longer had the numerical and moral forces to be able to repeat such an attack.
The plight of the Army was revealed to us by the
condition of the divisions which were sent to us as reinforcements for our Western Front. Their immediate
employment was quite out of the question if we were to
get any good work out of them later on. They needed
rest, training, and suitable equipment most of all. These
facts were admitted by the troops themselves as freely
as by the Austro-Hungarian General Staff. In the
relatively short time at their disposal all the Austro-
Hungarian officers took the greatest pains to train the
Austrian troops to be used in the West to the level of
their coming task. If they did not achieve their aim, it
was certainly not for want of energy and intelligence on

the part of the officers. The men also showed themselves extremely willing.

The great losses of the Austro-Hungarian armies in Italy, their precarious situation as regards drafts, the political unreliability of some parts of the Army and the uncertain domestic situation, unfortunately made a really effective and striking reinforcement of our Western Front impossible. In view of all this General von Arz had to grip the soul—in the most literal sense of the words—of every single division he wanted to send us. He himself was entirely convinced of the great importance of this reinforcement. I cannot say whether all circles in Austria-Hungary were permeated by the same desire to help, or whether everyone felt as grateful to us as General von Arz.

During the summer nothing of any note occurred on the Austro-Hungarian front. The only military event worth mentioning at this time took place in Albania. In that region the opponents had faced one another inactively for years : the Italians in the strength of rather more than an army corps at and east of Valona, and the Austrians in the north of Albania. This theatre would have been without any military importance if it had not had a certain connection with the Macedonian front. Bulgaria was always afraid that if the enemy pressed forward west of Lake Ochrida the right flank of their front would be enveloped. From the military point of view it would have been a perfectly simple matter to meet such a move on the part of the enemy by withdrawing the western wing from the region of Ochrida in a north-easterly direction. As I have said before, it was solely due to considerations of Bulgarian domestic politics at this time that the withdrawal of the Bulgarian troops from this conquered district was impossible. To that must be added Austro-Bulgarian jealousies in Albania, which we had great difficulty in composing.

The question has often been asked why the Austrians never drove their Italian adversary from Valona. The extraordinary importance of this naval base as a second gatepost of the Adriatic, a second point from which this sea could be closed, was obvious enough. However, for such an operation Austria-Hungary lacked the essential preliminary—effective communications with the battle area on the Vojusa. Such an enterprise could not be based on the sea, and there were no land communications through the desolate Albanian mountains before the war. Nor had Austria been able to make good this omission in sufficient measure during the war.

In their operations in Albania the Austro-Hungarians had played the part of a kind of Sleeping Beauty. The sleep had only been disturbed at intervals by raids on both sides, raids which were carried out with small bodies of troops and even less energy. The situation in Albania could be taken more seriously in the summer of 1918, when the Italians took the offensive on a broad front from the coast to the neighbourhood of Lake Ochrida. The weak, and to a certain extent very neglected, Austro-Hungarian detachments were driven north. There was great excitement in Sofia and on the Macedonian frontier immediately, and the Bulgarians demanded our intervention, as having supreme military control. This intervention took the form of a request to the Austro-Hungarian General Staff to reinforce their Albanian front so that they could continue to cover the Macedonian flank. The Austro-Hungarians at once decided on a counter-attack in Albania, and the Italians were thrown back again.

It is not easy to say whether this Italian offensive had any ulterior military and political goals. In particular, I must leave it in doubt whether it had any close connection with the subsequent Entente attack against the centre of the Macedonian front. In view of the amazing difficulties of the country in the Albanian mountains and the enemy's numerical superiority, the Austrian counter-attack represented a very remarkable achievement. It certainly deserved to be regarded as such by our Allies.

In the course of the year 1918 the domestic situation in Austria-Hungary had developed along the fateful lines which I have already discussed. The exceptional difficulties with the food supply occasionally threatened Vienna with a real catastrophe. It was thus hardly surprising that the Austro-Hungarian authorities, in their anxiety to lay hands on everything available, whether in Rumania or the Ukraine, proceeded to measures which very definitely conflicted with our own interests.

In the dismal political situation in which Austria-Hungary found herself, it was not a matter for wonder that we were informed again and again that it would be quite impossible for the Danube Monarchy to continue the war beyond the year 1918. Anxiety for the conclusion of hostilities found ever more frequent and stronger expression. I will leave undiscussed the question whether, as was alleged, the ambition of playing the part of peace-maker was not the prevailing motive in some quarters.

During the summer Count Czernin resigned the office of Foreign Minister. The reason the Count himself gave for this step was that the letters written to Prince Sixtus of Parma had created a gulf between himself and his master which could not be bridged. To me the Count was a not unsympathetic figure, in spite of the fact that his political views and mine were in opposition on many points, and though he expressed them as freely to us as we did ours to him.

To me Count Czernin was the typical representative of Austro-Hungarian foreign policy. He was clever, fully recognised the difficulties of our joint situation, and was a pointed and ruthless critic of the weaknesses of the political organism he represented. His political plans were directed far more to efforts to avoid disaster than to make full use of our victories. It goes without saying that the Count had an open eye and a warm heart for the interests of his country. The one great exception was that in his judgment of the general situation he could only see safety in renunciation. The result of this contrast was that he never ceased to work for an extension of his country's sphere of influence, even when he was asking us Germans to make great sacrifices for the interests of the whole Alliance. Like all Austro-Hungarian statesmen at this time, Count Czernin did not realise of what his country was capable. Otherwise he would never have talked to us in the spring of 1917—shortly after he took office—of the impossibility of going on any longer, although the resources of Austria-Hungary were destined to suffice for a long time yet, and Austria had not died of exhaustion even at the time he resigned. Count Czernin's processes of thought ran to a kind of mania for self-abnegation. It was not easy to ascertain whether the result of this was that he was unable to offer any opposition to the peace efforts of his Emperor, or whether he was in agreement with these at the bottom of his heart.   In any case the Count did not ignore the dangers of an exaggerated and much too frequently expressed insistence on our readiness to conclude peace, especially when we were dealing with enemies such as ours.   This alone can explain the fact that he lost his composure and suggested the Peace Resolution by the German Reichstag at the very time when our U-boat campaign was beginning to make itself felt, the spring offensive of our enemies had failed, and the political dissolution of Russia was having a serious effect upon them.

It was my opinion that Count Czernin never showed us anything but loyal frankness, even when he was facing us with a good many surprises in the peace negotiations at Brest-Litovsk and Bucharest.   There is no doubt that what he then feared was that the Danube Monarchy would never be able to survive the breakdown of these negotiations, and that the cry for bread in Vienna demanded an immediate compact with the Ukraine.

While Czernin was conducting the foreign policy of his country, there was no solution of the Polish problem between us and Austria-Hungary.   For reasons which I have already mentioned, the idea of surrendering the whole of Poland to the Dual Monarchy was and remained unacceptable.

I had made the acquaintance at Pless of Count Czernin's successor, Count Burian, when he was Foreign Minister in pre-Czernin times.   With Burian's dilatory methods, which were displayed in all questions of any importance, I could not hope that the Polish problem would be settled within a measurable period.   I must also

2 B

admit that at this time my attention was occupied with matters more important than these wearisome and futile negotiations.

On his recall to the office of Foreign Minister, Count Burian very naturally directed all his efforts to finding a way out of our political dilemma as soon as possible.

It was only human that under the impression of the military situation in the West, which was steadily growing worse, he should display the greatest obstinacy in pressing for peace. Personally, I was convinced that none of the Allied States ought to desert their posts on the common political front and make offers of peace to the enemy. It was an error to think that in so doing the State in question could secure substantially better terms for itself or all of us. The Turkish Grand Vizier, who visited us at Spa in the first half of September, shared our opinions entirely. The Tsar Ferdinand also expressed the view at this time that there could be no question of peace efforts for his country outside the framework of the whole Alliance. But perhaps the Tsar suspected even then how little importance Bulgaria had as a factor in the calculations of our enemies.

For these reasons I felt convinced that the Austro-Hungarian attempt to suggest a peaceful compromise with the Entente in the middle of September was unfortunate. In practice the enemy too showed strong disinclination towards such a step. They realised our situation at this time too clearly to wish to take the path of a peace by negotiation. To them the question of further sacrifice of life played no part. The enemy's attitude was completely dominated by the fear that we Germans might easily recover if we were allowed a moment's respite, so powerful was the impression which our achievements had made on our foes, and perhaps still make. This may well fill us with a feeling of pride even in the midst of what we are now suffering and will still have to suffer!

CHAPTER XXIV

TOWARDS THE END

1

September 29 to October 26

IN the book of the Great War the chapter on the heroism of the German Army may only just have been written, but with regard to the last fearful struggle it is written with the blood of our sons in letters that can never fade. What terrible demands were made in these few weeks on the physical strength and moral resolution of the officers and men of all Staffs and formations! The troops had now to be thrown from one battle into another. It was seldom that the so-called days in rest billets were enough to allow us to reorganise the decimated or scattered units and supply them with drafts, or distribute the remains of divisions we had broken up among other formations. Both officers and men were certainly beginning to tire, but they always managed to find a new impulse whenever it was a question of holding up some fresh enemy attack. Officers of all ranks, even up to the higher Staffs, fought in the front lines, sometimes rifle in hand. The only order issued in many cases was simply " Hold out to the last."

" Hold out! " What a renunciation after so many glorious days of brilliant victories. To me the vision of such deathless heroism can never be clouded by a few cases of despondency and failure. In such a conflict, which

426

meant the renunciation of our hopes and the absence of any feeling of victorious progress, human weaknesses inevitably play a larger part than at other times.

We had not the men to form a continuous line. We could only offer resistance in groups, large and small. It was only successful because the enemy, too, was visibly tiring. He seldom attempted a large operation unless his tanks had opened a way or his artillery had extinguished every sign of German life. He did not storm our lines directly, but gradually slipped through their many gaps. It was on this fact that I based my hope of being able to hold out until the efforts of our enemies were paralysed.

Unlike the enemy, we had no fresh reserves to throw in. Instead of an inexhaustible America, we had only weary Allies who were themselves on the point of collapse.

How long would our front be able to stand this colossal strain? I was faced with the question, the worst of all questions: When must the end be? If we turn in such cases to history, the great tutor of mankind, what we find is an exhortation to courage, not to caution. When I turned my gaze to the face of our greatest king the answer I received was, "Hold out." Yet times had certainly changed from what they were a hundred and sixty years before. Not a professional army, but the whole nation in arms was making war, was swallowed up in war, and bled and suffered. But men have remained fundamentally the same, with all their strength and weakness. Calamity would overtake him who showed himself weak when strength was required. I was willing to take responsibility for anything, but never for that.

Thus for us another battle was raging side by side

with those in the field. The other battlefield was in our hearts. In this mighty conflict we stood alone. We had nothing to guide us but our own convictions and conscience, nothing to support us but hope and faith. With me they were still strong enough to enable me to support others.

It was on September 28 that this inward battle raged most fiercely. Though German courage on the Western Front still denied our enemies a final break through, though France and England were visibly tiring and America's oppressive superiority bled in vain a thousand times, our resources were patently diminishing. The worse the news from the Far East, the sooner they would fail altogether. Who would close the gap if Bulgaria fell out once and for all? We could still do much, but we could not build up a new front. It was true that a new army was in process of formation in Serbia, but how weak these troops were! Our Alpine Corps had scarcely any effective units, and one of the Austro-Hungarian divisions which were on their way was declared to be totally useless. It consisted of Czechs, who would presumably refuse to fight. Although the Syrian theatre lay far from a decisive point of the war, the defeat there would undoubtedly cause the collapse of our loyal Turkish comrades, who now saw themselves threatened in Europe again. What would Rumania, or the mighty fragments of Russia do? All these thoughts swept over me and forced me to decide to seek an end, though only an honourable end. No one would say it was too soon.

In pursuance of such thoughts, and with his mind already made up, my First Quartermaster-General came to see me in the late afternoon of September 28. I could see in his face what had brought him to me. As had so often happened since August 22, 1914, our thoughts were at one before they found expression in words. Our hardest resolve was based on convictions we shared in common.

In the afternoon of September 29 we held a conference with the Foreign Secretary. He described the situation in a few words. Hitherto all attempts at a friendly compromise with our enemies had failed, and there was no prospect of getting into touch with the leaders of the hostile States through negotiations or mediation on the part of neutral Powers. The Secretary of State then described the internal situation. Revolution was standing at our door, and we had the choice of meeting it with a dictatorship or concessions. A parliamentary Government seemed to be the best weapon of defence.

Was it really the best? We knew what an immense strain we should put on our country with the steps we took to secure an armistice and peace, steps which would very naturally cause extreme anxiety about the situation at the front and our future. At such a moment, which meant the death of so many hopes, a moment in which bitter disillusionment would go hand in hand with even deeper anger, and every man was looking for some nucleus of stability in the State organism, ought we to let political passions be converted into some more violent agitation?

What direction would that agitation take? Surely not the direction of stability, but that of further chaos! Those who had sown the unholy weeds in our soil would be thinking that the time of harvest had arrived. We were on the slippery path.

Was it possible to believe that by concessions at home

we could make an enemy less exacting who had not yielded to our sword? Ask those of our soldiers who, trusting in the alluring promises of our foes, voluntarily laid down their arms! The enemy's mask fell at the same moment as the Germans lowered their weapons. The German who let himself be deceived was treated not a whit better than his comrade who defended himself to the last gasp.

We had also to fear that the formation of a new Government would further postpone a step which we had already delayed as long as possible. As a matter of fact, we had not taken it a moment too soon. Would it come too late as a result of the reorganisation of the State?

Such were my anxious thoughts. They were entirely shared by General Ludendorff.

As the result of our conference we placed our proposals for a peace step before His Majesty. It was my duty to describe the military situation, the seriousness of which was realised by the Emperor, to provide a foundation for the necessary political action. His Majesty approved our proposals with a strong and resolute heart.

As before, our anxieties for the Army were mingled with cares for the homeland. If the one did not stand firm the other would collapse. The present moment was to prove this truth more clearly than ever before.

My All-Highest War Lord returned home, and I followed him on October 1. I wanted to be near my Emperor in case he should need me in these days. Nothing was farther from my thoughts than to wish to control political developments. I was ready to explain the whole situation to the new Government which was in process of formation and answer their questions to the full extent that I thought possible. I hoped I could fight down pessimism and revive confidence. Unfortunately, the State had already been shaken too greatly for me to achieve my purpose as yet. I myself was still firmly convinced that, in spite of the diminution of our forces, we could prevent our enemy from treading the soil of the Fatherland for many months. If we succeeded in doing so the political situation was not hopeless. Of course it was a tacit condition for this success that our land frontier should not be threatened from the east or south and that the public at home stood firm.

Our peace offer to the President of the United States went forth in the night of October 4-5. We accepted the principles he had laid down in January of this year for a " just peace."

Our next concern was with the further operations. The failing energies of the troops, the steady diminution of our numbers and the repeated irruptions of the enemy compelled us on the Western Front gradually to withdraw our troops to shorter lines. What I told the leaders of the Government on October 3 can be put in the following words : As far as possible we are clinging to enemy soil. The operations and actions are of the same character as all others since the middle of August. A diminution of the enemy's offensive capacity is accompanying the deterioration of our own fighting powers. If the enemy delude themselves into believing that we shall collapse, we ourselves may make the mistake of hoping that the foe may become completely paralysed. Thus there could be only one *finale* unless we succeeded in creating one last reserve from the resources of our people at home. A rising of the nation would not have failed to make an impression on our enemies and on our own army. But had we still enough life left in us for that? Would the mass still possess the spirit of self-sacrifice? In any case our attempt to bring such a reserve to the front was a failure.

The homeland collapsed sooner than the Army. In these circumstances we were unable to offer any real resistance to the ever-increasing pressure of the President of the United States. Our Government cherished hopes of moderation and justice. The German soldier and the German statesman went different ways. The gulf between them could no longer be bridged. My last effort to secure co-operation is revealed in the following letter of October 24, 1918:

I cannot conceal from your Grand-Ducal Highness that in the recent speeches in the Reichstag I missed a warm appeal for goodwill to the Army, and that it caused me much pain. I had hoped that the new Government would gather together all the resources of the whole nation for the defence of our Fatherland. That hope has not been realised. On the contrary, with few exceptions they talk only of reconciliation and not of fighting the enemies which threaten the very existence of our country. This has had first a depressing and then a devastating effect on the Army. It is proved by serious symptoms.

If the Army is to defend the nation, it needs not only men but the conviction that it is necessary to go on fighting, as well as the moral impetus this great task demands.

Your Grand-Ducal Highness will share my conviction that realising the outstanding importance to be attached to the *moral* of the nation in arms, the Government and the representatives of the nation must inspire and maintain that spirit in both the army and the public at home.

To your Grand-Ducal Highness, as the Head of the new Government, I make an earnest appeal to rise to the height of this holy task.

It was too late. Politics demanded a victim. The victim was forthcoming on October 25.

In the evening of that day I left the capital, whither I had gone with my First Quartermaster-General to confer with our All-Highest War Lord, and returned to Head-quarters. I was alone. His Majesty had granted General Ludendorff's request to be allowed to resign and refused my own. Next day I entered what had been our common office. I felt as if I had returned to my desolate quarters from the graveside of a particularly dear friend. Up to the present moment—I am writing this in September, 1919—I have never again seen my loyal helper and adviser during these four years. In thought I have visited him a thousand times and always found him present in my grateful heart.

2
October 26 to November 9

At my request my All-Highest War Lord appointed General Gröner as my First Quartermaster-General. The general had become well known to me through holding previous posts during the war. I knew that he possessed a wonderful organising talent and a thorough knowledge of the domestic situation at home. The time we were now to spend together brought me ample proofs that I was not mistaken in my new colleague.

The problems which faced the general were as difficult as thankless. They demanded ruthless energy, utter self-denial, and renunciation of all glories but that of duty faithfully done, and the gratitude of none but his colleagues for the time being. We all know how great and critical was the work which awaited him. Affairs began to go from worse to worse. I will attempt to describe them in outline only.

In the East the last attempts at resistance of the Ottoman Empire were collapsing; Mosul and Aleppo fell, practically undefended, into the hands of the enemy. The Mesopotamian and Syrian armies had ceased to exist. We had to evacuate Georgia, not under military pressure, but because our economic plans there could not be realised, or at any rate made profitable. The troops which we had sent to help with the defence of Constantinople were withdrawn. The Entente did not attack it from Thrace. Stamboul was not destined to fall by some mighty deed of heroism or impressive manifestation of military power. I do not know the reason. It may lie in certain military considerations which were concealed from our understanding at the time. It is possible, too, that political motives played the dominant rôle in the decisions of the Entente.

All our other German reinforcements which were in Turkey were drawn in the direction of Constantinople. They left the land we had defended side by side, enjoying the respect of the chivalrous Turk with whom we had fought shoulder to shoulder in his life and death struggle. The outburst against us which now took place came from those circles which now saw their plans materialising and hoped by their manifestations of hatred of us to have a first claim on the good feeling of the newcomers. The true Ottoman knew that we stood ready to help not only in the present conflict but also with the subsequent reorganisation of his country. Enver and Talaat Pasha left the scene of their labours, insulted by their opponents but otherwise without a stain on their character.

Our last troops were withdrawn from Bulgaria also.

They were followed by the gratitude and honourable recognition of many, feelings which found their most vivid expression in a letter which the former Commander-in-Chief of the Bulgarian Army wrote to me about this time. I could not resist the impression that the lines expressed something which I had thought I detected so often in the words of this honourable officer : " Had I been politically free, my military actions would have been different." The revelation had come too late in his case, as in many others.

The political structure of Austria-Hungary went to pieces at the same time as her military organisation. She not only abandoned her own frontiers, but deserted ours as well. In Hungary rose the spectre of Revolution, inspired by hatred of the Germans. Can that be considered surprising? Was not this hatred an ingredient of Magyar pride? During the war the Hungarian had certainly had other sentiments when the Russian was knocking at his frontier. Mighty knocks and many of them! With what joy were the German troops greeted ; with what devotion were they looked after, nay pampered, when it was a question of helping to overthrow Serbia! What an enthusiastic reception we met with when we appeared on the scene to reconquer Transylvania! Gratitude is a rare blossom in human life, even rarer in political.

On the other hand in Rumania we often met with open expressions of gratitude. The Rumanian appreciated that without the destruction of Russia the free development of his country could never have been realised.

If certain circles in Germany now bring up the hatred of our former Allies as a reproach against us and a proof of our mistaken political and military principles, they forget that outbursts of hatred against an ally could also be heard in the enemy camp. Had not French soldiers insulted and shaken their fists at their English brothers in arms under our very eyes? Had not Frenchmen shouted to us: "Against you with England to-day; with you against England to-morrow!" In March, 1918, had not an angry French private, pointing to the ruins of the Cathedral of St. Quentin, cried out to an English soldier who had been taken prisoner at the same time: "*You* did that"?

I can only hope that the expressions of hatred between ourselves and our former Allies will gradually die away when the dark clouds lift which now veil the truth, and our former brothers in arms can once more gaze steadfastly at the scenes of glory we shared together, scenes in which German blood was poured out for the realisation of their plans and dreams.

By the end of October the collapse was complete at all points. It was only on the Western Front that we still thought we could avert it. The enemy pressure there was weaker, but weaker was our resistance also. Ever smaller became the number of German troops, ever greater the gaps in our lines of defence. We had only a few fresh German divisions, but great deeds could still have been done. Empty wishes, vain hopes. We were sinking, for the homeland was sinking. It could breathe no new life into us for its strength was exhausted!

On November 1 General Gröner went to the front. Our immediate concern was the withdrawal of our line of defence to the Antwerp—Meuse position. It was easy to decide but difficult to carry out the decision. Precious war material was within reach of the enemy in this line, but it was less important to save it than to get away the 80,000 wounded who were in our advance or field hospitals. Thus the execution of our decision was delayed by the feelings of gratitude which we owed to our bleeding comrades. It was plain that this situation could not last. Our armies were too weak and too tired. Moreover, the pressure which the fresh American masses were putting upon our most sensitive point in the region of the Meuse was too strong. Yet the experiences of these masses will have taught the United States for the future that the business of war cannot be learnt in a few months, and that in a crisis lack of this experience costs streams of blood.

The German battle line was then still connected with the lines of communication, the life-nerve which kept it in touch with the homeland. Gloomy pictures were certainly revealed here and there, but generally speaking the situation was still stable. Yet this could not last for long. The strain had become almost intolerable. Convulsions anywhere, whether at home or in the Army, would make collapse inevitable.

Such were my impressions in the first days of November.

Our fears of such convulsions began to be realised. There was a mighty upheaval in the homeland. The Revolution was beginning. As early as November 5 General Gröner hastened to the capital, foreseeing what must happen if a halt were not called, even at the eleventh hour. He made his way to his Emperor's presence and described the consequences if the Army were deprived of its head. In vain! The Revolution was now in full career, and it was purely by chance that the general escaped the clutches of the revolutionaries on his way back to Headquarters. This was on the evening of November 6.

The whole national organism now began to shake with fever. Calm consideration was a thing of the past. No one thought any longer about the consequences to the whole body politic, but only of the satisfaction of his own passions. These passions in turn began to foster the craziest plans. For could there be anything more crazy than the idea of making life impossible for the Army? Has a greater crime ever had its origin in human thought and human hatred? The body was now powerless; it could still deal a few blows, but it was dying. Was it surprising that the enemy could do what he liked with such an organism, or that he made his conditions even harder than those he had published?

Nothing more was heard of all the promises which the enemy propaganda had announced. The vision of revenge appeared in all its nakedness. "Woe to the vanquished!" A phrase which springs from fear as well as hatred.

Such was the situation on November 9. The drama did not conclude on this day, but took on new colours. The Revolution was winning. Let us not waste time on discussing the reasons. It first destroyed the very backbone of the Army, the German officer. As a foreigner has said, it tore the hard-earned laurels from his brows and pressed the thorny crown of martyrdom to his bleeding head. The comparison is moving in its truth. May it speak straight to the heart of every German!

The visible sign of the victory of the new powers was the overthrow of the Throne. The German Imperial House also fell.

The abdication of the Emperor and King was announced even before he had made his decision. In these days and hours much was done in the dark which will not always evade the fierce light of history.

The suggestion was made that we should use the troops from the front to restore order at home. Yet many of our officers and men, worthy of the highest confidence and capable of long views, declared that our men would unhesitatingly hold the front against the enemy, but would never take the field against the nation.

I was at the side of my All Highest War Lord during these fateful hours. He entrusted me with the task of bringing the Army back home. When I left my Emperor in the afternoon of November 9, I was never to see him again! He went, to spare his Fatherland further sacrifices and enable it to secure more favourable terms of peace.

In the midst of this mighty military and political upheaval, the German Army lost its internal cohesion. To hundreds and thousands of loyal officers and men it meant that the very foundations of their thoughts and feelings were tottering. They were faced with the hardest of all inward struggles. I thought that I could help many of the best of them to come to the right decision in that conflict by continuing in the path to which the wish of my Emperor, my love for my Fatherland and Army and my sense of duty pointed me. I remained at my post.

MY FAREWELL

IT was the end.

Like Siegfried, stricken down by the treacherous spear of savage Hagan, our weary front collapsed. It was in vain that it had tried to drink in new vitality from that fountain in our homeland which had run dry. It was now our task to save what was left of our army for the subsequent reconstruction of our Fatherland. The present was lost. We had only our hope in the future.

So to work!

I can quite understand the desire to leave the country which possessed many of our officers at the sight of the ruin of everything which they held dear. The longing " to have nothing more to do " with a world in which unbridled passions were mutilating the true heart of our nation until it was unrecognisable, was a very human one, and yet—I must say exactly what I think.

Comrades of the German Army, once the proud and mighty German Army! How can you talk of despondency? Think of the men who gave us a new Fatherland more than a hundred years ago. Their religion was their faith in themselves and in the sacredness of their cause. They built up a new Fatherland, not on the foundation of doctrines strange to them, but on those of the free development of the individual within the framework of the whole body politic, and on his sense of responsibility to the State. Germany will tread that path once more as soon as she is permitted to do so.

440

I have an unshakable conviction that, as in those days, our historical continuity with our great and glorious past will be preserved or restored where it has been broken. The old German spirit will descend upon us again, though it may be that we shall first have to go through the purifying fires of passion and suffering. Our enemies well know what that spirit means. They admired and hated it in peace, they feared and were amazed at it on the battlefields of the Great War. They tried to represent our strength to their peoples as the expression of the empty word " organisation."

They say nothing about the spirit which created this tenement and lives and works within it. With and through that spirit we will courageously build up our world again.

Germany, the goal and starting point of so much that is inexhaustible in human civilisation and culture, will count as naught only so long as she ceases to believe in her great historical mission. My faith is unshakable that the best among us, with their deep, strong thoughts, will succeed in fusing the ideas of to-day with the precious relics of ancient times and on them set the stamp of eternal qualities which will bring salvation to our Fatherland.

Such is the firm conviction with which I left the bloody battlefields of this War of Nations. I have witnessed the heroic struggle of my Fatherland, and I shall never believe that it was its death struggle.

I have often been asked the question on what I based my hopes of our ultimate victory even in the darkest hours of the war. I could only point to my faith in the justice of our Cause and my confidence in our Fatherland and the Army.

I passed through the serious crises of this long war and the days that followed it in a state of mind and feeling for which I can find no better expression than the words in which Field-Marshal Herrmann von Boyen, when he was Prussian War Minister in 1811, wrote to his Sovereign in the midst of the greatest military and political afflictions of our enslaved Fatherland :

"I am not in any way ignorant of the dangers of our situation, but where we have no alternative but subjection or honour, religion gives me the strength to do everything which right and duty demand.

"Man can never foresee with certainty the end of the task to which he has set his hand, but he who lives only for duty from inmost conviction has a shield about him which gives him peace in every situation in life, come what may, and indeed often brings him the success for which he strives.

"It is not the ravings of excited fanaticism, but the expression of a religious feeling when I thank those who taught me long ago to love my King and Fatherland as the most sacred possessions on earth."

For the time being a flood of wild political passions and sounding speeches has overwhelmed the ancient structure of our State, and apparently destroyed all our sacred traditions. Yet this flood will subside again. Then from the tempestuous seas of our national life will once more emerge that rock—the German Imperial House— to which the hopes of our Fathers clung in days of yore, and on which the future of our Fatherland was confidently set, nearly half a century ago, by our own efforts.

When our national ideals and our national conscience have resumed their sway among us, we shall see how moral values have been struggling to birth in our present grievous trials and the Great War on which no nation is entitled to look back with more pride than the German people, so long as it remained true to itself. Then, and then only, will the blood of all those who fell believing in the greatness of Germany have been poured out not in vain.

In that hope I lay down my pen and firmly build on you—Young Germany!

INDEX

AFRICA, East, the Protective Force in, 177
North coast of, German material for, 176
Africans on the Western Front, 384
Aisne, the, crossing of, 361
new line on, 389
Aisne-Champagne battle, 261, 375
Aisne—Vesle sector, the, 383
Albania, Austro-Bulgarian difficulties in, 420
operations in, 419 et seq.
Albert, capture of, 349
Albert of Prussia, Prince, 31
Aleppo, fall of, 434
Alexander of Prussia, Prince, 54, 60
Alexandretta, Gulf of, 294, 295
Allenstein, a thanksgiving service at, 99
castle of Teutonic Knights at, 91, 99
reserves at, 98
America, a lesson for, 437
enters the war, 257, 366
reinforcements for Western Front, 319, 386
(see also United States)
Americans penetrate line between the Argonne and the Meuse, 399
Amiens remains in enemy hands, 350-1
strategic importance of, 348
Amiens—St. Quentin line, enemy breach of, 390
Angerburg, Rennenkampf's march on, 94
Anglo-French front, lack of co-operation on, 330
Anglo-Indian Army in Palestine, 416
Arabs and, 303
Anthony of Hohenzollern, Prince, 26
death of, 27
Antwerp, escape of Belgian Army from, 242

Arabs fight under Turkish standard, 303
Argesch, the, battlefield of, 204
Armenia, mortality of Turkish soldiers in, 414
Russians suspend offensive in, 209
Turkish attack on Russians in, 411
Armenian Front in first half of 1917, 269
question, the, and Turkey, 229
Armentières, enemy evacuation of, 353
ground gained at, 352, 353
Arras, attack on east of, 349
failure of new defensive system at, 264
initial success of enemy at, 391
spring battle at, 266
Arz, General von, 259, 338, 419
Asia, events in first half of 1917, 269
overthrow of Turkish power in, 411 et seq.
the situation in 1916, 209
Asia Minor, Turkish deserters in, 306
Asiatic Corps, the, 299, 339
Asiatic Turkey, events in, 293
weakness of coast defences of, 294, 295
Auboué, 34
Augustovo, Forest of, a visit to, 147
Russian collapse at, 137
Augustus of Würtemberg, Prince, 36
Australian Cavalry in Palestine, 417
Austria, Polish policy of, 222
war with Prussia, 19
Austria-Hungary, and Germany, 78
and the war in the East, 135 et seq.
critical position of, 168
final attempt to help Bulgaria, 407
food supply in, 309, 421, 423
internal difficulties of, 309
longings for peace in, 310, 421
military and political issues in, 418 et seq.

Austria-Hungary, political difficulties of, 169

Austrian artillery, excellence of, 23

Austro-Hungarian Army at Lemberg, 110
critical frontal battles of, 101
headquarters transferred to Baden, 258
plight of, 418
retirement of: Germans to the rescue, 115

Austro-Hungarian Eastern Front, Russian offensive against, 154 et seq.

Austro-Hungarian field artillery, bravery of, 23, 279

Austro-Hungarians, and the Poland campaign, 173
despatched to Serbian frontier, 101
pessimism of, 174

Austro-Slav collapse near Stanislau, 275

Auxiliary Service Law, the, 238

Avesnes, as advanced headquarters, 342
memories of, 342

BADEN, Austro - Hungarian head-quarters at, 259
Grand Duke of, 66

Bagdad, German reinforcements for, 297
in the possession of the English, 269, 296
the Asiatic Corps, 299, 339

Bailleul, capture of, 354

Balkans, the, hostile attacks in Macedonia, 292
position in August, 1916, 165

Baltic Provinces, liberation of, 335

Bapaume in German hands, 349
line withdrawn, 397

Bartenwerffer, Colonel von, 58

Batilly, 33

Bavaria, Crown Prince of, 217

Beaumont, battle of, 40

Beersheba, English offensive at, 300

Below, General, 94

Beneckendorffs, the, 3

Berlin, a triumphal entry into, 51
author's studies in, 14

Berlin, Royal review at, 29
social life of, 54

Bernhardi, General von, 54
enters Paris, 48

Bernstorff, Count, memorandum to, 253

Bethmann-Hollweg and the U-boat campaign, 255
resignation of, 310, 311
visits Posen, 145

Beuthen, 115

Bialla, a fight at, 104

Bialoviesa, Forest of, a visit to, 147

Bischofsburg, fighting at, 94, 95

Bismarck, Prince, 42, 220
a prophecy of, 50

Blücher, Field-Marshal, 121
at Gonesse, 44

Blumenthal, General von, and the Crown Prince, 22

Bohemia, Prussian invasion of, 19

Bölcke, Captain, 193

Bolshevism, author's reflections on, 51
in Russia, 335-6

Boris, Crown Prince, 179, 408

Bosnian crisis, the, 78

Bothmer, General Count, 157

Boyen, Field-Marshal von, a letter to his Sovereign, 442

Breslau, 113

Brest-Litovsk, a conference at, 334
headquarters at, 158
peace negotiations at, 423
Treaty of Peace signed at, 335

Brody, German concentration at, 278

Bronsart, General von, 63

Brussiloff, 157, 273

Bucharest, an attempted break-through from Kronstadt, 203
fall of, 204
peace negotiations at, 423

Bukovina, the, clear of the enemy, 279
Russian success in, 156

Bulgaria, alliance with Germany, 225
and its sovereign, 179
and the Dobrudja question, 225
anti-Germanic factions in, 307
author's views on alliance with, 170
collapse of, 399, 400 et seq.

Bulgaria, concludes an armistice, 411
  declares war, 199
  food shortage in, 306, 400
  German troops for, 175
  German troops withdrawn from, 434
  political parties of, 400
Bulgarian Army, the, 175
  retreat of (September, 1918), 408
  Russophile sentiment in, 200, 212
  wholesale desertions from, 401, 404, 410
Bulgarians, and Salonica, 248
  capture Constanza, 203
  difficulties with their communications, 207
  forced back in Macedonia, 403
  suspicious of Turkey, 207
  ultra-sensitiveness of, 208
Bülow, Field-Marshal von, 54
  at Prince Leopold's jubilee, 68
Burian, Count, 231, 423
  recall of, 424
Burkersdorf, Austrian Uhlans captured at, 20

Cadorna and the Isonzo battles, 284, 285, 286
Cambrai, a conference at, 216, 217
  an enemy surprise at, 289
  enemy break-through held, 398
  initial success of enemy at, 391
  successful counter-attack at, 290
Camphausen, a picture by, 60
Canrobert, Marshal, 36
Carpathian front, situation in August, 1916, 165
Carpathians, the, fighting in, 138
  Russian operations in, 211
Cassel and its importance, 355, 356
Champagne, the operations in, 375 et seq.
Channel Coast in danger, 355, 356, 357
Charles, Emperor, 258
Chataldja lines, fortifications of, 417
Château-Thierry, 361
  Americans at, 366, 382
  left wing withdrawn from, 382
Chemin des Dames, the, 358, 359
  a surprise attack on, 359
  evacuation of, in 1917, 359

Chlum, fighting at, 25
Cholera, ravages of, 28
Classics, the, author on, 10
Clausewitz, 111, 112
Coblenz, unveiling of a monument to William I at, 66
Cologne cathedral, 8
Communist insurrection in Paris, 49
Compiègne, French reserves at, 371
Conrad, von Hötzendorf, General, 181, 247
  advocates a decisive operation in the East, 136
  and a projected attack on Bucharest, 198
  in command of South Tyrolese Front, 259
Constantinople, 417
  enemy's lost opportunity at, 418
  food shortage in, 304, 305
  German troops withdrawn from, 434
  Russians and, 212
Constanza, fall of, 203
Corbény, 44
Cossacks, brutality of, 97
Craonne, 44
  heights stormed, 363
Czecho-Slovaks, excellent work in Italy of, 284
Czechs, 19
Czenstochau, headquarters at, 122
Czernin, Count, 338
  a suggested Peace Resolution of, 423
  resignation of, 421

Danube, the, crossed by Mackensen, 280
Danzig, the 3rd Regiment of Foot Guards at, 18
Dardanelles campaign, the, 296
  Turkish losses in, 299
Dardanelles, the, Turkish troops at, 417
Deime—Angerburg line, the, 99, 101, 104
Denmark, war with, 15
Deutsch-Eylau, entrainment of 1st Army Corps for, 86
Deutschland and its commander, 193

Diplomacy and foreign policy, 219
Dobrudja, the, fighting for, 201
  question, the, 225, 226, 306, 307
  Southern, battles in, 212
Doiran, Lake, Bulgarian heroism at,
  404
Doncourt, 32, 33
Dormans, 361
Douaumont, loss of, 215
Dunker, Geheimrat, 54
Dvina, the, 280
Dvinsk, Russian attack at, 275

EAST PRUSSIA (see Prussia, East)
East, the, collapse in, 434
  hostilities resumed in, 335
Eastern Front, a counter-attack in,
  276 et seq.
  at end of 1916, 211 et seq.
  author leaves for, 81
  battle and operations on, 135
  in first half of 1917, 269
  plans for a decisive action on, 136
  troops transferred from the West,
  277
Eichorn, Field-Marshal von, 54, 136
Elbe, the, storming of, 21
Elizabeth, Queen, 14
England, her determination to conquer, 316
  " Trafalgar fame " of, 295
English retirement on Amiens, 349
  Army, insufficient preparation of,
  330
  High Command, the, faulty plans
  of, 290
  troops, the, élite of, 330
Entente, the, and the Russian collapse, 271, 274
  autocratic power of, 365-6
  Intelligence Service of, 319
  their " Propaganda in the Enemy's
  Camp," 314, 392
  ultimatum to Rumania, 194
Enver Pasha, 209, 434
  a conference with, 198
  and German troops on Syrian Front,
  339
  and neutrality of Turkey, 176
  and the protection of the Gulf of
  Alexandretta, 294

Enver Pasha, and the Rumanian campaign, 198
  his lack of military training, 182
  loyalty of, 181, 228, 229
  requests German help to recover
  Bagdad, 297
Epernay, 373
  advance towards, 376
Escherich, Forstmeister, 147
Estaires, fall of, 353
Evert, Adjutant-General, Army order
  of, 153
Eydtkuhnen, 108

FALKENHAYN, General von, 164, 223
  and the Bagdad enterprise, 297
  battle of Hermannstadt, 202
  secures the initiative, 202
Falkenstein, General von, 66
Ferdinand of Bulgariă, King, 179,
  180
  and the Dobrudja question, 226
  on German troops, 299
  refuses an armistice, 408
Finland, military assistance to, 336
Flanders, battle in, 288, 351 et seq.
  preparations for a new offensive in,
  371
Foch, Marshal, his decision in
  August, 1918, 397
  knowledge of German plans, 379
  reserves of, 371
France, as saviour of England, 357
  her determination to fight to a
  finish, 315
  opening of the " great battle " in,
  346
  self-abnegation of, 396
  signs peace treaty with Germany
  (1871), 49
Francis Joseph, Emperor, death of,
  180
Franco-German war, the, 32
François, General von, 94, 95, 97
Frederick Charles, Prince, 21
Frederick William II, King, 4, 14, 22
  announces surrender of Napoleon, 42
  death of, 62
  thanks his troops, 28
Frederick William IV, birthday
  celebration of, 14

French, the, a counter-attack on the Meuse, 215
  and battle of Sedan, 41, 42
  attacks in August, 1918, 397
  temperament of, 48
French Front, German retirement on Roye, 1918, 394
  in July, 1918, 371
Freytag-Loringhoven, 63

GALICIA, Austria and, 284
  clear of the enemy, 279
  collapse in, 165, 169
  fighting in, 284
  oilfields of, 213
  reinforcements from Eastern Front for, 157
  Russian front broken in, 139
  Russian operations in, 212
Gallwitz, 141
Garonne, Bois de la, 40, 41, 43
Gaza, English offensive at, 300,
  failure of enemy attack at, 269, 296
  Turkish troops at, 210
Georgia, evacuation of, 434
  troops sent to, 413
Gerdauen, Russian retreat from, 106
  17th Corps and 1st Reserve Corps at, 86
German Army, an enemy officer's tribute to, 365
  and the German nation, 71
  area of French spring offensive in hands of, 361
  author's farewell to, 440 et seq.
  author's tribute to, 364-5, 383 et seq.
  battle-worn troops and enemy propaganda, 392
  changes in defensive system of, 261 et seq.
  defects in structure of, 367
  disposition of, at outbreak of world war, 82
  enemy propaganda in, 369
  "feudal loyalty" of, 17
  General Staff of, 54 et seq.
  heroism of, on French Front, 381
  last weeks of war, 426 et seq.
  loses its internal cohesion, 439
  on the defensive (1918), 389 et seq.

German Army, peace-time work of, 71 et seq.
  reconstruction of, 53
  tactical training in, 332
  the great break-through (1918), 344 et seq.
  the Medical Services, 150
  vanquished on the defence, 393 et seq.
  withdrawal from French Front, 398
German Crown Prince, the, 216, 345
German defence lines, defects in, 395
German Empire, foundation of, 46-7
German foreign policy: difficulties of, 77
German Navy, the, von Tirpitz and, 146
Germans and the Flanders battle, 351 et seq.
  evacuate salient north of Lys, 398
Germany, abdication of the Kaiser, 438, 439
  accepts President Wilson's peace offer, 431
  alliance with Bulgaria, 225
  and Austria-Hungary, 78
  and Rumania's declaration of war, 167
  and the Allies: author on, 172 et seq.
  and the Polish problem, 221 et seq.
  announces her readiness to conclude peace, 232
  benefits conferred by her colonisation, 113
  blockade of, 314
  changed feelings of former Allies towards, 435
  collapse of the homeland, 432, 436
  compact with Turkey, 228
  concentrates forces for decision in the West, 339
  end of party peace in, 311
  fails to separate the Entente, 242
  her intentions and prospects for 1918, 325 et seq.
  introduction of Auxiliary Service Law in, 238
  Peace resolution approved by the Reichstag, 320
  privations in, 313
  resignation of Imperial Chancellor, 310

Germany, Revolution in, 437
tension in, 80
Glogau, a commemorative tablet at, 9
Gneisenau, 121
Goltz, von der, 109
Gonesse, 44
Gorlice, 139
Gradsko, fall of, 408
in peril, 403 et seq.
Grajevo, district of, 101
Graudenz, fortress of, 88, 89
Great War, change in High Command, 164
outbreak of, 80
West or East? the question of a
decision, 129 et seq.
Greece, mobilisation of, 293
the political situation in, 248
Greek Divisions, Royal, 402
Greek language, author on, 10
Groeben, von der, 5
Gröner, General, appointed author's
First Quartermaster-General, 433
interviews William II, 437
visits the front, 436
Gumbinnen, author's pledge of fealty
to William II at, 63
battle at, 82

HANNONVILLE, 32
Hanover, life in, 31
the King's visit to, 31
3rd Guards Regiment at, 30
Hazebrouck, advance on, checked, 354
Hedin, Sven, 145
Heiligenbeil, 4
Helldorf, Lieutenant von, 34
Hermannstadt, battle of, 202
Hertling, Count, and Brest-Litovsk
conference, 335
becomes Chancellor, 312
death of, 313
Hindenburg, Field-Marshal von, a
tiring march, 33
accepted for the Kriegsakademie, 53
additional duties for, 147
an echo of Königgratz, 24
an Imperial summons to arms, 81
ancestry of, 3 et seq.
and Count Czernin, 422
and last battles of Allies, 400 et seq.

Hindenburg, and Ludendorff's resignation, 433
and peace proposals, 424
and the attack on Italy, 283 et seq.
and the U-boat war, 250 et seq.
and the question of peace, 231 et
seq., 430 et seq.
appointed G.O.C., 12
as Staff officer, 54
at Königgratz battle, 21
at loggerheads with Government, 311
at proclamation of Emperor at Versailles, 45-47
attitude on political questions, 219
et seq.
awarded the Iron Cross, 32, 312
battle of Lake Narocz, 154
battle of Sedan, 40 et seq.
battle of Tannenberg, 86 et seq.
becomes a major, 59
becomes a second-lieutenant, 17
birth of, 5
campaign in the East, 77 et seq.
campaign in Poland, 110 et seq.
captures Austrian Uhlans, 20
Commander-in-Chief of the Eastern
forces, 123
commander of 91st Infantry Regiment, 64
commands 28th Division at Karlsruhe, 67
concentration in Thorn—Gnesen
region, 125
cosmopolitanism of, 48
enters Cadet Corps, 9
first glimpse of Paris, 44
first meeting with his future
Kaiser, 60
first visit to Berlin, 14
his farewell and hopes for the
future, 440 et seq.
his parents, 6, 28
home at Neudeck, 5
hostile offensive in 1917, 261 et seq.,
288 et seq.
impressions of political situation,
167
in battle for greatness of Prussia
and Germany, 17 et seq.
in command of a newly-formed
(9th) Army, 112

Hindenburg, in command of a Polish company, 58
in command of 4th Army Corps, 67
in Paris after Sedan, 48
joins the Foot Guards, 17
journeys to the Silesian capital, 113
jubilee of Army life, 148
leaves the 8th Army, 109, 110
life at headquarters, 186 *et seq.*
marriage of, 56
meets Count Burian, 423
meets Count von Moltke, 60
meets Grand Duke Nicholas, 119
meets Skobeleff, 56
meets von Tirpitz, 145
military situation with regard to Rumania, 199
objects to operations in Italy and Macedonia, 247 *et seq.*
on collapse of Bulgaria, 400 *et seq.*
on consequences of defeat on Aug. 8, 1918, 394 *et seq.*
on the Dobrudja question, 225 *et seq.*
on the Turks, 302-4
opposes Peace Resolution, 321
ordered to clear East Prussia of Rennenkampf's Army, 99
orders withdrawal of troops to north of Marne, 378
outbreak of Great War, and recall of, 77 *et seq.*
page to Queen Elizabeth, 14
perplexing orders from Main Head-quarters, 110, 111
preparations for 1917 campaign, 241 *et seq.*
presented to the Empress, 68
presented to William I, 15
promoted to rank of captain, 54
pursues the enemy, 107, 141
reasons for a last great offensive, 325 *et seq.*
receives Order of Red Eagle, 30
reflections on political events after his retirement, 77 *et seq.*
rejects idea of offensive in Italy and Macedonia, 247
relations with Ludendorff, 84 *et seq.*, 112, 123, 428 (*see also* Ludendorff)

Hindenburg, reports collapse of Russian Narew Army, 98
requests permission to resign, 311, 433
retirement of, 60, 70 *et seq.*
retrospect and prospects at end of June, 1918, 364 *et seq.*
schooldays, 8
seventieth birthday of, 16, 65, 259
studies military history, 12
summoned to a political conference at Spa, 396
summoned to Main Headquarters, 163
tactics teacher at *Kriegsakadamie*, 63
takes steps to secure armistice and peace, 429
the Franco-German war, and, 32 *et seq.*
the three great offensive battles, 344 *et seq.*
transferred to Great General Staff, 59
transferred to War Ministry, 64
tribute to, and criticism of, German Army, 364 *et seq.*
unchanged soldier instincts of, 365
visit to Laon, 358
visited by Bethmann-Hollweg, 145
visits battlefields of Laon, 361
visits his old regiments, 343
visits Rome, 11
visits Western Front, 216
wife and family of, 56, 57
work in peace-time, 53 *et seq.*
youthful days, 3 *et seq.*
"Hindenburg Programme," the, 237-8
Hohenstein, desperate position of Russian Army at, 96
Horonowes, 23
Hötzendorf, General Conrad von, 136, 181, 198, 247, 259
House, Colonel, 254
Hungary, revolution in, 435
Hutier, 63

Indo-Australian cavalry squadrons on Syrian Front, 417
Influenza, an outbreak of, at head-quarters, 191

Insterburg, enemy corps at, 105
  German headquarters at, 107
  Rennenkampf's headquarters at, 102
  Russian reserves at, 104
Irak, situation in, 210
Ismail Hakki, and the food supply of
    the Turkish Army, 304
Isonzo Front, repeated Italian attacks
    on, 165, 283, 284, 285
Italian soldiers, in France, 372, 376,
    384
  lay down their arms, 317
Italy and Germany, 79
  anxiety regarding, 156
  attack on, 283 *et seq.*
  Austro-Hungarian plan of attack
    on, 156
  author on, 247
  failure of Austro-Hungarian attack,
    and its consequences, 418
  her bitter fate, 318
Ivangorod, battle of, 116

JEKOFF, General, and Salonica cam-
    paign, 195
  and the plan of campaign against
    Rumania, 198
  and the Western offensive, 338
  confidence in his troops, 182, 200
  popularity of, 182
  the Dobrudja question and, 226
Jericho, a British break-through at,
    414
Jerusalem, fall of, 300
Johannisburg, 86
Joseph II, Emperor, a tribute to an
    enemy hero, 29

KALKANDELEN, capitulation of, 411
  reached by retiring Bulgarians, 411
Kammerar, Major, death of, 191
Karlsruhe, 67
Kemmel, Mount, collapse of English
    defence on, 355, 356
  French attempt recovery of, 356
  key-position in Flanders, 354
Kerensky, a counter-offensive against,
    298
  a deserter discloses plans of, 275
  offensive against German Front,
    273, 274

Ketzler, Colonel, 54
Kobelt, Herr, author's schoolmaster, 8
König, Captain, 193
Königgrätz, battle of, 21 *et seq.*
  an incident of, 60
Königinhof, 21
  death of Prince of Hohenzollern at,
    27
Königsberg, garrison of, retreat to
    the west, 86
  Rennenkampf's march on, 93, 95, 96
Kovno, 139
  fall of, 142
  headquarters at, 147
Kreuznach, author entertains heir-
    presumptive of Turkey, 415
  headquarters at, 258
  seventieth birthday celebration at,
    16, 259
Kronstadt, defeat of Rumanians at,
    202
Kulm, battle of, 7
Kurland, attack on, 139
Kut-el-Amara, Turks at, 302

LANSDOWNE, Lord, 317
Laon, a long-range gun at, 348, 357
  fighting (in 1814) in neighbourhood
    of, 358-9
  shells and bombs on, 361, 382
  the battlefields visited, 361
Latin language, author on, 10
Lauenstein, 63
Lautenburg—Bischofsburg line, the,
    94
Lemberg, a successful thrust at, 140
  perilous position of Austro-Hun-
    garians at, 110
Lenin at Brest-Litovsk conference, 334
Leopold of Bavaria, Prince, 68
Liége, fall of, 81
Limbsee, 4
Linsinger, Captain von, death of, 191
Lithuania, a cavalry sweep into, 139
Lodz, battle of, 127
Longchamps, a parade at, 49
Lorraine, victory in, 81
Lötzen, headquarters at, 186
  memories of, 144
Ludendorff, General, a brief separa-
    tion from, 135

Ludendorff, General, a conference with the Emperor, 188
a new appointment for, 112
and the Vistula operations, 82 et seq.
and the Winter Battle, 141
at Liége, 82
author's Chief of Staff, 81, 123
becomes First Quartermaster-General, 163
convinced of necessity of peace, 428-9
energy of, 147
his resignation accepted, 433
visits Army Group of Crown Prince Rupprecht, 378
visits Western Front, 216
Luttwitz, 63
Lyck, enemy defeat at, 105
Lys, the, battle on, 351 et seq.
reached and crossed, 353

Macedonia, attack of Entente armies in, 402
Bulgarian attack in, 196
hostile attacks on Bulgarian front in, 292
question of an offensive in, 247
Sarrail's renewed attacks in, 268
Macedonian Front, fighting on, 206 et seq.
German commanders on, 244
position in 1918 on, 402
transfer of German troops to West from, 338
Turkish reinforcements for, 207
Mackensen, General von, 94, 97, 198
at conference with Enver Pasha, 198
crosses the Danube, 280
in command of 9th Army, 123
on northern bank of the Danube, 204
successful advance of, 201
Magdeburg, 68
Margency, 45
Marienburg, headquarters at, 86
Marne salient, the, situation in, 370 et seq.
Marne, the, battle of, 130
crossed, 374, 380
withdrawal from, 382
Mars la Tour, 32, 33

Massenbach, Herr von, 8
Masuria, the " Winter Battle in," 137 et seq.
Masurian Lakes, battle of the, 99 et seq.
a general retreat of enemy in, 106
Medical Services of German Army, 150
Merville, capture of, 353
Mesopotamia, a lost chance in, 300
mortality of Turks in, 414
Turkish operations in, 211
Messines, a new attack on, 353
battle of, 266
Michaelis, Dr., resignation of, 312
succeeds Bethmann Hollweg, 311
Military operations and the encroachment of politics on, 111 et seq., 135, 220 et seq., 435
Miroslavsky, Polish leader, 7
Mlawa, Russian concentration at, 87, 93
Mohammedans, 176
Caucasian, 412
Moldavia, frontier of, an offensive comes to a standstill on, 279
Moltke, Colonel-General von, 82
Moltke, Field-Marshal Count von, 54
a brief toast by, 61
and General von Winterfeldt, 60
death of, 61
on military and political leadership in war, 220
resignation of, 60
Monastir, loss of, 206, 207
Montdidier, 350
Mont d'Hiver, 44
Mont Valérien, a French sortie from, 47
Montenegro, 242
Montmartre and the Communists, 51
Montmédy, a reception at, 216
Mosul, fall of, 434
Mulhausen, a victory at, 81
Myszaniec, 97, 99

Napoleon I, 5
Napoleon III, as prisoner en route for Belgium, 43
at Sedan, 41
surrender of, 42

Napoleonic campaign of 1806, 116
Narew Army, 82, 83, 86
    collapse of, 98
Narocz, Lake, 151, 152
    battle of, author and, 154
Neidenburg, 96
    advance on, 95
Neudeck, 4
" Nibelung Compact," the, 78
Nicholas, Grand Duke, 118
Nicholas II, Tsar, abdication of, 270
Niemen Army, the, 82, 86, 101, 139
    numerical superiority of, 103 (*see*
        also Russian Army)
Nish, 268
Nivelle, General, 265, 273
Nordenburg, Russian reserves at, 104
Novo Georgievsk, capture of, 142

Ochrida, Lake, Italian offensive near,
    420
Oesel, co-operation of Fleet with
    Army at, 281, 282
    in German hands, 282
Oldenburg, Grand Duke and Duchess
    of, 65
Opatow—Radom line, the, 117
Ortelsberg, 96, 97
Osterode, captured Russian Corps
    Commanders in, 96
Ostrolenka, 97
Ottoman Corps, the, 297, 298

Pacifism, French definition of, 315
Palestine, anxiety regarding, 210
Pan-Islamism, 229
    and the overthrow of Turkish power
        in Asia, 412, 413
Pape, Lieutenant-General von, 39
Pardubitz, 28
Paris, capitulation of, 47
    march on, 43
    shelled by long-range gun, 348, 357,
        358, 361
    the Communist insurrection in, 49
Passarge, the, 5
Passenheim, 96
Peace proposals, 232
    enemy's reply to President Wilson, 233
    German acceptance sent to Presi-
        dent Wilson, 431

Péronne, bombed by enemy aircraft,
    393
    fall of, 349
Persia, a Turkish Army Corps
    dispatched to, 210
    Turks and, 413
Petersburg, alarm in, at attack on
    Riga, 281, 282
Petersdorff, Colonel von, 56
Pinne (Posen), reminiscences of, 8
Pless, a consultation with Kaiser at,
    158, 163
    Count Burian at, 423
    headquarters at, 178
    life in, 186
Poland, author's views on, 221 *et seq.*
    Count Czernin and, 423
    the 1848 rising in, 7
Poland campaign, the, 110 *et seq.*
    a counter-attack, 124
    a curious strategic situation in, 117
    enemy's plans for, 118
    the advance, 114 *et seq.*
    the retreat, 120 *et seq.*
Poles, 58, 59
Polish Volunteers, 224
Politics and military operations, 111
    et seq., 135, 220 *et seq.*, 435
Portuguese troops in flight, 353
Posen, " French days " in, 7
    headquarters at, 124, 186
    Poles of, 58
Postawy, 151
Potsdam, author's regiment at, 18
Prilep, Bulgarian retreat on, 408
Prussia, East, celebrated visitors to, 144
    counter-measures against enemy in,
        87
    enemy force and armaments in, 87
    Rennenkampf's plunders in, 88
    Russian advance on, 86 *et seq.*
    the struggle for, 77 *et seq.*
Prussia, war with Austria, 19
Prussian Army, a favourite battle
    formation of, 24
    mobilisation of, 18
    triumphal entry into Berlin of, 29
Prussian Cadet Corps, life in the, 9
Prussian Corps of Officers, the, 17
Prussian Guard, monuments to, on
    heights of St. Privat, 39

Przasnysz, storming of, 141
Przemysl, 135

QUADRUPLE ALLIANCE, a Treaty of
    Peace with Russia, 335
    military situation of, changes for
        the worse, 366
Quérimont Farm, 43

RADOM, headquarters at, 122
Radoslavoff, Bulgarian Minister-
    President, 183
    Bulgarians and, 308
    loyalty of, 185
    overthrow of, 400
Rahovo, Rumanian disaster at, 201
Rappard, Frau von, 8
Rennenkampf, General, 82
    battle of the Masurian Lakes, 99
        et seq.
    his fame as soldier and general, 102
    marches on Königsberg, 93, 95, 96
    plunders and burns East Prussia,
        88
    presses on to Königsberg, 95, 96
    retreat of, 98
Revolution, French, 50
    in Germany, 437
    in Hungary, 435
    in Russia, 270
Rheims, 361
    its military importance, 377
    unsuccessful attempts for, 370
Rheims battle, 265, 266
    opening of, 374
    plan of, 370 et seq.
Rhine Provinces, 65
Richter, Professor, 54
Richthofen, Captain von, 193
Riga, alarm in Russia at attack on,
    281
    Russian attack at, 275
    Russian northern wing at, 280
Rome, 11
Roncourt, 36
    occupation of, 37
Roon, Field-Marshal von, 18, 62
Rosberitz, 25
Rumania declares war, 159
    defection of, 242
    enters war, 165, 194

Rumania, invasion of, 203
    plan of campaign against, 198
Rumanian Army, an unsuccessful
    attack against, on Moldavian
    frontier, 279
Rumanian campaign, the, 194 et seq.
Rumanian frontier, troops for, 166
Rumanians defeated at Hermann-
    stadt, 202
    retreat from Transylvania, 202
Rupprecht, Crown Prince, tactical
    objective of, 344
Russia, entire collapse of, 318
    fall of the Tsar, 270
    her designs on Constantinople, 212
    her position after the war in
        Eastern Asia, 79
    hopes of a separate peace with, 224
    in 1914-15, 132 et seq.
    in revolution, 270
    internal agitation in, 282
    out of the war, 335
    Treaty of Peace signed with, 335
Russian Army, a tribute to, 97
    enormous reserves of, 104, 105
    numerical superiority of, 103, 118,
        123, 127, 128, 138, 150, 151, 152,
        243
Russian Front, an armistice on, 333
    crumbling of, 269
Russian Poland, impressions of, 116-
    117
Russians, and the Rumanians, 212
    attacked by Turks in Armenia, 411
    enormous losses of, in 1917, 273, 274
    heroism of, 96
    plan a concentric attack against
        8th Army, 87
    plan invasion of Germany, 127
    pursuit of, 107, 141
    retreat of, 279
    their careless use of wireless, 123,
        127
    threatened with envelopment, 141
    wholesale shooting of horses by, on
        surrender, 142

ST. GERMAIN, 46
Ste. Marie aux Chênes, 34
Ste. Marie Roncourt, 36
St. Privat, battle of, 35 et seq.

St. Privat, losses at, 38
  monuments to Prussian Guards at,
  39
St. Quentin, a break-through at, 347
  a humane Englishman at, 363
Salonica, Bulgarians and, 248
  emergency measures at, 195
Samsonoff, General, 82
  defeated at Tannenberg, 94 *et seq.*
Sarrail, General, attack on Monastir
  by, 206
  renews attacks in Macedonia, 268,
  292
Schakir Bey, 63
Scharnhorst, a dictum of, 300
Schlieffen, Colonel Count von, 59
Scholtz, General von, 94, 95
Schwerin, Field-Marshal Count, monu-
  ments to, 28, 29
Schwichart, Surgeon-General, 5
Sedan, battle of, 40 *et seq.*
  the prelude to, 40
Seegenberg, Major von, 32
Seel, Major von, 31, 39
Senussi, supplies for, 176
Serbia, a rising in, 26
Serbian Army, the, reappearance of,
  242
Serbians capture Uskub, 411
Siberian Corps, the, 118
Siegfried Line, the, 245
  back to, 398
Sievers, General, 136
Silesia, critical situation in, 120 *et
  seq.*
  headquarters in, 115, 178
Sinai peninsula, Turkish defeat in,
  210
Sixtus of Parma, Prince, and Count
  Czernin, 421
Skaggerak, battle of, 146, 296
Skobeleff, General, author's meeting
  with, 56
Smorgon, Russian attack at, 275
Sofia, the American Consulate in, 400
Soissons, an initial enemy attack
  mastered at, 391
  enemy success and failure at, 391
  fighting at, 44, 265, 266, 292
  French defences at, 358
  heroic deeds at, 381

Soissons—Rheims, battle of, 356 *et
  seq.*
Somme battle, 244
Somme battlefield, the, 349
Somme, the, battle of, 346 *et seq.*
  critical position on both sides of,
  158
  fierce fighting on, 215
  indecisive struggle on, 164
  reached, and crossed, 348
Soor, battle of, 19
Spa, a political conference at (August,
  1918), 396
  headquarters transferred to, 341
Sperling, General von, 56
Stallupönen, an action at, 82
Stanislau, Russian offensive at, 275
Stein, 63
Steinmitz, General von, 22
Stettin, author's marriage at, 56
Strasburg, the Danube Monarchy and,
  338
Submarine warfare, President Wil-
  son's attitude regarding, 233,
  235-6 (*see also* U-boat campaign)
Suez Canal, the, Turkish attempt on,
  210
Suvalki, 107
Sweti, 25
Syria, Falkenhayn's visit to, 297
  food supply in, 211
  reserves sent to, 300
Syrian Front, English attacks on, 414

TALAAT PASHA, 183, 229, 434
Tank-warfare, 289, 291, 380, 382, 390,
  391
Tannenberg, battle of, 94 *et seq.*
Tarnopol, 278
Tartenau, 21
Teutonic Knights, 3
  castle of, 91, 99
Tewfik Effendi, 63
Thorn, fortress of, 88, 89
Thrace, weak protection of, 417
Tilsit, enemy march on, 105
Tirpitz, Grand Admiral von, 145
Tisza, Count, visits Pless, 192
Tolmino, 286
Trans-Caucasia, Turks in, 412
Transylvania, concentration in, 202

Transylvania, retreat of Rumanians
from, 202
Rumanian occupation of, 212
Trieste threatened, 284
Tripoli, war in, 79
Trotsky at Brest-Litovsk conference,
334
refuses to sign Peace Treaty, 334
Turkey, a new Sultan of, 415
an Army Corps for Persia, 210
and the Armenian question, 229
as " a cipher," 302
asked to return German troops :
their recall cancelled, 339
author's views on alliance with, 170
compact with, 228
Enver Pasha on critical position of,
182, 183
help to, 176
internal difficulties of, 415
loses her land defences, 417
Ottoman corps restored to, 297, 298
Sultan of, and his Army, 415
the domestic situation of her statesmen, 184
tragic end of Caucasus armies of,
250
Turkish Armies in the Asiatic
theatres, 209
Turkish Army, a surprise attack on,
in the coast plain, 417
condition of, 176
Turkish defeats in Syria, 300
Turkish reinforcements on the
Struma Front, 207
Turks, and Persia, 413
their services in the war, 302-4
under German protection, 297, 298
Tutrakan, 200, 201
Tyrol offensive, abandonment of, 165

U-BOAT campaign, 250 et seq.
and the peace proposals, 236
effect of, 274, 278, 288, 319
U-boats, von Tirpitz on, 146
Ukraine, the, why German forces
were necessary in, 336
United States, the, internal situation
at end of 1917, 318 (see also
America)
Usdau, Russian defeat at, 95

Usdau, strategical importance of,
94
Uskub, Bulgarian retreat on, 408, 409
captured by Serbians, 411

VALONA, importance as naval base of,
420
Italians at, 419
Venetian Alps, failure of attempted
capture of, 287
Venizelos, M., 293
Verdun, French attacks at, 292
hopeless efforts for, 214
initial success of enemy at, 391
its importance, 154 et seq.
Verdy, General von, 57, 64
Versailles, proclamation of William I
as Emperor at, 8, 45
Vienna, a compact regarding Poland,
222
difficulties of food supply in, 421,
423
Villaume, Captain, 54
Villers-Brétonneux, attacks on, 350
importance of, 350
renewed attacks at, 355
Villers-Cotterêts, 361
French reserves at, 371
Villers le Roi, 47
Vilna, 140
a conflict at, 143
advance on, 142
Vionville, battlefield of, 32
Vistula Front, the, 117
actions on, 139
disposition of rival armies on, 86
et seq.
failures of Austrian counter-attack,
121
operations on east of, 82 et seq.
Vogel von Falkenstein, Colonel, 59

WAHLSTATT a Royal visit to, 14
Cadets' Academy at, 3, 12
Waldersee, General Count, 26, 56
War, crises inevitable in, 264
demoralising effect of, 314
examples of humanity in, 362, 363
the miseries of, 91, 92
Warsaw, 116

Warsaw, an important capture at, 118
Governor-General of, 223
surrender of, 143
Wartensleben, General Count von, 69
Wehlau, Russian reserves at, 104
Wellington, Duke of, 44
Westar, 25, 27
Western Front at end of 1916, 211 et seq.
author's impressions of, 217
defects in defence lines of (Aug., 1918), 395
enemy retirement on, 349
enemy's weak leadership on, 216
German retirement on, 246
great offensive on entire, 344 et seq.
hostile attacks on, 213, 261 et seq., 288 et seq.
preparations for 1917 campaign on, 244
question of an offensive on, in 1918, 325 et seq., 340
situation on, at end of August, 1916, 164
the Siegfried Line, 245, 398
withdrawal of line of defence on (Nov., 1918), 436
Weyherrn, General Hans von, 56
Willenberg, 96
William I, German Emperor, author's presentation to, 15
death of, 62
proclaimed Emperor, 8, 45
reviews cadets, 14
thanks 2nd Army Corps, 56
visits his troops after battle of Sedan, 42
William II, German Emperor, abdication of, 438, 439
accession of, 63
addresses enemy prisoners, 363
and command of Eastern Front, 158
and the Army, 178
and the question of peace, 232
and U-boat campaign, 255
appoints author Chief of General Staff of Field Army, 163

William II, at Novo Georgievsk, 142
confidence in author, 188
congratulations on the author's seventieth birthday, 259
consents to an attack on Italy, 283
his "Hold out" command, 426, 427
in "Supreme Command," 171
manœuvres of 1897, and, 66
order for first "great battle" in France, 344
peace proposals placed before and sanctioned by, 430
receives news of collapse of Narew Army, 98
refuses resignation of author, 311, 433
train-life of, 343
witnesses Soissons—Rheims battle, 44
William of Prussia, Prince, manœuvres at Zossen, 59
Wilson, President, and the U-boat campaign, 233
Germany accepts peace principles of, 431
Germany's peace offer to, 431
peace proposals of, 232 et seq., 319
"Winter Battle in Masuria," the, 137 et seq.
Winterfeldt, a story of Königgrätz, 60
Wiszniew, Lake, 152
Wittich, Major von, 12, 54
Wolhynia, Austrian collapse in, 156, 169
Woyrsch, Ensign (afterwards Field-Marshal) von, 26, 115
Würtemberg, Crown Prince of, 217
Prince Augustus of, 36
Wytschaete, 266
attack at, 353
fall of, 354
initial success of enemy at, 391

Yorck, Count, 10
Ypres salient, the, enemy withdrawal from, 355

Zeppelin, Count, visits Pless, 193
Zingler, Lieut.-Colonel von, 56
Zossen, manœuvres at, 59

Printed by Cassell & Company, Limited, La Belle Sauvage, London, E.C.4
F.60.320

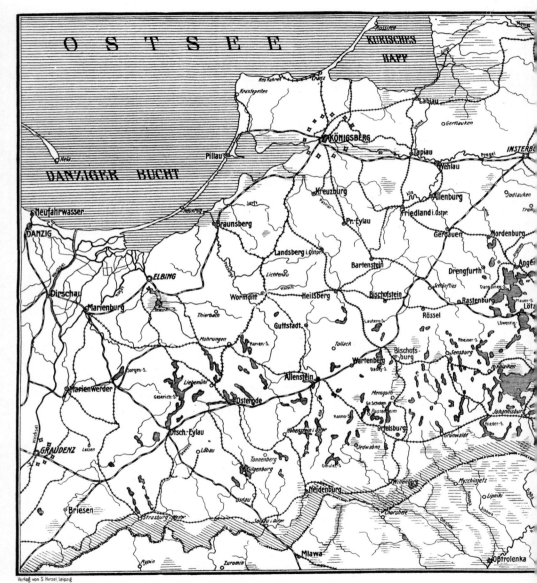

THE EASTERN FRONT

Map I

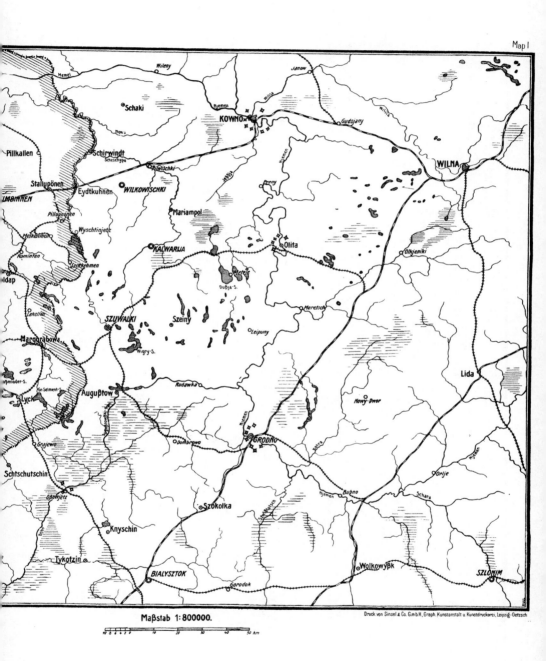

Maßstab 1:800000.

Druck von Sinsel & Co. G.m.b.H., Graph. Kunstanstalt u. Kunstdruckerei, Leipzig-Oetzsch.

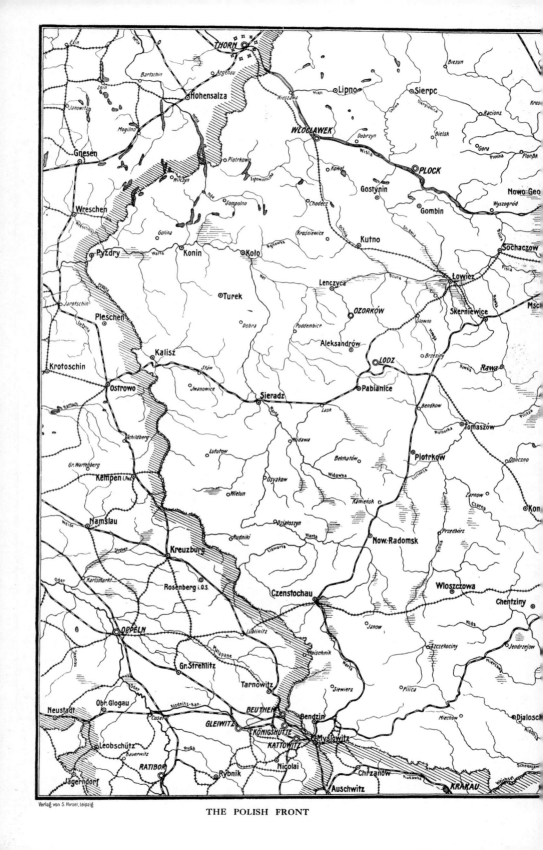

THE POLISH FRONT

Map II

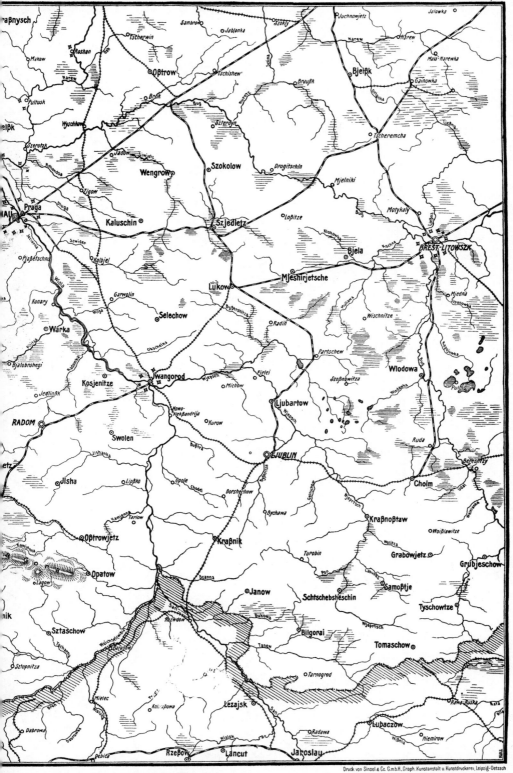

Maßstab 1:800000.

Druck von Singel & Co. G.m.b.H. Graph. Kunstanstalt u. Kunstdruckerei, Leipzig-Oetzsch

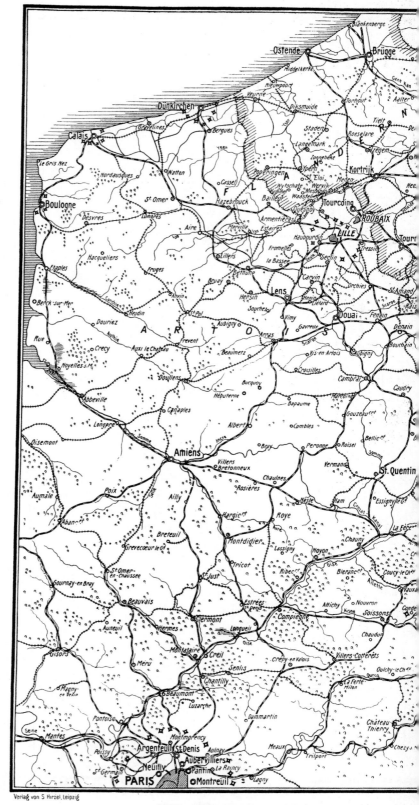

THE WESTERN FRONT

Map III.

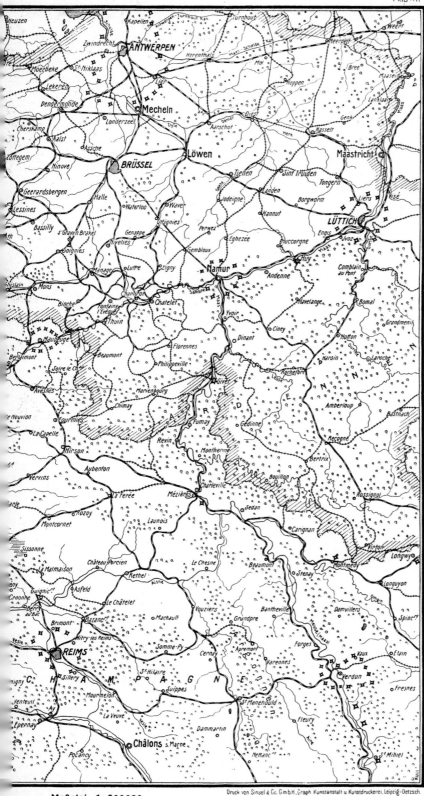

Maßstab 1:800000.

Druck von Sinsel & Co. G.m.b.H. Graph Kunstanstalt u. Kunstdruckerei, Leipzig-Oetzsch.